MW00441445

RICHARD PURVIS,
ORGANIST OF GRACE

James Welch

For additional information received since the original publication, please visit www.welchorganist.com.

Copyright © 2013 by James Welch. All rights reserved.

No part of this book may be reproduced or transmitted in any form or by any means, electronic or mechanical, including photocopying, recording, or by any information storage and retrieval system, without the written consent of the author.

James Welch
3330 Saint Michael Drive
Palo Alto, California 94306
www.welchorganist.com

Cover photo, Richard Purvis at the Alexander Memorial Organ, Grace Cathedral, 1960s. Photo by Proctor Jones. Courtesy the Proctor Jones Family.

ISBN: 978-1481278010
LCCN: 2013901478
version 1.2

Book design by Marny K. Parkin

Printed in the United States of America

CONTENTS

INTRODUCTION

Richard Purvis is probably the most prominent organist to come from California. For nearly 25 years he was Organist and Master of the Choristers of Grace Cathedral, San Francisco, the home of one of the most venerated organs in America and the source of some of the finest sacred choral music performed anywhere in the country. A prolific composer, he published in his lifetime over 100 compositions for organ and over 80 choral scores, many of which were performed widely; he was in constant demand as a concert organist throughout the United States; and he taught dozens of students, many of whom went on to brilliant careers, and all of whom revered him as a teacher and mentor.

That is the Richard Purvis most people knew. However, as is the case for almost all great artists, there is a much more complex story. A gifted and talented young man, he made his mark early on in his native San Francisco and the greater Bay Area. He pursued formal education at The Curtis Institute in Philadelphia, where he came under the influence of the finest teachers and musicians America had to offer in pre-World War II days; rarefied days of study followed in England and France; then military service, including imprisonment in a German concentration camp, the horrors of which he rarely acknowledged and which undoubtedly took their toll on his psyche. Developing strategies for coping with this type of adversity, he succeeded brilliantly as a musician. Toward the end of his tenure at Grace, a growing bureaucracy and changing musical tastes affected him, resulting in a slightly clouded departure from the place that meant so much to him. In his later years he reinvented himself, actively teaching students throughout

California, performing nationwide, and composing. In the end, he and his partner, John Shields, would die within a few months of each other.

Here then is not simply a biography of a legendary American organist and musician, but also a story of a man whose dogged pursuit of his craft made him such an icon. In ways this book is not just an account of Richard Purvis, but also a look at the life and times of an organist in a very different time in our country's musical history. Since one generation often fails to appreciate the immediately preceding generation, a major goal of this book is to help acquaint future generations with Purvis's legacy.

Unlike most of the people I interviewed for this study, I met with Purvis only three times that I can recall, each time towards the end of his life. However, I had listened to his recordings and played some of his compositions as a young teenager and organ student, and these caught my attention and stayed with me. I wonder how many others may have had the same experience I did. At the same time I was also listening avidly to recordings by E. Power Biggs and theatre organist Gus Farney—a rather eclectic mix. No one told me then that I shouldn't like Richard Purvis just as much as I did E. Power Biggs—it was all great organ music to me. I would fall into the academic routine before long as a university student. But as the years went by, I found myself coming back more frequently to the music of Purvis. I have programmed it frequently, because for me it evokes an earlier (and friendlier) era, when music was expected to be beautiful, emotional, and creative.

A few years ago, as I was writing some program notes about a Purvis composition, I realized that it was difficult to find detailed information. I soon discovered that not only had no book ever been written about Purvis, but not even a substantial article could be found. There is a master's thesis, written in 1967 while Purvis was still at Grace Cathedral, but the information contained in it is relatively brief. Purvis did not leave a journal of any kind. Existing documents were scattered to various locations. Certain parts of his life were better documented than others, but all of it was a challenge to locate and put in order.

My first thought was to collect information for an updated article about Purvis's life and work. As I began my research and interviews, I became absorbed in the project, which quickly grew from article to book length.

Confirming Purvis's popularity among his peers, a 1952 poll of more than 2,200 American organists conducted by Choral & Organ Guide *ranked Purvis among the top 10 organ virtuosos in the country.* The American Organist, *May 2004, p. 96. Copyright 2004, by the American Guild of Organists. Used by permission of* The American Organist *magazine.*

I could have pared it down to a more streamlined volume, but I was more inclined to include, for the benefit of future researchers, as many relevant documents as possible. As a result, readers will notice a certain amount of repetition. In some cases different people recalled an incident in Purvis's life, but the details varied somewhat. In other cases documents were very similar, varying only in certain details. Nevertheless, I have sometimes included them, because it is valuable to see which sources (and sometimes the inaccuracies in them) led to others.

One subject that deserved more attention in the book is an analysis of Purvis's compositions. After all, what would be the point of this history, were it not for the music itself? I made a conscious decision not to attempt much description or analysis of the music, which would have increased the length of the book substantially. Moreover, any attempt to "describe" Purvis's music would be a subjective exercise at best. The task for those who want to acquire published scores of his music is now even more difficult, because most of his music is long out of print. Some of his compositions have been recorded, but those recordings are also rare and difficult to locate. Fortunately, future readers and researchers now have at least the titles and complete publication information to work with. Perhaps some future devotee of Purvis's music will take up the next phase of this project—that of the music itself.

acknowledgments

I owe a great deal to those who shared their Purvis stories with me. Fortunately I began the process early enough that I was able to interview quite a few people who knew Purvis well. (Unfortunately, some key people had already passed on, notably Tom Hazleton.) The list of names is long, but I need to give special thanks to a few people in particular.

First, Edward Millington Stout III, who was the curator of the Alexander organ at Grace Cathedral, and a close personal friend of Richard's; and second, Donna Parker, one of Purvis's students, who rescued Purvis's papers and library just as they were about to be unceremoniously discarded shortly after his death. Donna and her colleague Jonas Nordwall were most generous with scores, documents, and anecdotes. On February 2, 2012, Donna donated the collection to the Archive of Recorded Sound at Stanford University, where it is now available to scholars.*

I am also grateful to the following: Douglas Metzler, former chorister at Grace and executor of Purvis's estate, for manuscripts and correspondence; Donald Braff, trustee of John Shields's estate, for many photographs; David Worth and Stephen Loher, assistants to Purvis, with their prodigious memories for detail; Lyn Larsen, a source of many anecdotes; Michael Lampen, Archivist of Grace Cathedral, who generously allowed access to a wealth of documents; William Ray, for his expert editing; Jack Bethards, for much information about California organ history; Jonathan

---

* This extensive collection includes Purvis's library of organ, piano, and choral scores; his own performance scores, many of them with his markings; manuscripts of his compositions; orchestral arrangements; recital programs; photos; and other memorabilia.

Ambrosino, Steven Bock, and Marshall Yaeger, for permission to quote from their publications; Susannah Thurlow and Helene van Rossum, archivists at The Curtis Institute of Music; Nelson Barden, for the transcript of an important interview; the late June Townsend, whose thesis and memoirs provided much source material for the book; Donald Corbett, who also wrote a thesis on Purvis; Jerry Butera of *The Diapason* magazine, for reprints of articles and photos; the Special Projects Committee of the San Francisco Chapter of the American Guild of Organists for two grants; Jerry McBride, Head Librarian, Music Library and Archive of Recorded Sound, Stanford University; the staff at *The American Organist,* for help in locating photos and articles; Tom L. DeLay, for information about various organs; Marny K. Parkin, for graphic design and indexing; Donald Braff, Steve Cohen, Stephen Loher, and others, for financial support; students, colleagues, and friends of Purvis who shared their stories; others whose names I have inadvertently omitted; and finally my family, who patiently allowed me to write for the better part of four years. They know how important this project was to me.

Most of all I owe a great debt to Richard Purvis. Even though I did not know him well when he was alive, I feel as though I do now. His music inspired in me a love of organ music and ultimately was one of the important influences that led me to my own choice of career.

chapter 1

EARLY YEARS,
1913–1935

Q: "When did you decide to make the organ your career?"

A: "When I heard my first organ recital at the age of four. The performer was Edwin H. Lemare at the console of the organ in the San Francisco Civic Auditorium."

The Very Beginning

Richard Irven Purvis was born in San Francisco, California, on August 25, 1913. His birth certificate states that he was born at home and records the birth as "legitimate." His parents were George Tunley Purvis and Jessie Marie Rivellie; they were 25 and 20 years old, respectively. His father was listed as "grocer" and his mother "at home."[1]

Purvis had one sibling, a younger brother named Robert, although through the years their relationship was a limited one. References to Purvis's family are rare and somewhat vague. Stephen Loher said, "I think the brother was a bit younger and there was something a bit strange about him. I saw him a few times. Unlike Richard, he was slender!"[2]

Douglas Metzler added, "Purvis had a younger brother who was 'not right.' Purvis talked very little about his own family. He later took care of his elderly mother who was in a nursing home in Alameda."[3]

During World War II, *The Diapason* reported, "Richard Purvis' only brother, Robert, has been overseas for two years and was in North Africa, but is now in Italy."[4]

While stationed in Germany in 1944 Purvis wrote to June Townsend,

> The pay-off is, I was born at the corner of 26th and Capp. The address is
> 1106 Capp St![5] Your speaking of the little Austin in the Mission Masonic
> Temple brings back a wealth of memories. You see my mother began her
> Eastern Star work there and Dad began his Masonic work there. The first
> time I actually played in public was in that hall and one of the first times I
> ever actually watched a person play the organ was in that hall. I used to pass
> the little Capp Street Church (to which you refer) every Sunday on my way
> to Sunday School and Church at the Presbyterian Church at 23rd & Capp.
> It was there I first touched an organ.[6]

First Music Lessons

Purvis's parents, though not musically inclined, recognized that their son
had a talent for music and started him with piano lessons at the age of four.
Purvis's first teacher, Beatrice Scrivener, was an associate of Trinity College, London.[7] At age eight[8] he went to study with Maybelle Sherwood
Willis, another teacher who had originally come from England; he studied
piano with her until the age of 11.[9] Some of his piano studies may also have
been at the San Francisco Conservatory of Music.[10]

Malcom Manson wrote of Purvis,

> His affection and interest swiftly transferred to the organ when the vicar of
> Good Samaritan Mission allowed him to play the wonderful old Whalley
> mechanical-action organ when he was nine. He gave his parents no peace
> until they took him to be interviewed by Wallace Sabin, who, with some
> misgiving, agreed to introduce him to the art of the organist only if the boy
> continued to study the piano.[11]

According to a brief biography found in Leonard Ellinwood's *The History of American Church Music*, Purvis "played his first service when nine
years old, in the Trinity Presbyterian Church of San Francisco."[12]

In January 1926, Purvis commenced organ study with Wallace Sabin,
organist of Temple Emanu-El and First Church of Christ, Scientist, San
Francisco.[13]

Helping to date the start of Purvis's study with Sabin is a reference
to a photo and short notice in *The American Organist* in 1935: "Here are

Wallace A. Sabin, eminent organist, and Richard Irven Purvis, who has been his pupil for the past nine years, since he was a boy of 13."[14]

Malcolm Manson continued,

> There were seven years of study with Sabin (one of the founders of the San Francisco chapter of the American Guild of Organists) augmented by piano study with Benjamin S. Moore, the organist at Trinity Episcopal Church here in San Francisco. During the time the Aeolian-Skinner organ was being installed at Grace Cathedral and through the interest of J. Sydney Lewis, the cathedral organist at that time, the young Purvis came under the musical influences of organ-builders Ernest M. Skinner and G. Donald Harrison.[15]

Purvis and his teacher Wallace Sabin, late 1920s. Courtesy Grace Cathedral archives.

The following anecdote about Sabin was contributed by Stephen Loher:

> Growing up he studied with Wallace Sabin who was organist at First Church of Christ, Scientist, in San Francisco, with the Kimball organ, and also organist at Temple Emanu-El. Richard tells of the place before they closed off the dome and that it had about five seconds of reverberation. He also tells about an incident with the new Skinner organ. Richard turned pages for Wallace Sabin on Saturdays at the Temple. One Saturday Sabin said that the console for the new Skinner had arrived and after the service they would have a look. When Sabin pulled up the roll top, Richard said it was the only time he ever saw Sabin angry. Skinner had changed some stops on the Great without asking. Later Sabin was consultant for the organ at Grace—and Richard claims that he was still angry at Skinner and therefore stipulated G. Donald Harrison be the tonal finisher (those were the days when both were still in the Company).[16]

In March 1926, Purvis was chosen as official pianist of the San Francisco Inter-School Orchestra.[17]

Purvis decided early that he wanted to be an organist. About a year before Purvis died, Ken Brown (who would later sell him a Rodgers electronic organ for his studio) interviewed Purvis.

> Ken Brown: When did you decide to make the organ your career?
>
> Richard Purvis: When I heard my first organ recital at the age of four. The performer was Edwin H. Lemare at the console of the organ in the San Francisco Civic Auditorium.[18]

Lemare, the most famous organist of the early 20th century, held the position of Civic Organist of San Francisco from 1916 to 1920.[19] It is likely that the young Purvis heard Lemare perform several times at the San Francisco Civic Auditorium.

The Symphonic Style of Organ Playing

In addition to his formal piano and organ lessons, Purvis gained an early appreciation for the theatre organ and the symphonic style of organ playing by hearing the great organists of the day perform in the large theatres in San Francisco.

In 2008 Ed Stout wrote the following reminiscence:

> Richard Purvis fell in love with the sound of a great theatre organ at the age of ten while attending San Francisco's Granada Theatre with his grandmother. He sat in the very front row in order to study how the legendary Iris Vining commanded the massive six-chambered style 285 Wurlitzer. From that day on, the Granada's organ was his favorite unit orchestra. One year later he began his organ studies with Wallace Sabin on the newly installed W.W. Kimball orchestral organ in the First Church of Christ, Scientist. That wonderful four manual, twenty-seven rank organ boasted nine sixteen-foot stops in the Pedal. Sabin agreed to instruct the eager lad if he promised to continue his piano studies. He also was in contact with other prominent San Francisco organists like Ben Moore [organist of Trinity Episcopal Church, San Francisco] and Uda Waldrup. These gentlemen provided Richard with the opportunity to play the finest instruments in Northern California, including the four manual Skinner organs in Trinity Church,

Temple Emanuel, and the orchestral giant in the California Palace of the Legion of Honor. That (impressively) scaled symphonic Skinner included a large percussion and trap assembly. Civic organist, Uda Waldrup played the Legion organ and a weekly "theatre organ" program over the radio.[20]

In a 2010 interview, Ed Stout expanded on the story:

His grandmother, who lived on Guerrero Street in San Francisco, would take him when he was 10, 11, and 12 to the various theaters to hear silent films accompanied on the organ. He mentioned in particular going to the New Mission where there was an organist by the name of Miss Perry. She wore an old sweater that had some holes in it, and she kept candies over on the key cheek and she'd be munching on candies while she played the movie and he got a bang out of that. His grandmother took him on occasion down to the Granada which was later renamed the Paramount. The Granada, on Market Street, was the premier theater on the West coast, if not the most famous photoplay house in the country. It had this legendary orchestral organ—it was more symphonic than it was a theatre organ—very symphonic in its tonal palette, much more than the Fox or the later organs that had an over-abundance of tibias. It was a Wurlitzer, almost a concert organ, and he used to go there with his grandmother and sit in the front row and then get out of his seat and go over to the rail and watch the legendary Iris Ethel Vining accompany pictures. She was probably one of the five greatest photoplay interpreters in the world. Purvis told me that she would play the organ *symphonically*. It was all sophisticated transcriptions of symphonic music she played—she had 800 pieces of classical music committed to memory. He got to know her later when he was a recognized talent, but as a 10- or 11-year old he was down there gawking. He said you couldn't distinguish the symphonic organ from the orchestra. The orchestra would phase out after the 7:30 show started, and if it was a long picture, the organ just took over. As the strings left the pit she'd put on the strings. That organ had 10 ranks of strings, an incredible string ensemble, and so he watched and studied what she did.[21]

Recitals by Lemare and Karg-Elert

Wallace Sabin encouraged Purvis to learn from the great recitalists who came to San Francisco. Among Purvis's papers was a fragment of a review of a recital given by Lemare, printed in *The San Francisco Call and Post* (which later merged with the *San Francisco Examiner*), dated September 16, 1925. In all likelihood, Purvis, age 12 at the time, attended this recital. The review paints a vivid picture of the event which would have undoubtedly made an impression on the young Purvis.

"Great Throng at Lemare Concert," by Charles Woodman

With a program consisting mostly of his own works, Edwin H. Lemare, former municipal organist, drew about 10,000 persons to Exposition Auditorium last evening and aroused them to repeated demonstrations of applause. Several "request" numbers were added during the concert and at the end Lemare was compelled to play again.

One of the notable features was the large number of young people in the audience, many of whom hardly could have known Lemare when he was playing here regularly, showing the wide appeal organ music has for all sorts of people, for it was not what one would call a regular concert crowd.

GREAT OVATION

Many of the leading musicians of the city joined in giving Lemare a great ovation. To an outsider it would have seemed as though the people were rejoicing with the organist over his reunion with the love of his life—the great instrument he created and over which he presided for years—giving the people a foretaste of heavenly music.

Bach's great G minor Fugue, which was played first, aroused much enthusiasm, as did "Moonlight and Roses," the popular adaptation of Lemare's Andantino in D flat, and there was a general demand for the original form of the composition.

Using the English designation of descriptive for what we call program music, Lemare gave his interpretation of his just published "Twilight Sketches," representing sundown, the thrush, the glow worm, the firefly and dusk, which follows the same lines as his "Summer Sketches," as well as his new "Humoresque," a rather rollicking number.

CALL FOR RETURN

He chose three rather military themes for his "Sonata" improvisation, all from one person, it appeared, and developed them in florid style with a finale suggesting "Way Down South in Dixie" that caught the ears of the crowd.

At the end the demonstration was renewed with more intense fervor. People crowded around the platform....[22]

Jonas Nordwall related the following:

> Dick's other passion was Karg-Elert. As a student he was allowed by Wallace Sabin to observe Karg-Elert practice at the San Francisco auditorium. Sabin insisted that Dick bring his copies of Karg-Elert's music and carefully note all of registrations that Karg-Elert used on the Austin. In the "Mirrored Moon", Karg-Elert made about 10 registration changes on one page alone not marked in the score. Additionally, Karg-Elert's daughter assisted him at the console as a registrant. Dick notated all of Karg-Elert's changes on his music, as he did on the Franck scores, which makes them very valuable as a key resource to how things were really played versus their publication.[23]

In February 1925, at the age of 11, Purvis entered a competition for the Boys Achievement Club of Northern California. In this competition he took first prize for piano performance.[24]

June Townsend wrote in her 1995 "Memories of Richard Irven Purvis,"

> He had won an award when quite young for his playing and when he did "Humoresque" the teacher asked why he phrased it a certain way—it just came naturally to him. The boy had talent to be cultivated and his parents saw that it was. In his teens he played for an Episcopal Church and a movie theater nearby. Now he was organist at the First Baptist Church in Oakland and studied with Wallace Sabin and accompanied for him as he directed the Chorus of the Tuesday Noon Club and Wednesday Morning Chorale under Wallace Sabin.[25]

Early Lessons at the Organ

Important information about Purvis's early training came from an interview Nelson Barden conducted with Purvis in October 1981. While the main purpose of Barden's interview was to obtain information about Edwin H. Lemare, Purvis also offered many details about his own early life as an organist.

> RIP: We were speaking of Lemare's "Twilight Sketches," of which "Sundown" is the first. It's awfully good Tchaikovsky. I heard Lemare play those at Temple Emanu-El when they were just published. I've got the old copy. I was still living with my family in Oakland then, I was about 12–13 years old. It was when Temple Emanu-El was still a magnificent

place acoustically and they hadn't ruined the organ. That was one of E. M. Skinner's best orchestral organs, and my old organ teacher, Wallace Sabin, knew how to play it. Lemare played a magnificent recital there—that's when I realized the legend was true.

NB: So even in your time he was a legend.

RIP: Oh yes, you see he had been the Civic Organist here, but I hardly remember being taken to some of those concerts. I remember the man coming out way up where the console used to be, but no other recollection of them at all....

NB: How did you get into organs?

RIP: I was four years old. There used to be concerts at the California Theatre here on Sunday mornings. The theatre had an orchestra, but for these concerts they supplemented it with members of the San Francisco Symphony who loved to play, because it was very lucrative at that time. They had a quite decent conductor, his name was Max Dalin. At one of these concerts there was a trio for one harp, one cello, and one organ, and I knew right then what I wanted to do. And guess what they were playing: Barcarolle from *The Tales of Hoffman*. That's what started it....

NB: You were born in Oakland?

RIP: No, San Francisco!

NB: A thousand pardons.

RIP: Good heavens, you may GO right now! I'm a third generation San Franciscan and a fourth generation Californian, and an Episcopalian. That lets me be quite a snob! I wanted to play the organ, but I was too small anyhow and my piano teacher, thinking tracker action, insisted that the organ would ruin my touch. My grandmother took a great interest in a little mission of Grace Cathedral which was called Good Samaritan, and they had the original organ built for the crypt of Grace Cathedral by Whalley somewhere around 1907–08. It was a tracker and a perfectly gorgeous little organ. Somehow she conned Father Turner into letting me practice. I was about eight or nine, had my first church job when I was 10. Isn't that scandalous? Must have sounded like hell. This would have gone on secretly for a long time. My grandmother lived in the old part of the Mission [district of San Francisco] when that was a nice place to live. I did this on the QT—my family and piano teacher never knew anything about it. Grandmother had three or four command appearances, one of them was the whole family to her house for Christmas dinner, and we preceded that by going to communion. We got there, and the organist had been in an accident, and Father Turner came and said, "Do you think you could manage the hymns and maybe a chant or two?" So that gave me away.

My dad and mother realized I was very interested, and so they trotted me up to Wallace Sabin. At the time, he was the best. There was a period when there were three outstanding teachers, Lynnwood Farnam on the East Coast, Palmer Christian in the Midwest, and out here it was Wallace Sabin. Of course there were others, but when you spoke to people you thought were good organists, they usually studied with one of the three. Sabin was from England. He had studied with Henry Wood at one time. He was at school the same time Lemare was, at the Royal College of Organists.[26]

High School

In the archives of The Curtis Institute is a "Certified Record of High School Work" submitted with Purvis's application to Curtis. From this application form we learn that in 1927 he attended the 9th grade at Hamilton Junior High School in Oakland, where he studied English, Algebra, French, Orchestra, and Physical Education, receiving "1" (A) grades in all subjects. From January to December 1928 (Oakland schools must have run on a calendar year at that time), he attended Fremont High School for the 10th grade; his courses were English, Geometry, French, German, Harmony, Glee, and ROTC, receiving "1" grades in all subjects. From January to December 1929, as an 11th grader, he studied English, United States History and Government, French, German, Harmony, Glee, and ROTC, with "1" grades in all subjects.

The form continues with the following notations:

This certifies that Richard Purvis has been a student in the Fremont High School from 1/9/28 to 12/29.... This candidate has 16-1/2 credits toward 19 credits required by this school for graduation and left before graduation. It is the opinion of the principal that this candidate possesses the character,

High school photos of Purvis, about 1927. Courtesy Grace Cathedral archives.

did a grade of work, acquired the habits of study and application, and possesses other qualities that merit recommendation to enter a higher institution of learning....

Richard Purvis completed three years of high school work. He enrolled as a Low Senior, leaving just 3 weeks before the close of the semester and enrolling with a private tutor. However, he has done the equivalent of high school work. He is an honor student, and was outstanding in a class of 157.

Highest standing in the class.[27]

First Positions as Organist

In December 1925, the sudden illness of the organist of Good Samaritan Episcopal Church, San Francisco, provided Purvis, at age 12, his first opportunity as a church organist, playing for services as a substitute.[28] Donald Corbett noted, "He probably did not realize that this experience would eventually culminate in a position at Grace Cathedral. However, the experience increased his interest in the organ and prompted him to seek training."[29]

Grace Cathedral under construction, about 1928. Courtesy Grace Cathedral archives.

Shortly thereafter Purvis's family moved to 7870 Garfield Avenue, Oakland, which remained the family home for many years.

Purvis was soon hired, at age 13, as organist of St. James Episcopal Church, 1540 12th Avenue, Oakland, in September 1926.[30] This job provided him with valuable experience and the full use of an organ that further improved his rapidly developing technique.[31]

In a booklet entitled *The Church of St. James the Apostle*, there is a mention of Purvis's being organist of that church, but with no dates. There is, however, a mention of a death "early in 1929" on the same page that lists Purvis as the church organist, so we can assume that Purvis was still organist there at least sometime through 1929.[32]

A document in the archives at St. James states:

> The organ at St. James, built in 1888 for the cost of $1500 by George Andrews & Son, is the oldest surviving church organ in the East Bay, and is the only

Grace Cathedral under construction, early 1930s. Courtesy Grace Cathedral archives.

one there that survived the 1906 earthquake. George Andrews (1832–1904) was an important organ builder in the East Coast. In 1886 Andrews and his family moved to Oakland; the organ at St. James Episcopal Church was the very first instrument that the firm built after the relocation. Originally a mechanical tracker, the organ was electrified during the 1920s by Thomas W. Whalley (1856–1931), a former associate of George Andrews.[33]

Purvis's next church position was at the First Baptist Church of Oakland, located at 534 22nd Street. The archives of First Baptist Church state: "On March 10, 1930, Richard Purvis became organist at $50 per month." Purvis would have been 16 years of age at the time.[34]

There is also documentation about the organ at First Baptist Church:

This was the second Murray-Harris organ for the Church; the first had been installed in the previous building just months before it burned down. Murray M. Harris was one of the great organ builders in this country, perhaps the greatest at the turn of the century, though he was active for only a short time. . . . It was electrified around 1924 and further remodeled in 1944, with the console being moved to its present location, at a cost of $6000. A new Austin all-electric console was installed in 1959.[35]

Purvis probably remained as organist of First Baptist Church of Oakland until he assumed the post as organist of Calvary Presbyterian Church, San Francisco, in 1933.

Chapel of the Chimes

Although Purvis had shown interest in symphonic and theatre organ music at an early age, his training and performance to date had probably been limited to the classic and sacred realm. Still, it is not surprising that he would also have the ability to play popular music. Purvis would soon find himself not only playing on a Wurlitzer organ, but performing on live radio broadcasts from the Chapel of the Chimes in Oakland.

The Chapel of the Chimes was founded in 1909 as a crematory and columbarium. The present building was rebuilt and expanded in 1928, based on designs by the legendary architect Julia Morgan, who designed over 700 buildings in California, including such landmark structures as Hearst Castle.

The basis for the organ at the Chapel of the Chimes is a seven-rank style "E" Wurlitzer, Opus 1239, shipped from North Tonawanda, New York, on December 31, 1925, to the State Theatre in Martinez, California. But silent films started going out of style around 1927. It may have been as early as 1927 that the organ was sold and moved to the Chapel of the Chimes, where it was assembled and installed by Oliver Lowe of the Oliver Organ Company in Berkeley. According to Tom DeLay, however, it wasn't until 1929 or 1930 that theatres began selling off their organs to churches. The Chapel of the Chimes organ was modified and enlarged considerably in 1939, but Purvis was already in Philadelphia by that time.[36]

According to the Biographical Data, Purvis was appointed in March 1927, at age 13, as one of the staff organists for radio station KRE, which broadcast from the Chapel of the Chimes.[37] Here Purvis provided music that ranged from classic to popular styles. His theme song was a jazzy "I'll Take an Option on You."[38]

Purvis's hire date of 1927 could not be verified; the Chapel of the Chimes has no record, nor do the archivists of KRE. Since the Chapel of the Chimes was under construction in 1928 and the acquisition date of

Chapel of the Chimes, Oakland, California.

Interior, Chapel of the Chimes. Wurlitzer organ on the right.

Wurlitzer organ, Chapel of the Chimes. Photos by James Welch.

the Wurlitzer was presumably around 1930, the 1927 hire date is probably incorrect; a logical start date might be closer to 1930.

Harrold Hawley was a long-time organist at the Chapel of the Chimes, playing on the air every night, and Purvis often subbed for Hawley.[39] Another organist who played for KRE at the time was a Maggie Murphy.[40]

June Townsend wrote in 1967:

> The first time I met Richard Purvis was at one of his recitals, about 1934, at the First Baptist Church in Oakland and subsequently started taking piano lessons from him at his home in Oakland. He had a piano class at this time. He was broadcasting daily from the Chapel of the Chimes over radio station KRE, and often I was privileged to turn his pages during a broadcast. At the 6:30 PM time, he played light classics while at the 8:00 o'clock spot he delighted his listeners with popular numbers. To protect his concert name, at the popular broadcast he altered his name to "Don Irving."[41]

KRE poster, 1930s. Courtesy Steve Kushman.

In 1995 Townsend reminisced:

When he had to drop our lessons because of his studies, I went to the Chapel of the Chimes Crematorium Columbarium in Berkeley [*sic*] and started organ lessons with Harrold Hawley. Richard was also on the staff and played for some evening broadcasts from station KRE. When he played popular music, he went by the name "Don Irving," and sometimes I sat on the organ bench and turned pages for him on a stack of songs of the day, such as "Stars Fell on Alabama" and "Take a Letter, Miss Brown" (my [maiden] name). Harrold introduced me to the pipes in the organ loft and tuning and allowed me practice time, "as it was better for organs to be in use." One Sunday a church service was being broadcast somewhere when it suddenly went off the air. The Radio Man rushed out shouting, "Play Something, Play Something!" I turned to Handel's Largo and started when Harrold appeared, climbed over the bench, pushed me aside, and said "You're not being paid for this!" When Dick arrived later, I told him I'd had my Big Moment and he asked, "Who was he?"[42]

Stephen Loher added: "I think he used the name Don Irving because he didn't want to be known as a theater organist at the time—the culture of the day may not have permitted both! Still, he was by no means a 'closet' theater organist—he played openly several times—one time at the Fox Theatre in San Francisco that I remember hearing about."[43]

Purvis was still under contract to KRE in late 1935. When he applied for admission to The Curtis Institute, he informed the school administration by telegram on December 1, 1935, that his "radio contract demands three weeks notice before cancellation." He must have given notice within a few days, because he left for Philadelphia in early January 1936.[44]

First Organ Recitals

Purvis's first public organ recital took place in May 1927, at age 13, when he appeared at the console of the 110-stop Austin organ at the San Francisco Civic Auditorium. The Austin organ had been built for the 1915 Panama Pacific Exposition and had been donated to the City of San Francisco. According to the Biographical Data, "This performance was in conjunction with the annual San Francisco Music Week Festival."[45] There is no record of the music Purvis played at this performance.

During his interview in 1981 with Nelson Barden, Purvis spoke of playing at the Civic Auditorium:

RIP: The first time I played that organ the Schoensteins were taking care of it, in the late twenties. They used to have a California Music Festival with a concert every noon during that week at the Auditorium. I remember Louis [Schoenstein] coming to get it going and asking me if I wanted help, and he was there during the concert.

NB: Did the pistons work?

RIP: Yes, they did. I didn't use that many, I used about five generals and about half the manual pistons and half the pedal pistons. If something didn't set right, I just substituted another one. I played two years, I think, and then the Festival went to pieces—too many politics. I played for conventions a couple of times, but you know the kind of playing that is. There was a convention of the Baptist young people and I played there for about a week, we had a choir of about a thousand. But you accompany the service, that was about it, and you do it on very broad lines, because there were about two thousand people there all the time, sometimes more than that. The last night all the Baptist churches in the area had their service there at once; no matter what I did it wasn't loud enough. Tremendous congregational singing of all the old cornhusks that the Baptists love. You could hardly hear the organ, and this was before the curtains and the acoustic tile. When the place was empty, it would bowl you over. It was big. The Tuba Sonora is a big baby, it's out in the open, a good English one.[46]

In June 1929, Purvis made his official debut as a recital organist when he played at First Baptist Church of Oakland under the auspices of the

American Guild of Organists.[47] One outcome of this recital was that he was invited to be accompanist for the Wednesday Choral Association of Oakland.[48]

In March 1930, Purvis was invited again by the American Guild of Organists to appear as recitalist for the Sacramento Chapter of the Guild. At age 16 he was the youngest person to have performed for the chapter.[49] It is not known what music he played on the recital. According to Purvis's application papers to The Curtis Institute, he also played for the Sacramento Chapter in 1932.

By this time Purvis had established himself as an accomplished piano accompanist. His reputation helped him to secure in September 1932 the position of rehearsal accompanist for the Loring Club of San Francisco, a distinguished choral society of the time.[50]

Purvis's application to Curtis mentions a "Bach recital" in 1933. While no details are given, this may have been the first of many all-Bach recitals to follow later in his life.

Construction on the San Francisco Bay Bridge, connecting Oakland and San Francisco, began in 1933; it was not opened to traffic until November of 1936. The Purvis family residence was in Oakland and remained so until the death of his parents. As a result Purvis would have crossed the Bay by ferry for every lesson, rehearsal, and performance in San Francisco.

Purvis and the Hammond Organ

With his interest in popular as well as classical music, Purvis would likely have taken interest in the Hammond organ, which was then in its infancy. June Townsend wrote in her memoir:

> He went back to Chicago for the big exposition [Chicago's "Century of Progress Exposition," 1933–1934], where he saw the new Hammond organ which had just been invented—the beginning of the electric organ age. Our SDA Church in Oakland got the first one, and since they were broadcasting, I got Richard and Harrold Hawley to play for a couple of them. Dick showed me how to set it up and I played for a song service and was told they could hear it clear out on the street. Beware of a heavy foot on the expression pedal![51]

Townsend also wrote: "When Elder Prout was holding an evangelistic broadcast from the Oakland Seventh-day Adventist Church he received the first Hammond Organ on the west coast and Richard Purvis played its premier radio broadcast."[52]

The following notice appeared in *The Pacific Union Recorder*, a monthly Seventh-Day Adventist news magazine:

> Already the instrument has attracted the attention of the musical world around the Bay district. Some of the finest organists have played upon it, offering their services. We had the honor of having the first instrument of its type to be installed in any church in California; and also the honor of being the first to broadcast with it over the air, west of Kansas City.[53]

Calvary Presbyterian Church, San Francisco

The archives of Calvary Presbyterian Church reveal that Purvis served as organist there from at least October 1, 1933, through December 31, 1935.[54] At Calvary he played for the 11 a.m. Sunday worship service and a service at 7:30 p.m. The evening service was preceded by a short recital of three or four pieces, followed by a song service, several more pieces by singers or the organist, and a sermon. The organ at that time was an Aeolian, Opus 1683, built between 1926 and 1928 and dedicated in 1929.[55]

An announcement in the church's October 8, 1933, bulletin reads: "MR. RICHARD IRVEN PURVIS, the rising young organist of the bay region has been appointed to play our beautiful memorial organ. Calvary is indeed fortunate in securing the services of this young artist."

Calvary Presbyterian Church, San Francisco, about 1957 (but the same Aeolian organ Purvis played in 1935). Courtesy Calvary Presbyterian Church.

It is enlightening to see the wide range of repertoire Purvis, now 20 years old, performed as preludes, offertories, and postludes. Note some of the interesting title alterations (i.e., Mulet's "Jehovah, Thou Mighty Rock," presumably "Tu es Petra"). Although not complete, this listing gives an idea of the music Purvis favored at the time.

11 a.m. Service	7:30 p.m. Evening Service
October 1, 1933	
Guilmant: Grand Choeur	Nevin: Toccata
Hollins: Meditation	Dethier: Intermezzo
Widor: Toccata (Symphony V)	Stoughton: Dreams
	de Falla: Chanson
October 8, 1933	
Karg-Elert: Now Thank We All Our God	Wallace Sabin: Bourree
Karg-Elert: O God, Thou Faithful God	Bonnet: Angelus du Soir
	Bonnet: Romance sans Paroles
October 15, 1933	
Bach: Lord, Unto Thee I Call	Handel: Royal Water Music
Corelli: Sarabande	Albert Snow: Distant Chimes
Widor: Allegro (Symphony V)	Saint-Saens: The Swan
October 22, 1933	
Batiste: Grande Offertoire de Saint Cecile	Clokey: California Mountain
Wolstenholme: Allegretto	Sketches (Canyon Walls, Jagged
	Peaks, Wind in the Pines)
	Stoughton: Softening Shadows
October 29, 1933	
Bach: Prelude and Fugue in D minor	Richard Hailing: Grand Choeur
Schubert: Ave Maria (organ solo)	Richard Hailing: A Highland
Widor: Toccata (Symphony V)	Pastorale
Ralph Kinder: In Moonlight	MacDowell: To a Wild Rose
November 5, 1933	
Anton Liadow: Prelude in E	Lemmens: Fanfare
Rubinstein: Kammenoi-Ostrow	Hugh McAmis: Dreams
Tschaikowsky: Andante (Symphony V)	Anthony Jawelak: Madrigale
Tschaikowsky: Marche Slav	Edwin H. Lemare: The Thrush
November 12, 1933 [Veterans' Day]	
Cesar Franck: Piece Heroique	Austin Dunn: American
Gordon Balch Nevin: In Memoriam	Triumphant

Van Denman Thompson: To an
  American Soldier
Roland Diggle: American Fantasy

Carl McKinley: Lamentation
Richard Irven Purvis: Prayer for
  Peace
Saint-Saens: Prelude to the Deluge

November 19, 1933
Handel: Allegro (Concerto II)
Cesar Franck: Adagio (Fantasy in C)
Salome: Offertoire
Jacques Lemmens: Triumphal March

Ernest Kroeger: Marche Pitteresque
Joseph Clokey: Twilight Moth
Alexander Guilmant: Allegretto
Tschaikowsky: Andante Cantabile

November 26, 1933
Karg-Elert: Now Thank We All Our God
Julio Valdes: Meditation
Stoughton: A Song of Autumn
Calkin: Thanksgiving Harvest March

Edward McDowell: A. D. 1620
Van Denman Thompson: Pastel
Percy Fletcher: Fountain Reverie
Frysinger: Autumn Night

December 3, 1933
Karg-Elert: Two Chorale Preludes
    O Lord, Most Holy
    Bedeck Thyself, O My Soul
Marcel Dupre: In dulci Jubilo
Karg-Elert: Marche de Triomphe

Karg-Elert: Legend of the Mountain
Wolstenholme: Allegretto
Arthur Poister: Bohemian Cradle
  Song
Percy Fletcher: Fountain Reverie

December 10, 1933
Bach: Jesu, Joy of Man's Desiring
Guilmant: Noel Languedocien
Dupre: In Dulci Jubilo
Mulet: Jehovah, Thou Mighty Rock

Stoughton: An Ancient
  Phoenecian Procession
Stoughton: Idyl "Pan in Revery"
James Rogers: Berceuse
Rachmaninoff: Serenade

December 17, 1933
Guilmant: Noel Polonais
Guilmant: Offertoire sur deux Noels
Stahl: Christmas Pastorale
Cesar Franck: Finale

Chubb: The Shepherd's Carol
Mulet: Noel
Poister: Bohemian Carol
Yon: Christmas In Sicily

December 24, 1933
Bach: Fantasy "In Dulci Jubilo"
Bonnet: Dream of the Infant Jesus
Bach: Toccata in F

Chubb: The Shepherd's Carol
Marcel Dupre: In Dulci Jubilo
Mulet: Noel
Handel: The Messiah (selections)

December 31, 1933
Joseph Jongen: Prayer
Gabriel Pierne: Cantilene
Edward d'Evry: Meditation
Eugene Gigout: Grand Choeur

Watch Night Service
   (7:30–12 midnight)
Deems Taylor: Dedication
Cyril Jenkins: Dawn, Night
Edward d'Evry: Moonlight

April 1, 1934 Easter
Farnam: Toccata on the Easter Carol
Karg-Elert: Pastorale, Recitative & Chorale
Bach: Rejoice, Good Christians
Candlyn: Prelude on "O Filii et Filiae"
Edward Johnston: Resurrection Morn
Pietro Yon: Hymn of Glory

James Rogers: Concert Overture
Enrico Bossi: Scherzo
Alexander Russell: The Bells of
   Saint Anne
Louis Vierne: Carillon
Messiah selections

While Purvis must have enjoyed the performance opportunities afforded him at Calvary, he had set his sights on further education on the East Coast. Sometime during 1935 Purvis applied for study at The Curtis Institute; his teachers Wallace Sabin and Benjamin Moore wrote letters of recommendation, as did Ezra Allen Van Nuys, one of the clergy at Calvary. In the fall of 1935, at the age of 22, he received his acceptance to Curtis, with an offer of a full scholarship.

June Townsend referred to a 1935 notice in *The American Organist*: "Mr. Purvis, who has just been awarded a scholarship in organ at Curtis Institute, will shortly leave for the East. He early displayed great talent for his chosen instrument, and although but 22 years now, has been for some years organist at Calvary Presbyterian Church, San Francisco, and has done a very considerable amount of recital work."[56]

On December 10, 1935, a Christmas concert was given by The Wednesday Morning Choral Club of Oakland at the Scottish Rite Temple in Oakland. Wallace Sabin was the conductor. In this variety program there was no solo organ music, but there were accompaniments (to Bossi's "Hymn to Glory" and Spross's "Let All My Life Be Music," with Purvis at the organ and Margaret Sherman Lea at the piano) and a four-hand piano accompaniment, arranged by Purvis, to "The Toymaker's Dream" by Golden-High.[57]

The final performance from this period of Purvis's life was a recital in Sacramento. A newspaper clipping with a photo of Purvis, dated

Will Give Concert

Richard Purvis, young San Francisco organist who is on his way to Philadelphia, to study at the Curtis Institute, will be presented by Sacramento Chapter, American Guild of Organists, in a recital at 8:30 o'clock to-night in the First Methodist Church.

Purvis's earliest known publicity photo. Sacramento, December 28, 1935. Courtesy Sacramento Chapter AGO.

December 28, 1935, reads: "Richard Purvis, young San Francisco organist who is on his way to Philadelphia to study at the Curtis Institute, will be presented by Sacramento Chapter, American Guild of Organists, in a recital at 8:30 o'clock to-night in the First Methodist Church.[58] No copy of the program could be located.

An announcement in the December 29, 1935, bulletin of Calvary Presbyterian Church reads:

> We appreciate the outstanding contribution Mr. Richard Irven Purvis has rendered as organist of Calvary Church. His masterly technique at the console of our great organ has been recognized not alone in Calvary and the Bay region, but in the Country at large. We congratulate him upon the honor conferred in awarding him a Scholarship in the Curtis Institute of Music, Philadelphia. We wish him God's blessing in this new opportunity.... The Choir is giving an informal reception to Mr. Purvis, in the social hall at the close of the Evening Service. Members and friends of the Church are cordially invited.[59]

Notes

1. The birth certificate gives the following additional information:
Father: George Tunley Purvis, born February 11, 1888; mother's maiden name Cole; no birthplace given [but the 1920 Census indicates that George was born in Kansas.]; died June 16, 1967, Alameda, California, age 79.
Mother: Jessie Marie Rivellie; born July 20, 1893; mother's maiden name Casadillio; California; died October 23, 1980, Alameda, California, age 87.

2. Stephen Loher, e-mail, November 2, 2010.

3. Douglas Metzler, e-mail, June 24, 2010.

4. "Hope Dim for Safety of Richard I. Purvis." *The Diapason*, April 1, 1945, 3.

5. His birth certificate gives the address as 1104 Capp Street.

6. Letter from Purvis to June Townsend, dated October 29, 1944, Germany. Cited in June Leora Townsend's 1967 master's thesis, "Richard I. Purvis: Contemporary American Organist-Composer," 1. Hereafter referred to as "Townsend thesis."

7. Corbett, Donald M. "The Life and Works of Richard Purvis." Master's thesis, 1969, 1. Hereafter referred to as "Corbett."

8. Age 6, according to an obituary compiled by Canon Malcolm Manson, Grace Cathedral School headmaster, January 5, 1995.

9. Corbett, 1.

10. Townsend thesis, 1.

11. Obituary compiled by Canon Malcolm Manson, January 5, 1995.

12. Ellinwood, Leonard. *The History of American Church Music.* New York: Morehouse-Gorham Co., 1953, 230. The book also lists Purvis's birth year erroneously as 1915. This may help explain the perpetuation of the inaccuracy throughout Purvis's lifetime.

13. "Biographical Data," 1. Anonymous typescript, on Grace Cathedral letterhead, covering Purvis's life from around 1925 through 1964. Possibly written by Purvis himself; or it may have been compiled by June Townsend. Hereafter referred to as "Biographical Data."

14. Cited in Townsend thesis, 2; original not available; month of issue unknown.

15. Obituary compiled by Canon Malcolm Manson, headmaster, January 5, 1995.

16. Stephen Loher, e-mail, May 30, 2009.

17. Biographical Data, 1.

18. Interview by Ken Brown in *Daffer Church Organs Newsletter,* Fall 1995, Vol. 7, No. 3.

19. Nelson Barden, e-mail, September 25, 2012.

20. Ed Stout, "Reflections about Richard Purvis, The Renowned Organist, Composer and Teacher," in "Professional Perspectives," *Theatre Organ, Journal of The American Theatre Organ Society,* May 1, 2008, 46–47. Used by permission of the author.

21. Ed Stout interview, Hayward, California, August 31, 2010.

22. Charles Woodman, "Great Throng at Lemare Concert," *The San Francisco Call and Post,* September 16, 1925.

23. Jonas Nordwall, e-mail, 2009. Many of Purvis's marked scores now reside in the Archive of Recorded Sound at Stanford University.

24. Biographical Data, 1.

25. June Townsend, "Memories of Richard Irven Purvis." Typescript, 1995. 3 pp. Hereafter referred to as "Townsend Memories."

26. Barden interview, 1981.

27. Curtis archives.

28. Biographical Data, 1.

29. Corbett, 1–2.

30. Townsend thesis, 1.

31. Biographical Data, 1.

32. Elizabeth Hanmore Francis, *The Church of St. James the Apostle,* no date, pp. 19 and 23; courtesy Rev. John Rawlinson, pastor of St. James. What is now St. James was originally the Church of the Advent, East Oakland. It merged with St. Philip's Mission in the Fruitvale District of Oakland, and the merged group took the name "St. James Church." John Rawlinson, e-mail, November 2, 2010.

33. Archives of St. James Episcopal Church, Oakland, courtesy John Rawlinson, pastor. Also http://stjamesoakland.org/en/organ.html, last accessed March 18, 2011.

34. The Biographical Data cites, probably erroneously, February 1929 as Purvis's start date. Biographical Data, 1.

35. Archives of First Baptist Church, courtesy Rev. Steven Reimer.

36. Tom DeLay, e-mail, September 8, 2011.

37. Biographical Data, 1.

38. Tom DeLay, e-mail, May 31, 2009.

39. Stephen Loher, e-mail, June 3, 2009.

40. Douglas Metzler, e-mail, June 24, 2010.

41. Townsend thesis, 2.

42. Townsend Memories.

43. Stephen Loher, e-mail, June 3, 2009.

44. Telegram, courtesy Curtis archives.

45. Biographical Data, 1.

46. Barden interview.

47. Biographical Data, 1.

48. Corbett, 5.

49. Biographical Data, 1.

50. Biographical Data, 1; also Corbett, 5.

51. Townsend Memories, 1995.

52. Townsend thesis, 2.

53. *The Pacific Union Recorder*, September 1935; cited in Townsend thesis, 3.

54. The Biographical Data gives March 1932 as the date of his appointment at Calvary Presbyterian, but this is probably incorrect. Biographical Data, 1.

55. Joe Beyer, archivist, Calvary Church, e-mail, September 13, 2011.

56. Cited in Townsend thesis, 2; original not available; month of issue unknown.

57. Concert program.

58. Name of newspaper unknown. Courtesy Sacramento Chapter AGO.

59. Calvary Presbyterian Church archives.

сḥартєʀ 2

CURTIS YEARS,
1936–1940

"I am indeed happy over the good fortune which has come my way and shall endeavor to prove myself worthy of the honor conferred upon me. I have long admired Curtis and its standards and to be within its walls is, indeed, an ambition achieved."

—*Richard Purvis to The Curtis Institute, December 1935*

Many Western and Midwestern musicians have gone "back East" for their education. Purvis was no exception. He had received excellent training from his teachers in the Bay Area, had performed widely, and had already held several church positions. Still, the lure of studying in the East, particularly at such a prestigious institution as The Curtis Institute of Music in Philadelphia, was strong. While there were other places in the country where he could have studied, there was really none equivalent to Curtis at the time.

It was Purvis's good fortune to be accepted for study at Curtis, where he came under the influence

Purvis during his Curtis days, mid-1930s. Courtesy Grace Cathedral archives.

of master teachers such as Alexander McCurdy. While there he found numerous performance opportunities in Philadelphia and New York; he played for major churches; he received experience in leading boy choirs (which would become an integral part of his career at Grace Cathedral); and he rubbed shoulders with fellow students who would become significant players on the American musical scene. He was also the recipient of an award to study in Europe, where he absorbed techniques that affected his style of composition and conducting.

On November 11, 1935, Curtis mailed to Purvis a catalogue and application form. Purvis acted quickly to gather the required information, returning it to Curtis on November 15. On December 1, 1935, only two weeks later, Purvis received word by telegram of his acceptance with full scholarship to The Curtis Institute. Due to his local contracts and obligations in the Bay Area, he was unable to leave for Philadelphia until January 1936. In December 1935, he played farewell recitals at Grace Cathedral, San Francisco; Trinity Methodist Church, Berkeley; and First Methodist Church, Sacramento.[1]

A memo from Susannah Thurlow, archivist at Curtis, gives additional background on Purvis's application:

> McCurdy recommended Purvis for the school in November 1935. There was an opening for an organ scholarship that year and it was at the request of McCurdy that Purvis received the application materials and eventually came East and was accepted at Curtis. Purvis mentioned discussing the prospect of Curtis with Mr. Wallace Sabin, who was a previous organ and piano teacher based in Berkeley. He studied with him from 1926 to Fall 1936. I don't see anything indicating a pre-existing relationship with McCurdy prior to the November correspondence.[2]

Through the authorization of Douglas Metzler, executor of Purvis's estate, access to Purvis's file in Curtis's extensive archives was granted. The file contains, among other things, letters of recommendation, correspondence, high school transcripts, records of his course work at Curtis, grades received, and photos. These documents, many of which are transcribed below, give insight into Purvis's personality and preparation.[3]

The Application Process

November sixth [1935]

Dear Mr. McCurdy:

Your letter arrived yesterday, and while I had entertained no intentions of going East this season, I am intensely interested in its contents. Especially after talking the matter over with my family and Mr. Sabin. (I'm sure you would not have wished me to exclude Mr. Sabin from the contents of your letter, despite the fact that you wished all information therein to be of a confidential nature.) It will be impossible for me to leave until the first of the year as there are many things that must be tied up before leaving. That is, of course, assuming that Curtis Institute will accept me.

There are two hitches, however. My funds will take me East and last six months, so I would have to find some kind of work within that period. Then, I should like to feel certain that my ability is worth such a scholarship, and that you are not overestimating what talent I have. However, I give you my word of honor that I will work to my utmost to prove worthy of [the] consideration you have given me.

Please accept my profound gratitude for your kindness in remembering me. If the thing seems at all feasible please let me know at your convenience.

My best wishes to you and Mrs. McCurdy.

Sincerely,

Richard Irven Purvis

[Carbon copy of letter from The Curtis Institute]
November 11, 1935
Mr. Richard Irven Purvis
7870 Garfield Avenue
Oakland, California

My dear Mr. Purvis:

At the request of Mr. Alexander McCurdy we are sending you a catalogue, under separate cover, and enclosing an application form in this letter.

We ask each student to place on file information concerning their previous preparation and experience. Will you please give us the required information in as much detail as possible, especially as to dates.

While vacancies in the Organ Department are filled, there is a scholarship available for a student of Organ who is qualified to meet the entrance requirements. Mr. McCurdy is recommending you for this scholarship. We understand that it will be impossible for you to come East before January first.

We shall be glad to have you complete and return this application blank as soon as convenient.

Very truly yours,

[   ]

November 15, 1935
Miss Helen Hoopes [administrative assistant]
The Curtis Institute of Music
Rittenhouse Square
Philadelphia, Pennsylvania

My dear Miss Hoopes:

Your kind letter of the eleventh with the enclosed application was duly received and I am returning the application with my latest photo, doctor's certificate, and birth certificate.

I am certain all the information I have given you is completely infallible and hope that I have answered all questions to your satisfaction.

In regard to the request for programs; I do not make it a habit of keeping programs and so those that you find enclosed are by no means choice examples, but merely stray ones that were about the house.

If there is any further information you desire, or should I have erred in my understanding of what was desired, I shall be glad, upon request, to give you any more data you may require.

Yours truly,

Richard Irven Purvis

[Application form to Curtis, dated November 15, 1935]

Permanent home address: 7870 Garfield Avenue, Oakland, California

Parent or Guardian: George Tunley Purvis; Father's occupation: Mechanic

Date of Birth: August 25, 1913

Religion: Presbyterian[4]

Height: 5 ft 5-1/2 in.; Weight 138 lbs.

Private Teachers and Dates of Study:
    Organ: Wallace Sabin, Berkeley, Jan 1926–present
    Piano: Maybelle Willis, San Francisco, Aug 1923–June 1926
    Piano: Wallace Sabin, Berkeley, Jan 1927–Dec. 1931
    Piano: Benjamin Moore, San Francisco, Jan 1933–Dec. 1935
    Harmony and Counterpoint: Wallace Sabin, two years work

High School Attended: Fremont High, Oakland, Cal., Jan 27–Dec 29
                See attached sheet*

Public appearances as a vocal or instrumental soloist:
    Handel Organ Concerto with Orchestra, Berkeley, 1931
    Recital for Sacramento A.G.O. 1932, San Francisco Music Week 1931
    Bach Recital 1933
    Regular Annual Recitals 1930–31–32–33–34
    Recital Convention of Local Guild Chapters (4), Grace Cathedral 1935

Name and Address of Organization
    Accompanist Wednesday Morning Choral Club, Aug 34–present
    Accompanist and Soloist Bach Festival Program by Steindorf Choral
        Society, Major work performed "Magnificat", Mar 35
    Organist for Various Church Choirs since 1928.

List some of the most important compositions which you have studied:
    Bach: Trio Sonatas, Chorale Preludes, Preludes and Fugues, Toccatas,
        Fantasie
    Handel: Two Organ Concerti
    Widor: Various movements from Symphonies V & VI
    Franck: Chorales in A and B min. Finale in B flat, Pastorale, Piece
        Heroique
    Vierne: Various Movements from Symphonies I, II, and III
    Karg-Elert: Four Pastels, Chorale Preludes, etc.
    Dupre: Prelude and Fugue in G min., Cortege and Litany

Above-mentioned attached sheet
General Education
    Although I have not graduated from a public High School and therefore
have no diploma,[5] I tutored for three years after leaving public school. The
following are the subjects studied:

English, Two Semesters
  Grammatical Analysis and Composition
Biology, Two Semesters
French (Continuation of Two years High School Work), Two Years
German (Continuation of three semesters High School Work), Three Years
  The English and Biology were taken at the Reid School which has since moved to another part of the State.

  The French and English were taken under Mme. Alwine Wilhelm of 2411 Dwight Way, Berkeley. Both she and Mrs. James Reid were recognized as credited [sic] teachers by Oakland Board of Education and University of California at Berkeley.

  I also have two Semesters of Conducting to my credit at the Golden Gate Junior College of San Francisco.

Both Wallace Sabin and Benjamin Moore filled out and signed a standard recommendation form for Purvis, which states: "I, _____, have known _____ for ____ years and consider (him or her) to possess musical talent likely to lead to a professional career. I cordially recommend (him or her) to the consideration of The Curtis Institute of Music." Rev. Ezra Allen Van Nuys, minister of Calvary Presbyterian Church, San Francisco, wrote a brief memo, dated December 5, 1935: "I, Ezra Allen Van Nuys, D.D., have known Richard Irven Purvis for two years and consider his talent sufficient to warrant a successful musical career." On November 15, 1935, George V. Cochran, M.D., Oakland, California, submitted a memo: "TO WHOM IT MAY CONCERN: This is to certify that I have this day examined Mr. Richard Irven Purvis of Oakland, California and find him to be in very good physical condition."

As part of his application Purvis submitted a Sunday bulletin, dated August 25, 1935, from Calvary Presbyterian Church. His 11:00 a.m. preludes that day: Marcel Dupré, Cortege and Litany; Carl McKinley, Andante Cantabile; postlude: Carl McKinley, Allegro Maestoso. For the 7:30 p.m. organ recital before the evening service: Karg-Elert, Soul of the Lake; Horatio Parker, Allegretto; Edward Sturges, Meditation.

  [Telegram, sent as a Night Letter]
  December 1, 1935
  Alexander McCurdy

Second Presbyterian Church
Phila

SHALL I OR SHALL I NOT MAKE DEFINITE ARRANGEMENTS TO GO
EAST JANUARY FIRST RETURNED APPLICATION TO CURTIS TWO
WEEKS AGO AND HAVE RECEIVED NO REPLY TO DATE RADIO CON-
TRACT DEMANDS THREE WEEKS NOTICE BEFORE CANCELLATION
PLEASE LET ME KNOW WITHIN A WEEK
      RICHARD IWEN [*sic*] PURVIS

(C O P Y) [typescript of text to be sent as telegram]
DAY LETTER
December 1, 1935

    The reason you have not heard further from the Institute is that the third recommendation has not been received. Tonight I arranged through Mrs. Bok directly for you to come. Your acceptance in the Institute is assured. Make all arrangements. I will expect you around January first.
    Alexander McCurdy

[Carbon copy of letter from Curtis Institute]
December 2, 1935
Mr. Richard Irven Purvis
7870 Garfield Avenue
Oakland, California

My dear Mr. Purvis:
    This letter will confirm the telegram sent you yesterday by Mr. Alexander McCurdy notifying you of your acceptance as a student of The Curtis Institute of Music for the season 1935–36.
    Will you kindly acknowledge receipt of this letter in writing and report to the Registrar for your schedule as soon after January first, 1936, as your duties in California will permit.
    May we suggest that you plan to arrive during the week so that we may be of assistance to you in finding a room.
    Very sincerely yours,
      [ ]
    Assistant to the Director

[Handwritten on Chapel of the Chimes letterhead]
December Seventh [1935]
Miss Dorothy Lynch
Curtis Institute of Music
Philadelphia, Pennsylvania

My dear Miss Lynch:

Please excuse this somewhat tardy reply to your letter of December second. Due to my absence from Oakland, I failed to receive the missive until yesterday.

I am indeed happy over the good fortune which has come my way and shall endeavor to prove myself worthy of the honor conferred upon me. I have long admired Curtis and its standards and to be within its walls is, indeed, an ambition achieved.

It is quite impossible for me to arrive in Philadelphia before January sixth or seventh, but I shall report to Curtis without delay.

Thank you for your kind offer of assistance.

Sincerely,

Richard Irven Purvis

[Handwritten on Chapel of the Chimes letterhead]
December Seventh [1935]
Miss Helen Hoopes
Curtis Institute of Music
Rittenhouse Square
Philadelphia, Pennsylvania

My dear Miss Hoopes:

I have at last discovered why you have never received my third reference. Dr. Van Nuys was out of town when the application arrived and in an endeavor to save time I mailed a reference blank to him but I must have erred in addressing it as he failed to receive it. However, under separate cover we are sending a written reference which we have tried to make as near the original as our memories would permit.

I do hope you will excuse this somewhat absurd delay.

Sincerely,

Richard Irven Purvis

[From The Curtis Institute]
December 10, 1935
Mr. Richard Irven Purvis
7870 Garfield Avenue
Oakland, California

My dear Mr. Purvis:

We have received Mr. Van Nuys recommendation by this time and you need have no further cause for worry.

Mrs. Lynch has also received your letter saying that you will reach Philadelphia about January sixth or seventh.

Very truly yours,

[   ]

The Saga of the High School Requirements

Among Purvis's application materials to Curtis is a "Certified Record of High School Work." Dated January 14, 1936, it was written on a form of the Commonwealth of Pennsylvania Department of Public Instruction Credentials Division (Harrisburg).

Purvis had not formally graduated from high school, and the administration at Curtis insisted that he make up the high school courses he lacked, concurrently with his college coursework at Curtis.

[From The Curtis Institute]
January 23, 1936
Mr. James G. Pentz, Chief
Credentials & Examination Division
Department of Public Instruction
Harrisburg, Pennsylvania

My dear Mr. Pentz:

I am enclosing the High School record of one Richard Purvis. I remember when you were here you said that we could credit something that was equivalent to High School. Do you think we can consider that he has completed the course? He is a very worthwhile student and will probably stay here long enough to be eligible for the degree if we can manage to credit him with the High School. If you wish, I will write to the individual tutors although I think the boy's word is not to be questioned.

Another question—must we be adamant about American History? One of our former students is eligible for the degree here except that he has not had this. Can we grant the degree with the provision that he does not teach in Pennsylvania? He probably will not anyway for he is a first class flutist and will be in a symphony orchestra all his life.

I wonder if it is as cold in Harrisburg as it is here? All the students are frozen and I am glad we can sit here all day and not go back and forth as they have to, to classes.

Very sincerely yours,
 J. F. H. [Miss Jane Hill]
 Registrar

January 24, 1936
Miss Jane Hill
Registrar, Curtis Institute of Music
Rittenhouse Square
Philadelphia, Pennsylvania

Dear Miss Hill:

I am returning herewith the high school record for Richard Purvis. According to our rating Mr. Purvis has credit for eleven units, or two and three-fourth years. In order to meet our requirements Mr. Purvis should furnish credit in a year of a laboratory science—Biology, Physics or Chemistry and electives to be selected from subjects not studied in high school.

Very sincerely yours,
 James G. Pentz
 Chief, Credentials & Examinations Division

For six weeks in July and August 1936, Purvis attended Temple University High School in Philadelphia, where he took Zoology, Latin, and Sociology, receiving "A" grades in each. His transcript was sent to James Pentz, who wrote to Miss Hill at Curtis on September 24, 1937, stating that "Mr. Purvis originally had 11 units. He has one additional unit or a total of 12 units at the present time."

Again in July and August 1938, Richard attended Temple University High School, this time studying Economics and Botany. These courses still failed to satisfy the high school requirement. On November 11, 1939,

Miss Hill wrote in a memo to the composer Randall Thompson, then Director of The Curtis Institute: "Board of Education in Harrisburg says that he has 11 units from High School and is lacking 1 unit of a laboratory science and 4 elective units. He has made up 2 units at Temple University High School but still has 3 to go before he has the required 16 for High School graduation." This appears to be the end of correspondence on the subject; somehow Purvis was allowed to graduate.[6]

The Advantages of a Curtis Education

All Curtis students since 1928 have been accepted on a full-scholarship basis. This policy was put into effect by Josef Hofmann, Director at Curtis 1927–1938, who wanted to model the school after European classical conservatories.[7] Purvis studied with financial support from the Cyrus Curtis Organ Scholarship during his four years at Curtis. Susanna Thurlow describes the precise nature of scholarship Purvis received:

> The Cyrus Curtis Organ Scholarship, as it is referred to in Vol. 7, No. 2 of *Overtones* [the semi-annual magazine of the Curtis Institute], is simply the name of the scholarship under which Purvis was studying. Each student since 1928 has been awarded a scholarship to study free of charge at Curtis. When Mary Louise Curtis Bok's husband, Edward Bok, died in 1930, Mrs. Bok endowed the Institute with 12 million dollars to help keep the Institute tuition-free. I assume when Cyrus Curtis died in 1933, himself an amateur organist, he left a certain amount to Curtis to further organ studies and Purvis was one of the recipients; in fact, in 1926–27 Cyrus Curtis funded the Aeolian Pipe Organ in the recital hall. In 1937 the organ was rebuilt and this probably used up a considerable amount of the fund, but this is speculation! Looking at a current program, I no longer see this particular scholarship listed, but each and every student is a "fellow" of some kind, studying under a specific scholarship, and each student is funded by a fellowship. The first mention I can find of the award is in *Overtones* from 1934. I assume that Purvis received similar treatment; the Cyrus Curtis Organ Scholarship most likely funded his trip to Europe. Many students during those days travelled to Europe for summer study, funded by the Institute, sometimes by Mrs. Bok herself. Today, a student awarded a scholarship studies under this name for the duration of his studies.[8]

Regarding the scholarship, the Biographical Data states, "This was the only time that an organist had been awarded this fellowship by the Curtis Institute."[9] The assertion is inaccurate, and Susannah Thurlow clarifies: "Your source stating that Purvis was the only recipient of this award is not correct as Paul Zuydhoek seems to be the first recipient [in 1933].[10] Although I can find no origination of this award and searched through clippings from 1933–34, I think, for posterity's sake, that the title of the award should continue to be the Cyrus Curtis Organ Scholarship, as mentioned in Curtis's *Overtones*."[11]

From the 1935–36 Admissions Catalogue:

Privileges Enjoyed by Students of The Curtis Institute

Free tuition.

Individual instruction by world-famous artists.

Financial aid when warranted.

Steinway grand pianos, string and wind instruments for home practice.

Preparatory public and radio performances.

Summer study for students of outstanding merit, under the artistic supervision of their major teachers.

Curtis Institute Graduates Who Qualify Receive

The Diploma of The Curtis Institute of Music.

The Degree of Bachelor of Music.

The Degree of Master of Music.

Introductory public appearances here and abroad.

Individual coaching in preparation for specific engagements.

Continued use of instruments owned by the Institute.

Continued use of music from the Library of the Institute.

Assistance in obtaining engagements by The Curtis Institute Concert Management.[12]

A look through the roster of Curtis students of that time reveals several famous names. Among them are Leonard Rose ('39), Lukas Foss ('40), and Leonard Bernstein ('41). Jonas Nordwall recalls hearing Purvis say that he sat across the aisle from Leonard Bernstein in composition class.[13] Vaughn Jones, a student of Purvis's, wrote, "I remember getting to his house and telling him that I had just heard on the radio that Leonard Bernstein had died, and Purvis started to cry. He said he had sat behind Bernstein in class at Curtis in Philadelphia."[14] (There was also a Frank Sinatra in the class of '36, but not the famous crooner.) With a small class size, Purvis probably knew most of his classmates well.

Course Work at Curtis

In the Curtis archives are complete records for Purvis's course work and private lessons. It is evident from these records that Purvis not only received very rigorous training, but that he excelled in all of his subjects. The curriculum stressed music theory and languages. Although Purvis seems not to have played the piano in recitals while at Curtis or after

Purvis in the cafeteria of The Curtis Institute, 1938. Photo by Fritz Henle. Courtesy The Henle Archive Trust.

graduation, he studied the piano seriously with Josef Levine, of whom he spoke often throughout his career. (He studied with other piano faculty as well while at Curtis; all of these teachers were students of Levine.)

1935–1936 [actually Purvis was there only for Winter and Spring of 1936]

(Private lessons were graded in the following four categories: Talent, Special; Talent, Native; Industry; and Progress.)

Organ, McCurdy	A, A, A, A–
Piano, Grade B, Levine	B+, B+, A, A
Solfège, Miquelle	A[15]
German, Turk	A–
Harmonic E. T. & P. [Ear Training & Practice?], Soffray	A+
Theory I, Soffray	A+
Faculty Recitals	

Compositions studied during year:
  Bach, Allegro from Sonata No. 6
  Vierne, Cantabile, Sym. 2, memorized
  Vierne, Scherzo, Sym. 2
  Handel, Concerto No. 5
  Bach, Vivace, Sonata No. 2, memorized
  Bach, Jesu, meine Freude
  Bach, Passacaglia
  Bach, Lord Jesus (Advent)

Purvis was given "A" grades for Previous training, General musical knowledge, and Technical ability; surprisingly, under "Special faults" is a notation of "General organ technique."

1936–1937

Organ, McCurdy	A, A, A, A
Piano, Grade B, Levine	
Piano, Grade B, Miss Behrend (after Levine left on tour)	B+, A, B+, B+
Instrumentation I, Mr. Scalero	C+, B[16]
Elements of Music I, Scalero	C+, B

Harmony & Counterpoint III, Miss Soffray	A, A, A+
Aural Harmony, Soffray	A, A, A+
Keyboard Harmony, Soffray	A, B+, A
Solfège, Mme. Miquelle	C–, A–, B
French II, Mr. Daudon	A, A, A+, A+
German IIIB, Miss Turk	A–, A–
Eurhythmics, Mr. deMontoliu (absent too much, dropped class)	
Faculty Recitals	
Student concert given (0.5 student hour)	
Radio: C.I.M. [Curtis Institute of Music] Broadcast, .1	

Purvis's residence at this time was 1207 Spruce Street, Philadelphia; telephone number, Pennypacker 7742.

1937–1938

Organ, McCurdy	A, A, A+, A
Piano, Grade B, Massena	B, B, C, C
("dropped him since he was so busy outside")	
Instrumentation II, Scalero	A–, A–
Elements of Music II, Scalero	A–, A–
Harmony & Counterpoint III, Soffray	B+, B+, B
Aural Harmony III, Soffray	A, B+
Keyboard Harmony, Soffray	B, B+, B–
Solfège, Miquelle	C–
French IV, Englander	B–, C+, A–, B
German IIIB, Turk	A–, A–
Radio: C.I.M. Broadcast	

1938–1939

Organ, McCurdy	A, A, A, A
Aural Harmony III, Soffray	A+, A+
Keyboard Harmony III, Soffray	B+, B
Written Harmony III, Soffray	B+, B–
Adv. French, Tabuteau	A, B–
German (Ind.), Turk	A–, A–

Purvis at the organ in Casimir Hall, late 1930s. The Aeolian organ was built in 1927 and was expanded by Aeolian-Skinner in 1937. Courtesy The Curtis Institute of Music.

German Conversation, Stöhr   P[ass]
Faculty Recitals
Radio: C.I.M. Broadcast, Christmas Broadcast

Compositions studied during year:
    Franck: Chorale in A minor
    Franck: Chorale in B minor
    Bach: Prelude and Fugue in G major
    Bach: Toccata in F
    Bach: Lamb of God
    Dallier: Electa ut sol

Notation, May 1940, from Miss Hoopes: "He is to play his graduation recital in May. Shall he get the Certificate of Excellence? Believe McCurdy will recommend this." Pencil notation: "Yes, if McCurdy approves."

Purvis's residence at this time was 2210 Sansom Street, Philadelphia; telephone number, Locust 5794.

1939–1940

Organ, McCurdy	A, A, A, A
Assembly	
Adv. French, Englander	
German, Turk	A–, A
Faculty Recitals	

May 7, 1940, Graduation Recital

May 10, 1940, "Received diploma and considered a graduate student. Will not return for season 1940–41"[17]

Course completed for diploma in Organ, May 10, 1940

Alexander McCurdy	recommends
May Bok	President approves
R[andall]. Thompson	Director approves

When Purvis graduated, his parents telegrammed Mary Louise Curtis Bok, expressing "gratitude for the opportunity you have given Richard in presenting him with a scholarship[;] also a trip to England to study there."[18]

Alexander McCurdy

The single greatest influence on Purvis while at Curtis was certainly his teacher Alexander McCurdy, who was born in California in 1905 and who also had been a Curtis student. Although McCurdy had completed his studies there in 1931, the first graduation at Curtis did not take place until 1934. All eligible students were invited back to Curtis to receive diplomas, and McCurdy received his diploma that year. He was then invited to join the faculty in 1935, and he was soon named head of the organ department.[19]

Shortly after McCurdy's death in 1983, his former student John Weaver wrote a short biography of McCurdy and a description of his teaching style. The following information is taken from Weaver's article in *The American Organist*:

> Alexander McCurdy was born in Eureka, California, in 1905. He became organist of a major church in Oakland, California, at age 15, and two years

Alexander McCurdy at unidentified organ, around 1937.
Courtesy The Curtis Institute of Music archives.

later he was appointed to St. Luke's Episcopal Church in San Francisco. McCurdy went to New York to study with Lynnwood Farnam and piano with Edwin Hughes. When Farnam was appointed the first head of the organ department at the Curtis Institute of Music in 1927, McCurdy was in his first class. That same year McCurdy became organist and choirmaster of the Second Presbyterian Church in Philadelphia.

In 1934 McCurdy graduated from Curtis, and a year later he joined the faculty. He was named head of the organ department, serving in that capacity until his retirement in 1972. He also was head of the organ department at the Westminster Choir College from 1940 until 1965. He was a legend among musicians in the Philadelphia area. He performed frequently as an organ soloist and with other instrumentalists, and for decades conducted weekly performances of major choral works. He died in Philadelphia in 1983.

As a teacher, McCurdy was demanding, and he did not suffer anyone foolish enough to come to a lesson unprepared.... Lessons and organ class were conducted with formality. The dress code was jacket and tie and well-polished shoes, and Dr. McCurdy never called a student by first name.

Dr. McCurdy's own playing style remained very much in the Farnam tradition, but he never forced his concepts upon his students. Each of us had great latitude to draw ideas from sources as diverse as Biggs and Fox. I never heard him say one negative thing about the various recitalists he presented at his church. He believed that each had something unique to pass on to us, and he would always point out what he appreciated about each one's playing. Consequently, each of his students developed a style which was individual and distinctive....

I think his students all regarded him with a sort of Old Testament combination of fear and love. To many of us he was like a second father—strict but supportive, prodding us when we failed but reveling in our successes, instilling in us his love of music and his high standard of humanity, and generous in both his admonitions and his blessings.[20]

On April 23, 1978, the choir of Virginia Heights Baptist Church in Roanoke, Virginia, performed Purvis's "The Ballad of Judas Iscariot." After receiving and listening to a copy of the recording, McCurdy wrote two letters to Richard Cummins, organist and director for the performance (and also a student of McCurdy's from 1954 to 1961): "Richard Purvis had <u>something</u> to say and he SAID it—he was so young when he wrote it ["Judas"],

Alexander McCurdy at the Aeolian-Skinner organ, Curtis Institute of Music, 1941. Photo by Kubey-Rembrandt Studios. Courtesy Curtis Institute of Music.

I am always amazed about the piece."[21] McCurdy continues, "I wish that you knew him [Purvis], he is quite a character. I have known him since he was a little boy, I guess he was fourteen or so,[22] then of course my experience teaching him was a rare privilege—he wanted to LEARN!"[23]

Many of McCurdy's traits as a teacher and mentor were adopted by Purvis, as can be readily discerned from comments by Purvis's students. (See Chapter 10, "Purvis as Teacher.")

Josef Levine[24]

During Nelson Barden's 1981 interview, Purvis spoke of his piano studies with Josef Levine:

NB: How was he [Levine] to study with? How old a man was he?

RIP: He must have been in his fifties. He played for me some, not a lot. "I think it would be a little better like this." Or, "Don't you think you could get a little more fluent like this? Does that have to stand out in that ugly way?" He spoke without very much of a Russian accent. I heard him play concerts, and I was also there when he made recordings in his New York studio....

He did one thing for me I'll never forget. Godowsky used to have these "Afternoons." It was in an apartment on West 57th Street, and the main room was two stories high. It was a buffet, there was food and drink, and they started about noon and went to all hours. I was able to go about twice with Josef Levine, and both times Rachmaninoff was there, drinking awful vodka. Not ours, but that potato stuff out of a water glass with no ice in it. Very slowly. Then get up and play the piano like three angels. I couldn't even find the piano! ... But that was a tremendous experience to have been there. Of course you're very impressionable. I didn't say a word, I just came and sat. The Levines were very proper leaving, and I never wanted to go! But I was beholden to them, I had to leave when they left. I could have stayed there until midnight!

NB: Did Levine teach you specific things, or was it just absorbing his spirit?

RIP: There were certain things about phrases. He spoke as though he had studied Gregorian chant. Every phrase does THIS. You had to do that in conception with the length of the phrase and the distance the phrase travels pitchwise.... Music was either going up, going down, or standing still. When it's standing still, meaning it doesn't move up or down on the staff, you have to give the illusion of movement by either a crescendo or diminuendo. And it's true....

What I did with [Benjamin] Moore and Lhevinne goes directly into organ technique. He made a point of pitch duration and spaciousness between notes. If you were playing staccato, Lhevinne would insist the silence between the notes would be as long as the note itself, or it wasn't staccato. That works on the organ, too. It's like the release. You don't worry nearly as much about the release on the piano as you do on the organ.[25]

Wanda Landowska

Douglas Metzler recalls hearing Purvis say that he had studied harpsichord with Wanda Landowska at Curtis, or at least had met her there. Metzler inherited from Purvis a beautiful record album personally autographed by Landowska, although he has no information about when or where Purvis may have acquired it.[26] Susannah Thurlow of Curtis added: "I do not know anything about Purvis' relationship with Landowska. Her last year at Curtis was 1928."[27]

Performance Opportunities While at Curtis

When he arrived at Curtis in January 1936, Purvis was immediately appointed organist and choirmaster of Tioga Methodist Church,[28] which was located at 18th and Tioga in Philadelphia. This was a wealthy church with a fine pipe organ. The church was demolished in the 1950s and has since moved to a new location.[29]

On April 9, 1936, Purvis made his first Eastern appearance as recitalist on the six-manual organ at the John Wanamaker store in Philadelphia.[30] As reported in *The Diapason*, his program included "Invocation" by Karg-Elert; "Allegretto" by Parker; "Cradle Song" by Dupré; "Scherzo Burlesca" by Bossi; and "Three Mountain Sketches" by Clokey.[31]

During the Barden interview, Purvis said, "At Wanamaker's it's fun to play the organ at night—they used to have concerts at night—this was when I was at Curtis. People came and sat, you had a card for admittance that said Men's Shoes, Women's Underwear, things like that. They put chairs around, and that's where you sat. The cards used to cause a lot of comment."[32]

It is obvious from the following 1936 postal card to June Townsend that Purvis enjoyed his studies at Curtis and was successful as a performer: "Curtis exceeds my highest expectations and I am enjoying the work immensely, though it is real hard and there is more than enough of it. I have a church job already and have been playing the harpsichord in the performance of the Bach 'Passion' at the Second Presbyterian Church. I'm crazy about the snow and sledding is great fun."[33]

Purvis also received notice in his hometown newspaper, *The Oakland Tribune*:

> When the "Curtis Institute of Music" of Philadelphia is in the national hook-up next Wednesday at 1:00 PM, Richard Purvis, Oakland boy, will be featured by the organ department. Young Purvis received a scholarship from the institute a year ago based entirely on the merits of his work in the bay area.
>
> He has been accorded numerous honors since going to the "Quaker City" in January. He appeared with the Philadelphia Philharmonic Symphony Orchestra soon after arriving there; played for the Democratic Convention of June; has given recitals on the largest pipe organ in the world at Wanamaker's, and is organist of the Tioga Methodist Church, largest Protestant Church in Philadelphia.[34]

It is unclear if the orchestra reference above is to the Philadelphia Orchestra or another orchestra. Darrin Britting, archivist of the Philadelphia Orchestra, supplied the following information:

> I was able to look on our list of full-time Orchestra members and Mr. Purvis was not among them. This is not unusual, however, as organists generally are not considered members of the Orchestra (and still are not to this day). He might have played with the orchestra in pieces that required organ as part of the instrumentation, but I would not have that information. I also looked on our list of soloists who might have appeared with the Orchestra and did not see Mr. Purvis mentioned there either. I don't know if there was a Philadelphia Philharmonic at any point. We have always been called The Philadelphia Orchestra.[35]

Among Purvis's papers was a typed schedule for the West Coast Convention of the AGO, held in the Bay Area June 25–27, 1936. Purvis was probably in England at the time, so it is unlikely that he attended this convention. Based on the convention venues and offerings, however, it appears that he may at least have had a hand in planning it. Included were a Cinema Organ Recital at the Paramount Theatre by Floyd Wright; lecture and recital at Stanford University; recital at Calvary Presbyterian Church, assisted by either the Loring or Wednesday Morning Choral Club; lecture at Temple Emanu-El; recitals at Grace Cathedral; Trinity Episcopal Church; First Church of Christ, Scientist; St. Paul's Church (Oakland); and a demonstration at the Chapel of the Chimes.[36]

William W. Carruth, a Bay Area correspondent who frequently wrote a column for the San Francisco Chapter of the AGO in *The Diapason*, often included notices about Purvis and his activities in the East. An example is found in the February 1937 issue: "In a recent coast-to-coast broadcast of the Curtis Institute of Music, Richard Purvis, formerly of Calvary Presbyterian Church and new organist of Tioga Methodist Church, Philadelphia, and a brilliant student at the institute, was heard in a program of Christmas music."[37] In March 1937, Carruth mentions in a notice titled "McCurdy Students in Recital" that Purvis performed the Cantabile and Scherzo from Symphony No. 2 and Sortie from 'Messe Basse' by Vierne."[38]

Classmate Clarence Snyder recalled that Purvis played the organ for occasional dances held in Casimir Hall at Curtis.[39]

Studies in Europe, Summers of 1936 and 1937

Purvis often spoke of his studies in England and on the Continent. Through the years, however, Purvis's own account of his European studies, as well as accounts by others in publicity releases and obituaries, became increasingly exaggerated.

The Curtis scholarships often paid for summer study in Europe, and with this funding Purvis spent the summers of 1936 and 1937 overseas. In England he spent time in London, in York, and on the Isle of Wight; he also visited Paris. However, it is not entirely clear during which of these two summers he spent time in which places.

While abroad Purvis was able to meet with many remarkable musicians, including Sir Edward Bairstow, Sir Ernest Bullock, Sir Sydney Nicholson, Sir William McKie, Sir Ralph Vaughan Williams, Marcel Dupré, and possibly Charles Tournemire.[40]

Various sources, including the Biographical Data, place Purvis in Europe for well over a year (June 1936 until the fall of 1937), but this cannot be correct. His class records show that he was in residence at Curtis for the 1936–1937 academic year and again starting in the fall of 1937. Other sources claim he spent four months on the Isle of Wight, was in Paris in January 1937, etc., but these, too, are inaccurate.

1936

Purvis spent the summer of 1936 in Chislehurst and York, England. It is not known exactly what he studied, but it probably included organ, conducting, and perhaps composition.

A notice in *The Diapason* gives the following report: "Richard Purvis, now organist of St. James [Episcopal] Church in Philadelphia, was the holder of the Cyrus H. K. Curtis European Traveling Fellowship of Curtis during the summer,[41] which enabled him to study in England. While at the School of English Church Music in Chislehurst he played a post-service recital."[42]

The Biographical Data states, "When he reached England, he studied first at the School of English Church Music in Chislehurst. Here he stayed from June through August of 1936.[43] Upon the advice of Sir Sidney Nicholson, Warden of the College of St. Nicholas, Richard went to York Minster cathedral in September 1936[44] for a full year [not accurate] of study with Sir Edward Bairstow. He admired and respected Bairstow, who was organist and Master of the Choristers at York Minster."[45]

Donald Sears wrote of Purvis's time in England:

Things got off to a rough beginning with Sir Edward, when at their first meeting, Bairstow lectured him severely about Americans coming over to England to "steal" elements of the English cathedral tradition for their own use. Even as a very young man, Purvis' irascible nature was evident when he took great exception to Bairstow's tirade. In his own words, which he told me many years later, "I said, 'I didn't come all the way over here to listen to this!!'" He returned to the hotel in a fury to begin packing for his return to America. While he was still packing, the phone rang. It was Madame Bairstow, who invited him to tea. Evidently things got smoothed over between the two antagonists, because Richard did finish out a year [not accurate] of study at York Minster."[46]

Douglas Metzler said that Purvis moved easily among the musicians of England, becoming acquainted with some of the great composers, and even taking walks with Vaughan Williams while he was visiting (and possibly living with) the Bairstows. Metzler also said that Purvis was more modest in his behavior in England than he was "back on his own turf" in the States, where he was likely to be "gruff and more arrogant in San Francisco."[47]

1937

Purvis spent most of the summer of 1937 at Quarr Abbey on the Isle of Wight, but he also visited London and Paris.

The following citations in *Overtones* tell of this sojourn in Europe (and confirm that he was in residence at Curtis during the academic years and not in Europe):

"The Curtis Institute will send Mr. Purvis to England during the summer for a two-months' pilgrimage of the famous old cathedrals and choir schools of that country."[48]

"The second student concert of the year was given by students of organ with Dr. Alexander McCurdy on Tuesday evening, February 9th.... Richard Purvis, the *Cantabile* and *Scherzo* from Vierne's Symphony No. 2, and the *Sortie* from 'Messe Basse' of the same composer."[49]

"Two students spent some time in Europe: Miriam Brunner visited Italy, where she studied composition with her teacher, Mr. Rosario Scalero. Richard Purvis, organist, made a pilgrimage of English cathedrals, observing the ritual and, in particular, the boy choir work. These students' European studies were financed by The Curtis Institute."[50]

The Biographical Data states, "Back in London, Purvis met with his friends Sir Sydney Nicholson and Sir Ernest Bullock. Both men advised him to study Gregorian chant with Dom Desroquettes of Quarr Abbey on the Isle of Wight. Upon his arrival[51] at Quarr Abbey, Purvis was not only exposed to the inspired teaching of Father Desroquettes but was "immersed in a sea of plainsong, hearing five services and one rehearsal daily."[52]

The following from June Townsend pinpoints the date of Purvis's voyage to England: "On a picture postcard [dated May 31, 1937] of the Wanamaker Organ, his mother writes the following: 'I heard Dick play on this organ and it is marvelous. Went to New York last Friday and Dick left Saturday noon for England.'"[53]

During Nelson Barden's 1981 interview, Purvis spoke of a return trip around 1968 to Quarr Abbey, more than 30 years after he had first lived there:

> RIP: The whole of the Isle of Wight is fun. That's where I studied Gregorian chant; I was at Quarr Abbey. It's just outside of Ryde, and not flourishing these days. I went there about 13 years ago.[54] Father Desroquettes, with whom I studied, was still alive, but it was pathetic. They were all old, old men and I went to evensong. They had no one to play the organ. It's a Cavaillé-Coll, incidentally, not a large two manual. The first time I played it I was disappointed because the Trompette was the only reed in the organ and was quite bland for a French reed.... I was there about three months, and I don't think I left the Abbey but once. They work your tail off. I didn't have to get up until 7, but by then they were all up and had said their individual masses already. I had a lot to do. In those three months I accomplished what it would have taken a year or two in the outside world. I had a lesson every day, and I had to be prepared.[55]

According to the Biographical Data, Purvis visited France during his 1937 trip abroad.[56] Corbett wrote, "He was determined to find out whether a study with the school of French organists would be advantageous to his study of church music. In Paris he met the distinguished Dupré, whom he greatly admired. Though Mr. Purvis respected the French school, he could not see its value in promoting his progress as an Anglican liturgical organist."[57]

It is unclear how much time Purvis spent in France; most likely he traveled several times from London to Paris for lessons with Dupré. According to Douglas Metlzer, Purvis had to go to an American Express office to get silver dollars, because Dupré demanded payment in silver.[58]

Ed Stout recalls distinctly hearing Purvis say that he met with Tournemire for lessons on several occasions. According to Stout, Curtis paid for Dupré's lesson fees, but Purvis had to pay Tournemire directly, and in cash.[59]

The Episcopal Academy, Overbrook

The May 1937 issue of *Overtones* announced:

> The Organ Department of The Curtis Institute is cooperating with St. James's Church (Philadelphia) and the Episcopal Academy (Merion, Pennsylvania) in establishing a choir school for boys to be under the direction of Dr. Alexander McCurdy. Plans have been worked out by the Reverend John Mockridge, Rector of St. James's Church, Mr. Greville Haslam, Headmaster of the Episcopal Academy, and Dr. McCurdy, Curtis Institute instructor of organ, for the formation of a boy choir for St. James's Church whose choristers will receive scholarships at the Episcopal Academy. A department of music is to be instituted at the Episcopal Academy, which Dr. McCurdy will head. These students of the Academy forming the choir of St. James's Church will have daily rehearsals with Dr. McCurdy.
>
> Preparations for the development of the choir school are already under way. Richard Purvis, Cyrus Curtis Organ Scholarship student in The Curtis Institute, becomes organist and assistant choirmaster of St. James's Church June 1st.... It is expected that the choir school will begin functioning in September.[60]

The Biographical Data states, "Upon his return to the United States in September 1937 to continue his studies at Curtis, Purvis, now 24 years of age, was appointed not only organist and choirmaster at St. James' Episcopal Church, Philadelphia, but also Assistant Head of the Music Department of the Episcopal Academy in Overbrook, Pennsylvania. These successive appointments resulted from the high recommendation of Alexander McCurdy, head of the organ department at the Curtis Institute."[61]

The Episcopal Academy in Overbrook, Pennsylvania, was founded in 1785 as a private secondary school for boys. In April 1937, a cooperative musical venture was established between the Episcopal Academy of Overbrook, St. James's Episcopal Church, and The Curtis Institute. A memo dated April 19, 1937, describes this new arrangement:

> Here then are three institutions, a central city Church, a Country Day School and a great Institute of Music. Each has a problem insoluble by itself. It is fortunate that personal friendship and "accidental" associations have brought them together in the development of a co-ordinated and cooperative plan.
>
> St. James's Church has arranged with the Episcopal Academy for the establishment of St. James's Choir School. Twenty boys will be chosen, and, in return for their services as Choristers, will be given their education at the Episcopal Academy. The boys become at once members of a great school with its high type of general education.[62]

An undated flyer entitled "The Choir School of St. James's Church, Philadelphia" made this statement:

> St. James's Choir School is the result of cooperative action on the part of St. James's Church, the Episcopal Academy and the Curtis Institute of Music through its Organ Department.
>
> The Church, by gifts of its members and friends, gives to each accepted boy a full Scholarship at the Episcopal Academy, a Country Day School of the highest standing, in return for his services as a Chorister at St. James's. At the Academy, in addition to their ordinary education, the boys are given daily training in Music under the direction of Dr. Alexander McCurdy, Head of the Organ Department at the Curtis Institute, and Mr. Richard Purvis, Organist of St. James's and Assistant Choirmaster. Mr. Purvis is the holder of The Cyrus H. K. Curtis Memorial Scholarship at the Curtis Institute.
>
> By the arrangement between the Church and the Episcopal Academy the boys form the Academy Chapel Choir at the service that begins every School Day.[63]

In his 1984 history of the school, Charles Latham, a former faculty member of the Episcopal Academy, wrote about the 1937 appointment of Alexander McCurdy as head of the music department. Latham elaborates:

> At the same time, the Rev. John Mockridge proposed a plan for a choir school: twenty boys would attend the Academy and also serve as the boys'

Purvis conducting a boys' choir, possibly at St. James's, Philadelphia, late 1930s. Courtesy The Curtis Institute.

choir at Mr. Mockridge's St. James's Church; the Church would pay a portion of their tuition, as well as the salaries of Messrs. McCurdy and Richard Purvis (the Academy's organist). In addition, arrangements were made to have other musicians give instrumental lessons at the Academy. The list of instructors was impressive, including Leonard Rose (cello), Joseph Levine (piano), Donald Sandifur (trombone), Frederick Vogelgesang (violin), and Richard Purvis (organ). By December it was reported that 28 boys were now taking lessons from eight different instructors. On the surface, it was a very impressive program. However, it rested on a shaky financial foundation. St. James's Church was losing members, and was disbanded in 1945. By December 1938 the church owed $435 in tuitions for the previous year, and $3000 for the first half of the current year. A modified arrangement for 16 boys was made for the following year. In June 1941 the choir school came to an end, with the church still several thousand dollars in arrears.[64]

Purvis, recently returned from England and steeped in his study of choirs of men and boys, must have been eager to work in a similar setting in the United States. His experience in England would also prove to be highly influential in his later establishment not only of a choir of men and boys but also of a cathedral school at Grace Cathedral.

Additional Performances at Curtis

Curtis's extensive online archives include course catalogues and recital programs; they also contain *Overtones*, a Curtis publication that began in 1929. Discontinued in the 1940s during the war, it was reinstated in 1986.[65]

Entries in the archived recital programs and *Overtones* show that Purvis performed on the following programs in Casimir Hall at Curtis:

February 9, 1937

Student recital shared with Walter Baker and Claribel Gegenheimer
    Purvis performed Cantabile and Scherzo from Vierne Symphony No. 2, and Sortie from Vierne "Messe Basse"
    "The Organ is an AEOLIAN"[66]

November 24, 1937

The Curtis Institute of Music Radio Programme, Columbia Broadcasting System
    Purvis performed Franck, Piece heroique; Bach, Vivace from Sonata No. 2 in C minor; Dupré, Cortège et litanie; Brahms, Es ist ein' Ros' Ent-sprungen; Schumann, Sketch in D-flat major; Vierne, Divertissement.[67]

October 17, 1938

The Curtis Institute of Music Radio Programme, Columbia Broadcasting System
    Purvis performed Bach, Prelude and Fugue in G major; Karg-Elert, Chorale Prelude "Thy Will Be Done;" and Vierne, Sortie from "Messe Basse." The program ended with Purvis accompanying soprano Florence Kirk in Franck's "O Lord Most Holy."[68]

December 19, 1938

The Curtis Institute of Music Radio Programme, Columbia Broadcasting System

Coordinated by Alexander McCurdy and performed by an ensemble of mixed chorus, string orchestra, organ, bells, and celesta and with the Choir Boys of St. James's, the program opened with "Silent Night," Gruber-Purvis arrangement; also on the program were Karg-Elert's "Glory be to God on High" and Dallier's "Electa ut Sol," probably organ solos by Purvis.[69] This program may have been an inspiration for Purvis's establishment of the Christmas Vespers concerts at Grace Cathedral, which used the same instrumentation and vocal resources.

February 21, 1940

Alexander McCurdy played a faculty recital, performing music of Bach, Schumann, Brahms, de Maleingreau, Arthur Egerton, and Purvis's "Communion."

"Aeolian-Skinner Organ"[70]

May 7, 1940

Purvis's Graduation Recital
    Franck: Chorale in A minor
    Bach: Allein Gott in der Hoh' sei Ehr,
              Liebster Jesu
              Prelude and Fugue in G major
    Karg-Elert: Ave Maria, from "Cathedral Windows"
    Langlais: La Nativité
    Mulet: Tu es Petra
      "Aeolian-Skinner Organ"[71]

A newspaper clipping dated May 8, 1940, probably from the *Philadelphia Bulletin*, contains the following review:

> Richard Purvis, organist, gave a graduation recital last night in Casimir Hall, Curtis Institute of Music. The substantial program embodying representative styles included the Cesar Franck "Chorale in A Minor," two choral preludes

and the Prelude and Fugue in G major by Bach, and a final group of pieces by Karg-Elert, Vierne, Langlais and Mulet. Playing with clarity and steady control, Mr. Purvis dealt effectively with the contrapuntal designs of Bach, and the problems of registration in the modern pieces. A large audience attended.[72]

Other Citations in *Overtones*

Overtones, Vol. VI, No. 1, May 1936, 61

"Three organ students obtained church positions: Claribel Gegenheimer, at the Bryn Mawr Presbyterian Church; Oscar Eiermann, at St. Ann's Episcopal Church, Willow Grove, Pennsylvania; and Richard Purvis, at the Tioga Methodist Church, Philadelphia."

Overtones, Vol. VII, No. 1, January 1937, 35

"The December 23rd concert was a Christmas program, featuring the organ and voice departments. Richard Purvis, organist, pupil of Dr. Alexander McCurdy, opened the program with the Bach Chorale Preludes *In Dulci Jubilo* and *Christians Rejoice*, and Dupré's *In Dulci Jubilo* and the Finale from *Variations sur un Noël*." ... "At the close of the program, Mr. Purvis played an improvisation on three carols: *Silent Night, Hark! the Herald Angels Sing, and Adeste Fidelis [sic]*."

Overtones, Vol. VII, No. 1, January 1937, 39

At a program on December 28, 1936, Richard Purvis accompanied baritone Lester Englander at The Barclay, a prominent hotel in Philadelphia.

Overtones, Vol. VII, No. 1, January 1937, 42

"Miss Thorne and Miss MacFarlane were soloists again at the Second Presbyterian Church on Sunday afternoon, December 13th, in a performance of Bach's *Magnificat*, with the chorus choir, Dr. McCurdy conducting. For this performance, Dr. McCurdy put two people at the organ: that is, one organist, Claribel Gegenheimer, played upon the organ proper, and a second organist, Richard Purvis, played upon an 'offset' console, being in fact a fifth manual. A harpsichord piano was used also, this part being played by Walter Baker. Miss Gegenheimer and Mr. Purvis are students under Dr. McCurdy at The Curtis Institute."

Overtones, Vol. VII, No. 1, January 1937, 44

"Richard Purvis is organist and choirmaster of the Tioga Methodist Church, Philadelphia.... All of these students are in complete charge of music at their respective churches."

Overtones, Vol. VII, No. 2, May 1937, 80

"The Curtis Institute will send Mr. Purvis to England during the summer for a two-months' pilgrimage of the famous old cathedrals and choir schools of that country."

Overtones, Vol. VII, No. 2, May 1937, 85

"The second student concert of the year was given by students of organ with Dr. Alexander McCurdy on Tuesday evening, February 9th.... Richard Purvis, the *Cantabile* and *Scherzo* from Vierne's Symphony No. 2, and the *Sortie* from 'Messe Basse' of the same composer."

Overtones, Vol. VIII, No. 1, November 1937, 28

"Two students spent some time in Europe: Miriam Brunner visited Italy, where she studied composition with her teacher, Mr. Rosario Scalero. Richard Purvis, organist, made a pilgrimage of English cathedrals, observing the ritual and, in particular, the boy choir work. These students' European studies were financed by The Curtis Institute."

Overtones, Vol. VIII, No. 1, November 1937, 29

"Richard Purvis (Organ), Donald Sandifur (Band and Orchestras), Joseph Levine (Piano), Frederick Vogelgesang (Violin), and Leonard Rose (Violoncello) are faculty members, headed by Dr. Alexander McCurdy, of the new Music Department of the Episcopal Academy, Overbrook, Pennsylvania. With the exception of Mr. Levine, all these members of Dr. McCurdy's staff are students of The Curtis Institute."

Overtones, Vol. IX, No. 1, December 1938, 3

John Simms—Lynne Wainwright—Frederick Vogelgesang—Richard Purvis with St. James's boy choir, p. 19 [an index entry]

Overtones, Vol. IX, No. 1, December 1938, 19

Photo with caption: "RICHARD PURVIS conducts the boy choir of St. James's (organist and assistant choirmaster)

Overtones, Vol. X, No. 1, December 1939, 24

"Richard Purvis, organist and assistant choirmaster of St. James's Church, Philadelphia, is presenting three organ recitals at the church in December, John Cooke and Clarence Snyder sharing one of them."

Overtones, Vol. X, No. 2, April 1940, 57

"Dr. McCurdy's program at the Cyrus Curtis organ the following week included a composition by his pupil, Richard Purvis, *Communion*."

Overtones, Vol. X, No. 2, April 1940, 58

"Graduation recitals have been given in the second half of our year by Abbey Simons, pianist, Noah Bielski, and Frederick Vogelgesang, both violinists. Richard Purvis, organist, will give his in May."

Overtones, Vol. X, No. 2, April 1940, 62

"Richard Purvis (graduating in Organ) has composed works for organ and church chorus: *Communion*, *Suite on Gregorian Themes*, three Christmas Carols, *Mass of St Nicholas*, and a *Magnificat*."

Purvis in *Life* Magazine

The December 12, 1938, issue of *Life* magazine featured an article entitled "Music: Ten Million Americans Become Musically Literate."[73] The article included several photographs taken by photojournalist Fritz Henle, many focusing on Curtis. On page 55 of the article is a photo in which Purvis appears at an organ console, accompanying a boys' choir. The photo on page 61 is very similar to the one in the *Life* magazine article.

Miscellaneous Activities, 1937–1938

According to Donald Corbett, Purvis met the Canadian organist-composer Healey Willan in late 1937. "At a later meeting with the English-born

Purvis conducting from the console in an unidentified Philadelphia church, 1938. Photo by Fritz Henle. Courtesy The Henle Archive Trust.

composer, a mutual friend persuaded Mr. Purvis to show Dr. Willan two of his organ compositions. The two became friends, and Dr. Willan encouraged Richard Purvis to continue his attempts at composition."[74]

On May 27, 1938, Purvis served as organist for the "Popular Meeting of The Board of Pensions of the Presbyterian Church, U. S. A.," held in Convention Hall, Philadelphia. He played three organ preludes for the meeting: J. S. Bach, Prelude and Fugue in G major; Dupré, "In Quiet Joy"; and Karg-Elert, "Invocation." Under the direction of Alexander McCurdy, he accompanied anthems by Thiman, Bach, C. L. Williams, Schubert, Franck, and Stainer.[75]

The following three listings appear in the Biographical Data but could not be verified:

> In July 1938 Purvis returned to his native Northern California. He appeared as a recitalist for the Northern California Chapter of the American Guild of Organists, playing recitals at Trinity Methodist Church, Berkeley. This Chapter was joined by the San Jose, Stockton, and Sacramento Chapters in sponsoring the event. His success secured a request by the Dean and Chapter of Grace Cathedral for another appearance in August of the same year.
>
> Also in July 1938 Purvis received from the Alumni Association of St. James' Episcopal Church's Liturgical Choir in Philadelphia an invitation to compose a Magnificat for male chorus. The composition was completed and first performed in September 1938 at St. James' in Philadelphia in the original form for two choirs. Upon the request of David McK. Williams, Organist and Choirmaster, St. Bartholomew's Church, New York City, this work was published for choir and baritone solo by G. Schirmer.
>
> In October 1938 Purvis was asked by Bishop Tait to teach a course on hymnology for the Winter Conference of the Dioceses of Pennsylvania. The success of this course warranted its repetition for the following two years.[76]

Studies with Courboin

During the summer of 1938, Purvis took the opportunity to study with Charles Courboin at the Peabody Conservatory in Baltimore. Courboin, a Belgian-born virtuoso, was organist at St. Patrick's Cathedral in New York

City from 1943 to 1973, succeeding Pietro Yon. He had also been organist for the John Wanamaker stores in Philadelphia and New York.[77]

In 1992 Jonathan Ambrosino interviewed Purvis about his experiences with Courboin. The interview was published in *The Erzähler, Journal of the Symphonic Organ Society,* in January 1995. The interview is reprinted here in its entirety, courtesy of Jonathan Ambrosino.

"Lessons with Dr. Courboin: A Conversation with Richard Purvis"

It was sad news indeed to learn that Richard Purvis passed away on Christmas Day. For the last few years, we were fortunate to spend many remarkable hours with this legendary San Francisco organist and composer, being regaled with reminiscences about his teachers, his favorite instruments, and the vibrant organ culture of the 1920s and '30s in which he grew up. Not only was Mr. Purvis invaluable in sifting fact from fiction, helping us to navigate through the nuances of other people's remembrances, but he was unfailingly generous with his time, his insights and his wisdom.

Mr. Purvis was a dramatic, colorful and individual organist—a rightful heir to the best of the late Romantic tradition. As a young man, he studied with two great Bay Area organists, Wallace Sabin (Temple Emanu-El) for organ and Ben Moore (Trinity Church) for piano. Afterward, he became a pupil of Alexander McCurdy at the Curtis Institute, Sir Edward Bairstow at York Minster, and the great pianists Josef and Rosina Lhevinne. He heard the best musicians of the day: on the organ, Edwin Lemare, Lynnwood Farnam, Courboin, McCurdy, Ernest Mitchell, David McK. Williams and the young Ernest White; on the piano, Sergei Rachmaninoff, Lhevinne, Josef Hoffman, and Leopold Godowsky, among many others. He even attended some of the famous weekly gatherings at Godowsky's New York apartment, at which Hoffman, Rachmaninoff, Godowsky and other pianistic wizards would play informally for each other's enjoyment.

As he talked, Mr. Purvis expressed how deeply he cherished having been a part of this era. He bemoaned the fact that, while more recent musical trends have been interesting and sometimes enlightening, very little modern music-making equaled the caliber of what he regularly heard as a young man. But he remained grateful. "I have no regrets," he said toward the end of our last conversation. "I had my time, and it was very good to me."

In our last discussion [September 1992], we specifically asked Mr. Purvis about his study with Dr. Charles Courboin, in order that it might be published with a series of articles on Courboin which Friends of the Wanamaker Organ President Ray Biswanger is preparing. As we were readying this piece for Mr. Purvis' pre-publication review, we learned of his passing. We regret that this conversation did not get far enough into the discussion of Franck, since Mr. Purvis went to Courboin specifically to study the works of this composer. However, Mr. Purvis offers us a valuable picture of this great musician and teacher.

The following is reconstructed from the notes of that last conversation, supplemented by quotations and recorded comments from prior discussions.

———

JA: What brought you to study with Charles Courboin?

RP: When I was an organ student at the Curtis Institute in the mid-1930s, I had already developed a great fondness for the music of César Franck. And yet I was very unhappy with the way I heard Franck's music being played. This sensation only became stronger after I spent time in Paris in 1937, and heard Charles Tournemire play Franck at Sainte-Clotilde. (At the time, I was on a scholarship from Curtis for two years, studying with Sir Edward Bairstow at York Minster in England.)[78]

The first thing I noticed was the especial warmth of the Sainte-Clotilde Cavaillé-Coll, especially in comparison with other Cavaillé-Colls I heard in Paris. The Sainte-Clotilde organ was very warm, and in a sense almost diminutive, like a large chamber organ. Although the organ had an unquestionable sense of energy, it was never actually loud. For example, the Swell Trumpet wasn't really all that large—just something to add a bit to the fat oboe, but it clearly performed its role coupled to the other foundations. Above all else, the organ was very beautiful, very lyrical, very warm.

The experience left a deep impression on me. When I returned to Curtis, I told my teacher, Alexander McCurdy, that I wanted to study Franck with someone who was more in tune with the practice of the idiom. Without a moment's hesitation, McCurdy said, "Courboin!"

When did you first meet Courboin?

I had heard him play before, and had perhaps shaken his hand at those recitals; at this point, I don't precisely remember. What I remember clearly, however, is that at no time was he anything less than extremely kind and gracious. He was very tall, a big man, very handsome and utterly charming. He spoke magnificent English, and did not seem foreign in any sense, at least not to me.

I learned from Alex that Courboin taught a summer course at the Peabody Institute [in Baltimore], and Alex convinced me that I should attend one. It was not exclusively organ study, but a full summer session in music, so I would be able to study things other than just organ. There would be as many as eighteen organ students in residence, and Courboin would come down from New York three to four days a week for teaching. I decided I would attend for the summer of 1938.

Commuting from New York to Baltimore to teach eighteen students? In summer?

You can see why there wasn't any question in my mind that Courboin adored his teaching. To him, every student was a different challenge, and in no sense did he want his students to play the same way, or in the way that he did. For instance, I remember that Claribel Thompson was there that year, a wonderful person and a beautiful player—entirely distinctive. When she played, you always knew exactly who was at the console. As the summer session was being organized, Courboin asked if I could take my lesson late in the afternoon, the last of the group. I thought it strange, but I soon found out why. Courboin had taken a liking to me; the schedule meant we could have a lesson as long as three hours.

Summer school was six weeks, one lesson a week. Naturally, with such long lessons, we covered many pieces each week. Furthermore, you were never finished with a piece. Out of the clear blue sky he'd ask you to play something you had prepared three lessons ago. He wanted to see if you had thought more about that piece and had come to a new point of view.

Were the long lessons tiring?

Not in the least. And besides, we often went out to dinner afterward. I learned as much then as I did during lessons!

Our dinners together were marvelous. Everything was very relaxed, although I would call him Dr. Courboin. He had a great sense of humor, and, like Ernest Skinner, he loved limericks. We never knew what we would talk about; conversation was spontaneous. He loved America, and had a real affection for this country. He especially liked the Pennsylvania

Dutch Country and its people. "They are so completely real and honest," I remember him saying, "there is no *guile* in them."

Courboin had an intense interest in anything artistic, and this shaped his entire outlook as a musician. In addition to his musical studies, he had taken a degree in engineering, and had become absorbed in matters of architecture. He was constantly using elements from these other disciplines to illuminate musical ideas. Anything that supported art could help us to a better understanding of music.

In such conversation, did he tend to avoid discussion of the organ?

No, not at all; we always returned to the organ and its music. He constantly spoke of the organ in relation to its variety and orchestral color—not imitative of the orchestra, but in an ensemble sense, how every voice related to every other between divisions and in the full ensemble. He wanted to play colorfully, but always logically and clearly. As he would critique my registrations, his first and last question was, "Does it make sense *musically*?" Beautiful effects were wasted if they stood out from the sense of architecture, if they violated the mood, if they clashed with the essential texture of a piece.

What elements of music-making did he emphasize?

In his teaching, Courboin always returned to three elemental principles in the consideration of any piece. First, one had to consider the architecture of the work; second was the texture; third was the emotional content.

The architecture was the most important, a point he would return to again and again. Where are the high points? he would ask, and how are you going to do them justice? What are the transitional points, at which you leave one mood and go to another? That was very important to him, that you should be able to carry the interest through from one point to the other, especially where the transitions were weakly written. At such a point he would say, "This is where the composer needs some help!" I remember this most especially in Widor's music, which Courboin admired and played a great deal of. But he felt that Widor occasionally had trouble with secondary themes, and would try to find ways to mold them and shape them, giving them greater interest so that the piece as a whole would not flag.

After architecture came texture. If the architecture defined the parameters of a piece, the texture was the actual landscape. Each section and the entire piece needed to be explored in a way that accentuated the intrinsic texture of the piece without violating the architectural unity.

How did he discuss his ideas about texture?

To describe texture, Courboin most often turned to visual imagery, as might be found in an oil painting, an etching, or a water color. To him, fugues were etchings, since the picture came from the lines. Franck's music was akin to fine oil paintings, where the rich colors blended together—Debussy, a wonderful watercolorist. At other times, he would discuss texture in more strictly musical terms. Was it contrapuntal? Harmonic? A combination of the two? And what tools were you going to use to emphasize the texture rather than obscure it?

What did he mean by harmonic?

A piece whose colors derive from vivid harmonies, to the extent that they become a dominant element in the character of the piece. Most of this music is homophonic in nature.

How else did he discuss texture?

For contrapuntal music, Courboin made a differentiation between what he called "linear" and "blockwise." If a fugue, to him, was linear, you had to register so that all lines were audible. Special attention must be paid to moving parts, because you can't rely on the organ to make them clear for you.

He would say over and over that to the listener, long notes take precedence over short notes; you had to pay attention how you apportioned them. On a Skinner of the early 1930s, for example, in a fugue you rarely if ever coupled Great to Pedal, since that would obliterate the tenor line. Couple the third manual instead, he would say. On that same thought, he would mention the long opening pedal-point in Bach's Toccata in F. To his way of thinking, in a reverberant room that note might build up over time in the inner ear of the listener, possibly growing out of balance and destroying the independence of the tenor and possibly the right hand as well. In that instance, Courboin would make sure to begin with a light pedal, feeling that its very duration would ensure that it would be heard. When the pedal line started moving, he would immediately change registration.

True to his word, he tried to avoid the Great to Pedal throughout these works, but he usually made an exception for the ending. By doing so, he was not trying to emasculate the pedal, but simply to get a different color and line, one that didn't interfere with the manuals. It follows that he was very interested in an independent pedal organ.

How did he describe texture in terms of touch?

He did talk about touch, but I learned the most simply by listening to him play. Courboin's touch was so natural that it always seemed right. It varied constantly. But we would explore the topic of texture, and it led us into long discussions about articulation and ornamentation.

Courboin knew well the value of silence in musical expression. He would often play quite staccato, even in a dead room; he used the term "detached" to describe that effect. If the room were live, he would detach even more. Also, he would say that sometimes you had to over-phrase to make the phrasing apparent in a reverberant building. He would use the acoustics of a live room in the same manner that a fine pianist uses the sustaining pedal. By doing so, he felt the listener would more readily grasp the sense of time and rhythm in a performance.

Courboin's ability to play tied notes was remarkable. He used to say, "A tied note is moving on itself, either growing (a crescendo) or regressing (decrescendo)." When he played, the melody always soared; he had a horror of things going sterile. In the same vein, he was very skilled at producing accents. (You can hear this on his recordings.) He likened accents to diving: the short note is like hitting the diving board. Accents were not solely produced by touch, but often through a tremendous swell pedal technique.

However, Courboin refrained from using the swell box in fugal work, because he felt that the addition of dynamic texture interfered with the contrapuntal texture. For episodic passages, he had a horror of going to the Swell after the Great and then closing the Swell, worrying that the counterpoint would get muffled if the contrast were too great. But in the big fugues, he would build up a steady crescendo, a growing torrent of volume—but it was not in any way to interfere with the structure of the piece. The result was incredibly dramatic without ever going too far.

Was he interested in bringing out the inner voices, like Josef Hoffmann or Lemare did?

Absolutely. *All* the best organists in that era did—the pianists too. For instance, in Widor Six, the slow middle section of the intermezzo, Courboin would thumb out the third voice—and he made *you* play it too.

Furthermore, where the pedal formed a fourth melody, you had to add to the pedal, then reduce once again after that phrase was complete. This was an important part of the texture's beauty, and he wanted to make sure it would be heard—not just as an exercise for the student, but for the benefit of the audience. He would say, "If it's important, bring it out." He wanted them to hear every part of the music.

Emotional content would seem difficult to teach.

I think Courboin was wise to place emotional content third. In that time, most poor playing was sloppy and overly sentimental. Courboin felt that emotional playing devoid of architecture or texture leads to a kind of meaningless sentimentality, and he felt that was irresponsible.

Once you had the foundation, and had done justice to the proper texture, you could then afford to explore the fine points of the emotions you were trying to communicate in a given piece. Courboin constantly asked, "What emotions does the piece involve, conjure up, portray?"

For example ... ?

Let's take the Bach Toccata and Fugue in D minor. In the toccata, drama had to be the dominant element. The opening phrases he classed as "menacing," and the passage work that follows as "fleeing"—as if you were fleeing from a menace. The big chords—they should be *terrorizing*. When he came to the fugue, the drama took second place, and contrapuntal texture took over. At the very end, the piece became dramatic once more, very large, very grand. He would extend the arpeggios at the end, in a way that emphasized them without stopping the flow. Again, he wouldn't do anything to compromise the architecture.

Take another kind of piece, the slow movement from Widor Six. He felt that it should convey, for the most part, a feeling of serenity, except in the middle portion. He used to say it was like an oration getting more dramatic, but returning to its serenity again.

Did he teach registration?

Some pupils he taught how to register. With Claribel Thompson and me, it was more or less a suggestion. "This should be more clear," "this should be more warm," "this should be more colorful." At the same time, he would suggest inner voices which might be brought out, and the best kind of color to contrast with the dominant theme. You see, this school of organist was very interested in putting the music forth very clearly to the listener, and they were imaginative in seeking clarity.

Another aspect he would stress was variety, not only in registration but in the phrasing of a certain repeated melody. Never play the same phrase the same way twice! When I would do this in a lesson, he would tell me, "You're repeating yourself. Say it differently this time."

With registration, he would use the word "transparency." In a sense, he really meant "projection," choosing a registration that an audience would need to hear in order to understand what you were playing. The color should be so much a part of the music that the music and sound become one thing. This was especially fascinating, since he had an idea that an organist should be able to have the music in front of him, and be able to see what was inherent without necessarily *making audible* what was inherent. He could scan through a score and hear it. (I later learned this technique in Fritz Reiner's conducting class at Curtis;[79] it's learned, not given. If you try to realize an orchestral score on the piano, you must learn to abbreviate it. This technique turned out to be very useful in scanning organ scores.)

On another occasion, I remember him likening the art of music to acting. Just like a good actor, as a good organist you had to convey to the listener the *meaning* of what you were doing.

Did he ever get on the bench and illustrate his ideas?

Sometimes he would play briefly in lessons. But his verbal descriptions were so good that this wasn't really necessary.

Did you learn much from watching him play while turning pages?

He played from memory, so I never got to turn pages for him. No one of that school really played from the music. However, I paid notice of his slight motion, all of which made his playing look superbly easy—which of course it wasn't.

He was always very nervous before a performance, though. At the recitals he gave at Peabody, I used to go down the street and get him an Irish whiskey. The bartender knew what I was there for, and gave it to me without my having to ask! Once Courboin got before his audience, all tensions seemed to disappear.

Where did you hear him play?

I heard him at Wanamaker's, New York's Academy of Arts and Letters, at Peabody. In San Francisco, when I was younger, I heard him play on the Aeolian at Calvary Church, where I also heard Lemare.

How well connected was Courboin to the San Francisco scene? For instance, did he know Ben Moore or Wallace Sabin?

He didn't know Moore or Sabin well, but he had been a guest of Sabin's at the Bohemian Grove one summer. Although they were both excellent organists, especially Wallace, they had a kind of West Coast complex. We all looked in awe at the goings-on of the East Coast, and by comparison we felt we were out of touch with things. It seemed that they did *so much more* than we were doing—although I found out later that they really weren't. But the quality was better in the East. For instance, although we thought our symphony was good, it really wasn't. It sounded more like a brass band with a string accompaniment. Opera was always good, even when we gave it in the Civic Auditorium. At any rate, I think that Ben and Wallace were a little too intimidated to look upon Courboin as a colleague.

Did Courboin improvise?

He did. Not in an Anglican style or "American," but rather French, and in its time very brilliant. I think that if he had really put his mind to it, he could have been a first-class improviser.

Did he encourage you to study one period of music specifically?

Courboin was so interested in teaching *music* that it didn't matter to him what kind. For instance, he thought Vladimir de Pachmann had earned himself great discredit by limiting himself to Chopin; he should have done Debussy, because he would have done it very well. Courboin admired all the great conductors: Koussevitsky, Furtwängler, Stokowski especially. He thought the Philadelphia Orchestra was the apex of fine orchestral playing.

What else was special about his recitals?

Courboin's programs were designed like a crescendo, with the main piece just before the intermission. He would say that organists played too many pieces of the same type. If we had the biggest repertory in the world, then we should use it.

Furthermore, his audiences reacted with their undivided attention. Even when Courboin played at Wanamaker's, the store noise was very slight. His demeanor was the antithesis of Virgil Fox; even David McK. Williams had more showmanship! In the end, the person he most reminded me of was Rachmaninoff. They knew each other, and he greatly admired Rachmaninoff.

This sounds like a marvelous experience.

It was *[sigh]*. He was a wonderful player and a wonderful teacher. He had so much to say musically, and so many ways to say it. To have been a part of that was ... it was very special indeed.[80]

Charles Heinroth

The program notes of a 1993 recital in Purvis's honor state that following his graduation from Curtis in 1940, he "studied the works of César Franck with Charles Courboin, and subsequently the music of Liszt, Reubke and Reger with Charles Heinroth (a pupil of Liszt)."[81] No further details about the encounter with Heinroth are available, nor can this statement be verified.

Organ and Choral Publications

The Biographical Data contains numerous entries about the publication and performances of Purvis's early compositions. This had to be a heady time for a young man in his mid-20s, performing in the some of the finest venues in the country and seeing his compositions, both organ and choral, accepted by respected publishing houses. Though much of this information is probably reliable, a number of details could not be verified. Nevertheless, it is included here as it appears in the original document.

December 1938: First performances of the "Scottish Carol" and "Iam Hiems Transiit," given by Second Presbyterian Church, Philadelphia, and the Choral Art Society of Philadelphia, respectively.

During 1939–1940: Due to the encouragement of Dr. Meekridge [name illegible], the Mass of St. Nicholas was written for the Midnight Mass of Christmas, 1939, at St. James' Church, Philadelphia. This was given in concert form by the combined choirs of the Second Presbyterian Church, First Baptist Church, and the Wylie-Chambers Memorial Presbyterian

Church, at the Second Presbyterian Church edifice in February 1940.

January 1940: The "Five Pieces on Gregorian Themes" (organ) was accepted for publication by Sprague-Coleman of New York City; "Iam Hiems Transiit" accepted for publication by the same company, and "Scottish Carol" accepted by C. Birchard of Boston.

March 1940: Two songs were accepted for publication: "Dream Vision" by Oliver Ditson of Boston, and "John Anderson My Jo" by Sprague-Coleman. Purvis appeared as soloist in a series of evening concerts given on the mammoth organ of the Philadel-phia Wanamaker Store.

Richard Purvis, around 1940. Courtesy Donald Braff.

May 1940: "Mass of St. Nicholas" and the "Magnificat" were performed in The Temple of Religion at the New York World's Fair by St. James' Episcopal Choir of boys and men. During same month Purvis appeared in recital at the Fair, playing a three-manual Aeolian-Skinner in same building.

Summer of 1940: "Four Carol Preludes" (organ) and "Ballad of Judas Iscariot" (soloists, choir and instrumental ensemble) were written. The former were accepted for publication by Sprague-Coleman of New York, the latter by Elkan-Vogel of Philadelphia.[82]

October 1940: Purvis named organist of Philadelphia Symphony Orchestra, Academy of Music, where he performed under the batons of Leopold Stokowski, Eugene Ormandy, Sir Thomas Beecham, and Arturo Toscanini.

December 1940: "Mass of St. Nicholas" performed at the Church of the Advent, Boston, and at St. James' Episcopal Church in New York City.

January 1941: Purvis made his first concert tour, playing Rollins College, Winter Park, Florida; First Presbyterian Church, Lynchburg, Virginia; Pennsylvania State Teachers College; Bard College, New York. At this time "Bene-dictus Es" in two versions for TTBB and SATB accepted for publication by

H. W. Gray of New York City. Purvis was named head of the Music Department at the Episcopal Academy [in Overbrook, Pennsylvania].

April 1941: First performance of his "Ballad of Judas Iscariot" at St. James's Church, Philadelphia.

Summer of 1941: Purvis appeared as a recitalist for the Northern California Chapter of the American Guild of Organists at Calvary Presbyterian Church, San Francisco. He also gave recitals at The Church of the Blessed Sacrament, Hollywood; Balboa Park, San Diego; and at Grace Cathedral, San Francisco.

Fall of 1941: Purvis commenced study of composition with Josef Schillinger, New York City, and named assistant organist under Charles Courboin at N.B.C., New York City.[83] "Jubilate Deo" composed for faculty and student body of the Episcopal Academy, accepted for publication by Sprague-Coleman. "Judas Iscariot" performed by choir of Second Presbyterian Church, Philadelphia and also in New York City.[84]

Purvis Becomes a Colleague of the A.G.O.

In the early days of the American Guild of Organists, it was necessary for two full members of the Guild to nominate a newer member for the status of "Colleague." ("Colleague" status was required in order to hold offices, sit for the AAGO or FAGO exams, etc.) This has nothing to do with the Colleague *exam,* which would be not be introduced in the Guild until June 1978. It is not known when Purvis first became a member of the Guild, but the following letter written in 1939 on letterhead of the American Guild of Organists confirms his election as a "Colleague" of the Guild. The identity of "Miss Fish" is unknown.

American Guild of Organists
RKO Building, Rockefeller Center
1270 Sixth Avenue, New York, N.Y.
May 15, 1939

Dear Miss Fish,

At a recent meeting of the Council, the following persons were elected Colleagues of the Guild [:]
Richard Purvis

5/39

American Guild of Organists

United States and Canada
(Name and seal registered in U. S. Patent Office)

ORGANIZED APRIL 13TH 1896

CHARTER GRANTED DECEMBER 17TH 1896

AUTHORIZED BY THE BOARD OF REGENTS OF

INCORPORATED DECEMBER 17TH 1896

AMENDED CHARTER GRANTED JUNE 17TH 1909

AMENDED CHARTER GRANTED JUNE 21ST 1934

THE UNIVERSITY OF THE STATE OF NEW YORK

RKO Building, Rockefeller Center
1270 Sixth Avenue, New York, N. Y.

MAY 15 1939

    At a recent meeting of the Council, the following persons
were elected Colleagues of the Guild.

Richard Purvis

Very sincerely yours,

RALPH A. HARRIS.
General Secretary.

Purvis elected a colleague of the AGO, 1939. Courtesy San Francisco Chapter AGO.

Very sincerely yours,
   Ralph A. Harris
   General Secretary

George Gershwin, Richard Purvis, and the Hammond Organ

Did Purvis ever meet George Gershwin and show him how to operate a Hammond organ? Jonas Nordwall recalls a conversation in which Purvis claimed that he had. Gershwin was a student of Joseph Schillinger, and the Biographical Data states that Purvis also studied with Schillinger, so it is possible that there was some connection.

Nordwall wrote, "Purvis did talk to me about meeting Gershwin and explaining mutations to him. I understood that the meeting was during Dick's time at Curtis."[85] Nordwall also said he understood that Gershwin owned an early Hammond organ (the Hammond organ was introduced to the public in June 1935, and Gershwin died in July 1937).[86] Nordwall continued: "Gershwin liked gadgets. Richard sat down with Gershwin and explained to him how the drawbars worked." Nordwall also said that Purvis told him that Gershwin had approached Purvis at the Moller organ at the Los Angeles Shrine Auditorium and "couldn't get over all the pitches. He went ga-ga over the mutations." Finally, Nordwall recalled Purvis saying that Gershwin had started to write a suite for organ for Purvis before he died.[87]

Vaughn Jones, a student of Purvis's in the late 1980s, wrote, "Purvis was always interested in chatting about popular songs, and having once been a theatre organist himself, he was quite knowledgeable about Gershwin, Kern, Richard Rodgers, and Broadway show scores in general. He told me that Gershwin had been composing an organ concerto, and that he [Purvis] had written to Ira Gershwin many years later to ask what had happened to the sketches, and Ira wrote back that he knew nothing about this project. Purvis also said that Rachmaninoff had also at one time started writing an organ concerto, which was never finished."[88]

The Next Step

Purvis had enjoyed four exhilarating years of study, travel, performance, and composition. Having traveled in Europe in the late 1930s, he must have been aware of the brewing political troubles there. Still, he probably could not have imagined how different his life would become within a few short months.

Notes

1. Biographical Data, 1; the Grace Cathedral and Trinity Methodist recitals could not be verified.

2. Susannah Thurlow, e-mail, November 9, 2010.

3. Documents courtesy Curtis archives.

4. Purvis had never definitively identified himself with any particular denomination, but as the organist of Calvary Presbyterian in San Francisco, he may have felt that was the most appropriate choice.

5. Purvis's lack of a high school diploma was rigorously dealt with shortly after his arrival at Curtis in January 1936.

6. Documents courtesy Curtis archives.

7. Susannah Thurlow, e-mail, November 2, 2010.

8. Susannah Thurlow, e-mail, March 23, 2011.

9. Biographical Data, 2.

10. "Paul Zuydhoek, organ student with Mr. Germani, received a special scholarship in memory of Mr. Cyrus Curtis, given by his daughter, permitting him to study in Italy with Mr. Germani during the summer of 1933 and continuing until December." *Overtones*, 1934, 71.

11. Susannah Thurlow, e-mail, March 23, 2011.

12. Curtis Admissions Catalogue, 1935–36, 10.

13. Jonas Nordwall, e-mail, September 27, 2010.

14. Vaughn Jones, e-mail, March 23, 2012.

15. Grades for second term only in Spring 1936.

16. Grades for first term and second term, respectively.

17. The commencement program can be seen in Curtis's archived recital files, p. 314ff.

18. Susannah Thurlow, e-mail, March 23, 2011.

19. Susannah Thurlow, e-mail, November 9, 2010.

20. John Weaver, "Alexander McCurdy 1905–1983." *The American Organist*, September 1983, 32–33. Used by permission.

21. Letter from Alexander McCurdy to Richard Cummins, May 17, 1978. Courtesy Richard Cummins.

22. This would have been around 1927, the same year McCurdy began his studies at Curtis.

23. Letter from Alexander McCurdy to Richard Cummins, November 15, 1978. Courtesy Richard Cummins.

24. Both "Levine" and "Lhevinne" spellings were used at Curtis, although "Levine" was the more common.

25. Barden interview.

26. Douglas Metzler, e-mail, June 24, 2010, and November 12, 2010.

27. Susannah Thurlow, e-mail, October 29, 2010, and November 9, 2010.

28. Biographical Data, 2.

29. Telephone conversation with Calvin Harris, Tioga Methodist Church, November 30, 2010.

30. Townsend thesis, 9.

31. *The Diapason*, 1936, 9; cited in Townsend thesis; original not available.

32. Barden interview.

33. Postal card from Purvis to June Townsend, February 7, 1936; cited in Townsend thesis, 4.

34. *The Oakland Tribune*, 1936; cited in Townsend thesis, 4; original not available.

35. Darrin Britting, Archivist, The Philadelphia Orchestra, e-mail, November 9, 2010.

36. Typescript.

37. *The Diapason*, February 1, 1937, 9.

38. *The Diapason*, March 1, 1937, 2. There are undoubtedly many such examples in other issues, but the hunt for these random notices is challenging.

39. Letter from Clarence Snyder to James Welch, November 1, 2010.

40. Corbett, 6.

41. Note reference to study in summer season only.

42. *The Diapason*, 1937; cited in Townsend thesis, 4; original not available.

43. Biographical Data states 1935, but this is not accurate.

44. Biographical Data states 1935, but this is not accurate.

45. Biographical Data, 2.

46. Donald Sears, "Richard I. Purvis: A Brief Biography in honor of the 90th Anniversary of His Birth," July & August 2003 issue of the San Francisco Chapter AGO newsletter.

47. Douglas Metzler, e-mail, June 24, 2010.

48. *Overtones*, Volume VII, No. 2, May 1937, 80.

49. *Overtones*, Volume VII, No. 2, May 1937, 85.

50. *Overtones*, Volume VIII, No. 1, November 1937, 28.

51. Biographical Data gives the date as April 1937, but this is not accurate.

52. Biographical Data, 2. According to Corbett, the period was four months, but this is not accurate.

53. Postcard dated May 31, 1937, from Richard's mother to June Townsend; cited in Townsend thesis, 4; original unavailable.

54. The date of this trip could not be verified.

55. Barden interview.

56. The Biographical Data states January 1937, but this is not accurate.

57. Corbett, 7.

58. Douglas Metzler interview, June 24, 2010, Bothell, Washington.

59. Ed Stout, telephone conversation, January 24, 2011.

60. *Overtones*, May 1937, Vol. VII, No. 2, 80.

61. Biographical Data, 2.

62. Typescript, April 19, 1937, courtesy Curtis archives.

63. Flyer courtesy Curtis archives.

64. Charles Latham, *The Episcopal Academy, 1785–1984*. Devon, Pennsylvania: William T. Cooke Publishing, 1984, 165–66.

65. Curtis's digitized collection can be accessed at http://www.archive.org/details/curtisinstituteofmusic.

66. Curtis Recital Programs 1937, p. 11; also mentioned in *Overtones*, Vol. VII, No. 2, May 1937, 85. An interesting discussion of the organ in Casimir Hall can also be read in "Some Additions to the Organ in Casimir Hall" by Alexander McCurdy, *Overtones*, May 1937, Vol. VII, No. 2, 78–80.

67. Curtis Recital Programs 1937–1938, p. 227.

68. Curtis Recital Programs 1939, p. 217.

69. Curtis Recital Programs 1939, p. 195.

70. Curtis Recital Programs 1940, p. 12; also mentioned in *Overtones*, Vol. X, No. II, 57.

71. Curtis Recital Programs 1940, p. 62.

72. Clipping courtesy Curtis archives.

73. *Life*, December 12, 1938: 49–57.

74. Corbett, 8; date and location of meeting unknown.

75. Meeting program.

76. Biographical Data, 2–3.

77. There are various biographies of Courboin; a good source is the article "Charles Marie Courboin 1886–1973," *The American Organist*, June 1994, written by his student Robert Arnold, with supplemental material compiled by Ray Biswanger.

78. As noted above, Purvis spent two summers in Europe, not two years.

79. Fritz Reiner, head of the conducting department and conductor of the Curtis Symphony Orchestra, was on the faculty at Curtis during 1931–1941. Susannah Thurlow, e-mail, March 23, 2011.

80. *The Erzähler, Journal of the Symphonic Organ Society*, Volume 4, Number 3, January 1995. Used by permission.

81. "An Organ Extravaganza Concert," Daly City, California, August 15, 1993; also in http://www.bach-cantatas.com/Lib/Purvis-Richard.htm, last accessed April 29, 2011.

82. Biographical Data, 3.

83. No details regarding this assistantship at NBC are available, so it is unclear whether it really happened.

84. Biographical Data, 4.

85. Jonas Nordwall, e-mail, November 7, 2010.

86. A simple Internet search will bring up a number of statements that connect Gershwin and the Hammond organ.

87. Jonas Nordwall, telephone conversation, September 27, 2010.

88. Vaughn Jones, e-mail, March 23, 2012.

chapter 3

war years,
1941–1946

"He holds the dubious distinction of being the only living American organist to have his obituary printed in The Diapason.*"*

—Biographical Data

"Composing organ music in a foxhole somewhere in Luxembourg is something that may aptly be described as 'unique.'"

—*The Diapason*

Following his graduation from Curtis in May 1940, Purvis apparently remained in the East for a while, continuing his church and recital work. According to Ed Stout, he also spent some time in California:

"Prior to the United States' involvement in World War II, Purvis returned to the Bay Area for a short time and during that era he was able to further investigate his longtime love for the theatre organ. He played a weekly theatre organ program from Oakland's Chapel of the Chimes."[1] But surprisingly little else is known about the 24 months between his graduation from Curtis and his enlistment in the army on June 20, 1942.

Sometime prior to enlistment, Purvis returned to Philadelphia. A newspaper clipping states: "He lived at the Chatham Hotel [on Rittenhouse Square, adjacent to Curtis] when he enlisted in August [*sic*], 1942."[2]

Purvis's former assistant Stephen Loher wrote, "He said that he 'got to flag waving' and joined. He was a committed San Franciscan. He told me that the day they shipped out for the War it was foggy and, due to the fog, his spirits were up!"[3]

An Internet search for Purvis's military records yielded the following enlistment information:

Name: Richard I Purvis

Birth Year: 1913

Race: White, Citizen

Native State: California

State of Residence: Pennsylvania

County or City: Philadelphia

Enlistment Date: 20 June 1942

Enlistment State: Pennsylvania

Enlistment City: Philadelphia

Branch: Branch Immaterial—Warrant Officers, USA

Grade: Private

Term of Enlistment: Enlistment for the duration of the War or other emergency, plus six months, subject to the discretion of the President or otherwise according to law

Component: Army of the United States - includes the following: Voluntary enlistments effective December 8, 1941 and thereafter; One year enlistments of National Guardsman whose State enlistment expires while in the Federal Service; Officers appointed in the Army of [sic]

Source: Civil Life

Education: 4 years of college

Civil Occupation: Musicians and teachers of music

Marital Status: Single, without dependents

Height: 66

Weight: 172[4]

The Biographical Data states, "After preliminary training, he eventually became assigned to the 76th Division where he attained the ranks of PFC (Private First Class) and Corporal as a lineman."[5]

The organ community was proud and very aware of its colleagues in uniform, and *The Diapason* would continue to report on the enlisted men.

The following article from August 1942 describes a decidedly optimistic Purvis; the mood would change before the war was over.

Richard Purvis, the Philadelphia organist and composer, is another of the prominent men in his profession who within the last month have joined the armed forces of the United States. He is a private in the 304th Infantry, 76th division, stationed at Fort Meade, Md., and reports that he has never been happier and never has felt better than at this writing. He is clerk and organist for the regimental chaplain and, though busy with basic training, finds time to play the Sunday services and is even organizing a soldier choir. Mr. Purvis has found a number of good players of instruments in his regiment and hopes to give programs in which orchestral instruments will be used in combination with the organ. A little later in the season he expects to give a series of recitals.

Mr. Purvis has been achieving note as a composer aside from his work as a recitalist. Among his works already published are a Magnificat, an *a cappella* carol, "Iam Hiens [*sic*] Transit," and a unison Jubilate. For organ there are "Five Pieces on Gregorian Themes" (three of which are in print and the other two soon to be issued by Sprague-Coleman) and a "Carol Rhapsody." There are various other pieces that have been accepted by Birchard, Oliver Ditson and Arthur P. Schmidt. In manuscript are a Festival Mass for the Anglican Church, "Missa Sanctae Nicolai," and a choral tone poem, "The Ballad of Judas Iscariot," for double choir, solo quartet, solo violin, two harps, celesta and organ.

Mr. Purvis had begun the study of composition with Joseph Schillinger when the war broke out and hopes to continue working with him by means of the mails as soon as he finishes basic training. He studied piano with Benjamin S. Moore in San Francisco.[6]

In 1942, while organist for an army show, Purvis was assigned to Army Music School in Arlington, Virginia. At that time his co-organist was Paul Callaway, who later became organist of the National Cathedral in Washington, D.C. In May 1942, Purvis graduated with honors from Army Music School and was assigned to the 28th Infantry Division as its bandmaster.[7]

Purvis asked the violinist Efrem Zimbalist, then Director of The Curtis Institute, to write a letter of recommendation for him. On September 21, 1942, Zimbalist wrote the following letter:

8th Class Band Leader Graduates, July 13, 1943. The U.S. Army Music School, Arlington, Virginia.
Purvis is on the second row, sixth from the left; Paul Callaway, second row, seventh from the left.
Courtesy Donna Parker.

Lieut. Harold V. Collins
Service Co. - 304th Infantry
76th Division
Fort George Meade
Maryland

TO WHOM IT MAY CONCERN:

I am told that Corporal Richard I. Purvis of the U. S. Army is in line for a promotion and it gives me pleasure to write a word of recommendation for him. Mr. Purvis was a student of organ at The Curtis Institute of Music for five years, where he did outstanding work both as a soloist and in all classes, and before graduating was competent enough to hold an excellent church position as organist and choir director. He is thoroughly musical.

As Director of the Curtis Institute, I consider Mr. Purvis worthy of any promotion permitting him to use his knowledge of music to the best ability.

[Efrem Zimbalist] Director[8]

October Eighth [1942]
Efrem Zimbalist, Director
Curtis Institute of Music
Rittenhouse Square
Philadelphia, Penn.

Dear Mr. Zimbalist:

Thank you sincerely for your great kindness in writing a letter of recommendation to accompany my application for entry into Army Music School.

If I am accepted, I'm sure it will be due to your backing in no small measure.

May I wish you a very happy and successful season at Curtis this year?

Sincerely,

Richard Purvis

On January 29, 1943, Zimbalist sent a letter identical to that of September 21, 1942, this time addressed to Purvis in Atlanta (3rd Corps, A.P.O. 303, Fort McPherson, Atlanta, Georgia), presumably for Purvis to give to one of his commanding officers.

A clipping dated February 15, 1943, most likely from the *Philadelphia Bulletin*, reads:

Music by Richard Purvis, young American organist and composer now in the Army, was featured on a special choral program under Alexander McCurdy's direction at the Second Presbyterian Church yesterday afternoon.

The principal offering, "The Ballad of Judas Iscariot," afforded interesting and effective treatment of a text by Robert Williams Buchanan. Mr. Purvis' scoring shows skill and excellent musical expression of the words which allows for a variety of moods. The solo parts were well interpreted by Barbara Stevenson, soprano; Nancy Fishburn, contralto; George Lapham, tenor, and Robert Grooters, bass. The choral passages were convincingly done by the church choir and the accompaniments and interludes engaged Dr. McCurdy, organist ...

The program also contributed Mr. Purvis' vigorous setting of the canticle, "Jubilate Deo." — W. E. S.[9]

In an undated letter to his parents Purvis sent two photos: one of himself playing a Hammond organ at Fort Meade, Maryland, taken in 1942 by Grant Anderson; and another photo with the notation "8th Class—Band Leader Graduates / The U. S. Army Music School, July 13, 1943." In the letter he wrote:

> Dear Mom 'n Pop:
>
> Here we are (sans officer's uniform).
>
> My gang comprised of
>
> Paul Callaway (the man next to me on the right)
>
> Louis Palmer (at whose home I stayed while in Chicago. He's second from the left on the very last row)
>
> Chuck Spurr (5th from the left on the next to the last row, right in front of Louis)
>
> Larry Grootins [illegible] (Left end man third row) and
>
> Jerry Perkins (fourth from the right, second row)
>
> The front row is comprised of the faculty.
>
> Weren't our 2 WACS good looking girls?
>
> Love,
>
> Dick[10]

In an undated letter to June Townsend, Purvis wrote: "Graduated in the top half of the class, and am now assigned to an Infantry Band. We're in the field (living in tents) and time is scarce."[11]

During 1943 the 28th Division was assigned overseas duty in England. This assignment created an extensive tour for the band that took them throughout England, Scotland, and Wales as "good-will ambassadors" for General Eisenhower and the United States of America.[12]

Eugene Dong compiled the following summary of Purvis's war experiences:

> Purvis joined the Army after the start of World War II. He was assigned to the 109th Infantry Band, 28th Infantry Division, the oldest division in the US armed forces and one of the most famous.
>
> On Feb. 17, 1941, the 28th Division was ordered into federal service for one year of active duty. The Japanese attack on Pearl Harbor on Dec. 7, 1941, led soldiers of the 28th to remain on active for the duration of the war. The Division entered combat on July 22, 1944, landing on the beaches

Purvis in the service, pictured here at a Hammond organ, Fort Meade, Maryland, 1942. Photo by Grant Anderson. Courtesy Donna Parker.

of Normandy. From Normandy, the 28th advanced across western France, finding itself in the thick of hedgerow fighting. In late August, the Division succeeded in trapping the remnant of the German 7th Army.

The famous photograph of American troops before the Arc de Triomphe, marching in battle parade down the Champs Elysees, shows the men of 1st Battalion, 110th Infantry Regiment, 28th Infantry Division. Then Corporal Purvis was the leader of one of the regimental bands. The Division moved on to some of the bloodiest battles of the War the day immediately following the parade. The Division fanned out into Luxembourg in early September. On September 11, 1944, the 28th claimed the distinction of being the first American unit to enter Germany.

Attacks in the Huertgen Forest began November 2, 1944. By November 10, the 28th held a 25-mile sector of the front line along the Our River. It was against this thinly fortified division line that the Germans unleashed the full force of their winter Ardennes "blitzkrieg" offensive. Nine German divisions stormed across the Our River over a few days. The division maintained its defense of this sector long enough to throw the German assault off schedule.

During this famous battle, members of the band were called to lay their instruments aside and fight. Many of the band members lost their lives in that battle. Purvis was captured and spent the rest of war as a German prisoner of war.

When allied forces could counterattack, the "Battle of the Bulge" ensued, inflicting heavy losses on the enemy forces. The division continued its devastating advance through Germany until VE day.

Over the duration of the war, the division suffered 1,901 killed, 9,157 wounded, 2,599 missing and 2,247 captured. The Division returned to the U.S. and was deactivated on December 13, 1945. Five campaign streamers—Normandy, Northern France, Ardennes-Alsace, Rhineland, and Central Europe—were earned during World War II, in addition to the Croix de Guerre."[13]

In 1944 the 28th Division Band was selected by General Omar Bradley as the official band for the Liberation Day Fête in Paris (August 19–25, 1944). During this time, Purvis composed his "Seven Chorale Preludes for Organ"[14] and the "Four Pieces" for piano.[15] According to Donald Corbett, the "Four Pieces" for piano were premiered in 1943[16] at the Royal Albert Hall in London. There they were featured at a concert of music composed by men of the Allied Forces and were played by the well-known Australian concert pianist Eileen Joyce.[17] At this time Purvis also wrote the songs "Discovery," "A Soldier's Prayer," and two pieces for women's chorus, "The Road's End" and "On the Streetcar."[18]

Rodgers Jenkins, president of the Rodgers Organ Company, recalled that Purvis played the Hammond organ while stationed overseas and that he played some jazz on Hammonds in the Bay Area.[19]

In late 1944, June Townsend received the following correspondence from Purvis:

> Yours of October 14th reached me here in Schickelgruber's front yard today (good time, what?) ...
>
> Since hitting the beach-head I have neither seen—heard, nor touched an organ! I'm dying to go into some of these churches I see, but everything

is VERBOTEN! It makes me so darn mad sometimes. Really you could commit mayhem—but c'est la guerre.

My band was the first American Band to play in Paris. On the day of the Liberation Fete—we gave out while the Division marched by in Battle Dress to the greatest display of acclaim—enthusiasm, and down-right excitement I've ever seen! Really it was a thrill.

Its been mostly mud, rain, foxholes, and non-musical duty, however, and its turned darned cold over here. We're pretty far north you know!

We've taken 5 prisoners, so we're not too much out of the combat picture. We also played a concert at Florisville (Belgium) less than 24 hours after Jerry left. Front-line serenade, what?"[20]

In December 1944, *The Diapason* printed the following article about Purvis:

Writes Organ Music in European Foxhole

———

Work of Richard I. Purvis

———

Band of Warrant Officer, in Peacetime an American Composer,
Is the First to March in Triumphal Procession in Paris.

———

Composing organ music in a foxhole somewhere in Luxembourg is something that may aptly be described as "unique." But Warrant Officer Richard I. Purvis, the young American organist now with the American invasion forces, finds time to pursue his peacetime work in the odd moments when apparently the Germans are not molesting our soldiers. His latest work, published this month by Sprague-Coleman, probably the only organ piece ever to be written under such circumstances, is the first of a series of four carol preludes on the well-known Christmas song "What Child Is This?" and advance proofs indicate that it is a very effective number suitable for the approaching Yuletide programs.

Under date of Oct. 7 Warrant Officer Purvis writes to The Diapason that "the censor says that at long last I may tell you what I've been burning to say a long while. The Twenty-eighth Division band was the first United States Army division band to play in a triumphal victory parade through the streets of Paris! From the L'Arc de Triomphe to the Place de la Concorde the division marched in battle dress in what I considered the greatest exhibition of combined welcome, enthusiasm and general excitement I've ever seen.

"Of course we just marched through; but we had our moment. We're back in pup tents (in Belgium), but our day was a pretty good one and we're eager to see what it feels like to march down the streets of Berlin."[21]

Prisoner of War

During the vicious Battle of the Bulge[22] at Wiltz, Luxembourg, Purvis was taken prisoner after evacuating most of his band.[23] He was held in a German concentration camp until being liberated on April 5, 1945.

Donald Sears wrote:

Richard served in the U.S. Army as a bandmaster and was captured by the Nazis during the Battle of the Bulge. He sustained serious injuries which he survived because his buddies took turns carrying him on their backs for four days to the prisoner of war camp where he remained until the liberation in 1945. I don't know exactly which camp it was but Richard spoke about his first decent meal being a can of cold baked beans after the Allies freed the prisoners.[24]

Although there is no record of Purvis's ever mentioning the name of the camp where he was interned, this information is available in his military record:

File Unit: World War II Prisoners of War Data File, 12/7/1941–11/19/1946

Serial number: W2129773

Grade, Alpha: Warrant Officer Junior Grade

Grade Code: Warrant Officer Junior Grade or Warrant Officer

Service Code: Army

Arm or Service: Infantry

Date Report: 23 March 1945

Racial Group: White

Area: European Theatre: Germany

REPRODUCED AT THE NATIONAL ARCHIVES

Name	Rank	ASN	PW No.
Pennick, Paul P	Capt.	01287579	160559
Pennington, Carl L.	2nd Lt	01645906	3244
Perkins, Cecil A.	1st Lt	01017907	097790
Perla, Peter J.	1st Lt	01042672	10157
Perry, Thomas C.	Capt	0450408	080884
Peters, Stanley H.	2nd Lt	01317665	270169
Pett, John Willis T.	1st Lt	01306142	15695
Peyton, Walter R.	1st Lt	01298123	12423
Pfeiffer, Paul E.	1st Lt	01298124	8037
Phelan, Lawrence J.	1st Lt	01298430	3015
Phillips, John C.	1st Lt	01060248	055074
Phillips, Melville M.J.	2nd Lt	0465385	095354
Piazza, Louis R.	1st Lt	01715319	10101
Pickering, John A.	2nd. Lt.	01110186	25352
Pickering, Louis R.	Capt.	0291933	87988
Piecuch, Michael J.	2nd.Lt.	01315612	3215
Pieros, Richard M.	1st.Lt.	0530059	11586
Pierce, Robert E.Jr.	2nd.Lt.	01115741	50955
Pierce, Stephen W.	1st.Lt.	01393311	3331
Pierce, Dean A.	2nd.Lt.	01052125	99106
Pike, Herbert M.	1st.Lt.	01304114	85598
Pitman, Robert M.	2nd.Lt.	01314413	99071
Pitman, Wilford G.	01998452	2nd.Lt.	15682
Pitts, Korn B.	2nd.Lt.	026718	25444
Plume, Stephen K.Jr.	Capt.	024054	15739
Pollock, Donald B.	1st.Lt.	01011644	97706
Pontlitz, Jack A.	Capt.	01297942	91210
Poplawski, Walter J.	1st.Lt.	01045559	25135
Porche, Stanley E.	Capt.	01030406	15678
Porter, Bernard V.	1st.Lt.0129	01291164	25234
Porterie, Louis B.	1st.Lt.	0588892	25347
Posz, Charles H.	1st.Lt.	01285494	80513
Potter, Franklin W.	01320178	1st.Lt.	55048
Powell, Frederick A.	2nd.Lt.	01313793	15694
Powell, George B.	2nd.Lt.	01181734	85032
Powell, Reuben F.	1st.Lt.	02048747	25364
Pratt, Page B.	1st.Lt.	0516117	25490
Prawdica, Rocco P.	2nd.Lt.	0885651	1555
Crell, Donald B.	2nd.Lt.	0551911	25563
Price, Wilbur H.	2nd.Lt.	01325669	15199
Prince, Altus E.	Capt.	025714	97893
Prior, Garnett J.	1st.Lt.	01316204	25344
Pritchard, John H.	2nd.lt	01310636	25334
Prusaitis, Joseph J.	Major	0422579	97718
Puett, Joseph F.	Lt.Col.	0288767	25271
Purcell, Frank P.	1st.Lt.	01297426	77782
Purvis, Richard I	WOJG	W2129773	97710
Regal, Raymond M.	2nd Lt.	01312445	097730
Reid, Chas B.	Capt	0341878	2522
Reid, Matthew J.	2nd Lt.	0549241	15736

Purvis's name can be seen on this roster of Americans interned at Oflag XIII-B, Hammelburg, Germany, dated March 25, 1945.[27]

Latest Report Date: 23 April 1946

Status: Returned to Military Control, Liberated or Repatriated

Detaining Power: Germany

Camp: Oflag 13B Hammelburg Bavaria 50-10[25]

Oflag 13

The revelation of Oflag,[26] or Stalag, 13B is significant because it would become the object of a failed liberation attempt ordered by General Patton himself. It is surprising that Purvis did not talk about this extraordinary event to which he was an eyewitness.

Two sources that provide information about the Battle of the Bulge and Oflag 13B are Alex Kershaw's book *The Longest Winter,* and *Raid! The Untold Story of Patton's Secret Mission,* by Richard Baron, Major Abe Baum, and Richard Goldhurst. From these sources we learn that Oflag 13B was located outside the Bavarian town of Hammelburg and about 70 miles east of Frankfurt. Used as a POW camp for Allied army personnel in World War I, it was used also as a German Army training camp during World War II. Consisting of 40–50 stone buildings, at first the camp housed Serbian officers, but in January 1945, American officers captured during the Battle of the Bulge arrived and were placed in a separate section. By January 23, there were 453 American soldiers, and by late March 25 the numbers would grow to 1,291. Officers were housed in areas apart from the enlisted men.[28]

Conditions at the camp were miserable for both the prisoners and their guards. The winter of 1944 was considered one of the coldest on record. Each five-room building was crowded with two hundred men. One fifty-square-foot room was to house 40 prisoners on bunk beds, while coal was rationed out to heat the furnaces at a rate of just 48 briquettes per stove every three days. Although some men were able to scavenge for wood nearby, it still was not enough to keep the soldiers warm. The average temperature in the rooms at any time was estimated to be 20° F.

Food was as scarce as heat. Initially the men in camps were given a diet of 1,700 calories a day, well below the 2,000-calorie recommended daily allowance for men doing no work. This was cut further as supplies ran low and the camp population increased, until an estimated 1,070 calories were distributed daily. Many men in the camp suffered dramatic weight loss of more than 50 pounds because of the lack of food and subsequent immobility. Dysentery due to unsterile conditions and utensils further weakened many men in the camp.

The normal daily menu consisted of one-tenth of a loaf of bread, one cup of ersatz coffee, one bowl of barley soup, and one serving of a vegetable a day. Toward the end of March, many officers were in a dangerous condition due to malnutrition, and the SMO [senior medical officer] credited the generosity of the Serbian Officers with saving many lives.[29]

Task Force Baum

Oflag 13B is perhaps best known for its connection with the "Task Force Baum," a secret World War II task force set up by U.S. Army General George S. Patton and commanded by Captain Abraham Baum on March 27–29, 1945. Baum was given the task of penetrating 50 miles behind German lines and liberating the POWs in camp Oflag 13B. Controversy surrounds the true reasons behind the mission, but it was probably motivated in part by Patton's desire to liberate his son-in-law, John K. Waters, who had been taken captive in Tunisia in 1943 and held at Oflag 13B.

Baum knew that his task was risky at best. He and the roughly 300 men of his task force first had to break through German lines. Lacking adequate maps, they had to rely on information obtained from civilians in order to find the camp. Due to heavy German fire, only about half of the company made it to Hammelburg. Baum quickly realized that the camp contained far more than the 300 officers he had been sent to liberate. He determined that he could take back no more than 200 men (field-grade officers O-4 and above) with what was left of his fleet. Any remaining men who wished to march with the columns would be allowed to do so, or they could try to travel cross-country on their own to the American line, about 50 miles to the west. Barely able to walk, the vast majority of POWs had little choice but to stay behind.

The mission was a complete failure; of the 300 men of the task force, 32 were killed in action during the raid and only 35 made it back to

Allied-controlled territory, with the remainder being taken prisoner. All of the 57 tanks, jeeps, and other vehicles were lost.[30]

The thousands of suffering POWs, Purvis among them, were elated when they first learned of the approach of the Allies. They must have been devastated, however, when they realized that they would be forced to remain in the miserable camp. But on April 5, 1945, barely a week later, the 14th Armored Division of the Seventh Army liberated Oflag 13B.

One can only speculate about Purvis's experiences while interned and at the time of liberation. Did he know Waters? Was he among the prisoners who walked out of the camp with Baum's forces, or did he remain behind until April 5? Following the liberation, most of the POWs were transferred to Nuremberg, and from there to a large camp in Moosburg, near Munich.[31] How exactly did Purvis find his way to safety? These dramatic questions may never be answered.[32]

Was Purvis One of Hogan's Heroes?

Hogan's Heroes, an American television sitcom, ran from September 17, 1965, to March 28, 1971, on the CBS network. The setting was a fictional version of Stalag 13 in Hammelburg. The TV version of Stalag 13 bore no resemblance, however, to its real-life counterparts, Oflag XIII-B and Stalag XIII-C. The show's premise was that the POWs were actually active war participants, using the camp as a base of operations for Allied espionage and sabotage against the Germans. They were aided by the incompetence of the camp commandant, Colonel Klink, and the Sergeant of the Guard, Sergeant Schultz.[33]

Composing in Foxhole and Prison Camp

In the preface to the 2004 reissue of selections of Purvis's music, we read:

> The famous setting of *Greensleeves* was actually composed during WWII as Richard sat under fire in a foxhole.... He was captured by the Germans during the Battle of the Bulge, given up as Missing in Action, and his obituary printed. However, like another organist/composer Olivier Messiaen, he was actually a prisoner of war. Suffering from hunger, cold, filth, and the endless marching for the POW columns, he was helped to survive a head

wound by a Jewish doctor who hid medication in his shoes. A friendly German soldier provided him with paper, which allowed many compositions to be created during his imprisonment.[34]

Douglas Metzler said that Purvis's German captors thought the music he was writing was some kind of "code."[35] Stephen Loher also reported that "The famous Seven Chorale Preludes were written in foxholes during battles."[36]

An Article about Hammond Organ Registration

In March 1945, an article by Purvis entitled "The Secret of Adding Orchestral Color To Hammond Registration" was published in *The Etude* magazine, ironically while he was still in prison camp. It is unclear when he wrote the article or submitted it for publication, although it includes the photo of him in army uniform shown on page 87. The full text appears in Appendix A.

Missing in Action

Communication from Purvis during the war was sparse. The reports below demonstrate not only the anguish of those who knew him, but also tell of his continued musical accomplishments as a soldier and prisoner.

From a clipping dated January 29, 1945:

> Also missing in Belgium is Warrant Officer Richard Purvis, 31, a bandmaster who formerly was an organist and choirmaster at St. James Episcopal Church, 22d and Walnut Sts. A native of California, he is the son of Mr. and Mrs. George T. Purvis, of Oakland, who were notified. He lived at the Chatham Hotel when he enlisted in August, 1942.
>
> He studied at Curtis Institute and was graduated in organ, piano and composition. He also was connected with several other churches. He was composer of several works.[37]

The following postcards from Purvis's mother to June Townsend demonstrate the highs and lows that families would suffer:

> Jan. 2, 1945. We, too, are dreadfully upset about our son, Dick. Have not heard from him for over a month, the last letter we received was written on Nov. 27. On Dec. 30th, we received a "V" mail letter written on Dec. 9th, have not heard a word from him since the big push of Dec. 16th.[38]

3/23/45. The most wonderful news just arrived. Dick is alive and German prisoner. We heard directly from Dick, a letter arrived yesterday afternoon from the Prison Camp.[39]

"Hope Dim"

A gripping article in the April 1945 edition of *The Diapason* caught the attention of the American organ community:

HOPE DIM FOR SAFETY OF RICHARD I. PURVIS

———

NO WORD COMES TO FAMILY

———

Young Organist and Composer Missing in Action in Luxembourg after Desperate Battle—Had Composed in Foxhole.

———

Hope for the safety of Warrant Officer Richard I. Purvis, the young American organist and composer, has been fading since no word from him has been received in March. Mr. Purvis' parents, Mr. and Mrs. G. T. Purvis of Oakland, Cal., were notified Jan. 10 that their son had been missing in action in Luxembourg since Dec. 22. In March the War Department sent the parents a letter stating that all recent lists received from the International Red Cross had been carefully checked but that Richard's name did not appear on any of them. His family and friends continue, however, to cherish the hope that word of his safety will come.

Warrant Officer Purvis was bandmaster of the Twenty-eighth Division band overseas. When Colonel Strickler found it necessary to hurl all his forces against the Germans he armed every one of the sixty members of the band, as well as clerks, quartermasters and ordnance men, and even convalescents, for the battle. From Sunday afternoon, Dec. 17, through Tuesday, Dec. 19, they defied the enemy and suffered heavy losses in the desperate fighting.

Before entering the service in the summer of 1942 Richard Purvis was organist of St. James' Church in Philadelphia. He was a private at Fort Meade, Md., and later was stationed at Fort McPherson, Ga. He studied at the army music school at Fort Myer, Va., in the spring of 1943 and entered the division headquarters band at Camp Pickett, Va., that fall. While in the midst of his war activities he continued to compose music for the organ in a foxhole, as told in the December issue of THE DIAPASON. Here he wrote what was to be the first of a group of four preludes on carols, the initial one being on the Christmas song "What Child is This?" The piece was published in America before Christmas. His band was the first to march in the streets of Paris after the liberation and Warrant Officer Purvis in his letters expressed the hope of marching down the streets of Berlin.

Before entering the armed forces Mr. Purvis had gained widespread fame as a composer for the organ and his compositions are issued by several of the leading publishers.

Richard Purvis' only brother, Robert, has been overseas for two years and was in North Africa, but is now in Italy.[40]

Donald Corbett wrote, "By 1945 the American Guild of Organists had become anxious over his fate. He had been able to smuggle some correspondence out, but they had not heard from him for over six months."[41]

The Famous "Obituary"

The following passage quoted in the Biographical Data and elsewhere probably gave rise to persistent rumors about the existence of a premature Purvis obituary: "Failing to hear of Purvis' survival for over six months, it was assumed he had lost his life, and he holds the dubious distinction of being the only living American organist to have his obituary printed in *The Diapason*, the official organ of the American Guild of Organists."[42]

This line about an obituary subsequently became part of numerous press releases and Purvis publicity over the years. The "Hope Dim" article from *The Diapason* may have looked like an obituary to many readers, and understandably so. Nevertheless, no actual obituary from the period has yet surfaced.

Rehabilitation and Discharge

June Townsend must have been relieved to receive this postcard from Richard's mother: "5/27/45. At last, we have heard from Dick again. The first since his liberation, which took place on April 29th [*sic*]. He is in a hospital somewhere in France. Said it was good not to be suffering from hunger, cold, filth, and the endless marching of the P.W. columns."[43]

According to the Biographical Data, "Purvis was liberated in June 1945 [actually April 5, 1945; V-E Day was May 8, 1945], going first to a convalescent camp for three months at Southampton, England. He was then transferred to the prisoner of war rehabilitation center in Santa Barbara, California, remaining there for an additional six months in order to regain his strength."[44]

The following newspaper clipping from *The Oakland Tribune* tells of his musical duties at the end of his military service:

> Warrant Officer Richard I. Purvis of Oakland, now at the Army Redistribution Center, Santa Barbara, is awaiting discharge after spending two years overseas.
>
> A former bandleader with the 28th Infantry Division, Purvis prefaced his first concert in Germany with the National Anthem. It was the first time in eight years that the strains of the Star Spangled Banner rang out over German soil and the fighting men in their fox holes stood at attention.
>
> From the 63 men who formed a complete concert orchestra, the Oakland veteran could make up two swing bands or a 56-piece marching band. With one of these orchestras he toured American installations during a year in England, and played for men drawn back from the front lines in France, Germany, Belgium, and Luxembourg. The band played marches, swing, and classics for battle-weary veterans in snow, rain, and mud.[45]

And finally this card from Santa Barbara, dated October 13, 1945: "Dear June: My discharge came thru okeh—so its 'hi-diddle-dee-dee', a civilian's life for me. Will have much copy work for you shortly. We must have a conference very soon. My very kindest regards to your husband, brother, and mother. Cheerio—Dick."[46]

In 1988, while I was living in Santa Barbara, Purvis wrote me a letter which ended with the following: "P.S.: Incidentally I was 'rehabilitated' for 2 months at Santa Barbara after my P.O.W. experience in W.W.II. I was billeted at the old 'Miramar.' Is it still there?"[47]

Lasting Effects of the War on Purvis

Purvis occasionally shaved a couple of years off his age, reporting his birth year as 1915 instead of 1913. One day R. Jay Williamson, visiting Purvis at his home, saw his real birthdate on his passport and asked Purvis why he sometimes fudged. Purvis answered, "The time I spent as a prisoner of war was not living!" He apparently felt justified in deducting that time from his life, even if he was a prisoner of war for much less than two years.[48]

Douglas Metzler reported that when Purvis returned from the war, he "couldn't even play a C-E-G" because his hands were so "out of it." Metzler said that Purvis wouldn't talk about his imprisonment and added that Purvis implied that he had been tortured.[49]

Ed Stout offered these sobering recollections regarding Purvis's war years:

> When he was young he wasn't heavy. He was slight in stature like me. I think 5'5". I think we were about the same height. He was a good looking lad, trim—he wasn't heavy. He was in the Battle of Bulge. He was a bandmaster, and he was captured. They took everybody. He was in a concentration camp, and he said they were experimenting on him and several others with drugs and diets, and it just destroyed his metabolism. He was completely messed up as a result of that when he came out of the war. He said he could barely play the organ. I believe he told me he was in a rehab facility in Monterey [actually Santa Barbara] for a while and he got to a piano and things began to come back, but he was pretty badly damaged. So he went from the rehab situation to St. Mark's [Lutheran, San Francisco] and got his footing back and then got the appointment at Grace Cathedral.[50]

In a letter recommending Purvis to Dean Bernard Lovgren of Grace Cathedral, W. Richard Weagly, choir director of The Riverside Church in New York, wrote, "His war experiences were of a shattering nature, yet in all his letters to me there was great faith and strength."[51]

According to Walter Bahn, it was Frederic Freeman (organist at First Unitarian Church in Oakland) who helped Purvis regain his health after his traumatic war experience. "Purvis was a basket case when he came back. When Purvis couldn't even play a hymn, Freeman would play duets with him." Bahn, who became a psychotherapist in the 1980s, says that now it would be described as post-traumatic stress disorder. "Today there are drugs, but post WW2 it was booze."[52]

June Townsend later recalled Purvis's war experience in this paragraph:

> World War II was on and Richard enlisted. He went from PFC to Warrant Officer and Chaplain's Assistant. He was in the Honor Guard for the President and the Queen, up close so he could see their faces. He and my brother were sent to Germany. He led his band in procession in the liberation of Paris. I copied his popular "Greensleeves" which he said he "wrote in a foxhole." Unfortunately he received a head wound and was captured by the enemy. There were endless marches and he was helped to survive by a Jewish doctor who hid medication in his shoes. He was Missing in Action and hope for him faded. However, he was liberated and hospitalized. He said the nurse said, Mr. Purvis, "Eat this," and I ate it. When he came home, his mother tried to stuff him, but he was afraid of getting a "spare tire."[53]

Return to San Francisco

After Purvis returned to the Bay Area, he was hired sometime in 1946 as organist at St. Mark's Lutheran Church in San Francisco. The organ at St. Mark's, built by Schoenstein & Co., had been in the church since its opening in 1895. Purvis would not stay long at St. Mark's; within in a few months he was hired as Organist and Master of the Choristers at Grace Cathedral, where he started in February of 1947.

During his brief tenure at St. Mark's, Purvis was involved in plans for a new organ there. The church's archives give the following details:

> On January 10, 1946, at the annual meeting, the congregation unanimously authorized "that the church council proceed, as soon as possible, to remodel the chancel and modernize and electrify the organ, (this was later changed to install a new organ).... [O]n April 27, 1947, the three-manual Moller Organ was dedicated, with Rev. H. Paul Romeis, First Church, Oakland, as the speaker, followed by the Dedicatory Organ Recital May 6, 1947, at 8:15 p.m., by Richard I. Purvis, Organist of St. Mark's when the contract was let.[54]

Bynum Petty offered the following information: "The organ at St. Mark's Lutheran when Purvis was organist was a Moller organ, Op. 7370. The Organ Historical Society archives contain correspondence between the Moller factory and Eugene Poole, who was the Moller sales representative at the time. Poole mentions in the correspondence that Purvis "wanted thumb pistons and a Swell Oboe."[55]

Purvis was a member of Musicians' Union Local No. 6, although it is not known when he joined or how long he remained a member. A form letter dated July 16, 1946, with the salutation "Dear Member" and a sample ballot were sent to him at 7970 Garfield, Oakland 3, California.[56]

Richard Purvis, late 1940s. Courtesy Donald Braff.

Back on the Bench

Judging from reviews of his recitals from this period, Purvis made a rapid comeback at the keyboard, and his listeners lost no time singing his praises.

In March 1946, the following review by Alfred Frankenstein appeared in the *San Francisco Chronicle*:

> Richard Irven Purvis returned to San Francisco Tuesday night after several years' military service and a long stretch as organist of Philadelphia churches, and gave one of the most brilliant organ recitals this city has ever had the privilege of hearing. And it is worth pointing out, at a time when the organ recital is supposed to be in decline, that Calvary Presbyterian Church held an extremely large audience for this occasion.

Unlike some of his colleagues, Purvis did not choose to stress any one phase of the literature, but touched on many phases, from Bach to Frederick [*sic*] Freeman of San Francisco, with works of the French school and the inevitable Karg-Elert by the way. He also presented Julius Reubke's rarely heard "Sonata on the 94th Psalm," which represents the baroque romanticism of Liszt applied to the organ, and was clearly intended to be played in a church adorned by Delacroix.

All this Purvis set forth with absolutely flawless manual and pedal technique, with subtle and highly effective registration, and with the utmost in intelligent musicianship. But what one particularly took away was a sense of youthful vitality, of resilience and enthusiasm and delight in playing the organ and playing it well, such as one takes away all too seldom from such events.[57]

Clarence Mader, a prominent Los Angeles organist, discussed with Purvis in the following letter certain details of the recital business:

Immanuel Presbyterian Church
Wilshire Boulevard and Berendo Street
Los Angeles 5, California
July 18, 1946

Dear Dick:

Your explanation is readily understood, and your offer to come some other time is appreciated. I'll do my best to help arrange it.

With three different programs, it sounds like a LaBerge tour. How do you do it? and why does he ask for three? Two programs are plenty. I often think one with substitutions should be enough. But I guess you must be famous like Horowitz or McCurdy to get away with it.

All good wishes for the success of your October tour.

As ever,
Clarence M.[58]

Robert Bennett reported that in the fall of 1946, Purvis played at First Presbyterian Church in Houston, Texas, for a regional convention of the AGO held there.[59]

On October 29, 1946, the Sacramento Chapter of the AGO presented Purvis in a recital at the First Methodist Church, 21st and J Streets. The program also specified a "Silver Offering" (a voluntary cash contribution).

Purcell: Trumpet Tune
Bach: Fugue in G minor
Dupré: Berceuse
Widor: Intermezzo (Symphony VI)
Karg-Elert: Invocation
Handel: Giga (Concerto V)
Purvis: Divinum Mysterium
Horatio Parker: Allegretto (Concerto in E-flat)
Frederic Freeman: The Wistful Shepherd
Vierne: Carillon de Westminster
Improvisations on Given Themes

The newspaper report that appeared shortly before the Sacramento recital states in part:

Purvis just recently resumed his concert career after four years of service in the army. He was division bandmaster for the 28th Division and it was his band which played the historic march through Paris on the day of the city's Liberation Fete. Purvis was among the Americans captured on the Belgian bulge and was a prisoner of the Nazis for five months.

Of Purvis' "comeback concert" early this year in San Francisco, Alfred Frankenstein wrote in The Chronicle: "It was one of the most brilliant organ recitals this city has had the privilege of hearing," and the critic lauded his "flawless manual and pedal technique, his subtle and highly effective registration and intelligent musicianship."[60]

The day after the recital, the following review appeared in the newspaper:

Organist Delights Listeners with His Tuneful Gems

by Mila Landis

A concert of tuneful music, played with imaginativeness and a sensitive poetic feeling, was that given last night by Richard Irven Purvis, young American organist, under the sponsorship of the Sacramento Organ Guild in the First Methodist Church.

The program consisted of brief compositions, rather than those of sustained interest, but each was a gem in itself. The Berceuse of Marcel Dupre and the Invocation of Sigfrid Karg-Elert were played with great delicacy of touch and depth of emotional feeling, as was the Divinum Mysterium, a composition by the artist himself. Variety was furnished to the program by the martial rhythms of the Trumpet Tune of Henry Purcell and the sprightly Allegretto by Horatio Parker.

The artist kept away from the numerous trick devices which many organists use for popular appeal. The sound of faintly echoing bells was an integral part of the melody when he used it, and the encore number, The Bells itself, by an obscure Dutch composer, was a little poem in itself rather than an organ show piece.

One of the pleasantest aspects of last night's recital consisted of the chatty, informative introductions which Purvis gave for each number. The hearers, too, particularly enjoyed his improvisations when from a quartet of heterogeneous notes suggested from the audience he sat down at the organ keyboard and produced an entertaining composition.[61]

Purvis performed again in Sacramento in January 1947:

Famous Organ Virtuoso Will Appear at Guild Concert

An added attraction to the affair will be the second appearance this season of the internationally famous organ virtuoso, Mr. Richard Purvis. Mr. Purvis was heard in a formal artist's recital here some three months ago. His magnificent press notices at that time were only fitting additions to the galaxy of unrestrained "rave" notices of his recitals from transcontinental tours and from his appearances in England, France, and Germany before and during the war. A pupil of three of the greatest organ pedagogues in America and in Europe, Mr. Purvis's hand and pedal technique and inspiring orchestration and interpretation of the traditional organ literatures is building greater organ audiences wherever he appears. In addition to his remarkable playing he is one of the few artists in America who is available for improvisation during the concert.[62]

This concert, entitled "Program of Roman Catholic Church Music," was held on January 14, 1947, at the Cathedral of the Blessed Sacrament, 11th and K Streets (again, with a "Silver Offering"). A "Mass in Concert Form" (as it was billed on specially printed invitation cards) was celebrated by the Most Rev. Robert Armstrong. Howard Scott directed the Cathedral Choir and soloists, and Purvis was the guest organist.

For his prelude, Purvis played J. S. Bach's Prelude in B minor, and may have written the following program note: "This prelude is said by the French organ maestro, M. Guilmant, to be the most sublime of all organ music, for its musical content is so great that the mechanics of composition and of performance are never obvious." The movements of the mass were sung by the choir. Purvis's concluding voluntary was the Sortie by Vierne.[63]

A review on January 15, 1947, by Mila Landis states in part: "Richard Purvis, organ virtuoso who was heard here recently in recital, opened the program with the inspiring Prelude in B Minor of Johann Sebastian Bach and closed it with the stirring Sortie (Messe Basse) of Louis Vierne. In both numbers he showed the same perfection of technique and sensitive interpretative qualities as in his previous appearance."[64]

Purvis, now 33, had spent eleven years on the road and far from home. Within two weeks of this performance in Sacramento, he would be named Organist and Master of the Choristers at Grace Cathedral, a post he held for almost 25 years.

Notes

1. Ed Stout, "Reflections About Richard Purvis," in "Professional Perspectives," in *Theatre Organ*, May 1, 2008, 46–47.

2. Clipping fragment, probably from the *Philadelphia Bulletin*; January 29, 1945.

3. Stephen Loher, e-mail, May 30, 2009.

4. http://search.ancestry.com/search/db.aspx?dbid=8939&cj=1&o_xid=0000584978&o_lid=0000584978, accessed June 10, 2011.

5. Biographical Data, 4.

6. *The Diapason*, August 1, 1942, 5.

7. Biographical Data, 4.

8. Curtis archives.

9. *Philadelphia Bulletin (?)*, February 15, 1943, F4.

10. Photos and letter courtesy Donna Parker.

11. Letter to June Townsend from Warrant Officer Richard I. Purvis, 109th Infantry Band, 28th Division, Camp Pickett, Virginia, undated; cited in Townsend thesis, 5; original unavailable.

12. Biographical Data, 4.

13. Eugene Dong, www.echoesofheaven.com, accessed March 2011; since withdrawn; used by permission.

14. The foreword to *Seven Chorale Preludes,* published in 1949, ends with the inscription "RICHARD PURVIS, England—1944."

15. Biographical Data, 5.

16. They had been published in 1941 and 1942 by Elkan-Vogel, so this may not in fact have been their premiere.

17. Corbett, 10.

18. Biographical Data, 5.

19. Rodgers Jenkins, telephone conversation, November 1, 2010.

20. Letter from Richard Purvis to June Townsend, October 29, 1944, Germany; cited in Townsend thesis, 6.

21. *The Diapason,* December 1, 1944, 1.

22. December 16, 1944, to January 25, 1945.

23. Biographical Data, 5.

24. Donald Sears, e-mail, May 30, 2009.

25. Internet search for "Richard Irven Purvis, <http://aad.archives.gov/aad/record-detail.jsp?dt=466&mtch=1&cat=WR26&tf=F&q=richard+purvis&bc=sl&sort=11673 desc&rpp=10&pg=1&rid=105491>, accessed June 8, 2011.

26. "Oflag" is a contraction of Offizierslager, or Officers' Camp.

27. POW list and other official information about Oflag XIII available at http://www .unforgettableveteran.com/POW_Camp__Oflag_XIII___Hammelburg_Prisoner_ List_p7.pdf; last accessed September 17, 2012.

28. Alex Kershaw, *The Longest Winter.* Da Capo Press, 2004. 178ff.

29. http://www.taskforcebaum.de/oflag13/report1.html, accessed June 2011. A full report by the International Red Cross of conditions at this camp can be read at http:// www.taskforcebaum.de/oflag13/report1.html, accessed June 2011.

30. Kershaw, 217–221.

31. Baron, Baum, and Goldhurst, *Raid!* New York: Putnam's Sons, 1981. 239–240.

32. On September 17, 2012, I spoke by telephone with Abraham Baum at his home in San Diego. Age 91 at the time, Baum chatted briefly about the raid but had no information to offer about Purvis.

33. http://en.wikipedia.org/wiki/Hogan's_Heroes, accessed June 24, 2011.

34. Musical Notes, *The Organ Music of Richard Purvis,* Vol. 1, H. T. FitzSimons, 2004, 5; this information was probably taken from June Townsend's 1995 "Memories." There is some question about the composition date of "Greensleeves": in December 1941, *The Diapason* reported that "What Child is This?" had recently been published by Sprague-Coleman.

35. Douglas Metzler, e-mail, June 24, 2010.

36. Stephen Loher, e-mail, May 30, 2009.

37. Clipping fragment, probably from the *Philadelphia Bulletin;* January 29, 1945.

38. Postcard, January 2, 1945, from Mrs. Purvis to June Townsend; cited in Townsend thesis, 6; original unavailable.

39. Postcard, March 23, 1945, from Mrs. Purvis to June Townsend; cited in Townsend thesis, 7; original unavailable.

40. *The Diapason*, April 1, 1945, 3.

41. Corbett, 11.

42. Biographical Data, 5.

43. Postcard from Mrs. Purvis to June Townsend, May 27, 1945; cited in Townsend thesis, 7; original unavailable.

44. Biographical Data, 5.

45. "Pianist Waits Discharge," *Oakland Tribune*, October 12, 1945; cited in Townsend thesis, 14 ; original unavailable.

46. Postcard from Richard Purvis to June Townsend, Santa Barbara, October 13, 1945; cited in Townsend thesis, 8; original unavailable.

47. Letter to James Welch, September 1, 1988. See the full text of this letter in Chapter 16, "Anecdotes and Reminiscences."

48. R. J. Williamson, telephone conversation, November 24, 2010.

49. Douglas Metzler, interview, Bothell, Washington, June 24, 2010.

50. Ed Stout interview.

51. Letter from Richard Weagly to Bernard Lovgren, September 21, 1946; courtesy Grace Cathedral archives.

52. Walter Bahn, telephone conversation, November 30, 2010.

53. Townsend Memories, 1995. Copies of Townsend's Memories were circulated among several friends. Sometime between 1995 and 1997 Townsend sent to Barbara Tonsberg a similar typescript—the only known copy—which contains the following variant: "About that time World War II needed America and he enlisted and soon worked himself up to Warrant Officer and Chaplain's Assistant. He even censored his own letters. He led a Band in the liberation of Paris and saw Queenies face (Holland) real up close. Unfortunately he received a head injury and was in a hospital when he was captured by the Germans...."

54. *One Hundred Golden Years, 1849–1949, A History of St. Mark's Evangelical Lutheran Church*, by Rev. J. George Dorn, pastor. Courtesy Marge Jencks, archivist, St. Mark's Lutheran, San Francisco.

55. Bynum Petty, archivist, Organ Historical Society, e-mail, July 26, 2011.

56. Courtesy Donna Parker.

57. Alfred Frankenstein, "Purvis Gives A Brilliant Organ Recital." *San Francisco Chronicle*, March 20, 1946.

58. Courtesy Grace Cathedral archives.

59. Robert Bennett, telephone conversation, November 29, 2010.

60. Unidentified clipping; no date; courtesy Sacramento Chapter AGO.

61. Unidentified clipping; October 30, 1946; courtesy Sacramento Chapter AGO.

62. Unidentified clipping, possibly the *Sacramento Shopping News*, January 1947; courtesy Sacramento Chapter AGO.

66. Concert program, courtesy Sacramento Chapter AGO.

64. Mila Landis, "Catholic Mass In Concert Form Is Successful Event," unidentified clipping, January 15, 1947; courtesy Sacramento Chapter AGO.

Richard Purvis at Grace Cathedral's Alexander Memorial Organ, 1960s. Photo by Proctor Jones. Courtesy the Proctor Jones Family.

Chapter 4

Grace Cathedral, 1947–1971

Richard Purvis served as Organist and Master of the Choristers at San Francisco's Grace Cathedral for almost a quarter of century, an era in which his name became synonymous with the iconic cathedral and its venerable Aeolian-Skinner organ. There he played and conducted music for services, gave recitals, composed most of his organ and choral works, instructed organ students, and established and taught at the Cathedral School for Boys. As anyone who knew, heard, or worked with him would attest, he became a San Francisco institution.

Purvis's Predecessors at Grace Cathedral

Prior to his appointment in 1947, Purvis had played at Grace Cathedral on several occasions and must have been well known there. Still, there is little information regarding his relationships with the previous cathedral staff or how he was notified of the availability of the position that would ultimately define him.

J. Sydney Lewis had been the cathedral organist from 1916 to 1942; he was followed by Hugh MacKinnon, who served from 1942 until his resignation on August 25, 1946. George H. Fairclough served as interim organist until Purvis was appointed less than six months later.[1] He would overshadow his predecessors, enlarge the Cathedral's reputation as a musical force, and embody the "agony and ecstasy" of rapid ecclesiastical evolution through a period marked by power and pain.

Purvis is Hired

On September 16, 1946, the Rt. Rev. Bernard N. Lovgren, Dean of the Cathedral, wrote to a number of high-ranking musicians in the country asking for their evaluation of Purvis as a candidate for the position. We do not have Dean Lovgren's letter, but several letters of response have survived.[2]

St. Bartholomew's Church, Park Avenue and 51st Street, New York 22, N.Y.
September 19, [1946]

Dear Mr. Dean, [sic]

I think very highly of Richard Purvis. He is an excellent organist. As far as I know his character is first rate. I know nothing of his work with choirs, I'm sorry. I should be persuaded to take him at his own evaluation.

Have you heard of Wm Coursen? He is an excellent service player & boy choir man—not so good as a recitalist. A man of fine character. I think we should invite a man to play a Sunday & to have rehearsals.

All my best to you.
David McK. Williams

The Riverside Church
Riverside Drive at 122nd Street
New York, 27, N.Y.
September 21, 1946

Dear Mr. Lovgren:

I appreciate the opportunity you have given me to write to you in regard to Mr. Richard Purvis, and it is gratifying to know that you are considering him for the position of organist and choirmaster of Grace Cathedral.

I have known Mr. Purvis for about ten years and have always found him a gentleman, refined and cultured, a sincere musician and Christian. His playing is brilliant and tasteful, and his reputation here in the East is outstanding as one of the top rank concert organists. During his years of study and development at Curtis Institute, he filled one of the leading church positions in Philadelphia. I cannot speak of first hand knowledge of his work there but heard often and consistently of his high standards, the regard and affection in which he was held by his boys, and the beauty of the work he did with them, from which I concluded that his personality was a winning one with the boys and his authority a recognized one throughout the choir. I know him also from his musical compositions for organ, choir and voice and they rank amongst the finest things being done by Americans today.

His character is a sterling one and his friendliness a great asset. His war experiences were of a shattering nature, yet in all his letters to me there was great faith and strength.

I trust that what I have written here answer somewhat your request, and I hope that it is of real service to Grace Cathedral and Purvis. Feeling as I do about the superior abilities Purvis has, I sincerely hope that he is given the opportunity of serving with you of Grace Cathedral.

Yours very truly,
W. Richard Weagly,
Choir Director

340 Penn Road, Wynnewood, Pa
September 22, 1946

Dear Dean Lovgren:

I have your letter regarding Richard Irven Purvis.

We, at the Curtis Institute, think that Richard Purvis is exceptional. He was one of our really distinguished students. His work as organist and choirmaster of St. James' Church was on the highest plain [*sic*]. His boy choir was the best in Philadelphia. The tone was clear and always on pitch. I have attended his rehearsals and his discipline is excellent. He gets magnificent results.

His organ playing is too wonderful. I am sure that you only need hear him play a few bars to know that he is on the top.

His improvisations were always a delight at St. James'.

We think that he is a composer of considerable ability. We are performing his Mass, his "Judas" and a number of his anthems this season.

This letters sounds very enthusiastic. It is exactly the way I feel about Mr. Purvis. I am sure that if you can get him that you will have something at Grace Cathedral in the way of music of which you have never dreamed.

If there is anything else that I can do, please feel free to call upon me.

Yours sincerely,
Alexander McCurdy
Head of the Organ Department
Curtis Institute of Music
Philadelphia 3, Pennsylvania

Washington Cathedral, Mount Saint Alban, Washington 16, D.C.
September 23, 1946

The Very Rev. Bernard N. Lovgren
Grace Cathedral
1055 Taylor St.
San Francisco 8, California

Dear Dean Lovgren,

I have your letter of September 16th requesting information about Richard Purvis, who has applied for the position of organist and choirmaster at Grace Cathedral.

It is a great pleasure for me to write to you recommending him unqualifiedly for the post. He is recognized throughout the organ profession as one of the outstanding organists of the country. I have often heard him play and I regard him a recital organist of virtuosic attainments.

While he was organist of St. James' Church in Philadelphia he developed a boy choir which was famous throughout this part of the country for its excellence.

He is a composer of great talent and his gift for improvisation is without equal as far as I know among the younger organists of the country. As a personality he has qualities of warmth and leadership which would endear him to any group of which he were director.

He has had the best of training. He has a real knowledge and love of the music of the Episcopal church and I am perfectly certain that he would bring distinction to any post he will ever fill.

I realized that I am going overboard in this letter in praise of Mr. Purvis but I assure you I would not write in this way if I did not feel that Grace Cathedral would be extremely fortunate indeed to secure the services of this outstanding musician.

Sincerely yours,

Paul Callaway, Organist and Choirmaster

The Riverside Church
Riverside Drive at 122nd Street
New York, 27, N.Y.
September 26, 1946

Dear Mr. Lovgren:

It is a pleasure for me to answer your inquiry of September 16th concerning Mr. Richard Purvis. In my estimation he would be the finest choice you could make for the position of organist and choir director of Grace Cathedral. His ability in church music is so widely known on this coast that I feel you could ask any competent church organist what you have asked me and get a similar answer. I feel that the fact that he composes so well, and incidentally so successfully, is one of his greatest assets in a position having the dignity of Grace Cathedral. His style in improvisation, his knowledge of the church service, and the very hard work that went into his studentship with Alexander McCurdy in Philadelphia, are more reasons why I would recommend him whole-heartedly. Never having heard his Boy Choir, I cannot speak but from reflected comments which were always of the highest order. Finally it seems to me that an artist like this can contribute to Grace Cathedral in such a way they both grow into each other and with each other. It would be a very great satisfaction to hear you had chosen Mr. Purvis.

Yours in complete sincerity,

Virgil Fox

NA11 NL PD=NEWYORK NY 28

BERNARD N LOVGREN=

    GRACE CATHEDRAL 1055 TAYLOR ST SFRAN=

RICHARD PURNIS FULLY QUALIFIED IN REFERENCE TO EVERY ITEMS
MENTIONED IN YOUR LETTER I CANNOT RECOMMEND HIM TOO HIGHLY=
    =CHARLES M COURLOIN.

Telegram from Charles Courboin recommending Purvis. September 29, 1946.

Purvis responded to Dean Lovgren's invitation in the following letter:

Richard Irven Purvis
7870 Garfield Avenue
Oakland 3, California
December 7, 1946

My dear Dean:

I have given the post of Grace Cathedral's Organist and Master of the Choristers most careful thought and serious consideration. I find that I may successfully fill that position only if the attached proviso is adhered to.

The Cathedral has the promise of a truly glorious and inspiring musical program, only if the proper foundation is laid now. I need not refer to the Cathedral's present musical status throughout the nation.

I am asking for $3,600.00 per annum. In view of the work entailed and the caliber of my abilities, I feel this is inadequate—but I am willing to start at such a small fee in view of the fact that I feel that Grace Cathedral is my Cathedral and that I would like to be among the builders according to my talents. If both the Los Angeles and Seattle Cathedrals can pay their incumbents $5,000 per annum—surely the Cathedral can manage the sum I have named. This will also include what fees it is necessary to pay the Deputy Organist.

I am sorry I have delayed so long, but if I were to come to the Cathedral I would want to be assured of the fact that I could do only outstanding, distinguished and dignified work. Nothing short of inspirational, reverent and truly artistic work will satisfy me.

No matter whom you choose for the post, I am hoping that a new musical era will begin for Grace Cathedral. One that is fitting for the worship and glory of God.

Sincerely,
Richard Purvis[3]

The following contract, dated February 1, 1947, was drawn up and signed by Dean Lovgren and his new organist-choirmaster. Presumably this was Purvis's official start date in his new position.

In order that the arrangements between Grace Cathedral Corporation and the Organist and Master of Choristers may be satisfactorily documented for future reference, the parties concerned have subscribed to the terms attached herewith.

It is understood that this arrangement may be terminated by either party upon 30 days notice.

Increased Rehearsal Schedule

| Trebles | Monday (Afternoon) |
| Altos | Tuesday (Afternoon) |

Trebles and Altos	Wednesday (Afternoon)
Men	Thursday (8:00 p.m.)
Full Choir	Thursday (7:00 p.m.)
Full Choir	Sunday (9:45 a.m.)
Men	Sunday (3:00 p.m.)

Jurisdiction of Organist and Master of the Choristers

The Organist and Master of the Choristers shall have full control of the Music Program of the Cathedral. Orders (as such) will be received only from the Bishop or the Dean of the Cathedral.

Discipline of the Choir

The Organist and Master of the Choristers is responsible for the discipline of the choir only while the choir is in the chancel or the choir room. (This does not include the robing room.)

Conversation between adult members of the choir and the boys is strictly forbidden at all times.

Assistant (Deputy Organist)

There will be a deputy organist chosen at the discretion of the Organist and Master of the Choristers. Said person (male) will be given a full scholarship in piano, organ, harmony, counterpoint, choral conducting, and composition by the Organist and Master of the Choristers. Services played by the deputy organist will be paid for by the Organist and Master of the Choristers. Deputy organist must be present at all rehearsals and services, unless excused by the Organist and Master of the Choristers.

Salary

The minimum salary to be considered by the Organist and Master of Choristers is $3,600.00 per annum. This is exclusive of wedding and funeral fees.

Wedding Fees

The minimum fee for a wedding shall be $15.00. Fees should be increased in accordance with the ability of the wedding party to afford a higher fee. Wedding rehearsals which require the presence of an organist shall be charged for at the rate of fifty percent of the wedding fee.

Concertizing

The Organist and Master of the Choristers shall be free to concertize in so far as his touring does not absent him from the Cathedral more than eight Sundays per annum. The Organist shall always be in the Cathedral Holy and Christmas weeks.

Personnel

The Organist and Master of the Choristers reserves the right to employ and dismiss members of the choir with the sanction of the Dean.

Use of the Organ

The Organist and Master of the Choristers reserves the right to use of [the] Cathedral Organ for practicing and teaching. In addition to the Organist and Master of the Choristers only the Deputy Organist may use the Cathedral Organ.

Public Appearances of the Choir

Under no circumstances may the Cathedral Choir sing elsewhere than in the Cathedral.[4]

The Appointment is Announced

The following announcement of Purvis's appointment appeared in the "Cathedral Chimes" newsletter on February 9, 1947, his first Sunday at Grace Cathedral. It reads in part:

> We are happy to announce that Mr. Purvis begins this week as Organist and Master of Choristers at the Cathedral.... We welcome Mr. Purvis most heartily and feel certain that he will give to the Cathedral an enviable musical position.... [W]e have every right to regard ourselves as tremendously fortunate in having Mr. Purvis associated with us. On the part of the Bishop, the Clergy, the Choir, and the Congregation we can assure him of our sincere cooperation. An expanded musical program is being planned which will include a full organ recital monthly and an Oratorio Society to be formed in the near future. It is our hope to establish the Cathedral as the focal point for musical activities in the Diocese.[5]

The *San Francisco Examiner* carried the following story on Sunday, February 9, 1947:

New Organist at Grace Cathedral Plays Today
Richard Purvis 'Master of Choristers'; Dean Announces Musical Plans

by Alexander Fried

Richard Purvis, distinguished new organist—or "master of the choristers"—at Grace Cathedral, will make his first appearance during cathedral services twice today. The services will be at 10:30 o'clock in the morning and 7:45 this evening.

"Master of the choristers" is the traditional formal title for the musician who presides over organ and choir music in a cathedral, as distinguished from a church.

MUSIC PROJECT

According to Dean Bernard N. Lovgren, the appointment of Purvis is part of a general plan to make the cathedral "a focal point for all musical activities of the diocese."

"I hope to build our choir—which now contains twenty-five boys and twelve men—to a more ideal balance of fifty boys and twenty men," said Purvis. "There is beautiful church music, ranging from Tallis and Gibbons to the present day, for just this type of ensemble, and we wish to give it fine and authentic presentation."

"At the same time, I should like to organize an oratorio society of mixed voices to perform the general choral repertory."

Purvis likewise envisages a special series of organ recitals—of outstanding ecclesiastical and secular music—at the cathedral the first Sunday of every month. Sometimes the organ may have the assistance of string instruments.

WON HIGH HONORS

Born in San Francisco, Purvis studied here with the late Wallace Sabin and with Benjamin Moore. He is the only young musician ever to have won the Cyrus H. K. Curtis memorial scholarship of the Curtis Institute of Music in Philadelphia.

Hence he studied at the institute three years and in England one year. He became organist of the Philadelphia Orchestra and held important church and educational positions in the East.

For four years he was in the Army. As infantry warrant officer, he was captured by the Germans during the "Battle of the Bulge." It was not until five months later that the advancing American forces liberated him from a prison camp near Munich.

As promised in the newsletter article, Purvis quickly became involved in the expansion of the music program in the diocese. In a memo to

Bishop Block dated September 28, 1948, Purvis discussed two new projects:

> The Right Reverend Karl Morgan Block
> Bishop of the Diocese of California
> Diocesan House
> 1055 Taylor Street
> San Francisco, California
>
> Dear Bishop,
>
> Thank you for your gracious note of recent date. If the choir gave you any pleasure at the service to which you refer, I am grateful, indeed. You may rest assured that I am expending every bit of energy and talent that I have in interests of not only the music program of the Cathedral, but that of the Diocese as well.
>
> Needless to say, I am happy to accept your Appointment as a member of the Youth Commission. The amount of time I can devote to such an endeavor is, I fear, somewhat limited; but Mr. Eastburn assures me that such service as I can render will be acceptable.
>
> In regard to our most pleasant conference of last Thursday, I am so happy that you are so enthusiastic about the formation of a Music Commission for the Diocese of California. I am attaching a list of organists and choirmasters who I think would be most helpful and discerning as members of that body.
>
> Again may I say how very pleasant it is to have you back in our midst and how very pleased I am that you will be with us at the Cathedral at least once a month?
>
> With every good wish for your continued health and happiness as our Bishop, I beg to remain
>
> Sincerely yours,
> Richard Purvis[6]

Purvis's appointment was announced in another San Francisco newspaper with a photo and profile:

> NOTED ORGANIST.—Richard Purvis, widely known composer and conductor, has been appointed organist and master of choristers at Grace Cathedral. A native San Franciscan, Mr. Purvis studied music in Philadelphia and Europe. He served 20 months overseas with the Army and was captured during the Battle of the Bulge near Luxembourg. After Allied victory

RICHARD IRVEN PURVIS

We are happy to announce that Mr. Purvis begins this week as Organist and Master of Choristers at the Cathedral. Through the following facts we introduce Mr. Purvis to our congregation. He is a native of San Francisco and was well known in local musical circles when he received the coveted Cyrus H. K. Curtis Memorial Scholarship granted by the Curtis Institute of Music in Philadelphia. While at the Institute he was given a fellowship for study abroad, particularly in that of the boy voice. His instructors included the late Sir Edward Bairstow of York Minster, Sir Ernest Bullock of Westminster Abbey and Sir Sidney Nicholson, founder of the School of English Church Music in the College of Saint Nicholas. Upon returning to America he was Organist and Choirmaster of St. James' Episcopal Church in Philadelphia; head of the Music Department of the Episcopal Academy; and Organist with the Philadelphia Symphony. He remained on the east coast until his enlistment in the Army in 1942, returning to the west coast about a year ago.

We welcome Mr. Purvis most heartily and feel certain that he will give to the Cathedral an enviable musical position. The highest recommendations were received from eminent organists. We quote from a few: Washington Cathedral, "He is recognized throughout the organ profession as one of the outstanding organists of the country;" Head of the Organ Department of Curtis Institute, "His work as organist of St. James' Church was on the highest plane and his Boy Choir was the best in Philadelphia;" Organist at Riverside Church, New York, "In my estimation he would be the finest choice you could make for Organist and Choirmaster of Grace Cathedral;" from the Choir Director of Riverside Church, "I have known Mr. Purvis for about ten years and have always found him a gentleman, refined and cultured, a sincere musician, and his reputation here in the east is outstanding as one of the top rank concert organists;" from the organist at St. Patrick's Cathedral, New York, "Richard Purvis is fully qualified, and I cannot recommend him too highly."

In view of the above opinions, we have every right to regard ourselves as tremendously fortunate in having Mr. Purvis associated with us.

On the part of the Bishop, the Clergy, the Choir, and the Congregation we can assure him of our sincere cooperation. An expanded musical program is being planned which will include a full organ recital monthly and an Oratorio Society to be formed in the near future. It is our hope to establish the Cathedral as the focal point for musical activities in the Diocese.

Newsletter article announcing Purvis as new Organist and Master of the Choristers, 1947.

he served as bandmaster for the famed 28th Division Band in the Liberation Day parade in Paris.[7]

The History of Grace

To understand Purvis, one must also understand the importance of Grace Cathedral's history, clergy, music program, and prominence in San Francisco. Appendix B provides a concise history of the cathedral, written in 2007 by Michael Lampen, Cathedral Archivist.

The Alexander Memorial Organ

Purvis was hired as Organist and Master of the Choristers at Grace, and he was devoted both to playing the organ and leading the choir. Nonetheless, due to his many compositions, recitals, and

NOTED ORGANIST.—Richard Purvis, widely known composer and conductor, has been appointed organist and master of choristers at Grace Cathedral. A native San Franciscan, Mr. Purvis studied music in Philadelphia and Europe. He served 20 months overseas with the Army and was captured during the Battle of the Bulge near Luxembourg. After Allied victory he served as bandmaster for the famed 28th Division Band in the Liberation Day parade in Paris.

The San Francisco Examiner announces Purvis's appointment as Organist and Master of the Choristers at Grace Cathedral.

recordings, he is better known as an organist than as a choral conductor. His relationship with the Alexander Memorial Organ—which he affectionately called "Gussie"—was intense, and the influence of this particular organ on his style of playing and composing was profound.

Appendix C contains Michael Lampen's detailed history of the organ played by Purvis, "Winds of God—75 Years of the Great Organ at Grace Cathedral."

The "Purvis Sound"

Anyone fortunate enough to hear Purvis play in person or through his recordings experienced an organ sound unlike any other in the world. Purvis developed his own colorful registrations and phrasing, as well as a skillful use of swell boxes and other expressive devices of the organ. The distinctive "Purvis sound" was also the result of the voicing of the organ at Grace Cathedral and the regulation of components such as the tremulants, all of which evolved over the years. Much of this was due to the expert technical know-how of Edward Millington Stout III, "Curator of Musical Instruments at Grace Cathedral"[8] from 1959 to 2004.

The following article by Stout describes Purvis's relationship with the Alexander Memorial Organ:

> Upon his return from the war, Richard Purvis was invited to be the Organist and Master of Choristers at San Francisco's Grace Cathedral. That began his long love affair with the great Alexander Memorial Aeolian-Skinner, installed in 1934. The four manual, ninety-three rank masterpiece became identified with Dick's masterful playing and his emotion-stirring music was written for an "American Classic" styled organ.
>
> Purvis knew the important role tremulants played in bringing romantic music to life and he insisted on having all of the tremulants set in what we called "the natural state", which of course meant in harmony with theatre organ settings, which remind the listeners of other musical instruments or in some cases, the uttering from a great singer. Ninety per-cent of classical organ tremulant settings are morbid. How can something have excursion after rigor mortis has set in?
>
> Much has been written about Richard Purvis' insight and ability to evoke the soul out of every whistle, but his very special contribution was in playing music from the French Romantic period. Many devoted music fans traveled from all parts of Northern California to attend his legendary Franck to Bach recitals in Grace, the instant Cathedral, "just add water, mix and pour."[9] Now and then the Nave was abuzz with the realization that George Wright was present. George and Richard held each other in the highest professional regard and they were long time friends.[10]

Donna Parker and Jonas Nordwall, both students of Purvis, co-authored the following preface to a 2004 reprinting of several of Purvis's organ works:

The Purvis Sound

Most of Richard's organ compositions were musically realized for the sound of the great Aeolian-Skinner Pipe Organ in San Francisco's Grace

Cathedral, where he was the Organist and Choirmaster for over 25 years. Regarded as one of the finest combinations of organ and building, this organ's tonal palette was enhanced in the early 1950s under Richard's guidance by his good friend, G. Donald Harrison, Aeolian-Skinner's Tonal Director. Careful refinement has continued throughout the years by the present curator, Edward Millington Stout III, who was also influenced by Richard's definitive desires. In the 1940s George Wright had named the famous San Francisco Fox Theatre's Wurlitzer *Ethyl*. Following suit, Grace Cathedral's organ became affectionately known as *Gussie*. Like George and *Ethyl*, Richard and *Gussie* were American musical institutions. George Wright and Richard were good friends and it was not uncommon for the two musical giants to attend each other's concerts.

To authentically interpret the music of Richard Purvis, an organist should imagine playing a romantic organ in a large gothic structure, where time can appear to stand still. Richard would often quote Charles Marie Widor's saying, "To be an organist, one must have a vision of eternity."

This type of space or its vision creates opportunities to focus on intense musical phrasing, articulation, very expressive use of the swell pedals, controlled tempi and most important, the use of unique, colorful sounds that define the Richard Purvis sound.

For example, a Purvis signature solo registration is a 4' Flute combined with a 2-2/3' Nazard with tremulant. This combination creates a haunting, lyrical sound. That sound will not occur if the Nazard has a Principal-like tone quality or if the 4' Flute is too colorful or has too much "chiff" in its character. It must also be in an enclosed division so musical nuance can be subtly enhanced. The distinctive flute stops used by Purvis are the 8' Lieblich Gedeckt, 4' Lieblich Flute and 2-2/3' Nazard. According to Ed Stout, "the secret for that renowned sound lies in the Choir division's tremulant, which is set in the 'natural' mode, thereby reminding the listener of a great singer or instrumental soloist. The deep and fast tremulant slightly overdrives the cut-up of the stopped metal pipes, thereby creating a feathery and colorful sound. Purvis insisted that all of the tremulants in the Grace Cathedral organ were adjusted to be in harmony with other musical disciplines and not like most church organ tremolos, which are most often set in a slow mortiferous mode."

When Richard's publications listed Strings, he always meant String Celestes. Grace's organ has four pairs of String Celestes varying in quality

Alexander Memorial Organ, North Choir façade. Photo by Proctor Jones. Courtesy Grace Cathedral archives.

from the thin, quiet Echo Celestes in the Swell Division to broad, soaring Gambas in the Solo Division. Organists must use their creativity to recreate those essential qualities on their instruments when performing Purvis compositions. As ever-changing color was important to Richard, all of his directions need to be followed as marked. It is just as important as using the appropriate sounds for other historical musical periods.

Early in his life Richard was greatly influenced by many of the 20th century's greatest musicians, whom he had enjoyed listening to, studying with or talking to. These included German organist Sigfrid Karg-Elert, French organists Charles Tournemire and Marcel Dupré, Belgian organist Charles Courboin, Dutch [*sic*] organist Flor Peeters, and American icon George Gershwin. Richard loved to tell the story about explaining the organ's mutations to Gershwin who was considering composing an organ concerto.

Richard was also greatly influenced by the Wurlitzer Theatre Pipe Organ. As a San Francisco native growing up in the 1920s, he heard the finest theatre organists of his time. A favorite was Iris Vining, who played the Paramount Theatre's 4 manual 33 rank Wurlitzer, his favorite theatre organ. Many of Richard's compositions were dedicated to theatre organ giants and good friends Floyd Wright, George Wright and later Bill Thomson, Tom Hazleton, Donna Parker and Lyn Larsen.[11]

In the following passages, Stout describes Purvis's knowledge of acoustics and how acoustics affect organ performance:

I loved watching him play the organ. There were certain people who knew how to play that room and make that organ sound clean and clear. Too many organists overload the room. Purvis knew how to play that room. He knew that you had to get OFF the keys and let the room be part of it. Let the room swallow, don't shove too much down its throat—it will just be murky. Purvis taught his students that how to deal with the acoustics.[12]

You know the room was slightly different before the building was finished. A lot of the music he wrote was written when we had the tin wall down at the end, only three bays deep when I started working there. I remember the organ in the acoustical setting Harrison worked with.[13]

The tremulants were probably fairly conservative when the organ was installed; Purvis had had them quickened after he began at Grace but before Stout arrived. Together they made more refinements to suit Purvis's taste.

Stout noted:

The Choir manual had the deepest tremulant and gave the organ one of its signature sounds, especially on the Choir flutes 8, 4, and 2-2/3. Richard also liked the color reeds (especially the English Horn) with a 4' Flute. The 4' Flute made the color reeds carry further and evened them out, gave them better carrying power, and made them smoother with the tremulants.[14]

Purvis's Registrations and Pistons

Purvis always had certain combination pistons designated for his signature sounds. Stout described them in the following interview:

JW: This is before the days of multiple memories. How many generals were on the original console?

ES: There were eight, lettered A B C D E F G H.

JW: Did Purvis play in the English style, using divisional pistons on the manuals?

ES: Yes, he used divisionals to create crescendos and decrescendos. Now and then he used the generals, but mostly he used divisionals. He said you could get a better buildup that way.

JW: What about his unique registrations?

ES: General D in the old days was super romantic, with all the flute and string celestes, tremulants, as slushy as it could possibly get. You know, that organ didn't have that many strings, but it had the effect of having a huge string ensemble. The reason was that the scaling and the voicing all contributed, there was no duplication, they all contributed, because they were radically different: Viola Pomposas in the Choir; and up in the Solo the Gamba and Gamba Celeste, a very good sound; and a pair called Echo Celestes, soft pencil strings. That was it for strings, but it had a Flauto Dolce and Céleste, a tapered Flute Céleste in the Swell and then the Erzähler and Kleine Erzähler in the Choir. That's it, but it worked! And the tremulants were right—they were fast and deep, and that's the way he liked them, because that's what we called "natural."

JW: The pistons were lettered in those days, correct?

ES: The generals were lettered instead of numbered. I kind of like that. It really sets it apart.

JW: What was on Choir 2?

ES: The Erzähler, Kleine Erzähler, and the 4' Lieblich Flute, and the way I had that tremulant set ...

JW: No Nazard in there?

ES: No, just three stops, two 8's and a 4'.

JW: Did he leave those pistons set up? What if there were a guest organist?

ES: He let them set the pistons, and he would reset them.[15]

Douglas Metzler added that General J (for "Joy") was always a "slush" registration on the Grace organ.[16]

Stephen Loher clarified: "When the Ruffatti console arrived it had 18 generals—again letters. On the original 'Gussie' general D was all lush strings. Richard decided to put that combination on the new general J. There never was a general J on the original Gussie."[17]

Purvis's Style of Service Playing

Most people who heard Purvis play a service have vivid memories of the experience. Fortunately, some recordings of services in which he played have survived. Below are a few commentaries on Purvis's service playing techniques.

Donald Sears wrote:

> His service playing was superb in what I would call the English/Purvis tradition. He usually began the prelude with a short improvisation followed by music from the organ repertoire. He did a lot with his hymn playing, putting in dramatic interludes between some of the verses and having the boy choristers sing beautiful descants. The last verse could be a free Purvis harmonization, such as the one he used with "O God, Our Help in Ages Past" which I heard him play, and he had arrangements of both "All Glory, Laud and Honor" and "Lyra Davidica" which he would frequently use.[18]

Stephen Loher responded to a question:

> You ask was the style British? American? Romantic? Theatrical? I would say yes to all. He used to do lots of improvising: i.e., when the procession came around, during communions, etc.
>
> His service playing was rooted in the English style with his unique touches—the color that we associate with him. Accompaniments were often masterful. Hymn playing was rather straightforward, though. He had a "hymn general" which was a basic pleno of Great, Swell, and Choir. For the second verse he would add the 8' and 4' reeds on the Swell; take them off for the third verse; put them on again for the fourth verse, etc. Sometimes he would do a free style accompaniment, but not very often. He

improvised before the service, so he had no prelude prepared. His improvisations sounded like his compositions.[19]

Clarence Snyder, a classmate at Curtis, shared the following memory: "Richard liked to make his anthem accompaniments colorful. He would often have me play on one manual a melody he wanted brought out while he was playing with two hands on another manual."[20]

Ed Stout said, "One of the reasons I'd go up there was for his improvs during communion. He would come up with these mini 'symphonettes' off the top of his head, often based on a hymn or something else that was in the service. He would take the organ all over the place in a symphonic way with some of the most beautiful harmonies. He knew how to meld and blend, and he knew how to work the boxes."

Stout summed up Purvis's unforgettable service playing as follows: "He was brilliant. He was accompanying and creating the drama and supporting emotionally everything that was happening in the service. Purvis knew that instinctively.... The organ potentially can be and is the perfect musical instrument for stirring the heart and the soul of the listener."[21]

The "Nob Hill Thrush"

In September 2010, I met with two of Purvis's former assistants, David Worth and Stephen Loher; joining us that day was Ken Dod, who had studied with Purvis.

At First Methodist Church in Salem, Oregon, Stephen Loher demonstrated for us on the Aeolian-Skinner organ what he called the "Nob Hill Thrush," improvising on the celestes and solo flute in the style of a Purvis prelude. Loher's highly descriptive phrase was probably used by other listeners to characterize Purvis's prelude playing style.

Interestingly, Loher added that in Purvis's time at Grace the choir entered during the prelude rather than during the processional hymn.[22]

Purvis and G. Donald Harrison

Purvis could get great music out of any pipe organ, but this was particularly true of the organ at Grace Cathedral.

RICHARD IRVEN PURVIS

ORGANIST AND
MASTER OF CHORISTERS
GRACE CATHEDRAL, SAN FRANCISCO

RECITALIST
CALIFORNIA PALACE OF THE
LEGION OF HONOR

Purvis's calling card during the 1950s and 1960s.

Stephen Loher said,

I think he favored the American Classic style of [G. Donald] Harrison the most. I am sure his favorite organ was Grace—but I don't think he had a least favorite. He seemed to find the best thing in any organ. I remember at a lesson he would say "I played a Wicks in Oregon that had a lovely Rohrflute on the Swell." The rest might be a disaster but that flute was lovely and that is what he remembered.[23]

Given his great affinity for the work of G. Donald Harrison, president of the Aeolian-Skinner Organ Company, Purvis made a visit in 1948 to Salt Lake City to hear the newly installed Aeolian-Skinner organ at the Mormon Tabernacle. Although he considered the organ at Grace Cathedral to be nearly perfect, he came away from the Tabernacle organ wishing for a few more stops on the Aeolian-Skinner organ at Grace.

Jonas Nordwall told his version of the story:

When Harrison did the Mormon Tabernacle, Dick was good friends with Schreiner and Asper [then Tabernacle organists]. Dick went over to play in 1948 when the organ was new, and a couple days later, Don said, "How do you like the Mormon Tabernacle organ?" Typical Purvis said, "Well, Don, we need to have a talk. I think it's a very stunning organ, but basically Grace is a better sound. Now if Grace only had a flute céleste and the echo string céleste in the Swell, if it had that extra terrace to go from the big pair of strings to echo strings down to the flute céleste, we could do even more magic than you can at the Tabernacle."

And about four months later these crates show up, and probably this could have been the beginning of the conflict, and Purvis is called into the Dean's office. "What is all this stuff here from Boston? We didn't order this. Did you order this? We don't have any money to pay for it." So Dick got on the phone with Harrison and Harrison said, "Well, you said it was going to be a better organ and we want to have our organs as good as they can possibly be. This is a gift from me and we'll get a hold of Paul Schoenstein and he'll do the installation and we'll pay the expense of that." And they did. And that was added—a flute céleste and echo string céleste.[24]

The Biographical Data has this to say about the encounter:

Following a visit to Grace Cathedral during a service, Mr. G. Donald Harrison, president of the Aeolian-Skinner Organ Company, was so impressed by its musical standards that he offered to rebuild the Alexander Memorial Organ, free of charge. At the same time, William Crocker had given Mr. Purvis a grant of $10,000.00 to rebuild the Crocker Memorial Organ in the Chapel of Grace. G. Donald Harrison immediately agreed to extend the facilities and talents of his company, producing an organ which would have normally cost many times the price of this grant, which was sent air freight to San Francisco, in order that it might be completely installed for the 1952 Convention of the American Guild of Organists.[25]

Stephen Loher added the following account:

Richard told me that he was at a convention and Harrison was saying that the Tabernacle was his finest so far. Richard said that he was overlooking Grace, so Harrison came out later on a trip. That is when it was decided to do some tonal work, and he used the 5-rank Swell mixture (plus an additional rank) to create a 3-rank Plein Jeu and a 3-rank Cymbal, and added the Viola Pomposa Celeste, among other things.[26]

Yet another version of the story was recounted by Bob Tall of Los Angeles, who had studied with both Schreiner and Asper:

Alex [Schreiner] and Frank Asper didn't get along too well. Alex was always telling Frank, "I'm a trained organist and I'm the principal organist here." But after radio shows on Tuesday when they'd deliver the mail,

40–50 cards would come to Alex, and there would be a big sackful of mail for Frank. Not great friends.

When Purvis went there to play a recital on the new Tabernacle organ in the 1950s, he didn't know about Asper and Schreiner's rivalry. He invited them both to dinner at the Hotel Utah, and they both accepted. When they found he'd invited both of them, neither showed up. Purvis waited impatiently and that made him angry. The entire experience was a negative one for Purvis, and he couldn't wait to get back to San Francisco and play his organ again.

G. Donald later said, "How did you like the [Tabernacle] organ?" Purvis answered, "It's all right, it's the room that makes the sound, but my organ at Grace Cathedral is better." G. Donald was taken aback, since the Tabernacle was considered his magnum opus.

Not long after, G. Donald went out to Grace Cathedral and listened to Purvis play for an hour and a half, had dinner with him, and, according to Purvis, G. Donald agreed with him that Grace Cathedral had the better organ.[27]

Modifications to the Alexander Memorial Organ, 1955–1957

According to Ed Stout, John C. Swinford maintained the Alexander Organ from the time of its installation through the mid-1950s, when Purvis proposed changes that Swinford probably didn't approve. At that point Purvis brought in his friends Bill Swain and Bob Kates, who took over the maintenance until around 1957, when they resigned or were let go. Starting at that time and until Ed Stout took over in 1959, the organ was maintained by William Reid of Santa Clara, California.

Several of the changes made to the organ by Swain and Kates reflected Purvis's strong interest in Wurlitzers. Removing the 16' Fagotto in the Swell, they put it on heavy wind and renamed it Military Trumpet (playable from the Solo division but located in the Swell box); they added a Trompette Provençale (like a Wurlitzer post horn) on 15 inches of wind, installed outside the Solo box; they augmented the Swell division with a 2' Waldflute (classically an open flute, but in this case a stopped flute because Purvis liked the 2' Wurlitzer piccolo sound). They also used the Gross Tierce pipes on the Great to create a 1' Italian Principal, and they turned the Gross Tierce in the Pedal into a 4' Choral Bass. G. Donald Harrison apparently approved of this last transformation, if not others. The additions ordered by Purvis remained intact until Purvis left Grace in 1971.[28]

Rebuilding of the Alexander Memorial Organ, 1966–1968

By the early 1960s, the Alexander Memorial Organ, installed in 1934, was in serious need of releathering and other work. Sometime in 1966, a gusset in the high pressure reservoir, which fed the Solo Tuba and Clarion as well as the console's combination action, blew out. Ed Stout says that it could have been satisfactorily releathered, but Purvis wanted a new five-manual console and seized the opportunity to arrange for one.[29]

Loher recalls that the gusset blew on the day of a Diocesan Convention. He said that Ed had to force some stops out so Purvis could accompany hymns, but due to the lack of wind in the console, there was no way to change registrations.[30]

Purvis may have already been consulting with various firms for a new console. In the Dean's Report of a meeting on November 6, 1966, there is mention of bids having been received from Aeolian-Skinner, Schantz, and Ruffatti. There was also the following notation: "Mr. Purvis on his trip East soon is to play a recital on an organ they [Ruffatti] have installed there. He is reserving comment on this company until he has seen and played the console."[31]

In 1964 Purvis's former student Ted Alan Worth had become a U.S. representative for the Italian-owned organ company Fratelli Ruffatti.[32] Worth was also organist at St. Mary's Episcopal Church in Wayne, Pennsylvania, and when his church signed a contract for a new Ruffatti organ, it became the first organ built by the firm in America. For the dedicatory Festival Evensong and Blessing of the Organ at St. Mary's, held on November 29, 1966, Purvis composed a choral setting of Psalm 150 entitled "Laudate Dominum" (described by Worth as "a boisterous and jazzy affair that ended with a terrific crash from the organ, tympani, brass, and cymbals"). Worth was organist for the program. Purvis had gone to St. Mary's a few days before the dedication to hear the choir and brass rehearse his new composition. Although he couldn't remain for the service or for the dedicatory recitals (by Worth on December 9 and by Virgil Fox on December 14), he inspected the new Ruffatti carefully while he was in Wayne. He must have been pleased with what he saw, for soon after, Grace Cathedral signed a contract with Ruffatti for a new five-manual console.[33]

Ed Stout said that Ruffatti boasted the latest in solid state organ technology, which may have influenced Purvis's decision. Grace's 30-year-old Skinner console was shipped to Italy, where Ruffatti removed the stop jambs, replacing them with rocker tabs and altering the case sufficiently to make room for a fifth manual.[34]

Purvis's first call to arrange for an interim electronic organ for Grace was made to Jerome Markowitz of the Allen Organ Company. Markowitz was happy to supply an organ, but only for a fee. Purvis then contacted Rodgers Jenkins at the Rodgers Organ Company, who, sensing a public relations opportunity, offered to lend a Rodgers organ to Grace Cathedral at no charge.[35] In 1966, Purvis accepted Rodgers' offer, a decision that resulted in a close relationship of many years. Purvis performed recitals on numerous Rodgers organs, including dedication concerts; he taught at Rodgers studios throughout the state; and he owned two Rodgers organs in his home studio.

Ed Stout remembers that during this interim-organ period a concert was given by the Air Force Choir. At one point part of a local taxi driver's conversation was picked up and broadcast over the sound system of the Rodgers organ![36]

Meanwhile, the Bishop and Cathedral Trustees passed a resolution on June 20, 1967, recognizing and honoring Purvis's 20 years of service at Grace.[37]

The new Ruffatti console was installed in 1968, initially with a system that allowed the console to be moved sideways, but only with considerable difficulty. Soon, however, a fully mobile console was fabricated, enabling the console to be moved more freely in the choir area.[38]

Stephen Loher said that Frank Roseberry, Ruffatti's West Coast representative, had told him that "on the four posts at the sides of the console were to be carved the faces of Richard, G. Donald Harrison, and two current choirboys."[39] To this Stout responded, "That may have been a conversation with Dick where in jest he said he was going to turn the console into Mt. Rushmore West, but I do not believe there was any serious consideration."[40]

The inaugural program on the Ruffatti console occurred on April 21, 1968. Purvis played the Toccata and Fugue in D minor of Bach; two miniatures that had been performed at the 1934 Skinner inauguration ("Fidelis"

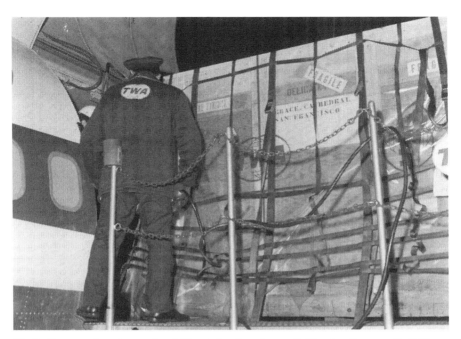

The Ruffatti console on its way from Milan to San Francisco, 1968. Courtesy Francesco Ruffatti.

Purvis at the newly installed Ruffatti console, 1968. Courtesy Francesco Ruffatti.

by Percy Whitlock and "Allegretto" by William Wolstenholme); "A Solemn Melody" by Sir Walford Davies; and "Toccata Festiva" by Purvis.[41]

Purvis on Organs and Organists

In 1975, four years after he had left Grace Cathedral, Purvis wrote a letter to David Worth with his thoughts about the Skinner organ designed by G. Donald Harrison at All Saints Episcopal Church in Worcester, Massachusetts.[42] Worth, then organist at All Saints, was contemplating changes to the Harrison instrument. It is informative to read Purvis's wide-ranging thoughts on organs and the organ profession:

> May 28, 1975
>
> Dear David:
>
> Forgive my not answering sooner, but I have just returned from a concert tour and found your letter awaiting me.
>
> About the organ rebuild:
>
> 1ˢᵗ The Organ is there for the <u>service</u> which is Anglican in ethos. Do not let anyone change its character to French Roman Catholic or German Lutheran. These misguided enthusiasts are ruining music in the Episcopal Church.
>
> 2ⁿᵈ The Organ should be restored as near as is possible to its original design (including the Solo Organ). To my mind it has been greatly altered and not to its advantage.
>
> 3ʳᵈ <u>No way</u> should slider chests be used! The Organ at St. Thomas in New York City was greatly harmed by so doing.
>
> 4ᵗʰ Roy Perry is one of the very few men in the Organ Field whom I admire and trust; tonally, musically and mechanically. You couldn't do better than to seek his help.
>
> 5ᵗʰ The Organ is there as an <u>aid</u> to <u>Worship</u>. It should be a thing of beauty and should <u>enhance</u> the liturgy—not detract from it.
>
> 6ᵗʰ The Organ Profession (as a whole) has regressed and not progressed in America during the past twenty years. Organ builders have done nothing creative since G. Donald Harrison. The Guild has become a harem of "antiquarians" who are divorcing the organ from the main stream of music. A friend of mine (who is a magnificent pianist) attended a recent Guild

Convention and what she encountered horrified her. She now describes the AGO as a "coterie of nasty individuals who are devotees of ugliness and boredom."

Win a Victory for the Organ, Music, Church and God and <u>Restore</u> (not rebuild) the Organ at All Saints. The church needs <u>Glory</u> in all its facets of Worship. The tide is <u>turning</u> musically among young organists—they are returning to sanity and musicality. Join Them!

(You might consult Joe Dzeda as well as Perry.)

All the best.

Keep me posted.

　　　Dick[43]

What Became of Grace's Skinner Console?

When Ruffatti built the new console for Grace Cathedral, installed in 1971, the Italians used the shell of the original 1934 Skinner console, adding new stop jambs and keydesks. This console remained in place until 1998, when Schoenstein & Co. installed the console that is in use to this day.

In 1998 organ enthusiast Martin Lilley purchased the Ruffatti console. He installed it in his home in Fremont, California, where it currently plays a combination of Willis pipes and electronics. Unfortunately, the original bench disappeared before Lilley bought the console.[44]

John Shields

A key person in Purvis's life was John Shields, who was born January 6, 1913, in Bethlehem, Pennsylvania. After graduating from Duke University in the mid-1940s, Shields moved to San Francisco. He sang bass in the choir at Grace Cathedral throughout the time that Richard played there; he also assisted Richard in the choir library and in other ways. At the Cathedral School, he taught music and P.E.

Purvis dedicated his "Four Prayers in Tone" to John in 1951. According to Donna Parker, Purvis considered this set of pieces his favorite work, and he performed it frequently.[45]

Some people have speculated on the exact nature of Purvis and Shields's relationship. Whatever the reality, they remained discreet and guarded,

John Shields and Richard Purvis, 1950s. Courtesy Donald Braff.

even though same-gender relationships such as theirs had become commonplace, especially in San Francisco.[46] Until 1971, when Purvis left the Cathedral, they had maintained separate residences (Richard in several different apartments, John at the Warrens' home at 70 Balceta Avenue). In 1971 Richard moved to join John at the house on Balceta, where they lived together until Richard's death on December 25, 1994. Less than six months later, on June 14, 1995, John died of heart failure.[47]

Purvis's Assistants

Over the years Purvis had the benefit of assistant organists for certain periods. When he didn't, according to Ed Stout, Purvis "just worked sunup to sundown."[48]

Purvis's early assistants were Tom Nicholson in 1948 and 1949,[49] and Carl Bonelli from 1950 until approximately 1952.[50] His long-term assistants were Robert Hunt, 1955–1959; Bill Duncan, 1959–1963; David Worth, 1963–1967; and Stephen Loher, 1967–1971. Tom Hazleton, while never officially an assistant, played for numerous services and performed so many other duties that he was often thought of as an assistant as well.

Other organists who filled in for Purvis occasionally were Jack Harder, 1949–1951; William Stone, 1951; Paul Fitzgerald, 1954; Ted Alan Worth, 1958; David Rothe, summer of 1962; and Alonzo Price, 1963.[51] Tom Rhoads frequently played for Diocesan choir festivals and choral concerts.[52]

Robert Hunt

From 1955 to 1959, Robert ("Bob") Hunt served as "Deputy Organist." Because Hunt was also the organist-choirmaster at St. John's Episcopal Church in Ross, California (where Purvis would later design the new organ), he wasn't available to play for Grace's Sunday morning services. Stephen Loher wrote, "When Purvis began at the Legion of Honor [in 1952], every other week they put Bob Hunt in as Deputy to do the first half of Evensong until Richard could get back around 4:30 p.m. You would always see him swing on to the console. I always thought he was sending a message out to the Nave that he was back!"[53]

Bill Duncan

Bill Duncan began as Purvis's assistant in 1959, and the two became close friends.[54] David Worth called Duncan "probably RIP's most notable assistant," adding that Duncan played for Evensong services and that Duncan and Purvis performed duo recitals every season.[55] Duncan remained Purvis's assistant until 1963.[56]

Ed Stout wrote,

Bill Duncan was a very fine organist, but he was also a professional railroad man. He was in charge of the Burlington Railway's interests out here. Bill

Bill Duncan and Richard Purvis, 1950s. Courtesy Donald Braff.

played the 9 o'clock service in the chapel and he would cover weddings and other extraneous services for Dick. He registered the organ beautifully. He was a very solid and competent musician and a very sweet man, and hardly anyone knows that he was ever involved there, but he really was a right hand man for Dick Purvis. He was already there when I started in 1959.[57]

David Worth

David Worth (no relation to Ted Alan Worth) began organ studies with Purvis in 1959 at age 14. He attended boarding schools in Lodi, California, and later in Napa, California, commuting to San Francisco for his lessons (Purvis's lesson fee: $20). Worth was the first full-time assistant to Purvis, serving from 1963 to 1967. His duties included setting up Purvis's music on the organ rack, playing for services during the summers and when Purvis was on vacation or out of town, and teaching in the Cathedral School for Boys.

David Worth recalls: "Ted Worth did some assisting one season, probably about 1957. I had been studying with Robert Flood and Nita Akin in Wichita Falls, Texas; had just started playing and Ted and John Shields were at the cathedral the day of our visit, showed us the organ and then let me sit down to play; I played Ein feste Burg, I think."[58]

Prior to studying with Purvis, Worth had studied with Barbara Tonsberg and had become a good friend of June Townsend, both of whom had studied with Purvis. "My mother finally decided to call him in 1959, and when he answered his office phone, she said, 'Is this Dr. Purvis?' He answered something to the effect of, 'This is Mr. Purvis; there is no doctor here!' Truly in his own imperious, definitive way!"[59]

Tom Hazleton

While Tom Hazleton never held the official post of staff assistant, Purvis relied on him to play for certain services, most notably the consecration of the newly completed Cathedral on November 20, 1964. Ed Stout wrote,

Tom was never an official assistant to Richard, but he was one of the few organists Dick could trust to keep the show going when the clergy's gowns were caught up in the gears. For that reason, Richard requested that Tom be the official organist for the huge service celebrating the completion of the Cathedral in 1964. Purvis was conducting and Tom played the daylights out of the organ, again, covering for the delays and expected problems.[60]

When asked why Tom played the organ for this service although David was already in place as Purvis's assistant, David responded: "The only reason was that I had been taking lessons from RIP for about three years, but I was still 'a work in progress' and RIP had at the moment been encouraging me to attend Curtis. Later that season he changed his mind about Curtis, saying that he wanted me to take Bill Duncan's place. (Took me to Blum's at the Fairmont to tell me what was up.)"[61] David was also busy during that service playing the carillon for the prelude and during certain parts of the service, such as during the Te Deum.[62]

Tom Hazleton was born in Monterey, California, on September 27, 1942. He began studying with Purvis at age 12 and became one of Purvis's most illustrious students. Ed Stout wrote, "Like his famed teacher Richard Purvis, Tom was a multi-faceted talent, playing both classical and theatre organ with equal ease." In demand as a recitalist, Tom served as organist at prominent Bay Area churches, including St. Andrew's Episcopal Church, Saratoga, California; St. Mark's Episcopal Church, Palo Alto; and Menlo Park Presbyterian Church. For years he was a fixture at Capn's Galley Pizza and Pipes in Redwood City, playing the theatre organ there. On September 7, 2003, he played a celebrated concert at Grace Cathedral in Purvis's honor.[63]

Donna Parker remembers that on one occasion Purvis and Hazleton played a duo arrangement of the Lemmens Fanfare in D, with the secondary part written by Purvis. Because one was at the console in the Chapel and the other at the organ in the chancel, they wore headphones to hear each other play.[64]

(Tom Hazleton would have been a major source of material for this book, but he died unexpectedly of a heart attack at the age of 64 on March 14, 2006.)

Stephen Loher

Stephen Loher, born in 1941 in San Francisco, studied with Purvis for five years, starting at age 14. Later he attended Peabody Conservatory in Baltimore, where he received a bachelor's degree in organ in 1965; and in 1967 he received an M.A. degree in organ from San Francisco State University. From August 1966 to May 1967, he was organist at All Saints' Episcopal Church in Palo Alto.

Loher wrote:

> Then I went to St. Gracie's. During this time I was practicing on a piano in the Crypt of St. Gracie's—I knew that David was going to leave, and the rumor was that Richard was going to appoint me. I was going to choir rehearsals all during that year and also finishing a Masters degree at San Francisco State. After a choir rehearsal in April Richard said to me, "Get your book out, you have some weddings." That was his way of telling me I was hired!

As Purvis's staff assistant, Loher played the organ and conducted choir rehearsals and services for the choir of men and boys. When Purvis was away for concerts three or four times a year, Loher took over for him. He was also a Music Master at the Cathedral School for Boys, teaching music and conducting boys grades 1–8 in singing for daily chapel services. Loher continued as staff assistant at Grace until Purvis's resignation.[65]

Douglas Metzler

Douglas Metzler supported Purvis in a variety of duties, such as helping with Purvis's paperwork, traveling with him on concert tours, and serving as his driver (his "roadie," as Metzler put it) when Purvis could no longer drive. Ultimately, Purvis appointed Metzler as executor of his estate. Douglas Metzler was born Douglas Stephen Cortright, changing his name at age 21 when he was adopted by his stepfather. (This explains why the name Cortright appears in some dedications of compositions by Purvis.) Born and reared in Inglewood, California, he moved to San Francisco, where he was "smitten by the music and choir there." Metzler recalls that when he auditioned for the choir at Grace Cathedral, it took Purvis three months to get back to him. He started as a chorister in 1964. After a year and a half in the choir, Metzler asked Purvis to give him organ lessons, which he took at the Cathedral through high school. He sang in the choir at Grace until 1971 but continued organ lessons until 1985 at Purvis's San Francisco home on Balceta. Following his graduation from San Francisco State in 1972 he joined the Navy.[66]

Grace Cathedral, unfinished, about 1960. Courtesy Grace Cathedral archives.

Services at Grace Cathedral

Like other great cathedrals, Grace held numerous services on Sunday and weekdays. Over the years, new services were added and the schedule changed, but Grace remained a center for memorable liturgy and music without interruption. The service schedules below were taken mostly from service leaflets.

Michael Lampen reported, "Sunday 11 a.m. services and Choral Evensong were in the main church. Weekday Morning Prayer services were also in the main church. All of the other services were held in the Chapel of Grace, and occasionally in the Chapel of the Nativity."[67]

1947–1956:
Sundays
    Holy Communion at 8 a.m.
    Holy Communion at 11 a.m. (but only on the first Sunday of the month)
    Morning Prayer at 11 a.m. (except the first Sunday)
    Choral Evensong at 4 p.m.
Weekdays
    Holy Communion every day at 8 a.m.

Starting in 1951:
> Holy Communion at 10:30 a.m. on Wednesdays
> Holy Communion at 10:30 a.m. on Holy Days

In 1957 an expanded schedule began under the new Dean, Julian Bartlett:

Sundays
> Holy Communion at 8 a.m. and 9 a.m.
> Holy Communion at 11 a.m. (but only on the first Sunday)
> Holy Communion at 12:15 p.m. (except the first Sunday)
> Morning Prayer, 11 a.m. (except the first Sunday)
> Choral Evensong, 4 p.m.

Weekdays
> Morning Prayer at 7:45 a.m.
> Holy Communion at 8 a.m.
> Holy Communion at 10:30 a.m. on Wednesdays and Holy Days
> Holy Communion at 7 a.m. on Thursdays
> Evening Prayer at 5:30 p.m. (except Saturdays)
> Evening Prayer at 5:00 p.m. on Saturdays

The service schedule evolved under Dean Julian Bartlett and Bishop James Pike in the years that followed, adding additional weekday services.

By 1967:

Sundays
> Morning Prayer and Holy Communion, 8:00 a.m.
> Holy Communion and Sermon, 9:00 a.m.
> Morning Prayer and Holy Communion, 11:00 a.m.
> Sunday School, 9:00 a.m.
> Evening Prayer and Sermon, 5:00 p.m.

Weekdays
> The Holy Communion
>> Daily (except Saturday), 7:30 a.m.
>> Wednesdays, 7:30 a.m. and 12:10 p.m.
>> Thursdays, 7:00, 7:30 a.m., and 5:30 p.m.

Purvis in the Grace Cathedral robing room, early 1960s. Courtesy Donald Braff.

Saturdays, Morning Prayer and Holy Communion, 10:00 a.m.
Morning Prayer (except Saturday), 8:30 a.m.
Evening Prayer, 5:15 p.m.

David Worth recalls the following details regarding Sunday services:

9:00 a.m., Eucharist in Choir, played by the assistant. As soon as the 9:00 a.m. service was over, the choir came into the chancel for warm-up and rehearsal, usually 10-10:30, prior to the 11 a.m. service. Between 10:30 and 11 the boys went to the choir room and the men retired to the choir-men's lounge.

The assistants set up Purvis's music on the rack prior to the 11 a.m. service.

11:00 a.m., Morning Prayer in the Church. Purvis did most of the playing and conducting (from the console) at this service. If there was a big anthem, the assistant played and Purvis conducted.

4:00 p.m., Evensong in the Chapel with the men of the choir, played and conducted by Richard.

He had played the Sunday Evensong service in the chapel, but eventually I was given that task.[68]

Around the summer of 1963 I started playing the 9:00 a.m. Eucharist (no Morning Prayer). Then at 11:00 a.m. it was always a conflation of Morning Prayer and Holy Communion. He often played a short 8-bar improvised fanfare on the Solo reeds preceding the Gospel. He also played the "Judas March" [exit music for people who didn't want to stay to receive Holy Communion] (usually a Handel Aria, or St.-Saëns III theme) after the Whole State of Christ's Church, improvising for about 45 seconds until the remaining congregants were settled down. Damn, I wish we had the old BCP HC [Book of Common Prayer, Holy Communion] back![69]

David Worth also played for midweek Evensong: "Always on Thursdays at 5:15, I think. Always in the chapel. Usually 25–40 people there. People walking home from the day's office work. Playing that service was how I began with RIP. Must have done that for a year before I began playing 9:00 a.m. Sunday."[70]

Stephen Loher elaborated:

11:00 was Matins and 4:00 was Evensong with just the men.

When I arrived we had 8:00 service in the Chapel said, 9:00 service in the Church with just the organ and later that was moved to the Chapel.

Choir arrived in the stalls at 10:00 to 10:30 for rehearsal—then boys to choir room to vest with John Shields and men to the lounge.

In my time, Evensong had been moved to the Chapel with just the organ.[71]

The choir did not normally sing for Evensong; at times a small group of four to five men sang for Evensong. After Evensong on some summer evenings, there were recitals at 8 p.m. These recitals, part of the Cathedral Concert Series run by Frank Roseberry, were always played by other artists, not Purvis. "We would put out a sign and ring the bells and would have about 800 show up."[72]

Under Bishop Pike in the 1960s, liturgical innovations occurred and the 11 a.m. Morning Prayer service became a Eucharist.

Organ Music at Services

Below is a brief sampling of service music from Grace Cathedral service bulletins.

June 7, 1964

Morning Prayer and Holy Communion, 11:00 a.m.
(no published prelude music at this service)
Offertory Anthem: "Lonesome Valley," "freely arranged by Richard Purvis"
Concluding Voluntary: Canticle of the Sun, Richard Purvis

Choral Evensong and Sermon, 5:00 p.m.
Concluding Voluntary: Earth Carol, Richard Purvis

June 14, 1964

Morning Prayer and Holy Communion, 11:00 a.m.
Concluding Voluntary: Ascription, Richard Purvis

Choral Evensong and Sermon, 5:00 p.m.
Concluding Voluntary: Soul Adorn Thyself With Gladness

Christmas Eve, 1964

Gallery Chorales, 10:45 p.m.
   Wie Schon Leucht Uns, Johann Sebastian Bach
   O Jesulein Suss, Johann Sebastian Bach
   Brich an, Du Schones Morgenlicht, Johann Sebastian Bach
Organ Interlude: Gevaert Carol, Richard Purvis
Fanfare for Christmas Day, Martin Shaw
Offertory Anthem: "Unto us a child is born," Richard Purvis
Communion Motets
   Gevaert Noël, Sowerby-Purvis
   Divinum Mysterium, Plainsong
   Rosa Mystica, Michael Praetorius
Postlude: Trumpet Voluntary, John Stanley

December 20, 1970, 4 p.m.

Annual Carol Concert
The Fourth Sunday in Advent
Grace Cathedral
    Organist, Stephen Loher
    Conductor, Richard Purvis
Gallery Carols
    The Annunciation (Basque Carol)
    The Bell Carol (Thoinot Arbeau)
    Sing Lullaby (Basque Noel)
Organ Interlude: Forest Green (Richard Purvis)
Fanfare for Christmas Day (Martin Shaw)
Veni Emmanuel (Plainsong)
Carols
    Sing Gloria (Katherine Davis)
    Gevaert Carol (Sowerby-Purvis)
    A Carol for Our Times (Richard Purvis)
    Christians Awake (Richard Purvis)
    Sleeps Judea Fair (Hugh A. MacKinnon)
    A Scottish Carol (Richard Purvis)
Offertory: Ave Maria (Bach-Gounod)
Sussex Carol (Willcocks-Purvis)
Carol of the Little King (Caldwell-Purvis)
Carol of the Bamboo Flute (Richard Purvis)
A Cradle Carol (Kirkpatrick-Purvis)
Christmas Day (Gustav Holst)
Gallery Carols
    Stille Nacht (Franz Gruber)
    O'er the Cradle of a King (Brenton Noel)

Easter Day, April 18, 1965

Procession and Holy Communion, 8:30 a.m.
(No published prelude)

Richard Purvis at the Alexander Memorial Organ, Grace Cathedral, about 1960. Courtesy Grace Cathedral archives.

Offertory Anthem: "O Filii et Filiae," Fifteenth Century French
Postlude: Toccata "Christ ist Erstanden," Richard Purvis

Procession and Holy Communion, 10:45 a.m.
Gallery Carols
   Personent Hodie, Piae Cantiones
   O Filii et Filiae, XVth Century French
   Christ ist Erstanden, XIIth Century German
   Entrata Festiva, Flor Peeters (organ, brass, choir, and tympani)
Processional: Lyra Davidica "as composed for organ, brass choir, and tympani, by Richard Purvis"
Postlude: Toccata "Christ ist Erstanden," Richard Purvis

Easter Day, March 26, 1967

Procession and Holy Communion, 8:30 a.m.
Offertory Anthem: "O Filii et Filiae," Fifteenth Century French [the same music done in 1965]
Postlude: Toccata "Christ ist Erstanden," Richard Purvis

Procession and Holy Communion, 10:45 a.m.
Gallery Carols
   Personent Hodie, Piae Cantiones
   O Filii et Filiae, XVth Century French
   Christ ist Erstanden, XIIth Century German
   Fanfare and Alleluia, Richard Purvis
Offertory Anthem: "Laudate Dominum," Richard Purvis
Postlude: Toccata "Christ ist Erstanden," Richard Purvis

December 17, 1967, 4 p.m.

Annual Carol Vespers
"Forest Green," Purvis; Gevaert Carol, Sowerby-Purvis; Sussex Carol, Willcocks-Purvis; A Scottish Lullaby, Purvis; Long, Long Ago, Williams-Purvis; A Scottish Carol, Purvis; Torches, Joubert-Purvis; Carol of the Little King, Caldwell-Purvis; Carol of the Bamboo Flute, Purvis; A Cradle

Purvis at the Alexander Memorial Organ, Grace Cathedral, also around 1960. Courtesy Grace Cathedral archives.

Carol, Kirkpatrick-Purvis; Carol of the Drum, Davis-Purvis. "All orchestrations made expressly for this service by Richard Purvis."

The Cathedral School

It is uncertain when Purvis first became interested in the music for choirs of men and boys. He would have heard this type of choir at its best in England during the summers of 1936 and 1937. He gained further experience at the Episcopal Academy at St. James's in Philadelphia, where he not only conducted such choirs, but also worked in a choir day school setting.

Regarding Purvis's involvement in the founding of the Cathedral School, Michael Lampen wrote, "Discussions were underway in 1956, as he was then going around to public schools to audition boys, and needed a steadier and more reliable supply. The school was founded September 10, 1957, with 13 boys and grew to about 30 during the term. Founders were Dean C. Julian Bartlett and Canon David Forbes."[73]

David Worth provided further details:

> Richard began it under Bishop Block and Dean Bartlett, early on in his tenure. David Forbes was headmaster and a canon at the Cathedral. They wanted a choir school, but it was decided that they'd be more successful if they made it a day school. They developed the Cathedral School for Boys, and the choristers would be on partial scholarship (although most of the kids came from wealthy families in Pacific Heights anyway and didn't need the scholarship money). There were 22 boys in each class at that time. The ideal was to have in-school rehearsals during the day, but this wasn't possible because only a few of the boys in each class were choristers.[74]

Judging by the coverage given in the three newspaper articles below, there was public interest in the concept of a boy choir in San Francisco. From the *San Francisco Examiner,* 1947:

Protestant Boy Choir of 70 Voices To Be Organized by Richard Purvis

by Claire Leeds

SOME FIFTY BOYS, ages 8 through 12, are going to add something new to musical tradition in this city.

Richard Purvis, master of the Grace Cathedral Choristers, is now conducting auditions in one of the first large scale endeavors to establish a Protestant Boy Choir in San Francisco. When the group is fully organized it will include fifty boys' and twenty adult male voices.

For the boy choristers, it will mean more than an opportunity for expert musical training. Besides electing their own officers, the boys will receive prizes, to be awarded by the cathedral for outstanding work. Upon completion of a year's participation in choir activities, each one will be offered a week at a boys' camp (either Y.M.C.A. or Boy Scout), or a $25.00

Government savings bond. There will also be parties and other special activities throughout the year.

* * *

PURVIS, A NATIVE San Franciscan, has long wanted to organize such a group here. Before coming to Grace Cathedral, earlier this year, he was choirmaster at St. James Choir School in Philadelphia, where he trained one of the finest boy choirs on the east coast. He was also organist with the famous Philadelphia Symphony Orchestra.

The new choir is being organized in accord with traditional cathedral precepts. Training methods to be employed are those used in the oldest choir schools in the world. Purvis has studied production for the unchanged boy's voice both in England and on the European Continent.

"Singing in a choir is in many ways excellent training for a boy," he points out. "He learns to co-operate with others in group participation. His alertness is greatly quickened through interpreting a conductor's signals, and it is a well established fact that proper vocal training develops greater breath control and finer posture."

Boys from all section of the city are eligible for auditions, and no previous musical training is necessary.

"While only boys of 9 or older will be admitted immediately to the choir, 8 year olds will be enrolled in a probationers group for training, until such time as they are eligible," Purvis explained.[75]

From the *San Francisco Examiner,* November 2, 1947:

Fine Boys' Choir Being Trained for Cathedral

Grace Group Has Openings for 18 More Voices in 9-12 Bracket

THEY MAY LOOK like the cherubic choir boys one sees pictured on Christmas cards, but it's entirely an illusion.

Actually, the thirty-two boy choristers at Grace Cathedral are not a bit different from any other group of San Francisco youngsters, aged 9–12.

Most of them come from average or above average income homes in various parts of the city. Some belong to the Cub Scouts. Many are active in athletics—(one is a star on his school soccer team).

* * *

TWO THIRDS of these boys, who are now singing at all the regular Cathedral services, have had no previous musical training. But they learn rapidly under direction of Richard Purvis, former choirmaster at St. James Choir School in Philadelphia, who trained one of the finest boy choirs on the East coast.

***

"THERE ARE openings for eighteen more boys," Purvis announced last week. "Although only boys of 9 or older will be admitted immediately to the choir," he explained, "acceptable 8 year olds will be enrolled in a probationers group for training."

When it reaches its full size, the choir will include fifty boys and twenty adult male voices. It represents one of the first large scale endeavors to establish a Protestant boy choir in San Francisco.

***

MEMBERSHIP in the Grace Cathedral Choristers means more for a boy than an opportunity for musical training. Upon completion of a year in the choir, each one will be offered a week at a boys' camp (either Y.M.C.A. or Boy Scout), or a $25 government bond. There is at least one special party a month, and prizes are awarded by the cathedral for outstanding work.

***

THE GROUP is now rehearsing special programs for Thanksgiving and Christmas...."

The article included a photo of nine boys, with the following caption:

REHEARSAL GROUP of Grace Cathedral Choristers includes, front row, left to right, John Joys, age 8; Jay Faurot, 11; center, Stewart Davis, 10; John Warren, 11; Kenneth Geisslar Jr., 8; back row, Morgan Littlefield, 10; Daniel Clark, 13; William Chisum, 10; Kenneth Bakken, 11. They are members of one of the first large Protestant boy choirs to be established in San Francisco.[76]

On July 16, 1950, a photo of Purvis conducting a small group of choristers appeared on the front page of the *San Francisco Examiner*. The caption under the picture reads:

SONGSTERS—Some of the members of the widely known chorister group of Grace Cathedral perform under the direction of Richard Purvis, cathedral organist and choirmaster. The choristers, a group of about fifty boys and young men from all Protestant denominations, are joined principally by a love of singing. Those shown above with Purvis are: John Warren, Karl Jacobs, Tom Newcomb, Dan Clark, Butler Minor and Pat Rankin.

Purvis conducting choristers. San Francisco Examiner, *July 16, 1950.*

Purvis conducting the choristers in the Mural Room of the St. Francis Hotel, Christmas 1948.

The accompanying article on the same page reads, in part:

Fine Record by Choir

50 Boys in Group At Cathedral

Fifty Bay area boys who would rather sing than sleep late on Sunday morning comprise San Francisco's Protestant liturgical choir.

The Choristers of Grace Cathedral are unique in that they are a self governing group. They come from all denominations of the Protestant Church and they love their singing so much that even on sunny spring afternoons they seldom miss rehearsals.

Each Sunday morning from September through mid-June they don purple vestments, white surplices and Eton collars and serenade the churchgoers of Grace Cathedral.

The liturgical choir—a choral group comprising only males and singing only ecclesiastical music—is a novelty in northern California and was formed by Organist Richard Purvis of Grace Cathedral with the support of Bishop Karl Morgan Block.

The church long ago had a chorus, but it included female members and also did not restrict itself entirely to the music of the Anglican cathedral.

POPULAR

The Choristers' success was instantaneous and they have appeared before clubs throughout the Bay area and regularly perform at the annual Union Square Christmas celebration. Next season the choral group plans a trip to Fresno and a tour of valley churches.

"Only boys interested in singing turn out for the Choristers so we have little trouble with dropouts. Most of the boys who stay through the two month trial period remain with the group for years," points out Purvis, a native San Franciscan who formerly was director of music at St. James Episcopal Academy in Philadelphia.

More than 50 per cent of the boys who apply for the Choristers are accepted. Those rejected lack clear voices or pitch perception, according to Purvis.

"American boys are much more musical than most people think. I haven't found one yet that is tone deaf," he adds.

To remain a Chorister, a boy—their ages range from 8 to 20—must attend two rehearsals a week, each one hour and a half long, which takes a good nip out of the day of the average schoolboy. However, the majority of the choir still manage to participate in school athletics—the biggest truancy from rehearsal occurred this year on the day of the city-wide track meet.

Twenty-seven of the younger boys are trebles—so called boy [remainder of article unavailable].[77]

Before long, Purvis took the Choristers outside the Cathedral to perform at other venues. As early as Christmas 1948, they performed in a public recital, probably at the Fairmont Hotel, which faces Grace Cathedral.[78]

One of Purvis's choristers remembered that in 1953 Purvis had taken the boys of the choir to sing a Christmas program at the University Club, also not far from Grace Cathedral. The businessmen in attendance wouldn't stop talking during the music, so Purvis marched the boys off the stage and that was the end of the concert![79] In the Fairmont photo, however, the listeners appear to be in rapt attention.

Beginning in 1948 and continuing through 1970, Purvis traveled with the boys of the choir each summer to The Bishop's Ranch in Healdsburg, California. There, during the last two weeks of August, the boys received further musical training and enjoyed outdoor recreation. See Steve Cohen's account of this, as well as many other personal recollections by various choristers ("The Old Boys") who sang at Grace Cathedral in the period 1948–1960, in Chapter 16, "Anecdotes and Reminiscences."

The Cathedral School Schedule

Most but not all of Purvis's choristers were enrolled in the Cathedral School. And not all of the students at the Cathedral School were choristers. Scholarships for the choirboys were available: one fourth of tuition for the first year and one third for the remaining years.[80] During the week, the boys at the Cathedral School attended various chapel services, rehearsals, and music classes.

At some point after the School was established, Purvis arranged to have "in-school" rehearsals, beginning at 1 p.m. and lasting for approximately 45 minutes. On Mondays and Wednesdays, 4th and 5th graders attended music class while the choristers from those grades rehearsed in the choir room. On Tuesdays and Thursdays, 6th and 7th graders, and on Fridays 8th graders, followed the same routine.

Stephen Loher commented:

> Richard usually did those rehearsals because I was doing the school music my last two years (1969–1971). From 1967–1968 John Shields did the School music and I accompanied for him during the classes. He wasn't really up to it, and from 1968–1969 Richard and I co-directed the School music. He did some school classes and I did some. From 1969–1971 I did all of the School music. Many times we did combine the choristers and the School boys together for these in school rehearsals during that year. For example, we had a School Christmas service on the last day of School before the Christmas break. For this I would often combine the Choristers with the School, and that would mean one or two rehearsals with the entire Upper School in the Church.[81]

Starting in the early 1960s, all choristers in the Choir School attended rehearsals conducted by Purvis on Tuesday and Wednesday afternoons from 3:30 to 5:00 p.m. in the choir room.

On Thursdays the choristers remained after school for study and recreation until 5:30, p.m., when they had dinner in Gresham Hall, prepared by choir parents on a rotational basis. From 7:00 p.m. to 8:30 p.m. Purvis conducted a full rehearsal with the men and boys, who left at 8:30 p.m. The men would stay for further rehearsal as required.[82]

David Worth explained his involvement:

> As for classes at the school, I have no recollection of [Purvis] teaching any. I did in 1966. I played the two matins services, one for the upper school in the chancel and then a very brief one for the lower school in the chapel. After that I had a couple of music classes for the general school population (vocal training, such as it was, and some music theory and music history). John Shields taught physical education. David Forbes was Canon Headmaster. I eventually attended choir camps and played the daily Evensong when he was there (with John Shields riding herd on the boys). When Richard was around, I often canted the Evensong at camp. Of course, John Shields was around in the music offices, helping as librarian, etc.[83]

David Worth recalls that Purvis played for daily chapel for the entire school, "which he always finished with a big concluding voluntary." Worth continues: "I remember coming in one Friday for a 9:00 a.m. lesson and that voluntary was glorious as usual. I went up to the chancel for my lesson and had the temerity to ask him what it was, to which he replied: 'It's my Toccata on "In Babilone," but you don't need to know that because it's too hard for you!'"[84]

Apparently the service was divided during Loher's time. Loher said that daily chapel was held in the chancel at 8:30 a.m. for the Upper School (grades 4–8), and at 9:00 a.m. in the chapel for the Lower School (grades 1–3). Loher played for all of these services.[85]

Purvis continued to teach in the Cathedral School until 1969, two years before he left Grace Cathedral in dissatisfaction.

Purvis, Master of the Choristers

Purvis was responsible for the choir and services, but he shared these duties with his assistants. Continuing the tradition he observed in England and established at St. James's in Philadelphia, his choir at Grace Cathedral was comprised exclusively of men and boys.[86]

Donald Corbett wrote that when Purvis arrived at Grace, he found the choir "lacking in the qualities he had so admired, such as blending, clarity of tone, and cohesiveness." He began working immediately to bring the choir up to his standards.[87]

Purvis devoted himself to the choral music of the Cathedral, but Loher explains his true allegiance: "Richard was mostly organ oriented. The choir was another stop on the organ. But he loved the choir, mind you, as well as the Anglican tradition and the service music. He was a wonderful service player."[88]

David Worth recalls Purvis's conducting:

> In my time he almost invariably played and conducted, and I was "observing." But there were times when I played for Carol Vespers, Choir Tea and the like. We also often did the series of four anthems which utilized an obbligato part (Judica Me Deus, Psalm of Ascents, etc.) for which I played the obbligato part on the Solo manual. I found that his combined

Purvis with the Grace Cathedral Choir, 1960s. Courtesy Donald Braff.

playing/conducting was remarkably skilled and still remember it that way to this day.[89]

Loher described Purvis's style as follows:

His rehearsals were precise and formal. In my days at the Cathedral the music to be rehearsed was written on the blackboard and he would say "next" and not mention the piece. This was for the full rehearsal on Thursday evenings with the men. The boys' rehearsals (Tuesday and Wednesday after School for 90 minutes) were different. He would often get off on tangents about topics of interest (he was a born teacher!). These were always fascinating excursions about social studies, geography, history, etc. Richard was very well read and what you might call a "generalist." Because we only did about 20 pieces (and kept repeating and repeating them during the year), he had time in the boys' rehearsals to go off on these tangents. During the full rehearsal it was very formal. The men were referred to as "Mr." as were the boys—this comes from the English public school culture (English public schools are what we would call private schools—the English refer to what we would call public schools as "state schools").

I would say that people more "feared" him but they also respected him. He wouldn't take any crap, if you know what I mean. He had excellent discipline from the boys. I remember that during my second year as Assistant, he and I shared running the School music. He was scheduled to run a rehearsal for the School Christmas Service and this was to happen after School Chapel (which we had daily in the Cathedral—in the quire). After the School service ended we waited, in complete silence for five minutes, waiting for Richard to appear—including some of the faculty. Everyone was afraid to make any noise![90]

When asked what the choir in those days was like, David Worth responded:

Well, it was well-disciplined. But the tapes tell the story; the boys had a predictable tendency to sing under pitch, and the tapes seem to suggest that the treble sound was pushed rather hard. Men were OK, though the altos (counter-tenors) were a bit anemic. Interesting how our reflections of the experience are modified by Life-after-Grace! I probably wasn't smart enough to make those observations at the time.[91]

Loher commented further: "He never toured with the choir. He didn't seem to believe in it. He was also not so much a team player in that we never had joint choir festivals nor did he favor having guest choirs sing.[92]

Still, Purvis took his choir work seriously. In a handwritten memo to the Bishop dated October 20, 1949, Purvis apologizes for a sub-par performance:

"My dear Bishop:

I am heartbroken over the utterly wretched musical service of Sunday last. My life's blood went into the preparation of that music, and the only possible excuse I can offer is that we have had absolutely no rehearsal time in the chancel and the boys and men felt strange and uneasy in their new surroundings and singing to the accompaniment of an instrument they hadn't heard for months.

Please accept my humblest apologies. I am most unhappy about the entire thing.

Dick[93]

Special Services

Purvis preferred to do all the "High Altar" weddings. These paid $100, an increase of $85 since 1947, and were held in the main church. Chapel weddings, of which there were as many as three on a Saturday, paid $35. Purvis's assistants played most of those.[94]

According to Loher, Richard had different responses on the telephone to prospective brides, depending on whether they were planning a wedding in the Chapel of Grace (in which case he was very gruff, said there would be no rehearsal, and got off the phone quickly) or in the main church (in which case he was very polite: "Yes, definitely, I will be at the rehearsal," etc.)[95]

Because of the size of the Cathedral, most memorials were held in the Chapel, reserving the main church for services when space for a large congregation was needed.[96] Unless he was away concertizing, Purvis played

Grace Cathedral completed, 1964. Photo by George Shimmon. Courtesy Grace Cathedral archives.

Grace Cathedral nave, 2010. Courtesy Grace Cathedral archives.

most of the services in the chancel, and the assistants usually played in the Chapel.[97]

Purvis played hundreds of memorial services, many of them for illustrious citizens. On August 17, 1951, for example, Purvis played for the memorial service held for William Randolph Hearst. Columnist Edd Johnson commented on the event in his front-page story in the *San Francisco Chronicle*, "At 11:48, Richard Purvis, church organist, began to play a group of selections from Bach and Cesar Franck." Burt Weaver noted, "It must have been somewhat humbling for Richard to read his name just as 'church organist,' but then to have it listed at all in a major newspaper was cause for celebration, especially considering Richard's young age at that time."[98]

David Worth described other notable services during his time at Grace:

> [Richard] played for a big Greek Primate visitation during my time there, but insisted I do the 50th Anniversary of the Armenian Martyrs Requiem Eucharist. He also did the Archbishop Michael Ramsey visitation service (the processional music was the Campra "Rigaudon"!). He also played the service for the visitation of Princess Margaret and Lord Snowdon. And then there was the modest involvement he and the choir played in the first Duke Ellington Concert. There were other regular dignitaries at the 11:00 a.m. services: Martin Luther King, Jr., Martin Buber, Barry Goldwater (my goodness, his visit upset Charles Agneau [verger at the Cathedral]!), and Casper Weinberger was a regular reader at services.[99]

The Consecration of the Cathedral

Certainly the most significant service during Purvis's tenure was the consecration of the completed Cathedral, which took place on Friday, November 20, and Sunday, November 22, 1964.

On November 20, the service began with carillon music played by David Worth. Selections included "A Festal Pean [*sic*]" by Richard Purvis. This was followed by "Psalm XVIII" by Benedetto Marcello, played on the organ and augmented by brass and tympani. Hymns and anthems included Veni Creator Spiritus, "I Was Glad" by Parry, "Christ is Made the Sure Foundation," "Glorious Things of Thee Are Spoken," "Pange lingua," and "O Worship the King." The postlude was "Processional on Lyra

Davidica" by Purvis, again augmented by brass and tympani. Organists for the service were Richard Purvis and Thomas Hazleton.

On November 22, the prelude consisted of "Psalm XVIII" by Marcello and "Processional" by Sir Martin Shaw, played on the organ and accompanied by brass and tympani. The printed program does not identify the organist, but David Worth believes it was probably Purvis and not an assistant who played that day. Anthems included Parry's "I Was Glad," "O God, Our Help in Ages Past" by Ralph Vaughan Williams, and "Sing We Merrily" by Sidney Campbell. The postlude was "Processional on Lyra Davidica" by Purvis, again augmented by brass and tympani.[100]

The Duke at Grace

For Duke Ellington's historic "Sacred Concert" at Grace Cathedral on Thursday, September 16, 1965, all of the music was by Ellington, except for a choral piece listed in the program as having been composed by Purvis. Entitled "Purvis a la Jazz Hot," it was orchestrated by Louie Bellson and Duke Ellington; the Grace Cathedral Choir performed it under Purvis's direction.[101]

Michael Lampen wrote of the event:

Ellington commented at a Cathedral House press conference that he considered the *Concert* to be (quoting from Dean Bartlett's memoires) "the most significant musical statement he will have made in his life." ... The Grace Cathedral Choir also participated, with a piece by organist/choirmaster Richard Purvis entitled "Purvis a la Jazz Hot." It took a quiet word from Ellington to get Purvis' beat *in sync* with Ellington's beat, this writer, then a chorister, recalls.[102]

Lampen elaborated:

I was there, in the choir, for the Ellington concert. Purvis directed the choir (standing in the sanctuary near the pulpit) in this piece, which he had trouble coordinating with Ellington who was directing the orchestra (up in the main floor of the choir). At one point Ellington came down and cooled down a rather frustrated Purvis, and they began again, in sync. I don't recall anything about the [Purvis] piece, and have not seen it since that day, looong ago![103]

Purvis conducting his choristers at the Duke Ellington "Sacred Concert," September 16, 1965. Courtesy Donald Braff.

The "Sacred Concert" has been reissued several times on CD and DVD, notably on a recording entitled "Duke Ellington: Love You Madly / A Concert of Sacred Music at Grace Cathedral." The "Purvis a la Jazz Hot," however, is not included on any of these recordings, and there is no known recording or score of the piece.[104]

Purvis at Work

Purvis typically did not attend Tuesday morning staff meetings, preferring to send an assistant in his place. There was no music librarian, so his assistants handled these duties as well. Stephen Loher and Steve Bowes, who acted as a kind of organ scholar, helped with copying scores.[105]

Ed Stout described Purvis as an administrator: "One thing I can tell you about Dick: he was incredibly focused and a hard worker—one of the most disciplined. He had no full-time assistant. He had no secretary. He did all his own work, correspondence, everything."[106]

Purvis at Home

Beginning in the late 1940s, Purvis lived at 1360 Clay Street, San Francisco. In the 1950s he lived at 1060A Filbert Street, and in the 1960s at 2140 Hyde Street #303. From December 1971 until December 1994, his residence was 70 Balceta Avenue.[107]

Stephen Loher wrote, "When I came on the scene in 1955 he had an apartment on Filbert, on the eastern side of Russian Hill. In the '60s he moved to Hyde Street and had an apartment with a commanding view from the Golden Gate Bridge to the San Francisco–Oakland Bridge. I loved being in there and taking in the view of pastel buildings spilling down hills to blue bays!"[108]

On Rockaway Beach, San Mateo County coast, 1950s. Courtesy Donald Braff.

As Stout recalls, "Fairly early on Dick moved from Filbert Street to a much larger and much more palatial place on Hyde. He lived on one of those streets that went over to North Beach. I helped him move, because I had a panel truck and he had an enormous collection of records and books. He loved throwing parties there."[109]

Concerts in the Cathedral

Purvis established a tradition of choral and organ concerts at Grace Cathedral that would become legendary in their time. The choral concerts at Christmas and Easter were the main attractions, and Purvis's annual cycle of organ recitals comprised an important part of the Cathedral's public event series.

After the Cathedral organ was completed in 1952 with the addition of several new ranks (see above), Purvis initiated an innovative program that he called "Worship Through Music." At the National Convention of the AGO held in San Francisco in 1952, the Grace Cathedral choristers and members of the San Francisco Orchestra performed this program, which comprised a historical survey of sacred music from Gregorian chant to contemporary compositions. An honored guest, Sir William McKie, Organist and Master of the Choristers at Westminster Abbey, was in the audience. He declared this program "the most comprehensive survey of an art ever produced in one hour and fifteen minutes."[110]

Stout recalled Christmas Vespers, one of Purvis's most popular innovations:

> He started the Christmas Vespers tradition there. That was in the classy old days—it was free! It was billed as "Grace Cathedral's gift to the community." They filled the place. This choral vespers, the annual Christmas concert that Purvis established, with an orchestra and the organ and the men and boys choir, Dick started that. Dick wrote some wonderful music for it. I remember one, "Carol of the Bamboo Flute," and it called for marimba. He had a great sense of what would please the public. His stuff was theatrical; it wasn't stoic or uptight or rigid, just festive and good fun. He knew what the word rubato meant and he'd tear their hearts out. I'll say this: I think that the choir of men and boys was actually perhaps a little better trained later on when Fenstermaker was there, but when Purvis was there it was very heartfelt and warm. He understood what was necessary to sell a piece without it being cheap or shoddy. He understood drama and emotion.[111]

Starting in 1948, Purvis offered a monthly "Masterpieces of Organ Literature" concert series from October through May. The last recital officially designated as part of the series was presented on March 10, 1957. However, Purvis continued to give similar programs in the following months and years, as well as programs of his own works, or combinations of both.[112] Below is a typical sequence of concerts:

Season of 1963–1964

Alexander Memorial Organ, Sundays at 5:30 PM.
October 13th   From English Chancels and Quires
November 10th   Bach-Franck, Cycle I
December 8th   Gloria in Excelsis Deo

February 9th	Bach-Franck, Cycle II
March 8th	From the Organ Lofts of Paris
April 12th	Bach-Franck, Cycle III
May 10th	Original Compositions [by Purvis][113]

There was also an active guest artist series, with recitals every other Sunday at 5:30 p.m. Appreciative audiences got in the habit of attending these recitals, which drew large crowds.[114]

In 1965 the American Theatre Organ Society held a regional convention in San Francisco that included a "Hi-Jinks" recital by Purvis at Grace Cathedral. Until then, concert attendees were typically not permitted to sit in the choir stalls. Ed Stout asked Purvis to make an exception so that theatre organ enthusiasts could watch Purvis play. From then on Purvis allowed people to sit in the choir stalls at all his recitals.[115]

Stephen Loher questions this theory, however:

> We sat in the quire for Richard's recitals in the 50s. He would give those of us who sat up there a card with a note saying to admit. I remember I lost mine and was worried that he might not give me another, but he did. Therefore I don't think the statement about 1965 being the first time watching in the quire is accurate. I remember Freddie Freeman who was organist at First Unitarian in Oakland would be up there with us![116]

Commenting further on the 1965 ATOS concert, Ed Stout related the following:

> I said to Dick, "We ought to do something that will tickle their funny bone. Is there any way we could use a Wurlitzer percussion, a trap, something like a sleigh bell?" Purvis was planning to play his newly composed "Fanfare," and he encouraged me to play the sleigh bells in rhythm with the opening pedal passage of the piece. I went over to the Paramount Theatre on Market and borrowed a sleigh bell strap in the right key. Then Dick said, "Well, we have to practice it, so we'll do it at the 11 a.m. service, and I'll play it as the postlude." I crawled in among the big pipes where I could look down at the console and follow him. So during the 11 a.m. service, you could see all the clergy looking up at the organ. He did have a great sense of humor.[117]

Composer of Grace

Purvis's most prolific period of composition coincided with his tenure at the Cathedral. Full information about the titles and dates of his organ and choral compositions can be found in the chapters on his compositions.

The Legion of Honor

In addition to his duties at Grace Cathedral, Purvis also played the E. M. Skinner organ at the California Palace of the Legion of Honor, one of San Francisco's premier art museums. From its commanding location overlooking the City, the Bay, and the Golden Gate Bridge, the "Legion" hosted recitals every Saturday and Sunday afternoon at 3 p.m.

In 1952 *The Diapason* ran the following notice:

PURVIS APPOINTED ORGANIST OF LEGION OF HONOR PALACE

Richard Purvis, organist of Grace Cathedral, San Francisco, has been appointed to the staff of the Palace of the Legion of Honor as organist. His recitals on the first and third Saturdays and Sundays of the month present an opportunity to bring to the public the finest in organ literature in an atmosphere that is both inspiring and intimate. Mr. Purvis is arranging his programs so that they will take cognizance of current art exhibits in regard to both period and style. The organ is a four-manual E. M. Skinner of 105 stops, built in 1924.[118]

Stephen Loher said that Purvis enjoyed playing at the Legion; in addition, he "liked the money."[119] Purvis alternated weekends with Newton Pashley, organist of First Presbyterian Church, Oakland; and Ludwig Altman, organist of San Francisco's Temple Emanu-El.[120]

Loher wrote, "[Purvis] played Saturday and Sunday every other weekend. On Sundays Phoebe Cole would drive him back to the Cathedral so he could finish evensong. You would see him swing on the console about 4:30 (evensong was at 4:00 and the Legion concerts were at 3:00)." John Shields drove him on Saturdays.[121]

Because Purvis was often chauffeured to events, some have assumed he did not know how to drive. Donald Braff said that Purvis had a driver's license, but that when he lived on Hyde Street there was no parking and he had little use for a car, so he gave up his car and license.[122]

Donald Braff recalls Purvis's description of the Legion organ: "The Legion organ was a very expensive installation, but it speaks through a blanket." Braff said that Purvis was careful not to denigrate the organ, but the truth was that it spoke through canvas painted to look like stone.[123]

Undaunted, Purvis continued to perform at the Legion until around 1969.

An Offer from Boston

In 1954 Purvis received a tempting invitation from Trinity Church in Boston to become the historic church's organist. Although the letter offering the job appears to be lost, a short, undated handwritten memo from Purvis to Bishop Karl Morgan Block survives:

> Dear Bishop,
>
> The enclosed letter requires a careful answer and I'm asking your help. Dr. Ferris is doing me a great honor in considering me and I feel Trinity in Boston is too important not to be considered. As usual, when I need help I turn to you.
>
> May we discuss this on Friday?

The Bishop responded in a letter dated May 17, 1954:

> Mr. Richard Purvis
> Grace Cathedral
> 1112 Jones Street
> San Francisco, Calif.
>
> Dear Dick,
>
> It is very kind of you to give me the opportunity to talking with you in anticipation of our luncheon meeting. I assume that you want to send an answer to Dr. Ferris as soon as may be. Hence, I am writing my impulsive judgment.
>
> First, you know that the very thought of the possibility of your leaving leaves me in disquietude of spirit that I cannot well describe. We cannot and we must not prevent you having the recognition that your great talents literally demand. But I hope you will give the thought of a move the most

serious consideration. With the coming of a new dean, and the one I have in mind is keen about music and the boy choir, I feel sure that there will be greater stability in achieving more adequate support for you and your choir. That is all I care to say about that until I see you.

Dr. Ferris is a charming person and Trinity Church is quite the best known, I should think, of the parish churches in America. It is a huge barn of a structure built for Phillips Brooks a half century or so ago. I know that you [would] be able to get boys in Boston but it would be the same struggle that you have here, aggravated, I suspect, by the preponderance of Roman Catholics and Unitarians in Boston, and the fact that Trinity Church is way down town some distance away from the residential areas that might provide boys for the choir. It would be better in my judgment if one wished to have a mixed choir which I strongly suspect you do not. New Englanders are initially a cold hearted lot apparently, but this is a mannerism. After you get to know them well they are as responsive and warm hearted as any group I know, but it takes time. If you should go to Boston you would want to walk the ties back to San Francisco for the first two or three years.

The choir budget does not seem at all impressive to me with the large endowments Trinity has, nor do I think the salary is at all adequate for life in Boston. It is very expensive to live there. I know that as I owned a house fifty miles away and lived there for seven summers. All off-season vegetables, fruits, etc., have to be shipped in, and from great distances. Meat is prohibitive and you will have to live largely off of fish, although I envy anyone who lives near the lobster pots.

Could you write Dr. Ferris and tell him that I will be out of town for most of next week and that you would wish to speak to me before writing to him, thus giving me time through this delay to discuss this matter and our musical future with you? My first job after the completion the current Centennial Fund campaign is to make secure the finances of the Cathedral, and our musical program is an integral part of that.

I need not tell you how I feel about you personally, as well as professionally. I am sure you would never suspect it, the depth of affection I have for you and my gratitude for your unique and brilliant service at the Cathedral. What I have not said to you I have said often and enthusiastically to many others.

Until Friday, then.

With warm affection,

[   ][124]

In all likelihood, Purvis's meeting with Block, private and unrecorded, was a reiteration of the skillful pressure exerted by the Bishop in his letter to his organist. In any event, we have Purvis's response to Trinity Church, dated May 24, 1954:

The Rev. Dr. Theodore Ferris
Trinity Church Rectory
233 Clarendon Street
Boston 16, Mass.

Dear Dr. Ferris:

I deeply appreciate your recent letter and I feel that you have paid me the highest compliment a clergyman can tender a musician in asking him to be organist of his church. For your appreciation of what I am attempting to do in Church Music, I am deeply grateful. Furthermore, I would be greatly honored to have my name associated with Trinity Church and with Theodore Ferris. Nothing would give me greater joy than to work with you.

However, I am loathe to leave Grace Cathedral. Bishop Block, to whom I am greatly devoted, has been most appreciative of my work. Our relationship has been one of mutual admiration and affection and since he plans to retire within the next several years, I feel that it would be most inopportune and a breach of loyalty for me to leave at this time. Then too, I feel that I have barely scratched the surface here musically, and while the course I have chosen is a rugged one and involves much pioneer and missionary labor, I want to see it more firmly established. It would be cowardly to leave in the midst of the battle. I feel that there are great possibilities for Church Music in California and particularly here at Grace Cathedral and since I am one of those rarities (a native of San Francisco) I should like to contribute to its growth.

Nevertheless, one of my fondest hopes is that someday we may be able to work together and I sincerely hope that you do not feel that the foregoing means that I am not interested in coming East or that I am deprecating the vital and historic role Trinity Church has played and continues to play in the Episcopal Church. I truly hope that at some future date circumstances may prompt you to prefer a similar offer. Please believe me when I say that the honor you do me makes me truly humble.

With every good wish for your continued success and happiness, I am,
Very sincerely,
Richard Purvis[125]

An Honorary Doctorate?

As early as 1963 or 1964, Dean Julian Bartlett suggested to Bishop James A. Pike that Purvis be recognized with an honorary doctorate for his many accomplishments. In a memo to Bishop Pike dated May 14, 1964, the Dean requested that the Honorary Degree Committee of the Church Divinity School of the Pacific consider the request for a possible award in 1965. In a memo dated March 15, 1965, the Bishop responded, stating that although he had presented Purvis's name for consideration, Purvis had been passed over in favor of Vernon de Tar, organist and choirmaster at the Church of the Ascension, New York City, while strongly suggesting that an award for Purvis "will come through next year." In another memo of August 19, 1965, the Bishop stated again that he would recommend Purvis at the next meeting of the seminary trustees, but suggested that Dean Bartlett "should be lobbying with any trustees that you know—thus bringing some more force to bear in this matter."

Bishop Pike spent time in England during this period, and it appears that he did not follow through on the Dean's request. Bartlett continued his quest for a degree for Purvis, however, and in a memo dated March 29, 1966, he wrote to the Bishop:

> I assume that your absence from the country these past winter months [means] that we have "lost another year" in obtaining an honorary degree for Richard Purvis from CDSP.... Actually, you have also told me that there was a question of some personal feelings toward Richard on the part of certain members of the Honorary Degree Committee. I would hate to accept this situation as decisive in the matter, for I would hope that institutions like CDSP would not be small enough to let personal likes and dislikes for a particular candidate be determinative. Richard Purvis has received in recent years, and is now in receipt of current tremendously complimentary invitations, both to compose and to play for major events—both Episcopalian and interdenominational. He is a man of international stature—as we both know—and I would hope that CDSP would be big enough to recognize that."

Apparently, this time Pike failed to respond. In a final memo to the Bishop, Bartlett wrote on May 19, 1966: "I have not heard from you regarding my memo of March 29th concerning the possible honorary degree for Richard Purvis. I gather that this will not be given him by CDSP this year. Perhaps we should forget about CDSP giving him this recognition. As one familiar with 'the intricacies of honorary degrees' can you give me a suggestion as to another institution which might be glad to award such a degree to Richard?"[126]

Thus it appears that no honorary degree was ever awarded to Purvis.

In honor of his 20 years of service at Grace Cathedral, Purvis was feted at the Cathedral on Mother's Day, May 14, 1967:

Grace Cathedral Choir Guilds'
Concert and Tea
Honoring
Mr. Richard Purvis
in his twentieth year
as
Organist-Master of Choristers
featuring
the West Coast Premiers
of
"Paean of Praise"
"Laudate Dominum"
Composed and Directed
by
Mr. Richard Purvis

The program also included Purvis's "A Canticle of Light," "Magnificat," and "The Song of Simeon." David Worth was organist; Stephen Loher played the celesta.[127]

Purvis Decrescendos at Grace

Purvis left Grace Cathedral in April 1971. However, his dissatisfaction, and probably that of certain clergy, was already in the air. Some of it had to do with changes in the liturgy that had begun as early as 1963. In Purvis's opinion the traditions of the Anglican service were being eroded, and his outwardly brusque nature didn't always endear him to the clergy. And there were issues of money, a subject that made Purvis uncomfortable.

Ed Stout explained:

> I think it's something that happens to everybody. You're in these institutions for close to 30 years and things change. They start having more layers of bureaucracy, and direct lines of communication aren't there. When I started at Grace Cathedral—I got the appointment in 1959—I was the ninth person on staff, and I was considered on staff there. It was up to 43 [on the staff], and the attitude in the later years was, "Well, nothing happened here until I arrived." Poppycock!

Stout continued: "It was time for Dick to leave. He stayed maybe two years too long. He resigned. We talked about it and he said, 'It's time for me to go.' He didn't like the changes in the liturgy. He didn't like the changes in the church and the way they were making it commonplace, taking the magic out. You start watering it down and taking the theatrics out of it and making it commonplace. He saw this happening and he didn't like it."[128]

Resignation Theories

Anecdotal accounts of Purvis's resignation vary, and there may be elements of truth in each. Even among his former assistants and closest friends, the details remain mysterious. For example, David Worth said simply, "No one really knows about the resignation details. He didn't have any farewell party."[129]

According to Donna Parker, part of the problem was Purvis's reluctance to discuss money. Parker wrote,

> Every year he would go in for his job review with Dean Bartlett and say, "Unless I get a raise, I'm leaving." But Dick hated to talk money. He would always say "No, no, no, I don't need extra, don't pay me that much for a concert." He hated to ask for a raise from his students. He would go through a big explanation instead of just telling us. It was always a lot of talk. So to think he got fired from Grace for asking for more money is the most ironic thing, because it's the one thing he never asked for—money!

So he went in and said, "I want a raise," and the raise was denied. And he said, "Then I'll quit," and Dean Bartlett said, "Goodbye." That's what we always heard. They [Dean Bartlett and Richard] didn't get along well. This had been going on for several years.[130]

Michael McCabe, who served as interim organist immediately following Purvis's departure, said: "About a week into the job the Dean told me that every time Richard wanted something, he'd threaten to resign. The Dean said, 'He did this probably 15 times. This was the 16th time and I accepted, but this time Purvis said he really didn't want to leave.' But the Dean said, 'We're on a collision course and I'm accepting your resignation.'"[131]

Stephen Loher, who was on staff until Purvis's resignation, remembered the story differently:

> [Donna Parker] says that Richard always asked for money and that on the "last time" the Dean said goodbye—I don't think that is true. Richard had a good relationship with the Dean—to suggest that they did not is not accurate. I am sure there were tensions at times and Julian could be peculiar. But Richard was enough of an Anglican to obey the Dean. I don't think they were "drinking buddies," but the picture that is suggested that they had an adversarial relationship is not true. Remember, I was there day after day.

Loher continued:

> I happened to be at Richard's place the night of the day he resigned. I had friends from Baltimore in town and we had planned to have dinner with him. We arrived at his place on Hyde for drinks before going to dinner. When we walked in he announced that he had resigned that day. His story was that there were going to be further budget cuts (the finances of the Cathedral were most precarious at that time) and that he decided he did not want to be around with half a choir. That was his story.[132]

In his resignation letter of July 1970, Purvis included a notice date of April 1971 to give the Cathedral nine months to find his replacement, who would then have the last six weeks of the choir season to get acclimated and plan for the coming year.

Stephen Loher wrote,

Because Stanley Rogers, Canon Chancellor, had come from Christ Church Cathedral in St. Louis, they offered the job to Ronald Arnatt—but he turned it down because of the salary offered ($6,000 from the Cathedral and $4,000 from the School—the new job description included teaching at the School) was not equal to what he was making in St. Louis. That is when the search was broadened and ended in John [Fenstermaker] being chosen.[133]

Prior to his departure Purvis was making exit plans. In demand as a teacher throughout California, he had already begun a regular multi-stop teaching tour. Donna Parker said, "Probably Bill Thomson encouraged him to do that." Bill had a lucrative career teaching in multiple locations, and Purvis followed his lead, giving organ lessons in Burbank, Glendale (at Bob Tall's house), San Diego, Hemet, Fresno, and other locations, typically in connection with Rodgers Organ Company sales representatives, a practice that continued for a number of years.[134]

An undated letter from Purvis to Eric Hubert, a Cathedral Trustee and music program donor, reads:

My dear Mr. Hubert:

I was a bit vague in my salary situation yesterday. So that you may have the facts, here they are.

Rather than take my deputy from the payroll, I agreed to take a cut of $1,063 for the rest of the year. This amounts to $212.40 per month. Per annum this comes to $2,548.80. My base salary is roughly $11,000 (it's taken me 24 years to get there!) $11,000 less $2,548.80 is $8,452.20 [*sic*], which is now my base salary. This is, I realize, a time of financial crisis for the Cathedral, but since my composing, teaching, conducting and concertizing are taking more and more of my time, I feel in fairness to myself and the Cathedral I should leave. Hence, I have resigned and my tenure will terminate April 30th.

There are so many things I want to do and I feel I shouldn't tie myself to the Cathedral any longer. I need more time and freedom for the work I want to do and should be doing.

I hope you will understand my reason for leaving the Cathedral is more for the latter factors than those financial, though finances must be considered, however.

I am deeply appreciative of your interest, cooperation and patronage in the "Cathedral Exchange." It's most kind and generous of you.

The best of everything to you always in all ways.
Richard Purvis[135]

Resignation Correspondence

The following memos document Purvis's fall from Grace. Despite Purvis's sometimes negative comments, Dean Bartlett, who had advocated for Purvis with Bishop Pike, always answered him graciously.[136]

July 28, 1970

Dear Julian,

The time has come for me to "pull up stakes." I've been here too long. I've done the job I came to do and should have left at least ten years ago. My whole career has changed (and so has the Cathedral) and despite the fact local critics neither like my playing nor my music, my fame and reputation as a composer, teacher, performer and conductor are now international. I cannot be "tied down" to such a constricting position as the one at the Cathedral any longer.

I shall be teaching and playing in England and Germany next year and have accepted several commissions for compositions in large forms, besides teaching in Los Angeles, Monterey and Seattle, possibly Vancouver. Consequently I can no longer assume the more than full-time duties of the Cathedral.

(You may be interested in what a critic, whom I class as second only to Paul Hume, has to say about my writing.)

Consequently, I am terminating my tenure with the Cathedral as of April 30th, 1971. I shall be in my 25th year and that's a long enough sentence for any man.

As my deal old teacher, Dr. David McKay Williams was wont to say, "Enough is enough."

All the best,
Dick

August 5, 1970

Dear Richard,

While we had opportunity for personal conversation yesterday, I do want you to have this note formally acknowledging your letter of July 28th, in which you submitted your resignation effective April 30, 1971. I accept it with reluctance.

I understand the reasoning which has brought you to this action and I must confess that looking at the matter from the standpoint of what will be best for you I believe you have made the right decision. However, from the standpoint of the Cathedral the separation at the end of your formal association with us will mark an unhappy event in our history. I need not try to recite here what your signal accomplishments have been and how much we owe you in terms of gratitude for having established Grace Cathedral as a solid leader in the finest quality liturgical music in this country. Moreover, your own virtuosity at the organ and tremendous talent as a composer, widely recognized as they are, have reflected distinction on this Cathedral—a distinction seldom enjoyed by churches large or small.

I shall have more to say about the above publicly before your departure, but these thoughts "between thee and me" are genuine and sincere. I wish you the greatest success and deep satisfaction in the coming years.

Affectionately,

[Julian Bartlett]

[about April 10, 1971]

Dear Dean Bartlett,

Now that the time for my departure is upon us, there are a few things needed to "wind up."

1. Two of the ranks in the organ are my personal property. The Solo French Horn (given to me as a birthday present by Joseph Whiteford) and the Military Trumpet (given to me on my 18th anniversary by Bob Kates). If the organ is suitably maintained I am willing for these two ranks to remain, until such time as I build my own organ.

2. I am forced to sell much of the music, book and record library, as I have no place for them in my present dwelling. This is a slow, painful process but I will have the office and studio cleared by late August or early September.

3. Because of the indefinite nature of my future locale, I should like to use the Cathedral as my mailing address until I have a real permanent address. (I just don't know when I will settle after my mother leaves us.)

4. I am so internationally identified with the Grace Cathedral Organ (which was all but unplayable when I came) that I should like to use it for practice and teaching purposes two Fridays a month (namely, the first and third). This seems to be the least disturbed day in the Cathedral schedule.

Due to the long tenure of my service to the Cathedral at a very minimum salary, I don't think these simple requests are overly presumptuous. Your consideration will be greatly appreciated.

Richard Purvis

[undated, probably March or April 1971]

Dear Dean Bartlett,

Since writing the attached letter, two things have materialized.

1. I am under option to make two recordings this Fall and would like permission to use the Cathedral Organ.

2. I leave May 2 for New York where I am performing my Concerto (which is now published)[137] at Columbia University on May 9.

I can't tell you how displeased and horrified I was at that garbage which preceded last Sunday's Service.[138] It was unspeakably rotten! I was ashamed to be forced to listen to such trash. Have you all taken leave of your senses? I'm glad I'm leaving, for I want no part of such cacophony and chaos. (I'm not, at all, alone in my stand.) It was unforgivable!

R. Purvis

April 20, 1971

Dear Dick:

This comes in response to the letter you left at my office a week or two ago. I shall comment in order upon your several paragraphs.

1. I must say that if I ever knew that the solo French Horn and the Military Trumpet ranks were your personal property it had escaped my memory. At least for the time being the Cathedral would like to have the two ranks remain here. My judgment is, however, that we should get together at an early date—hopefully before you leave for the East—and work out quite specific understandings as to responsibility, etc., so that this matter may now be formally a matter of record. Please call Miss Doig to arrange an appointment so that we may come to these understandings. Meanwhile, I thank you for offering to allow these ranks to remain in the organ.

2. I know you must be very reluctant to dispose in part of your music, books and record library. It is entirely possible that the Cathedral may wish to acquire much of which you wish to dispose of for our permanent music library—music, books and recordings. At such time as may be convenient

to you I would welcome a conversation with you on this subject and would ask that you give us first refusal. In this connection, I infer that these items are now in your office and studio here on the Close. I think it would be well if we segregated this material so that it could be appropriately marked and secured. This is the only way we could accept responsibility for having it remain here until either we procure it from you or you dispose of it in other ways. This then should be the second important item on our agenda.

3. It will be quite all right for you to have your mail delivered to the Cathedral until you have a more suitable permanent address. ...

4. I am well aware of your special feelings respecting the Alexander Organ. In one way I am sorry you asked for the privilege of using it for practice and teaching because I had hoped to volunteer that privilege as evidence of our great debt of gratitude to you. You are welcome to use the organ and, indeed, we will consider it an honor to have you thus continue your relationship to the Cathedral as well as through your honorary title. I request that you schedule your time with Miss Rudokas in the Master Calendar. This promise is granted, of course, with the following conditions which I am sure you will agree are appropriate:

a. The matter will be subject to review, confirmation and times allowable when the new Organist-Master of Choristers is in residence. While I am confident there will be no problem here, I am sure you agree it would be a matter of courtesy to come to a new arrangement in accordance with this method of operation.

b. This promise is granted subject to the Cathedral's reserving the right to preempt your scheduled times if important services or other functions should unavoidably conflict.

5. You are granted permission to use the Cathedral Organ for your two recordings which will be scheduled for this Fall, subject to the following conditions:

a. That the times to be arranged shall be agreeable to the new Organist-Master of Choristers and not in conflict with other important events scheduled by the Cathedral.

b. I request that the jackets of your recordings and other publicity indicate that the recordings were done on the Alexander Memorial Organ in Grace Cathedral.

c. If the recordings are to be made at hours which require the Verger's responsibility for security, etc., of the building at other than working hours that you make an appropriate arrangement with Canon Rodgers respecting an honorarium for the Verger.

I look forward to seeing you to work out the details of the several items indicated above.

Sincerely,

[Julian Bartlett]

April 20, 1971

Dear Dick:

It is my great pleasure to inform you that at the April 14th meeting of the Bishop and Trustees of the Cathedral it was my privilege to nominate you and you were unanimously elected to be Organist-Emeritus of the Cathedral effective at the termination of your tenure, April 30th. It was our pleasure to extend to you this honorary relationship to the Cathedral.

The enclosed copy of a resolution passed by the Trustees attempts to express, however inadequately, the tremendous sense of gratitude we all have for your years of faithful devotion to building up a great tradition of music here at the Cathedral. You should feel free to use your honorary title in all publicity and program notes, etc., as you continue your distinguished professional career.

In behalf then of the Trustees I express our gratitude and a fond "au revoir".

Sincerely,

[Julian Bartlett]

The following is an excerpt from the April 14, 1971, minutes of the Meeting of the Bishop and Trustees of Grace Cathedral:

WHEREAS, the Bishop and Trustees recognize the imminence of the termination of Mr. Richard I. Purvis' twenty-four years tenure as Organist-Master of Choristers and wish therefore to take appropriate formal notice thereof; and

WHEREAS, we are singularly aware of the great talent and ability of Mr. Purvis as well as the distinction he has brought to this Cathedral Church in establishing an outstanding tradition of the finest music over the years; and

WHEREAS, we regret his departure which has been brought about on his own volition;

THEREFORE BE IT RESOLVED that the Bishop and Trustees express to Mr. Purvis the lasting gratitude of the people of this Cathedral, of the Episcopal Diocese of California and of the community at large for his many contributions both as an instrumental virtuoso and as a Master of Choristers and we commend him in the highest possible terms for his accomplishments here; and

BE IT FURTHER RESOLVED by unanimous vote that the Bishop and Trustees hereby confer upon him the honorary title of Organist Emeritus of Grace Cathedral with all rights and privileges appertaining thereto; and

BE IT FURTHER RESOLVED that the Bishop and Trustees express to Mr. Purvis their hope that his distinguished career will continue to the great satisfaction of himself and all who shall be benefited by his great talent.

April 30, 1971

Dear Ex Boss:

On the eve of my departure for New York two things come to mind.

1. The Cathedral chime which I wrote for Bishop Block has never been copyrighted. This means anyone can duplicate it. I think it would be wise for the Cathedral to hold a copyright on it.

2. I really think I am entitled to one month's vacation pay. Especially so, since there is no severance pay, no retirement, and your pension plan was activated too recently to be of any service to me. Nothing was mentioned about this, but I think it is my due.

I will contact you on my return.

Cheerio,

Dick

June 21, 1971

Dear Richard:

According to the doctor I am now sprung from my long incarceration. I expect to be on deck full time from now on. Inasmuch as there are a number of matters which need clarification between us I ask that you call Miss Doig as soon as possible to make an appointment.

Now, to a problem which has arisen. In your letter (undated but written about the middle of April) you requested permission to use the Cathedral organ two Fridays a month—the first and the third. In my reply of

April 20th I granted such permission based on two conditions: first, that the matter would be subject to review, confirmation and times allowable when the new organist is in residence; and second, that the Cathedral would have to reserve the right to pre-empt your times if important services or other functions should conflict. Having been away from the office since the second week of May with this vexing laryngitis I have just learned some disquieting news. At my request Miss Rudokas prepared a schedule for me showing the dates and times you have reserved practice and/or teaching time since your departure April 25th. Review of this schedule quickly reveals that you have booked many Saturdays since May 15th and on into August. Moreover, I understand from Canon Rodgers that there were one or two occasions in which your Saturday times raised some problems with respect to Cathedral activities and while these apparently were settled amicably enough the fact is that they posed problems to be settled.

Now, Richard, I must hold you to our first understanding: the first and third Fridays of July and the first Friday of August. Mr. Fenstermaker will be in residence about August 10th. The arrangements must be subject to review between him and me when he arrives. I do not understand your not following the first and third Friday arrangements and I do not understand your booking so many Saturdays without clearance from me or in my absence Canon Rodgers. I am sure this request presents problems for you, but at least from my point of view it appears the problems were really created by you.

The point is not whether or not the Cathedral has anything booked on such days as you might inquire about. The point is that you have booked days well into the future which presents us with problems if anything arises in conflict and which pre-empts the Cathedral organ for use by our interim organist, Michael McCabe. He deserves to have as much flexibility as possible because he is holding down a full time job with the Army as you know. I want the organ to be available to him. Other activities come up from time to time and I wish us to be flexible. . . .

Sincerely,

[Julian Bartlett]

cc: Canon Rodgers
    Canon Wilmington/Miss Rudokas
    Capt. McCabe
    Canon Forbes

August 2, 1971
To: Canon Forbes and Canon Rodgers
From: The Dean

I had a clarifying session with Richard Purvis the other day. The following points were made very clear to him:

1. The interim arrangement which has allowed him to use the organ for practicing and for teaching on the first and third Fridays is definitely to be up for reconsideration once Mr. Fenstermaker is here.

2. I advised him that once Mr. Fenstermaker is in residence that he will not be able to teach students at this organ. If Fenstermaker approves of his continuing to have two days per month at the organ that it will be strictly for purposes of his own practicing. No students.

3. He advised me we should copyright the Carillon Chime which is struck on the hours. He composed this for the Cathedral. I have initiated correspondence with Bill Orrick respecting copyright procedures.

4. A bit of clarification, and again some further confusion respecting the two "ranks" of the organ which Richard alleges are his: he claims that the solo French horn was given to him by Mr. Joseph Whiteford, formerly president of Aeolian-Skinner, in 1949. He said the pipes were from an old E. M. Skinner organ which had been taken out of a residence somewhere. The wind chest which was built for this rank was done by the late John Swinford of San Mateo, who at the time was the organ maintenance man. Mr. Swinford gave the chest to the Cathedral. Richard estimates that the pipe work could be worth approximately $2,000 but, of course, that estimate might be changed radically one way or another by an appraiser. Now for the confusion: confidentially, Mike McCabe told me he had a visit with Mr. Whiteford when he was in San Francisco recently. Mr. Whiteford is now retired and lives in Palm Springs, California. Mr. Whiteford told Mike that he had not given the rank to Mr. Purvis but to the Cathedral. I have not mentioned this to Richard yet. Before doing so I wish to talk to Joe Whiteford.

In any case, Richard has said that he would be prepared to sell the French horn rank to the Cathedral at an appropriate appraised price. The military trumpet rank Richard claims was given to him by Swain and Kates when they were the organ maintenance people at the Cathedral (twelve to fifteen years ago). Richard says that he will be glad to give this rank to the Cathedral.

I expected to get back on to these matters when I return in September and get clarification and termination of the negotiations.

5. Purvis will have cleared the Cathedral of his piano and all other belongings by the end of last week, except four wooden boxes of sheet music for choirs. Charles Agneau assured Richard he could find a place to store these. Stan Rodgers should make sure that the boxes are clearly marked and when they have been stored address a letter to Richard informing him where the boxes are stored and disclaiming any responsibility whatsoever for the music. The letter should be sent in duplicate. Richard should be asked to sign the carbon copy and return it.

6. Richard is leaving in the cabinets in the organist studio a good deal of organ sheet music, some of which he says is quite rare and valuable. It is likely that Mr. Fenstermaker would like to have some if not all of it. He will be glad to give whatever is wanted. He will have it appraised so that he can obtain a tax deduction on the gift. He has suggested and I have relayed on to John Fenstermaker that Fenstermaker have a session with him at his convenience so that he may go through the music with John.

cc: Canon Wilmington

Organist Emeritus of Grace and Successors to Purvis

Purvis's tenure at Grace Cathedral ended on April 30, 1971, when he was named Organist Emeritus. A search for his replacement had begun when he announced his resignation nine months earlier, and the announcement of the selection of John Fenstermaker was made on April 19, 1971. Michael McCabe filled in as interim organist from May to August of 1971, when Fenstermaker was scheduled to begin.[139]

Michael McCabe, a native of Iowa, was a member of the U.S. Army working as a nurse anesthetist at Letterman Hospital in San Francisco. He came to Grace Cathedral from St. Mary the Virgin in San Francisco, where he had served as Dale Wood's assistant.

McCabe had been introduced to Grace Cathedral through David McK. Williams, whom he had met earlier at the Evergreen Music Festival in Colorado. After Williams retired to San Francisco, McCabe continued his studies with the older organist. They had lunch weekly, and one week they invited

Stephen Loher to join them. Loher was then Purvis's assistant, and the connection with Purvis began shortly before Purvis announced his resignation.

According to McCabe, Dean Bartlett had expected Loher to stay on until there was a replacement, but when Loher decided to leave concurrently with Purvis, the Cathedral had to find an interim organist fast. Both Loher and Williams suggested to the Dean that he contact McCabe. After a casual audition at the organ, Bartlett offered McCabe the temporary position.

Purvis had kept his office at the Cathedral and still had teaching privileges there. McCabe spoke to him on many occasions and found him mostly cordial. Still, Purvis could be difficult. McCabe recalls the following encounter:

> The bishop decided instead of going out to all the parishes in the diocese for confirmations, he wanted everyone to come to his Cathedral at 10 a.m. on every first Saturday for confirmations. One Saturday I walked in at 9:30 for the 10 a.m. service. Purvis was teaching a lesson, and Cathedral was half full. I sat down and waited. He was walking up and down the sanctuary; a student was playing the Franck Chorale in E major on General J (with all the strings). I walked over to them at quarter of 10, and said, "I'm going to play now." Finally at five 'til he got off the bench, and he had changed every piston on the organ.

Understandably, the Dean decided that they couldn't have this sort of thing when Fenstermaker arrived, and that Purvis would have to leave.

McCabe related another pair of stories that demonstrate Purvis's Jekyll and Hyde personality:

> When I was visiting San Francisco once from Omaha, I introduced myself and he asked if I would like to play the organ. He was as cordial and sweet as he could be. That afternoon I was at the Legion of Honor and Purvis was the organist. He was just finishing his rehearsal and I went up to him and said, "I see you're going to play today." He said, "No, I'm just going to sit here and watch the people walk around."
>
> Some poor woman from "Lower Slobovia" went up to Purvis after a service to tell him how much she enjoyed playing his music, etc. When she told him that she was organist at the Baptist church in her town, he replied, "That's not my fault."

McCabe concluded diplomatically by saying of Purvis, "He certainly had his gift and made his mark."[140]

John Fenstermaker had served for four years as assistant to Paul Callaway at the National Cathedral in Washington, D.C. When the position at Grace Cathedral was announced, he was working with Alan Wicks at Canterbury Cathedral in England.[141] Purvis's last service was April 25, 1971, and following McCabe's interimship, Fenstermaker's first official Sunday was August 15, 1971;[142] he would serve as Organist and Choirmaster at Grace Cathedral for 30 years.

Fenstermaker said that when he arrived at Grace, Purvis made it a point to stay away. "He wanted to give me space to be my own person, a respectful kind of distance." He said that they spoke from time to time until Purvis died, but didn't meet often.[143]

Stephen Loher wrote, "When John arrived their relationship was not good for several years. I tried a couple of times to get them together but to no avail. However, when the School was thinking of putting in girls, Richard was against this move and that is when he and John had a common cause and became good friends."[144]

David Worth drew a poignant conclusion: "The relationship between Purvis and the organ of Grace Cathedral was a spousal relationship."[145] It must have been painful for Purvis to see the instrument he knew so well in the care of anyone else, even a fellow organist as distinguished as his successor.

Notes

1. Michael Lampen, e-mail, September 21, 2011; see also Grace Cathedral history in Appendix B.

2. Letters from Grace Cathedral archives, courtesy Michael Lampen.

3. Grace Cathedral archives.

4. Grace Cathedral archives.

5. Grace Cathedral archives.

6. Grace Cathedral archives.

7. *San Francisco Examiner*, no date.

8. Stout said that Dean Bartlett invented this title as a joke, but soon thereafter many organ technicians across the country started referring to themselves as "curator." Stout interview.

9. Ed Stout's humorous reference to the fact that Grace Cathedral was made of concrete rather than stone.

10. Ed Stout, "Reflections About Richard Purvis, The Renowned Organist, Composer and Teacher", in "Professional Perspectives," in *Theatre Organ*, May/June, 2008, pp. 46–47. Used by permission of the author.

11. Donna Parker and Jonas Nordwall, "The Purvis Sound," Preface to *The Organ Music of Richard Purvis*, Vols. 1 and 2, H. T. FitzSimons, 2004. Used by permission of Steven Bock, Fred Bock Music.

12. Ed Stout interview.

13. Ed Stout, e-mail, August 31, 2010.

14. Ed Stout interview.

15. Ed Stout interview.

16. Douglas Metzler, e-mail, June 24, 2010.

17. Stephen Loher, e-mail, September 23, 2011.

18. Donald Sears, e-mail, May 30, 2009.

19. Stephen Loher, e-mail, May 30, 2009.

20. Clarence Snyder letter to James Welch, November 1, 2010.

21. Ed Stout interview.

22. Meeting at First Methodist Church, Salem, Oregon, September 27, 2010.

23. Stephen Loher, e-mail, May 30, 2009.

24. Jonas Nordwall, e-mail, September 27, 2010.

25. Biographical Data, 6.

26. Stephen Loher, e-mail, June 3, 2009.

27. Bob Tall, telephone conversation, October 12, 2010.

28. Ed Stout, telephone conversation, October 20, 2011.

29. Ed Stout, telephone conversation, October 20, 2011.

30. Stephen Loher, e-mail, October 5, 2011.

31. Michael Lampen, e-mail, October 10, 2011.

32. Nancy Daley, Director of Marketing for Fratelli Ruffatti in North America, e-mail, February 1, 2012.

33. *Virgil Fox (The Dish)*, by Richard Torrence and Marshall Yaeger, based on a memoir by Ted Alan Worth. New York: Circles International, 2001. 247.

34. Ed Stout, telephone conversation, October 20, 2011.

35. Jonas Nordwall, telephone conversation, January 27, 2012.

36. Ed Stout, telephone conversation, October 20, 2011.

37. Michael Lampen, e-mail, October 10, 2011.

38. Ed Stout, telephone conversation, October 20, 2011.

39. Loher, e-mail, December 18, 2011.

40. Ed Stout, e-mail, December 18, 2011.

41. Michael Lampen, e-mail, October 10, 2011.

42. The Worcester Skinner organ was on the factory floor at same time as the Grace Cathedral Skinner and was very similar in size. David Worth, e-mail, April 30, 2011.

43. Letter courtesy David Worth.

44. Martin Lilley, e-mail, August 1, 2011.

45. Donna Parker, interview, September 27, 2010.

46. Donald Braff characterized Richard and John's relationship as "very discreet and dignified." Interview with Donald Braff, October 5, 2010, Palo Alto.

47. For more details regarding the end of John's life, see Chapter 5, "Later Years."

48. Ed Stout interview.

49. Michael Lampen, e-mail, September 17, 2012.

50. Vaughn Jones, e-mail, March 23, 2012.

51. Michael Lampen, e-mail, September 26, 2011.

52. David Worth, e-mail, April 5, 2011.

53. Stephen Loher, e-mail, November 8, 2010.

54. Ed Stout interview.

55. David Worth, e-mail, July 22, 2010.

56. After leaving Grace, Duncan moved to Chicago. He died there on June 25, 1968. Death certificate, Cook County Vital Statistics.

57. Ed Stout interview.

58. David Worth, e-mail, July 21, 2010.

59. David Worth, e-mail, September 20, 2011.

60. Ed Stout, e-mail, April 26, 2011.

61. David Worth, e-mail, April 27, 2011.

62. David Worth, email, April 26, 2011.

63. Ed Stout, "Some Thoughts about Tom Hazleton," *The Stentor*, Fall 2006, 7.

64. Donna Parker, e-mail, September 2, 2012.

65. Stephen Loher, e-mail, November 7, 2010.

66. Douglas Metzler interview, Bothell, Washington, June 24, 2010.

67. Michael Lampen, e-mail, April 11, 2011.

68. David Worth, e-mail, November 8, 2010.

69. David Worth, e-mail, April 5, 2011.

70. David Worth, e-mail, April 6, 2011.

71. Stephen Loher, e-mail, April 6, 2011.

72. Stephen Loher, e-mail, November 8, 2010, and September 23, 2011.

73. Michael Lampen, e-mail, March 28, 2011.

74. David Worth, e-mail, November 8, 2010.

75. *San Francisco Examiner?*, 1947.

76. *San Francisco Examiner*, November 2, 1947.

77. *San Francisco Examiner*, July 16, 1950.

78. The accompanying photo is dated March 14, 1949, but the event was clearly a Christmas concert, probably in 1948.

79. Old Boys Interview, Healdsburg, California, June 7, 2011.

80. Stephen Loher, e-mail, April 6, 2011.

81. Stephen Loher, e-mail, November 8, 2010.

82. David Worth, e-mail, November 8, 2010, and Stephen Loher, e-mail, September 26, 2011.

83. David Worth, e-mail, November 8, 2010.

84. David Worth, e-mail, November 8, 2010.

85. Stephen Loher, e-mail, November 7, 2010.

86. Stephen Loher, e-mail, November 7, 2010.

87. Corbett, 12.

88. Stephen Loher, e-mail, November 7, 2010.

89. David Worth, e-mail, November 8, 2010.

90. Stephen Loher, e-mail, May 30, 2009.

91. David Worth, e-mail, November 8, 2010.

92. Stephen Loher, e-mail, May 30, 2009.

93. Grace Cathedral archives. Michael Lampen clarifies: "That September, the General Convention of the Episcopal Church had met in San Francisco (having met here only once before, in 1901), with several major services at the Cathedral. There were new choir furnishings in place, which is why the choir is mentioned as being out of sorts. I expect the choir (and Purvis) were exhausted after this Episcopal Church onslaught and gave a less than standard showing on this particular Sunday." Michael Lampen, e-mail, November 9, 2010.

94. Stephen Loher, e-mail, November 7, 2010.

95. Stephen Loher, conversation, Salem, Oregon, September 27, 2010.

96. Stephen Loher, e-mail, November 7, 2010.

97. David Worth, e-mail, November 8, 2010.

98. *San Francisco Chronicle*, August 18, 1951, p. 1 ff; Burt Weaver, e-mail, January 2, 2012.

99. David Worth, e-mail, November 8, 2010.

100. From "The Consecration of Grace Cathedral Church in San Francisco," official program booklet. Courtesy David Worth.

101. Concert program.

102. Michael Lampen, "Friends of Grace Quarterly," Fall 1999, Vol. I, No. 3, p. 4.

103. Michael Lampen, e-mail, May 8, 2011.

104. For further discussion of "Purvis a la Jazz Hot," see Chapter 9, "Choral and Vocal Works."

105. Stephen Loher, e-mail, November 7, 2010.

106. Ed Stout interview.

107. Donald Braff, letter, September 24, 2011.

108. Stephen Loher, e-mail, May 30, 2009.

109. Ed Stout interview.

110. Biographical Data, 6.

111. Ed Stout interview.

112. Michael Lampen, September 25, 2011.

113. Cited in Townsend thesis, 14.

114. Jack Bethards, telephone conversation, October 13, 2011.

115. Stout, telephone conversation, October 20, 2011.

116. Stephen Loher, e-mail, October 20, 2011.

117. Ed Stout, telephone conversation, October 20, 2011. See also Chapter 12, "Purvis and the Theatre Organ."

118. *The Diapason*, February 1, 1952, 17.

119. Stephen Loher, e-mail, April 6, 2011.

120. Douglas Metzler, e-mail, June 24, 2010.

121. Stephen Loher, e-mail, April 6, 2011.

122. Interview with Donald Braff, October 5, 2010, Palo Alto, California.

123. Donald Braff, conversation in Palo Alto, California, October 5, 2010.

124. Grace Cathedral archives.

125. Grace Cathedral archives.

126. Grace Cathedral archives.

127. Concert program.

128. Ed Stout interview.

129. David Worth, e-mail, September 27, 2010.

130. Donna Parker, e-mail, September 27, 2010.

131. Michael McCabe, telephone conversation, April 7, 2011.

132. Stephen Loher, e-mail, September 25, 2011.

133. Stephen Loher, e-mail, September 25, 2011.

134. Donna Parker, e-mail, September 27, 2010.

135. Undated but probably mid-1970s. Grace Cathedral archives.

136. All documents from Grace Cathedral archives.

137. Purvis may be referring to his "Pièce Symphonique" for organ and orchestra; however, it was never published.

138. It is not known which service Purvis was referring to here, but Lampen wrote: "There were ballet performances February 3 and 4, 1971, and a Whale, Pelican and Pygmy Forest Sensorium on March 7, 1971. It was a time of musical and performance experimentation that upset traditionalists." Michael Lampen, e-mail, October 11, 2011.

139. Michael Lampen, e-mail, September 23, 2011.

140. Michael McCabe, telephone conversation, April 7, 2011.

141. Ed Stout interview.

142. Michael Lampen, e-mail, September 23, 2011.

143. John Fenstermaker, telephone conversation, November 30, 2010.

144. Stephen Loher, e-mail, May 29, 2009.

145. David Worth, e-mail, September 27, 2010.

chapter 5

Later Years,
1971–1994

Following his departure from Grace Cathedral, Purvis continued actively with his composing, recital work, and teaching. Further details regarding each of these aspects of his life are found in subsequent chapters of this book.

The Move to 70 Balceta Avenue

At the time of his resignation, Purvis lived alone in his apartment at 2140 Hyde Street #303, San Francisco. John Shields had previously rented a room at the home of Mrs. Grace Warren, located at 70 Balceta Avenue, San Francisco. Mrs. Warren, whose sons Tom and John had been choristers at Grace Cathedral, was a violinist and deeply devoted to the music program at Grace. Purvis moved to the Balceta house in December of 1971, joining John there.

Purvis at the Rodgers organ in his home studio, 1970s. Courtesy Donald Braff.

70 Balceta Avenue, San Francisco. Photo by Jonathan Dukes.

RICHARD PURVIS

Organist - Composer - Conductor

ORGANIST AND MASTER OF CHORISTERS EMERITUS
HONORARY CANON - GRACE CATHEDRAL

(415) 564-4406

70 BALCETA AVENUE   SAN FRANCISCO CA 94127

Purvis's calling card, 1970s–1980s.

Purvis with two unidentified students, 1970s.

Mrs. Warren moved to a nursing home around 1974 and died in 1980. Upon her death her heirs decided to sell the house quickly. Shields came home from a summer trip in the Sierras to find some of his belongings being discarded. He and Purvis decided on the spot to buy the house, which had been built around 1925.[1]

Teaching Studio

At his home on Balceta, Purvis converted the garage into a teaching studio, where he taught on several different Rodgers electronic organs through the years.

In 1988 Purvis purchased a new Rodgers model 925 organ for his home studio. It was sold to him by Bob Daffer, then the Rodgers dealer in San Francisco, who had taken Purvis's Rodgers model 330 in on trade.[2]

Purvis wrote the following letter to Daffer on February 28, 1988:

My dear Bob:

The new 925 has been in my studio some 3 weeks now, and while we are nowhere near finished with voicing and regulating, I am more than delighted with the instrument, both musically and technically. It is truly a joy and inspiration and since you are in large measure responsible for its being here, I want to express my sincere gratitude to you.

Ed [Galley, salesman] and Mark [McCauley, salesman] and Bill Petty [local technician] have been most helpful and cooperative, and all three have gone far beyond the call of duty in getting things to sound as I wish them. We are truly making progress.

I understand you've been to England (my musical Mecca) and like the sound of British Cathedral Organs. As you know, most of my Anglican Training was on the "Fair Isle," and to me men like Willis II, Hill, Norman and Beard and the original Harris can do no wrong. I worship at their Tonal Shrines.

Needless to say, I hope you'll visit us again soon. In the interval, rest assured of my sincere gratitude, admiration and appreciation.

The best of everything to you always, in all ways.

Dick

Purvis Endorses Rodgers Organs

Sometime during Purvis's retirement years, the Rodgers Organ Company ran the following promotional brochure featuring his name.

Richard Purvis. Organist. Composer. Conductor. For 25 years he served as Organist and Master of Choristers at Grace Cathedral, San Francisco. And for at least ten years was first organist of the California Palace of the Legion of Honor (one of the West Coast's finest art museums).

Today in his San Francisco residence, Mr. Purvis maintains a busy schedule teaching and composing. His residence music studio isn't exactly Grace Cathedral or the Palace of the Legion of Honor. But some of his best works have been inspired there.

What organ did he choose? RODGERS. An impressive three manual specification designed and installed to complement the particular acoustics of his studio.

Not everyone can afford to be inspired on an instrument like Grace Cathedral. Or the Palace of the Legion of Honor. Or a custom three manual Rodgers.

But you might be surprised to know that you can have a complete two manual RODGERS organ—with AGO pedal clavier, optional Tracker Touch keyboards, and Computer Combination Action—all for under $10,000.

Visit your nearest Rodgers Organ representative today. You'll be inspired, too![3]

Travels and Leisure Activities

During the 1950s and '60s, Purvis returned several times to England, one of his favorite destinations. In his later years he also enjoyed traveling in the United States and abroad, including two cruises with Shields to Alaska and at least two trips to the British Isles. In May and June of 1976, he visited Wales and Scotland, sending postcards to Shields at home in San Francisco from Conwy and Betws-y-coed in Wales, and from Glencoe and the Isle of Iona in Scotland. From August to October of 1986, he traveled to Britain for the last time, again sending postcards to John from Edinburgh, Loch Katrine, Melrose Abbey, and the Isles of Mull (where he rode a steam locomotive), Orkney, and Skye, in Scotland; and from Blenheim

Passport photos from 1959 and 1963. Courtesy Donald Braff.

Martin Lilley, Richard Purvis, and Ed Mullins at the Royal Festival Hall, London, October 8, 1986.
Courtesy Martin Lilley.

Palace, Fountains Abbey (Yorkshire), Leeds Castle (Kent), Canterbury
Cathedral, the Vale of Rheidol Railway (Wales), Fowey (Cornwall); and,
most meaningfully, from York Minster, where he had studied as a young
man. On a postcard showing the interior of the York Minster choir he
wrote, "Dear John, Despite a few <u>minor</u> changes, this is still one of the
greatest organs I know. Heard a lovely Evensong, including a most beautiful anthem by Sir William McKie! This place certainly holds a magical aura
for me."[4] During his 1986 trip he also made a visit to the Royal Festival Hall
in London.

Closer to home, both Purvis and Shields enjoyed driving to Yosemite
and the Sierra Nevada. Nearly every summer Shields camped there in his
VW bus, and Purvis, who liked to walk the hills and mountains of the Bay
Area (sometimes taking the ferry to Angel Island for day hikes), joined
him at Yosemite when he could.

John Shields's VW bus. Sierra campout, 1970s. Courtesy Donald Braff.

Purvis contemplating the Pacific Ocean, San Mateo County coast, 1980s. Courtesy Donald Braff.

But one of Purvis's greatest pleasures was dining and drinking with friends at favorite restaurants in the Bay Area. Starting when he retired in 1990, Donald Braff, a student of Purvis's from about 1960 to 1970 and a close friend of both Richard and John's, had a lunch engagement every Wednesday ("like clockwork") with the pair. They especially enjoyed the San Mateo County coast, and they often drove north of the Golden Gate Bridge on Highway 1 for lunch in Olema, California.

Purvis at the Olema Inn, Marin County, 1990s. Courtesy Donald Braff.

Purvis liked to cook; Shields didn't. Braff's wife Marian was a gourmet cook, and the two couples dined together frequently at one another's homes.[5]

Among Purvis's papers was found the following menu plan, in his own handwriting:

S[aturday]
Mix Meatloaf
L   Spaghetti & Ravioli
D   Casserole,
Zucchini-Succotash

Sun (1st)
L   Eggs, Canadian Bacon,
Rolls

Purvis grilling, late 1980s. Courtesy Donald Braff.

Purvis relaxing on an Alaskan cruise, 1980s. Courtesy Donald Braff.

Douglas Metzler, Richard Purvis, and John Shields enjoying drinks in the revolving restaurant atop the Space Needle in Seattle, Washington, 1980s. Courtesy Donald Braff.

Richard and John aboard a Liberty Ship in the San Francisco Bay with other World War II veterans, early 1990s. Courtesy Donald Braff.

Ed Stout, Richard Purvis, and Dick Taylor, on the occasion of Ed's 25th anniversary as Curator of the Organs at Grace Cathedral, October 1985.

D   Cornish Hen, Yam, Broccoli

   M[onday]

L

D   Meatloaf, Mushroom Gravy, Baked Potato, Sour Cream & Chives, Zucchini

   T[uesday]

L

D   Pork Tenderloin, Spinach, Red Potato

   W[ednesday]

L

D   Meatloaf, Broccoli

Of Purvis's film and TV preferences, Vaughn Jones wrote, "Purvis loved to talk about Masterpiece Theatre programs on television: 'Upstairs, Downstairs;' 'I, Claudius;' 'The First Churchills.' He would have loved Downton Abbey. But I don't think he ever went to see a movie."[6]

1976 Festival of Virtuosos

From September 10–26, 1976, Ted Alan Worth promoted a concert series at St. Mary's Cathedral in San Francisco entitled "A Festival of Organ Virtuosos & Illumination." In addition to recitals by Virgil Fox, Joyce Jones, and Anthony Newman, Purvis performed on September 18. The Festival concluded on September 26 with a program called "A Tribute to Richard Purvis." This ambitious concert included a Festival Choir and members of the San Francisco Symphony (brass, tympani, harp, and organ), all conducted by Richard Purvis.[7]

Poster for "A Festival of Organ Virtuosos & Illumination," St. Mary's Cathedral, San Francisco, September 1976. Courtesy Christoph Tietze.

Richard's 80th birthday celebration, Grace Cathedral, August 15, 1993. Courtesy Donald Braff.

Purvis with John Fenstermaker, 80th birthday celebration, Grace Cathedral, August 15, 1993. Courtesy Donald Braff.

80th Birthday Recitals

In honor of Purvis's 80th birthday, friends and colleagues performed recitals of his organ music within a period of four weeks.

The first was given on August 15, 1993, at Grace Cathedral by local organists Kenneth Matthews, J. Stephan Repasky, and John Fenstermaker:

Organ Recital of Music by Richard Purvis

In honor of the Composer on the occasion of his Eightieth Birthday
St. Francis Suite
Capriccio on the Notes of the Cuckoo
Four Prayers in Tone
Prelude on "Forest Green" "composed in England, 1944"
Partita on "Christ ist Erstanden"[8]

The second occurred on September 10, 1993, at Our Lady of Mercy Catholic Church in Daly City, California. Entitled "An Organ Extravaganza Concert," it was performed by five of Purvis's former students: Ted Alan Worth, Lyn Larsen, Donna Parker, Jonas Nordwall, and Tom Hazleton.

Their program included the following Purvis compositions: Thanksgiving, Romanza, Dialogue Monastique, Of Sea and Skye, Fanfare, Of Moor and Fen, Spiritual, Fanfare in D (Lemmens-Purvis), Marche Grotesque, Les Petites Cloches, Toccata Festiva, Capriccio on the Notes of the Cuckoo, Symphonic Suite for Three Organs (California premiere), I'll Take an Option on You (Purvis's theme song on radio station KRE), and Processional on "Lyra Davidica."

Nunc Dimittis

During the last year of his life, Purvis battled colon cancer. On November 29, 1994, he underwent his final operation, a colon resection, at San Francisco Presbyterian Medical Center.[9] Returning from the hospital, he was at home from December 5 to 24, under the care of John Shields. Purvis wanted to die at home, but at the end John was physically unable to lift or care for him. On Christmas Eve, Richard was taken back to the Presbyterian Medical Center, where he died on December 25, 1994, at 8:31 a.m.[10]

John Shields and Richard Purvis, 80th birthday celebration, Grace Cathedral, August 15, 1993. Courtesy Donald Braff.

80th birthday concert, Daly City, September 10, 1993. From left to right: Gary Kibble (Rodgers Organ Company Western Regional Manager), Ted Alan Worth, Jonas Nordwall, Richard Purvis, Donna Parker, Lyn Larsen (behind Donna), Tom Hazleton, George Kirwood (Rodgers Organ Company's Senior Engineer).

Purvis's certificate of death states that the immediate cause of death was "cardiac arrest due to aortic stenosis." Under "other significant conditions contributing to death" is listed "metastatic colon carcinoma." The certificate was signed by William T. Armstrong, M.D., Purvis's personal physician (and former organ student).[11] Donna Parker wrote, "Dick passed away from congestive heart failure in the hospital on Christmas Day. Lee Pare, his long time friend and the organ technician, called me on Christmas morning as we were opening our gifts to tell me that Dick had passed away."[12]

Interment

Purvis's ashes are inurned in the Saint Francis Chapel of Grace Cathedral, the cathedral columbarium, on the gallery level of the north tower (also called the Singing Tower, named for its carillon). His niche is 15-6-B. The plaque on the cabinet door reads simply, "Richard I. Purvis 1913–1994."[13]

John Shields survived for less than six months, passing away on June 14, 1995 (see details below in "Richard's Estate").

Obituaries and Tributes

Numerous obituaries, tributes, and articles were released to the media following Purvis's death. Canon Malcolm Manson, Headmaster at the Cathedral School for Boys, 1990–1999, compiled the following obituary, from which most of the other obituaries and notices were excerpted. Not all of the information contained in this obituary and those that follow is absolutely accurate, in part because it was based on the Biographical Data and other sources which contained minor errors. It is nevertheless included here in its original form; the reader can find the correct data in previous chapters.

Mr. Purvis's Obituary
compiled by Canon Malcolm Manson, headmaster
For Immediate Release: January 5, 1995
RICHARD IRVEN PURVIS

Richard Purvis, organist and choirmaster at Grace Cathedral from 1947 to 1971 and a noted composer of sacred music, died on Christmas Day, 1994, after a long illness. He was 81. A Memorial Service will be held at Grace Cathedral on January 25 at 2:00 p.m. Gifts in his memory may be sent to the Purvis Memorial Fund at Cathedral School for Boys, 1275 Sacramento St. SF CA 94108.

Richard Irven Purvis was born in San Francisco on August 25, 1913. He began the study of piano at the age of six with Maybelle Sherwood Willis, but his affection and interest swiftly transferred to the organ when the vicar of Good Samaritan Mission allowed him to play the wonderful old Whalley mechanical-action organ when he was nine. He gave his parents no peace until they took him to be interviewed by Wallace Sabin, who, with some misgiving, agreed to introduce him to the art of the organist only if the boy continued to study the piano. There were seven years of study with Sabin (one of the founders of the San Francisco chapter of the American Guild of Organists) augmented by piano study with Benjamin S. Moore, the organist at Trinity Episcopal Church here in San Francisco. During the time the Aeolian-Skinner organ was being installed at Grace Cathedral and through the interest of J. Sydney Lewis, the cathedral organist at that time, the young Purvis came under the musical influences of organ-builders Ernest M. Skinner and G. Donald Harrison.

In the winter of 1934, he was awarded a full scholarship to the Curtis Institute of Music in Philadelphia and there studied the organ with Alexander McCurdy, and conducting with Fritz Reiner. In addition he made weekly trips to New York to study the piano with Josef F. Levine.

In 1936, he received the Cyrus H. K. Curtis Memorial Fellowship, which permitted further study in Europe and England. Here he was greatly inspired by Sir Edward Bairstow at York Minster. He journeyed to Paris to work with Marcel Dupré and also studied Gregorian chant with Dom Desroquettes of Quarr Abbey on the Isle of Wight.

He became organist and choirmaster of Saint James Episcopal Church in Philadelphia and Director of Music at the Episcopal Academy at Overbrook, Pennsylvania, still continuing his studies at Curtis until his graduation in 1940. He then studied the works of César Franck with Charles Courboin, and subsequently the music of Liszt, Reubke and Reger with Charles Heinroth (a pupil of Liszt).

The war saw him as a bandmaster for the 28th Infantry Division. This ended by his becoming a prisoner of war during the Battle of the Bulge.

After the war was over and Mr. Purvis regained his freedom, he returned to the West Coast and became organist and choirmaster of St. Mark's

Purvis at home, 1990s. Courtesy Donald Braff.

Lutheran Church in San Francisco and from there, at the invitation of the Episcopal Bishop, Karl Morgan Block, came to Grace Cathedral in 1947. He immediately established the Christmas Vesper Concert, which has become such a strong local tradition in the city. In 1957, he and C. Julian Bartlett, Dean of the Cathedral, founded Cathedral School for Boys, thus enabling the tradition of the Men and Boys' Choir to continue at Grace Cathedral. After a long career of playing services, conducting singers and instrumentalists, composing, and playing organ recitals through the west, Mr. Purvis retired from the cathedral in 1971.

He continued to give recitals and to compose well into the 1980's. Among his best-known compositions are the *Partita on 'Christ ist erstanden'* for the organ, written for E. Power Biggs in 1951, *Four Prayers in Tone* for the organ; and *The Ballad of Judas Iscariot*, for choir and organ.[14]

Though Purvis's most famous "obituary" was printed in *The Diapason* in April 1945 during World War II (see Chapter 3, "War Years"), true death notices were printed in the following journals, newspapers, and newsletters, all based on Canon Malcolm Manson's obituary:

San Francisco Examiner, January 13, 1995
San Francisco Chronicle, January 14, 1995
San Francisco AGO Newsletter, February 1995, p. 3
The Diapason, April 1995, p. 6
The American Organist, April 1995, p. 54

To the obituary in the San Francisco Chapter AGO Newsletter, John Fenstermaker added the following:

"In Memoriam: Richard Purvis 1913–1994"

Richard Purvis, composer, recitalist, teacher and organist of Grace Cathedral from 1947 to 1971, died on Christmas day. He was eighty-one.

The author of *Le Petit Prince,* Antoine de Saint-Exupéry, wrote

"It came to me that when a man dies, an unknown world passes away … The hard bone of his skull was in a sense an old treasure chest."

Not long ago, Mr. Purvis told me about his first trip to England in the 1930s and his first stormy meeting with Sir Edward Bairstow, organist of the vast York Minster. A youth spent in San Francisco, studies at Curtis with Alexander McCurdy, time in the armed forces, and a long cathedral tenure with his beloved Aeolian-Skinner organ: all these comprised a unique and fascinating life from which Mr. Purvis richly shared his anecdotes, humor and philosophy. He was an independent thinker—he was especially irritated by those who were sanctimonious or pretentious. Because of this, his time as a church musician was filled with energetic and memorable encounters, as he strove to bring to the institutional church his vision of the holiness of beauty. The world is richer for his being with us.

Into paradise may the angels lead him.
At his coming may the martyrs receive him,
and bring him into the holy city Jerusalem.
May the choirs of angels welcome him,
and with Lazarus who once was poor,
may he have everlasting peace.

—John Fenstermaker[15]

Memorial Service

On January 25, 1995, a Service of Thanksgiving for the Life of Richard Irven Purvis was held at Grace Cathedral. The musicians who performed were John Fenstermaker, Canon Organist and Choirmaster; Christopher Putnam, Assistant Organist and Choirmaster; and the Grace Cathedral Choir of Men and Boys.

The service included the following:

Prelude: Repentance, Supplication, and Adoration, from Four Prayers in Tone, Richard Purvis

Psalm 23, sung by the choir (Chant, Bairstow)

Hymn: St. Denio

Greeting: The Rev. Canon Malcolm Manson

First Reading: Isaiah 25:6-9

Psalm 121, sung by the choir (chant, Richard Purvis)

Second Reading: Revelation 7:9-17

Winter Passes Over, Richard Purvis

Gospel: John 14:1-6

Homily: The Rev. Canon James McLeod

Nunc dimittis, Horatio Parker

Hymn: Darwall's 148th

Postlude: Thanksgiving, from Four Prayers in Tone, Richard Purvis

The homily was given by one of Purvis's former choristers, the Rev. Dr. James W. McLeod, and is reprinted here in its entirety:

> Immortal, invisible, God only wise
> in light inaccessible hid from our eyes,
> most blessed, most glorious, the Ancient of Days,
> almighty, victorious, thy great Name we praise.
> > Hymn 423, St. Denio

Jack Chism and I were late getting to choir rehearsal on that Thursday night in early February 1947. As we walked into the choir room the dark-haired young man reminded us of our tardiness. I gave a lame excuse. He didn't buy it and went on to tell us that from henceforth we were to address him as "Sir!" Also, we were trebles, not boy sopranos. Thus began my 10-year career as a Purvis chorister.

After a brief warmup, he called in the tenors and basses and the most difficult choir rehearsal in that or any year began. We rehearsed a simple hymn for the offertory on his first Sunday as Organist and Master of the Choristers.

"Immortal, invisible, God only wise
in light inaccessible hid from our eyes"

The words of the hymn describe the wonder and majesty of God. Mr. Purvis was determined to make us sing that hymn as though we ourselves had experienced the mystery of the Invisible Godhead.

Over many years as a parish rector I have come to realize and appreciate the power given to the church musician to help a congregation enter into the divine reality of God. We preachers fashion ourselves as wordsmiths, as communicators, but we never approximate the power of music to touch the emotions and convey the Gospel. In ways beyond the spoken word, music penetrates our filters and defenses and touches our souls. The music of the church gives life to the worship of the church. For twenty-five years in this place that mighty work was entrusted to Richard Purvis, and he did nobly.

Two days before last Christmas I found myself humming and singing the words and music of Dick's, "Mass of St. Nicholas," and his "Magnificat" for organ and choir. I had sung these last as a young tenor nearly forty years ago. I remembered Dick's Christmas Scottish carol, "What strangers are these?" The music brought back a wealth of pleasant memories. How mightily that music had moved me as a young person and it still does. Nearly two weeks later, I learned that Dick Purvis had died on Christmas Day. This was not the first time I had experienced such recollections of singing with Mr. Purvis since leaving the choir so long ago. The music and the man have left a strong impression on my life and the lives of many others.

It is important that we talk not only about the musician, but about the man. The greatest teachers not only convey a subject matter or train a skill, but give insight into our common humanity. I can name many boys over the years who found something of a father figure in Richard Purvis. But I'd best speak for myself. I was a poor kid, son of a widow, who was invited to sing in the Choir two years before Dick came to Grace Cathedral. I lived in Visitacion Valley, one of many boys who came on public transportation from throughout the City to sing in the choir. From Pacific Heights to the Excelsior, rich and poor, we came. At 13, I had never met such a powerful, dynamic and bright man as Richard Purvis. His stern attitude and dynamic leadership attracted me even more. Yet, Dick had a problem with the adulation he received from all of us. He did not want us to get too close. His temperament frustrated all of us at times, particularly the men of the choir. Yet we would follow him anywhere. He had a power over our lives which he may not have wanted, but which he could not prevent. He was respected. He was loved.

I am reminded of a popular movie of some fifteen years ago, "The Blues Brothers," with John Belushi and Dan Aykroyd. Two mobsters break out of prison. Their old Catholic school principal, a nun, finds out where they are and orders them to come to her office. Because of her nun's habit and her personal power, the whole student body called her the Penguin. Our two hoodlums obey the Penguin's command. These two hardened criminals walk into her office, hat in hand with knees knocking, perspiring, in sheer fear and solemn respect. That was the power the Penguin had over their lives. Some of us old choir boys have felt something of that same trauma even as middle aged men when we met Dick Purvis. He impacted our lives deeply and none of us has been the same. We might have joked about him; we might have griped about his demanding ways; but we loved him.

Dick was born in San Francisco and went to high school in Oakland. He studied at the Curtis Institute in Philadelphia and with Sir Edward Bairstow in England before World War Two. In December 1944 as an Army warrant officer he was captured in the Battle of the Bulge and landed in a German prisoner of war camp. He remarked one evening at the Bishop's Ranch after a picnic dinner of canned baked beans and hot dogs that his first food as a liberated prisoner was a can of cold baked beans. A month or so later after his liberation, Dick led one of the great U.S. Army marching bands through the Arch de Triomphe in Paris to celebrate the Allied victory in Europe, one of his personal great moments. After the war and recuperation he taught in Philadelphia before being called to the choir and great Alexander Organ of Grace Cathedral.

In a time when relationships between men were unspoken, we were aware of the special bond between John Shields and Richard Purvis. No one understood Dick better or supported him more strongly than John. John's style was to stay behind the scenes and to be constant in support. Their friendship was essential to our understanding Richard Purvis. Their companionship continued for over 40 years. We are grateful to John and our love goes out to him at this time of loss.

What about the legacy? Richard Purvis cannot be separated from music, and music cannot be separated from God. It was a joy, it was thrilling to hear him play the organ works of J.S. Bach and César Franck. Or to hear Dick improvise on a theme. It was both exhausting and joyful to sing a concert with him.

The legacy of Richard Purvis is more than I can describe. Certainly, his organ literature is one of his great legacies to us. "In Babylon," "Christ ist erstanden," "Thanksgiving," "Supplication," and so many others. And the music he wrote for boys' and men's voices. But musical works were not his only legacy. From his earliest days on the Cathedral Close we heard from him his hopes and dreams for a choir school. The Cathedral School for Boys began in his dreams and after ten years those dreams took fruition. But Dick's most important legacy, I believe, was the lives that have been reached, enriched and changed by this teacher.

Today, we gather to give thanks for the life and ministry of Richard Irven Purvis, musician of the church, teacher and friend. We commend him to God's love and care. May Jesus the Good Shepherd greet him with open arms. May Gabriel the Archangel welcome him with a mighty fanfare. May David the Master of the Heavenly Choristers share with Dick the music of praising God. And may the altos always come in on time and in tune.

Almighty God, we are grateful to be called Dick's friends. Amen.[16]

Other Tributes

Douglas Metzler, a student and friend of Richard's for more than 30 years, wrote the following "appreciation":

Pacific Church News, February/March 1995
Published by the Diocese of California, the Episcopal Church in the Bay Area

"An Appreciation of Richard Purvis"

Richard Purvis, organist and Master of Choristers at Grace Cathedral from 1947 to 1972 [*sic*], and a profoundly important contributor to music in the Anglican heritage, was born in San Francisco in 1915 [*sic*] and died there on Christmas Day 1994. His memorial Eucharist took place at the cathedral on January 25.

RICHARD PURVIS told me often that "life is for the living." And this very kind and gentle man certainly did just that! His musical talent was recognized early: he began his training at age 4 [*sic*]. By the time—at 12—he played the organ in San Francisco's Civic Auditorium, he had already been appointed a church organist and the staff organist for Bay Area station KRE, where he played both classical and pop music.

Richard's teachers included some of the greatest names of the period, and he traveled far and wide to work with them: Wallace Sabin and Benjamin Moore in San Francisco; Dr. Alexander McCurdy in Philadelphia; Joseph Lhevinne and Joseph Schillinger in New York; Sir Edward Bairstow at York Minster in England; and Marcel Dupré in Paris.

Richard served in the Army and was captured during the Battle of the Bulge. Following his return to the U.S. and recovery from internment by the Nazis, he was named Organist and Master of Choristers at Grace Cathedral in San Francisco. His tenure there lasted a quarter of a century. During that time, Grace Cathedral witnessed one of the richest and most productive eras in the history of American church music. The magnificent Aeolian-Skinner organ, with its peerless acoustical surroundings, inspired some of Richard's finest creations and provided a colorful palette for his improvisations during cathedral services.

Richard was a prolific composer, and his work has contributed enormously to church music, encompassing every conceivable medium available to church performance. He composed and published more than 200 works for organ, organ and brass, choir and organ, voice, piano, piano and organ, two organs, organ and harp, and a concerto for organ and orchestra. Some of his most noted commissions were a complete English liturgy, written for the Church of England and a partita on the chorale "Christ ist Erstanden," written for E. Power Biggs.

Richard appeared with the Philadelphia Orchestra, the Houston Symphony, the Oakland Symphony, and the Peninsula Symphony, and in broadcast on NBC, CBS, BBC, and the Canadian Broadcasting network.

Richard loved to have picnics around the Bay Area, especially at Samuel Taylor State Park and Angel Island. He enjoyed entertaining guests and listening to music. His quick wit always made him fun to be with. He enjoyed living, and living, and living.[17]

The July–August 2003 issue of the San Francisco Chapter AGO newsletter featured an article by Donald Sears, entitled "Richard I. Purvis: A Brief Biography in honor of the 90th Anniversary of His Birth." Excerpts appear elsewhere in this book. Sears credited June Townsend (who died in 2002), Donald Braff, and Jean White for providing the information used in the article.

Michael Lampen, archivist at Grace Cathedral, wrote the following remembrance, probably in 2006:

Richard Purvis Remembered—by a Chorister Alumnus

As a chorister in the late fifties, I well remember Mr. Purvis. He was famous for his practice room discipline, and any boy who crossed him had to endure his rage. Still, he had a soft heart under that hard exterior, and was as apt to make quips as to become angry. "You sound like death warmed over" usually followed the first notes sung by the boys after a long vacation. A particularly squeaky boy might be compared to "a chicken with the pip." Mr. Purvis detested "cold shower" singers like Lily Pons. When learning a new piece, he would give the choir a bit of leeway with the words "If you fall off the wagon, just climb back on." A portly man for most of his life, Mr. Purvis had in his office a caricature of an equally large cigar-chomping Brahms, playing happily away on a piano. The drawing still hangs in the choir house. It is the way I like to remember him.[18]

A 90th Birthday Tribute

The July–August 2003 issue of the San Francisco AGO newsletter ran the following notice:

Purvis Celebration

In recognition of the valued contribution by Richard Purvis, who was one of America's foremost musicians in the field of church music, in celebration of the 90th year of his birth, you are invited by Grace Cathedral and the San Francisco Chapter of the American Guild of Organists to a gala recital of Purvis music for the organ, played by Thomas Hazleton, 3:00 p.m., Sunday, September 7, 2003, Grace Cathedral, San Francisco.[19]

Hazleton performed the following on this all-Purvis program: Fantasia on Ton-y-Botel, Supplication, Thanksgiving, Of Moor and Fen, St. Francis Suite, Dies Irae, Fanfare, Night in Monterey, March Grotesque, and Partita on "Christ ist Erstanden." His encore was an improvisation on Harold Arlen's "Over The Rainbow."[20]

John Shields and Richard Purvis in front of their home, 70 Balceta Avenue, on their way to Richard's 80th birthday celebration, August 15, 1993. Courtesy Donald Braff.

Purvis's Estate

Richard did not have a trust, but in his will he left his estate to John Shields. Douglas Metzler was the executor.[21]

According to Donald Braff, John had a premonition that he, too, would die soon. Following Richard's death, John gathered many items from Richard's library, located on the first floor of their home, and put them on tables. He then invited various organist friends to come by and take any sheet music and manuscripts that they wanted.[22] John had also intentionally stopped taking his medications. He received a call one day from his doctor's office, asking why he hadn't come for a recent appointment. John had told Braff, "No more doctors."

Following Richard's death, Braff continued his weekly lunches with John. On June 14, 1995, when Braff arrived for their lunch, he found John fully dressed in a suit and vest and sitting in a chair, but barely alive. Braff said, "I think he knew what was coming."[23] Donna Parker wrote, "He had his will and insurance policy at his side, everything on the table, for whoever found it."[24] Braff called the paramedics, but when they arrived they found no pulse. They rushed John to the hospital, but Braff received a call about an hour later saying that John had died.[25]

Throughout their time together, Richard and John had been discreet about their relationship, whatever its true nature. Poignantly, Donna Parker wrote: "During Dick's memorial service at Grace Cathedral, they referred to John as Dick's lifelong partner. I was sitting next to John, holding his hand, and he turned to me and said, 'That's the first time that has ever been mentioned in public.'"[26]

John had a trust, and Braff had been appointed successor trustee. The proceeds from Richard's estate went to John's trust (although Richard's estate was still in probate until about a month after John died).

The proceeds of John's trust, which consisted mostly of the Balceta home, were left to John's sister, Louise Geiser, who lived in upstate New York. Most of John's family were in the East, except for Louise's son Tom Geiser, who lived near Vacaville, California.[27] Donna Parker claims, "Tom's mother had no regard for Purvis, because she felt he had stolen her brother." Louise wanted to sell Richard's sheet music, but Tom said there was no money in it.[28]

Tom Geiser lived at the Balceta house part-time until Braff, as trustee, sold it. While Tom was at the house, he began to dispose of the accumulation, giving various items to Goodwill. A dumpster had also been rented for what was left. When Braff, who still visited the house frequently, realized that certain items, including Purvis's collection of manuscripts and sheet music, might be discarded, he asked Tom to hold off until they could find someone to take it.[29]

In the first week of October 1995, Lee Pare called Donna Parker and Jonas Nordwall to advise them about Richard's possessions. Parker relates, "Jonas and I were in Portland. Lee had been helping us with the music project, so he was well aware we needed to get the music out of the house— legally, of course. He and Don [Braff] worked with Tom Geiser (Louise's son and John Shields's nephew) to help him understand the situation. He did. Lee called one day and said that Tom had asked his mother (Louise) about the Purvis music. She asked, 'How much can we get for it?' Tom told her not much, that it was valuable only to a select group of organists, so she said to get it out of the house. We had about a two-day window to accomplish this. When Lee called with the okay, Jonas and I drove down in my mom's Ford Explorer, and loaded it with all the boxes of music. Tom was most happy to see it go to us, and Lee helped load the SUV.... On the way home, Jonas and I were listening to the radio to hear if O. J. Simpson was guilty or not. I remember the verdict coming over the radio and not believing it! So whatever day that was [October 3, 1995], we were driving back to Portland from San Francisco with the library."[30]

Had it not been for Braff, Richard's library and other materials would have been lost. Credit is also due to Tom Geiser for helping to save Purvis's papers. Donna said, "He loved his uncle and would do anything he could for John."[31]

Included in Purvis's estate were his three-manual Rodgers organ and a Steinway piano from around 1910. John had sold the organ for $10,000; he had offered the Steinway to Grace Cathedral, where the gift was declined. The piano was given away or purchased by someone locally.[32]

On February 2, 2012, Donna Parker donated much of Purvis's library, along with other papers and memorabilia, to Stanford University's Archive of Recorded Sound. These materials are accessible to researchers. Most of the original documents used for this book will eventually reside in the Stanford collection as well. Other individuals are encouraged to donate relevant materials to the growing collection.

Purvis's Will and Testament

Although Richard's will did not specify the beneficiary of the royalties from his previous publications, Douglas Metzler, his executor, arranged for these residuals to go to a fund for the organ at Grace Cathedral. This arrangement continues.[33]

Discussions regarding the republication of some of Purvis's organ music began as early as 1992 between Purvis and Fred Bock. In the late 1990s, Tom Hazleton, Donna Parker, and Jonas Nordwall, with input from Lyn Larsen, established an entity called "Friends of Richard Purvis" to perpetuate Purvis's music and memory.[34] Most of Purvis's music was already out of print, and obtaining permissions from the various copyright holders posed a serious challenge. To date the group has been successful in compiling three volumes: *The Organ Music of Richard Purvis,* Vols. 1 and 2, and *Three Christmas Preludes.* They were published by Fred Bock in 2004 and 2006.

Louise Geiser, John Shields's sister, apparently had a change of heart regarding Purvis and gave her blessing to the project in the following memos:

October 4, 2001

Dear Donna,

We have heard from Don Braff concerning the republishing of Dick Purvis' music. I certainly do agree with the republishing of Dick Purvis' music and all the royalties going to the Grace Cathedral's Music department. I'm sure I agreed to this some time ago, so I'm reinforcing that decision with this letter.

I hope you are successful with this endeavor and his music becomes available once again.

Yours truly,

Louise Geiser

Mrs. Louise Geiser

21 Bishops Court

Pittsford, New York 14534-2882

[no date, but envelope postmarked March 10, 2002]

To Whom It May Concern:

I, Louise Geiser, executor to the estate of Richard Purvis, do hereby grant authority to Friends of Richard Purvis, Donna Parker, Executive Director, the right to contact the publishers and copyright holders of Richard Purvis' music, to request that the copyrights be assigned to the Friends of Richard Purvis. In the event that any of these pieces become published or made commercially available, wherein monies are received, all royalties will be payable to the Grace Cathedral Music Department.

Sincerely,

Louise Geiser[35]

Donna Parker wrote: "The proceeds from the newly published music were intended to go to a scholarship/education fund. This was what Stephen Bock and the Friends of Richard Purvis discussed before we began the publishing through Fred Bock Music, but it is my understanding that those proceeds never amounted to very much—at least not enough for a fund. My understanding is that proceeds from his music would go to Grace Cathedral's music department—not necessarily just the organ. This was stated in both letters from Louise Geiser."[36]

Jonas Nordwall clarifies: "Donna may have had conversations with Steve Bock regarding any profits from the three books published by Fred Bock Music. Technically, a portion of the Vols. 1 and 2 should go to the education fund as there were previously unpublished works in those two books. Any profits from the Christmas book goes directly to Grace."[37]

Some of Richard's compositions have never gone out of print, and through the efforts of the Friends of Richard Purvis and others, a number of his out-of-print compositions and recordings are again being made available. Thanks to their dedication, the legacy of Richard Purvis lives on.

Notes

1. Donald Braff, interview, Palo Alto, California, October 5, 2010.
2. Ken Brown, e-mail, December 17, 2010.
3. Rodgers brochure, no date.
4. Postcard postmarked September 20, 1986; postcards courtesy Donald Braff.
5. Donald Braff, interview, Palo Alto, California, October 5, 2010.
6. Vaughn Jones, e-mail, March 23, 2012.
7. Series poster.
8. Recital program.
9. Certificate of death.
10. Donald Braff, interview, Palo Alto, California, October 5, 2010.
11. Certificate of death.
12. Donna Parker, e-mail, September 27 and 30, 2010.
13. Michael Lampen, e-mail, September 26, 2011.
14. Grace Cathedral archives.
15. San Francisco AGO Newsletter, February 1995, 3.
16. Grace Cathedral archives.
17. Grace Cathedral archives.
18. Typescript, courtesy Michael Lampen.

19. San Francisco Chapter AGO newsletter, July & August 2003, 4.

20. Ed Stout wrote, "Tom had last played at Grace Cathedral the week Judy Garland died [June 22, 1969]. He asked Richard Purvis if it would be all right to create a special arrangement of 'Over The Rainbow' in tribute to Garland. Richard said, by all means do so." Ed Stout, e-mail, September 2, 2012.

21. Copy of the will not available.

22. Donald Braff, e-mail, September 17, 2010.

23. Donald Braff, telephone conversation, April 25, 2011.

24. Donna Parker, e-mail, September 27, 2010.

25. Donald Braff, telephone conversation, April 25, 2011.

26. Donna Parker, e-mail, September 26, 2011.

27. Donald Braff, telephone conversation, April 25, 2011.

28. Donna Parker, e-mail, September 27, 2010.

29. Donald Braff, telephone conversation, April 25, 2011.

30. Donna Parker, e-mail, April 27, 2011.

31. Donna Parker, e-mail, September 27, 2010.

32. Donald Braff, telephone conversation, April 25, 2011.

33. Douglas Metzler, telephone conversation, September 23, 2011.

34. Donna Parker, e-mail, September 26, 2011.

35. Letters courtesy Donna Parker.

36. Donna Parker, e-mail, April 7, 2011.

37. Jonas Nordwall, e-mail, April 8, 2011.

chapter 6

purvis as composer

"Composing is a crazy occupation. Some days it goes so fast you can't keep up with it. Others you just sit and stare at a sheet of blank manuscript paper."

"My music is all corn on the cob, but it is GOOD corn on the cob!"

—*Richard Purvis*

Richard Purvis was multi-talented. Many musicians would be satisfied to become proficient in any one area, such as performance or teaching or composing. Purvis excelled in each, and achieved success early in his life. He concertized nationwide; he was known for his inspired service playing; and he was in demand as a teacher. Additionally, he was a widely published composer, with over 100 organ compositions, sacred and secular, and nearly as many vocal works, for both choral and solo voices.

Purvis was a gifted orchestrator, and, according to Ed Stout, he received invitations from Hollywood studios to write for the movies. It must have been hard for the young musician, in the heyday of Hollywood pictures, to decide between studio offers and writing music for the church. But his heart was in sacred music, although it's worth noting that he could have made much more money writing film scores and musicals.

Stout makes this leap in a clever comparison: "He told me that he had been invited to come down to the motion picture industry and write film music. He had been invited by Alfred Newman at Fox and by Max Steiner, but Newman was the more powerful. He didn't do it, and of course he would have been a millionaire had he. I said, 'Well, all you did was spend 40 years writing film music for the Episcopal church, because your Easter partita—I'm sorry—is the perfect score for the silent Ben Hur.' "[1]

Purvis the composer at his writing desk, 1993. Photo by Donna Parker.

Praise for Purvis's Compositional Style

In 1947 Alexander McCurdy wrote an article for *The Etude* magazine, placing his former organ student Purvis alongside other well-known composers:

> For an offertory, for which so many of us must be prepared, there is generally only one type that is effective and appropriate: that is the short, melodious piece with perhaps a soft ensemble of 8' solo with accompaniment. We find that almost every great composer has given us appropriate music for this. "The Little Organ Book" (Orgelbüchlein) by J. S. Bach can be our most important help. Then there are the works of the pre-Bach composers, the wonderful preludes of Brahms, Choral Improvisations of Karg-Elert, and works of Max Reger, and so forth. Americans such as Seth Bingham,

Carl McKinley, Cochrane Penick, Richard Purvis, and many others have written excellent things on chorales and hymns which no organist should be without.

I am perfectly sure that it is much more important to play a simple beautiful thing well which will move the congregation to worship than to play some large work well which will not help them.[2]

A 1953 Aeolian-Skinner "King of Instruments" record jacket states:

Music is usually written because there is an irresistible creative urge to express on the part of the composer or because there seems to be a need for certain types of composition which the composer feels he can fulfill with some degree of success. The latter type bears the somewhat mundane "canard" of "utilitarian" and it is in this category that Richard Purvis classifies himself. Every composition heard on this record was written, either because someone requested he write a specific type of piece, or because he himself needed a definite type of composition for a particular occasion....[3]

This note was included in a 1980 recital program in Fresno, California:

His composing style is marked by rich orchestral color and chromaticism balanced by a distinct modal flair, especially in his solo organ works. The music contains utilitarian warmth and forthright romantic lyricism. His more current compositions consistently appeal to the sophistication of the times but retain sensitivity gained from great cathedral acoustics, their choirs of men and boys and the magnificent Skinner organs."[4]

Stephen Loher wrote:

Richard was a superb orchestrator. I learned so much about orchestration from him. The ones I was most exposed to were his arrangements of the carols we did for the Carol Vespers each year on Advent 4. These included 22 strings, harp, celesta, and organ. He also arranged for brass (again, learned so much!) for the Easter Services—both his own pieces (Lyra Davidica, which was the Easter Procession we used) and arrangements of the hymns we did.[5]

I would describe his compositional style as "mid century" American with a very definite English influence (i.e., the use of triplets which he said gave breadth, and open fifths). He often said the English were the most musical.

He seemed to favor many sources—chant tunes, folk tunes, chorales, hymn tunes—but especially the English style.

I don't know where he developed the "colorist" but I suspect it came from Sabin, McCurdy, and the English influence—they were all into color. Also he grew up during the symphonic organ times and was exposed to many transcriptions and all their color. Then there is the theater organ influence!

His registrations: basically English, but theater organ influences at times in registration. There was a 4' Flute (Lochgedeckt) on the choir with a tremulant on the choir close to a Wurlitzer (thanks to Ed Stout!). It made for a very unique sound in several combinations. That I would say was a signature of his on the Cathedral organ.

As to needing a 4-manual Skinner to perform his music: remember, the 7 Chorale Preludes were written in a foxhole! I remember being a bit astounded at that because I grew up hearing all these things on the Cathedral organ in those acoustics and with all that reverb. But the few times Richard played outside the Cathedral and did his pieces, I saw that they can come off on a smaller, less color-oriented organ. I have also heard other organists play them—that would either bring a smile or make me cringe![6]

In his academic thesis Donald Corbett made astute observations:

Throughout the compositions of Richard Purvis contemporary rhythmic patterns prevail. Besides these, he incorporates modality into his harmonizations and melody. Because improvisation is his main approach, Mr. Purvis chooses to utilize the pedal fully, contrary to traditional literature of the organ, to create dramatic, dynamic, and rhythmic effects. He prefers to treat pedal and manual equally, so that neither can be termed subservient to the other.

There is a spontaneity about Mr. Purvis's sacred choral music. It is unhampered by limitations which would be induced through a strict adherence to an orthodox ecclesiastical style and there is no suggestion of triteness, nor does it descend to the level of the mundane....

The greater portion of his composition uses contemporary rhythmical and harmonic idioms, coupled with medieval modes.[7]

June Townsend also wrote at length in her thesis:

In endeavoring to analyze Purvis' compositions and style, we must consider the reason they were written. Like Bach, creating music for the church service and recital was part of his job. His teachers, Wallace Sabin and Sabin's pupil, Dr. Alexander McCurdy, imbued Richard with the idea that music should do something for the hearer. It should be simple, understandable, satisfying and inspiring so as to direct his mind in worship. Recital playing must have audience appeal and "showmanship," which to Purvis meant of the *music*, not of the performer.

Perhaps his popular broadcast at the Chapel of the Chimes developed the facility that he had as a child to "come home from the movies and play everything I'd heard." Of course, a radio broadcast features the music, not the performer. Popular or theater organ styling involves the taking of a tune and arranging it extemporaneously by ear or by reading the melody and chord symbols from the song sheet and setting up various rhythmic and "voicing" patterns. Styling devices include solo melody above or below the accompanying harmony, duet melody, closed or open harmony, counter-melody and harmonic changes; to say nothing of exploiting all the tonal resources of the organ as an orchestra.

The idea can be extended and elevated into the composition of hymn tune arrangements. (Was not the great J. S. Bach accused of thus "confounding the congregation" and reprimanded?) Following in such a tradition, Purvis has composed the majority of his organ pieces as Chorale Preludes or Fantasias. In the main, his work is in the style of the late German and French Romantic School of Wagner, Reger, Karg-Elert, Franck, Dupré, and Vierne.

His study of Plainsong in the Anglican tradition gives a modal flavor of "High Church" setting to numbers using such canti firmi, while he is just as much at home in writing less austere chorale preludes for organists of freer Protestant services. In fact, one of his latest albums, *Folk Hymn Orisons for Organ*, includes charming arrangements of gospel songs such as "Dwelling in Beulah Land" and "Jesus, Savior, Pilot Me." As a rule his works lie within the range of the ability of the parish organist and student, and have a pleasing, inspirational quality.

His pedal passages are not excessively difficult, although in the toccata-type numbers, the solo is often in the pedal. The pedal ostinato is used in many of his pieces. It gives effective tone painting in the "rocking of the cradle" in "Resonet in Laudibus" (Joseph Dearest, Joseph Mine, Help me Cradle the Child Divine), and in "Greensleeves" (What Child is This?).

Changing rhythms are reflected in successive time signatures. "Introit" employs 5/4, 6/4, and 2/4, which aids the inflection of the Sarum Plainsong, "Christe Redemptor Omnium."

Shifting accents, in keeping with the exuberant character of the text in the "Capriccio" (Burlesca) of the Partita, combined with the startlingly dissonant opening chords (double fifths) of the Toccata of the same work, caused quite a reaction in the staid AGO Convention in San Francisco over a decade ago.

Contrapuntal imitation and canon are employed in some numbers. In "Eklog," the melody follows exactly at an octave lower, forming an interval of a fifth at the third note of the subject. The middle section of the piece places the melody in the pedal with two voices moving in duet style above. The "Prelude" of the Partita has a two-voice canon with pedal ostinato. "Tallis Canon" is quoted in "Contemplation," while "Gevaert" and "Carillon" use rather free three- and four-part imitation. "Ton-y-Botel" has an interesting fugal section. Mr. Purvis' effective arrangement of Bach's "Arioso" adds a beautiful counter-melody above Bach's tune, an effect similar to "Air for the G String."

Chromatic harmonies, of course, are Purvis' trademark. I recall expostulating with him for using a strange chord in the "Wedding March" at the Chapel of the Chimes." His defense was, "Richard Wagner used it," to which I replied, "It sounds like 'Ricard' Purvis to me!" His chromatic chords are generally used for color and modulation, but his cadences establish the feeling of key and basic tonality. Since his compositions are based on a given cantus or hymn tune, the tonality of that tune "brings you down to earth" even though the shifting clouds and rainbows of chromaticism are overhead. Examples of this are: "Liebster Jesu" and the quotation of "Silent Night" in "Carol Rhapsody." "March Grotesque" lives up to its name with a reed fanfare on chords of D answered by the French horn stop on E-flat.

The form used by Purvis is seldom complex, although it often mirrors the text and mood of the cantus or hymn. Sometimes motifs are taken from the tune and developed.

Nothing could be more sublimely simple than "Pax Vobiscum," a late work for the wedding service, in giving the quiet feeling of a blessed benediction. An A and a B melody in the same quarter and half note values sustain the mood. Their repetition changes only at the cadences, contributing to the hypnotically restful effect. There seems to be one melody throughout,

Purvis perusing a musical score, 1993. Photo by Donna Parker.

as the B melody is so much like the A. The melodic phrases are eight bars in length, forming the pattern: Introduction (A₁A₂) (A₁A₂) (B₁B₂) (A₁A₂), Coda. Another simply laid out number is "Les Petites Cloches." One would expect the little tinkling bells to repeat, almost like a music box.

When Purvis sent me the manuscripts of "Four Prayers in Tone," he said, "These are the best things I ever wrote." "Adoration" on the plainsong "Adoro Devote" illustrates his style and incorporates the stylistic features discussed. It opens in D major in 2/2 time with a statement of the first phrase of the cantus in the pedal, ending on an F#. The manuals answer with two sequential phrases starting on an F# chord with chromatic harmonies and expanded intervals a la Cesar Franck. The pedal repeats its cantus, this time starting on B instead of D, and is answered by two phrase motifs from the cantus in chromatic chords starting on G. The hymn phrase is then played in four parts in the dominant G, ending on an F# chord. A pedal passage leads into the "Lento Cantabile" in 4/4 time with melody and accompaniment in modal or chromatic harmony modulating into a return to the pedal statement of the cantus, this time in D minor. This is answered as at the beginning on the manuals with an E-flat chord and chromatic harmonies. The pedal phrase this time starts with E-flat and leads into a complete statement of the hymn in C major in 6/4 to 4/4 time accompanied in the pedal by the theme of the "Lento Cantabile." This modulates to a new section in A-flat major in 2/2 rhythm with a pedal ostinato motif of the first two measures of the cantus against a 34-measure crescendo of chromatic chords that climax on B major and then slowly decrescendo for 34 measures, restating the ostinato motif in the manuals, instead of the pedals, toward the end; and modulating back to the key of A-flat near the close. An orchestral gamut of tone color such as Trumpet, French horn, English horn, Oboe, Strings, and Flutes, Unda Maris and Flute Celeste is used in the decrescendo after the "tutta forza," and Bourdon 32', 16', and Flute 8' give the "Quasi timpani" in the pedal.

One might say that Purvis uses tone painting in this number. The text of the cantus "Adoro Devote" reads: "Humbly I adore thee, Verity unseen, Who thy glory hidest 'neath these shadows mean; Lo, to thee surrendered, my whole heart is bowed, Tranced as it beholds thee, shrined within the cloud." The piece begins with "Adagio mistico" denoting humility; the slow crescendo typifies the glory of the Lord; the decrescendo, the heart bowing in surrender; and the high mystic chords at the close, the "shrined within the cloud."

The style of Purvis' choral writing is similar to his organ works. Frequently he utilized simpler harmonies and unison writing for Boy Choirs. Still, however, there are examples of shifting time signatures, imitation, and tone painting. The latter as used in the "Mass of the Holy Resurrection" (for Bishop Pike) depicts sorrow and joy ("and was buried" and "ascended into heaven"). His recent use of Brass, Tympani, Harp, Piano, Celesta, Finger Cymbals, and Cymbals makes these works more colorful.[8]

June Townsend, Purvis's Trusted Amanuensis

For many years, June Townsend helped Purvis prepare his manuscripts for publication. She made the now-famous "foxhole" reference in her thesis:

> This writer had the privilege of getting in on the "ground floor" of Richard Purvis' career as a composer in doing his manuscript copy work to be sent to the publisher. The first piece was a youthful "Pastoral," also "Dream Vision," a song. After he went to Curtis, "Communion," "Idyl," "Romanza," came; and then he began putting his numbers into groups of Suites. His organ pieces are generally written on a hymn tune and are for church use. Many pieces were dated from his war years, and he says that his popular "Greensleeves" was written in a "foxhole."[9]

In 1995 Townsend reminisced:

> He liked my music copy work, and showed me one of his first pieces called "Dream Vision"—"I see her face, my lady fair with rose hued hands and silken hair, And through she smiles and beckons to me, I sigh, for 'tis but a Vision I see." He said it was why organists stay awake nights. He said, when half asleep he could hear beautiful music; but if he got up to write it down, it was gone.
>
> After my father died and our house burned down,[10] he said I could do copy work for him to pay for my lessons.[11]

Below is correspondence regarding her collaboration with the composer:

All Saints Day

> Here we go again and as usual, I'm in a hurry. I promised a score to the Church of the Advent, Boston, by September fifteenth and just looked at the calendar! However, I've completely rewritten the Sanctus—added a

Benedictus Qui Venit and a Gloria in Excelsis and done the whole of the accompaniment over. So I haven't been asleep.

Please do (as quickly as you can) a full score (large paper) for Charles [George] Faxon, Church of the Advent, Boston, Massachusetts.[12]

Townsend says that the ledger gives the date of this work as November 1948.[13]

July 31, 1951

Enclosed please find MS. of Divertissement,[14] of which I would like to have two copies made. I have written it for E. Power Biggs, and I want to get a copy off to him as soon as possible.... Perhaps I should warn you that there will be some more things coming along in the near future.[15]

September 7, 1951

On the enclosed MSS. will you please make one copy each of "Marche Grotesque" and "Les Petites Cloches." I would like to have these just as soon as possible as Virgil Fox wants to use them on his tour starting in October. On the other MS. will you please make one copy each of "Introit" and "Elevation" only.... I would like to have these as soon as possible as well, as Mr. William Teague wants to use them in his programs.[16]

Donna Parker noted that, after Townsend died, Dale Wood (who achieved success as a composer) also did transcription work for Purvis.[17]

Purvis on Composition

In the early 1970s, Purvis's former organ student Keith Chapman conducted the following interview with Purvis on a radio program:

> Keith Chapman: Richard Purvis's music has always been very greatly accepted and admired by congregations and listeners at organ recitals; however, organists have often felt that his music lacks the technical display and intellectual depth that they would like in their music. Whether this is effete snobbery or a true professional judgment is difficult to say; however, I discussed this with Mr. Purvis this past summer when I met with him in August, and here are his views on his aims in composition.

Richard Purvis: I believe that music is for people, and we should consider the average man in the pew as our sort of modicum of measure. There is a great temptation, when you're writing, to be clever, and as you get clever, you get more clever, and the more clever you become, the more ingenious and the more involved becomes your writing, so that it takes a performer who has the music before him to comprehend what you're doing. I am more on a trend of simplify, simplify, simplify. I think that probably this is going to win a good deal more friends for the organ than if we get overly active in contrapuntal devices and that sort of thing. It's very difficult to write simply. It's much more simple to write in a complex manner because it covers up flaws. When you write simply, every note counts.[18]

Donna Parker recalls Purvis's description of the process of composing: "You get a package of well sharpened pencils, a trash can, and lots of paper!"[19]

In a letter to Lamont Crape, dated Thanksgiving 1991, Purvis wrote:

Here's your piece [Soliloquy]! I hope you enjoy playing it with as much pleasure as I had writing it. This one did not come easily at first, but once the conception solidified, it progressed with greater ease. I've tried to use the organ's colors to the greatest advantage, but don't hesitate to change any registration you deem fit.

As usual I have to apologize for my terrible manuscript. I hope with the aid of a magnifying glass and two pairs of glasses you may be able to decipher my hieroglyphics. I have not employed many expression marks and no phrasing, leaving this up to your own good taste.

Since this is the only copy, sometime along the line (when it's convenient) would you please send me a Xerox for my collection? However, I want you to have the original.

May you and Marie enjoy a Happy and Blessed Thanksgiving Season.
All the best, Dick[20]

In another letter to Lamont Crape, dated June 9, 1992, Purvis again wrote:

Here are the "Fountain" and the "Moon."[21] (Imagine my giving you the "moon" when I've never owned it myself! (Such arrogance!)

Purvis at his writing desk, 1993. Photo by Donna Parker.

Sorry to be so slow in getting it to you, but I seem to go "Molto adagio" these days. But thanks be to God, at least I go!

When you see Nick [?], please tell him I'm not at all happy with the first two drafts of his piece and that I'm about to start a third. Composing is a crazy occupation. Some days it goes so fast you can't keep up with it. Others you just sit and stare at a sheet of blank manuscript paper.

My love to Marie and yourself.

Dick[22]

Purvis's Creative Techniques

Following are selected passages from the prefaces to two volumes of Purvis's music, republished in 2004. No authorship is given; however, Donna Parker and Steven Bock stated that they represent the collaboration of Donna Parker, Jonas Nordwall, Tom Hazleton, and Ed Stout.

Richard Purvis did not limit his visions to only traditional organ sound, but always looked at the possibilities to create the best musical results. He taught his students how to make music that was meaningful, full of interest and performed with the highest musical integrity. . . .

The Chorale "O Sacred Head Now Wounded" was composed using four staves. Richard routinely would prepare each rough draft using a single staff for each manual, later condensing the manuscript to the standard three stave copy. Tom [Hazleton] felt that the range of notes exceeded the practical printing range on three staves, so the original four stave version was retained.[23]

Many agree with Tom Hazleton that only Richard could write such a soaring, intoxicating melody as found in *Romanza*. Both Virgil [Fox] and Ted [Alan Worth] frequently used this piece in many of their concerts. The Purvis orchestration requires a very romantic Clarinet for the main section's melody. As a musical foil, Purvis uses Flutes at 4' and 1-3/5' for the scherzo section.

Manual bridging is a trademark Purvis manual technique, requiring playing two manuals with one hand. Sometimes on four manual organs, Richard would play all four manuals simultaneously. This was learned from carefully watching the great early 20th century organists who created the symphonic, orchestral style of organ playing.[24]

Further Observations on Purvis as a Composer

Purvis's music clearly draws on a variety of sources as diverse as folk tunes, Gregorian chant, European cathedral music, and Hollywood film scores. Whether dramatic or simple, there is often a strong rhythmic pulse in the organ pedal, and usually a harmonic surprise somewhere in the piece.

Townsend wrote about the dichotomy of styles popular in Purvis's day: "Some musicians criticize Mr. Purvis' style as being reactionary in tonal language while others say that he is bringing the popular idioms of our day into the church."[25] Townsend also cited the following passage from a 1967 article by G. C. Ramsey in *The American Organist*:

> Mr. Purvis is obviously a not-too-modern 20th century Romanticist at heart, and his music often shows the problems of trying to update a previous historical period—harmonies which once were daring, pass quickly into the possession of popular composers and of people writing for films, television, and so forth. Possibly one of the problems of 20th century

organ music in America is that we have never quite decided whether the organ is a purely sacred instrument, or whether it is a concert instrument as well. An attempt to reach both a sacred and a secular audience is frustrating, and one often wishes that Mr. Purvis' harmonies would do one or the other.[26]

Clarence Snyder, a classmate of Purvis's at Curtis, wrote: "I was in Dr. Alexander McCurdy's organ class with Richard Purvis, Walter Baker, Claribel Thompson, and Jack Cook from 1935–1936.... He [Purvis] had perfect pitch, you know, and could play anything he heard. He and I went to see Robin Hood [*The Adventures of Robin Hood,* 1938, score by Korngold]. We came back to St. James and he played most of the score on the organ by ear."[27]

Rodgers Jenkins, the Rodgers Organ Company executive who often hosted Purvis as a houseguest when Purvis concertized in Portland, Oregon, said that Purvis would go upstairs to the office and compose music without a piano or keyboard.[28]

According to Donna Parker, Purvis "never cared about getting his music published. It was John Shields who asked him to and encouraged him to get his music published." Parker also said that Purvis didn't ask for enough money for his commissions. "He had come through the Depression, and got by on as little as possible, on limited resources."[29]

Jack Bethards recalls a self-effacing remark made by Purvis during a talk at the San Anselmo Organ Festival: "I am what might be called a *utility composer*—I try to write music that people can use."[30]

Lyn Larsen commented, "Because of his whole gorgeous Anglican tradition and male choir, a lot of his organ writing reflects Vaughan Williams, a little bit of Delius."[31]

In the lighthearted vein of Ed Stout, Jonas Nordwall quipped: "Richard wrote 'Episcopal cocktail music.' He was never conservative about the texture." He also said that Richard was fascinated by MIDI and other technological advances on organs.[32]

Carrying the "corny" comparison even further, Vaughn Jones, a student of Purvis in the late 1980s, wrote, "About his own compositions he told me more than once: 'My music is all corn on the cob, but it is GOOD corn on the cob!'"[33]

Notes

1. Ed Stout interview.

2. Alexander McCurdy, "Helping the Congregation to Worship through Organ Music," *The Etude*, January 1947, 17; cited in Townsend thesis, 25; original unavailable.

3. Author unknown. Aeolian-Skinner Presents The King of Instruments, Vol. 5, "The Music of Richard Purvis," Made by the Aeolian-Skinner Organ Company, Inc., Boston, Massachusetts, 1953.

4. Anonymous program notes in recital program, University Presbyterian Church, Fresno, California, March 9, 1980.

5. Stephen Loher, e-mail, June 6, 2009.

6. Stephen Loher, e-mail, May 30, 2009.

7. Corbett, 30, 44.

8. Townsend thesis, 43–50.

9. Townsend thesis, 24.

10. Date unknown; ironically she would lose her home a second time to fire in the 1980s.

11. Townsend Memories, 1995.

12. Memo from Richard Purvis, cited in Townsend thesis, 30.

13. Townsend thesis, 30.

14. No composition by this title survives; he is probably referring to the Capriccio from *Partita on "Christ ist Erstanden,"* composed in 1951.

15. Townsend thesis, 30.

16. Townsend thesis, 31.

17. Donna Parker, e-mail, September 27, 2010.

18. Audio file of radio program from early 1970s, courtesy Ray Biswanger.

19. Donna Parker, interview, September 27, 2010.

20. Copy of letter in possession of the author.

21. "Jeu d'eau" and "Claire de lune" for organ and harp, commissioned by Kenneth Starr; unpublished. Crape was also a harpist, and Purvis shared these pieces with Crape.

22. Copy of letter in possession of the author.

23. Musical Notes, *The Organ Music of Richard Purvis*, Vol. 1, H. T. FitzSimons, 2004, 5.

24. Musical Notes, *The Organ Music of Richard Purvis*, Vol. 2, H. T. FitzSimons, 2004, 4.

25. Townsend thesis, 51.

26. G. C. Ramsey, "The Aeolian-Skinner Record Series," *The American Organist*, March 1967, Vol. 50, No. 3, 21–23.

27. Clarence Snyder, letter to James Welch, November 1, 2010.

28. Rodgers Jenkins, telephone conversation, November 1, 2010.

29. Donna Parker, e-mail, September 27, 2010.

30. Jack Bethards, telephone conversation, November 30, 2010.

31. Lyn Larsen, telephone interview, December 1, 2010.

32. Jonas Nordwall, e-mail, September 27, 2010.

33. Vaughn Jones, e-mail, March 23, 2012.

Interior view of the unfinished Grace Cathedral, 1961. Photo by Proctor Jones. Courtesy Proctor Jones Family.

chapter 7

The Organ Works of Richard Purvis

Perhaps it is well that the "King of Instruments" can bring forth a chuckle as well as a mood of exaltation.

—*Richard Purvis*

Most of Purvis's early works were published by Sprague-Coleman, Inc., and Leeds Music Corporation, both located in New York City. Lou Levy (1912–1995), whose career began on Tin Pan Alley in the 1930s, established Leeds Music in 1935. (The name "Leeds" came from the name of a suit he and his famed colleague Sammy Cahn took turns wearing "in their hungry early days.")[1] In 1946 Levy purchased the Sprague-Coleman catalogue,[2] and in 1964 MCA Music bought out the Leeds Music Group.[3] Beginning in the 1950s, Purvis used numerous publishers elsewhere in the U.S.A.

This chapter lists all of Purvis's known organ compositions. Each entry includes the title of the piece, the subtitle if any, the name of the dedicatee if there is one (in parentheses), and other descriptive information as given in the publication; the publisher, date, and text of the foreword if one appears.

Following this section, beginning on page 250, is an alphabetized list of the individual compositions and movements, with publication details for each.

A note of explanation regarding the complicated chronology of some of Purvis's early and most frequently published pieces may be helpful:

The collections *Five Pieces on Gregorian Themes* and *Four Carol Preludes* were not published as bound sets, but rather as single pieces released separately within a few months.

The April 1940 issue of *Overtones* at Curtis reported that Purvis had composed a "Suite on Gregorian Themes" and "three Christmas Carols," although it does not specify the carol titles.[4]

According to the Biographical Data, *Five Pieces on Gregorian Themes* was accepted for publication in January 1940 by Sprague-Coleman, and in the summer of 1940 *Four Carol Preludes* was accepted by Sprague-Coleman.[5]

The Diapason reported of Purvis in December 1941: "His latest work, published this month by Sprague-Coleman ... is the first of a series of four carol preludes on the well-known Christmas song 'What Child Is This?'"[6] This assertion conflicts with subsequent statements by June Townsend and others that Purvis wrote "Greensleeves" "in a foxhole" during the war. Furthermore, no 1941 publication of "Greensleeves" has been located.

In August 1942, *The Diapason* reported, "For organ there are 'Five Pieces on Gregorian Themes' (three of which are in print and the other two soon to be issued by Sprague-Coleman) and a 'Carol Rhapsody.'"[7]

When Leeds took over Sprague-Coleman in 1946, the company probably continued to distribute some of the Sprague-Coleman singles, while beginning to publish others under the Leeds name. Leeds also continued to publish all nine of the pieces as singles well into the 1950s.

In 1957 Leeds combined the two anthologies, supplementing them with "Romanza" and "Carol Rhapsody" to create *Leeds' Organ Selections by Richard Purvis*. When MCA Music acquired Leeds in 1964, the collection was renamed *Eleven Pieces for the Church Organist*, although it continued to show the year 1957 as the copyright and publication date in subsequent editions.

Detailed commentary about individual compositions, as well as complete prefatory material to the anthologies, is found in the notes at the end of this chapter.

Published Works for Organ Solo

All Glory, Laud and Honor (Processional)
Leeds, 1963
(For the Very Reverend C. Julian Bartlett, Dean of Grace Cathedral)
"Organ Solo With SATB or Unison Chorus"
(Introduction, accompaniment, and interludes)

An American Organ Mass[8]
> Flammer, 1953
> Based on Carols and Hymns
> (Dedicated to Joseph Whiteford, Vice President of the Aeolian-Skinner
> Organ Company)
>> Prélude Solennel (Veni Emmanuel)
>> Introit (Christe Redemptor Omnium)
>> Offertory (Resonet in Laudibus)
>> Interlude (Corner)
>> Elevation (Vom Himmel hoch)
>> Communion (Gevaert)
>> Carillon (Puer Nobis Nascitur)

Andante Cantabile (for Douglas Steven Cortright [Metzler])
> Apogee Press, 1971
> Arranged by the composer from his work "Pièce Symphonique" (a con-
> certo for organ, strings, harp and timpani)

Carol Rhapsody (1941)
> see *Leeds' Organ Selections by Richard Purvis*, Leeds, 1957

Dialogue Monastique, for 2 organs (based on plainsong "Te Deum" and
"Dies Irae")
> Apogee Press, 1972, sole distributor, World Library Publications,
> Cincinnati
> ("For Earl Ness and William Whitehead, who first recorded it")[9]

Eleven Pieces for the Church Organist
> MCA Music, copyright date 1957 (but probably published 1964 and
> after)
> (Except for some brief program notes added to this MCA edition, con-
> tents are identical to *Leeds' Organ Selections by Richard Purvis*, Leeds,
> 1957; see below.)

Five Baroquisms
  Gentry, 1972
    Air for Flute Stops (Arne)
    Andante Sostenuto (Bach)
    Les Fifres (d'Andrieu)
    Musette en Rondeau (Rameau)
    Siciliano (Bach)

Five Classical Airs for Organ
  "Freely Transcribed and Edited by Richard Purvis"
  Sacred Songs, Waco, Texas, 1966
    Rigaudon (Campra)
    Aria (Handel)
    Trumpet Tune (Purcell)
    Arioso (Bach)
    Psalm XIX (Marcello)

Five Classical Airs for Organ, Vol. II
  "Freely Transcribed and Edited by Richard Purvis"
  Sacred Songs, Waco, Texas, 1967
    Trumpet Voluntary (Stanley)
    Larghetto (Handel)
    Sketch in D Flat (Schumann)
    Psalm XVIII (Marcello)
    Trumpet Voluntary (Purcell)

Five Classical Airs for Organ, Vol. III
  "Freely Transcribed and Edited by Richard Purvis"
  Word, 1972 (Waco, Texas)
    Trumpet Tune (Stanley)
    Largo (Vivaldi)
    Noel (Balbastre)
    Sicilienne (van den Gheyn)
    Caprice (Greene)

Five Folk Hymn Orisons for Organ
>   Sacred Songs, 1966
>> A Prayer of Aspiration (Beulah Land)
>> A Prayer for Guidance (Jesus Savior, Pilot Me)
>> A Prayer of Confidence (Dwelling in Beulah Land)
>> A Prayer of Consecration (Have Thine Own Way, Lord)
>> A Prayer of Patriotism (America, the Beautiful)

Five Pieces on Gregorian Themes
>   Leeds (not published as a bound set but as singles)
>> Vexilla Regis (for Palmer Christian) (Leeds, 1943)
>> Dies Irae (for Virgil Fox) (Sprague-Coleman, 1942)
>> Divinum Mysterium (for Richard Keys Biggs) (Leeds, 1942)
>> Kyrie Eleison (for Dr. Charles M. Courboin) (Sprague-Coleman, 1943)
>> Communion (for Alexander McCurdy) (Sprague-Coleman, 1941)

Four Carol Preludes
>   Leeds (not published as a bound set but as singles)
>> Greensleeves (for Claribel G. Thomson) (Leeds, 1944)
>> Spiritual (for Claude Murphee) [actually Murphree] (Leeds, 1947)
>> Chartres (Noël Varié) (for Marshall Bidwell) (Sprague-Coleman, 1946)
>> Gwalshmai [sic; Gwalchmai] (for Dr. C. Harold Einecke) (Leeds, 1948)

Four Dubious Conceits[10]
>   Flammer, 1952
>> Cantilena: Green Boughs (for Harold [actually Harrold] Hawley)
>> Les Petites Cloches (for Sister M. Carola, C.S.A.)[11]
>> Nocturne (Night in Monterey) (for Janie Craig)[12]
>> Marche Grotesque (for Carl Mueller)

Four Prayers in Tone (to John W. Shields)[13]
>   M. Witmark & Sons, 1951
>> Repentance (La Trobe) (finished July 25, 1950)
>> Adoration (Adoro devote)
>> Supplication (Eisleben)
>> Thanksgiving (finished October 5, 1950, Grace Cathedral)

Gentle Moods[14]
    Gentry, 1971
        Autumn Soliloquy (for Larry Vannucci)
        Lilliburlero (for Donna Parker)
        Plaintive Blue (for Helen Dell)
        An Erin Lilt (for Patricia O'Leary)
        Melody in Mauve (for Bill Thomson)

Greensleeves (for Claribel G. Thomson)
    Leeds, 1944[15]

Idyl (for Gaylord Carter)[16]
    Oliver Ditson, 1943 (later published as "A Sylvan Idylle," Gentry, 1973)
    Includes registrations for Pipe and Hammond Organ

In Retrospect (Three Miniatures for Organ)
    in *Artists' Performance Collection*, Volume One, Sonos, 1984 (From the
    Rodgers Organ Company Library of Music, Edited by Darwin Wolford)
        1. A Joyous Procession (for Darwin Wolford)
        2. Rimembranza (for Joyce Jones)
        3. Roundelay (for Dan Semer)

Introspection (1969)
    in *Quiet Reflections*, an Anthology Compiled by Dale Wood
    Sacred Music Press, 1994

Leeds' Organ Selections by Richard Purvis, Leeds, 1957*
    Greensleeves (for Claribel G. Thomson) (Leeds, 1944)
        Spiritual (for Claude Murphee) [actually Murphree] (Leeds, 1947)
        Chartres (Noël Varié) (for Marshall Bidwell) (Sprague-Coleman, 1946)
        Gwalshmai [sic; Gwalchmai] (for Dr. C. Harold Einecke) (Leeds, 1948)
        Kyrie Eleison (for Dr. Charles M. Courboin) (Sprague-Coleman, 1943)

---

* Includes contents of *Four Carol Preludes* and *Five Pieces on Gregorian Themes* and two
additional pieces. Compare with *Eleven Pieces for the Church Organist*, MCA, 1957.

Vexilla Regis (for Palmer Christian) (Leeds, 1943)
Dies Irae (for Virgil Fox) (Sprague-Coleman, 1942)
Romanza (for Roland Diggle) (Sprague-Coleman, 1943)
Carol Rhapsody (for Floyd Wright) (Leeds, 1941)[17]
Divinum Mysterium (for Richard Keys Biggs) (Leeds, 1942)
Communion (for Alexander McCurdy) (Sprague-Coleman, 1941)

Lyra Davidica (Processional)
Leeds, 1963
Dedicated to the Reverend Canon David Forbes, Headmaster, Cathedral School for Boys
Organ solo (not a choral accompaniment)
(Also arranged for Organ, Brass, and Tympani)

Meditation on "Rockingham"
in *Impressions*, Organ Service Music, Vol. 1 (Communion, Lent Easter)
Fred Bock Music Company, 1985

Organ Music from Grace Cathedral
The Sacred Music Press, 1969
Cortège (A Solemn Processional) (In Memoriam Alma de Bretteville Spreckels)[18]
Three Novelettes (Dedicated to Reginald Greenbrook)
Novelette I[19]
Novelette II
Novelette III[20]
Undulato (for Bill Thomson)[21]
Toccata Marina (for George Thalben-Ball)[22]
A Retrospection (for Richard Thomasson)[23]

The Organ Music of Richard Purvis, Vol. 1[24]
H. T. FitzSimons [Fred Bock], 2004
O Sacred Head, Now Wounded [previously unpublished]
Gwalshmai [*sic*; Gwalchmai] (for Dr. C. Harold Einecke)
Greensleeves (for Claribel G. Thomson)

Carol Rhapsody (for Floyd Wright)
Lilliburlero (for Donna Parker)

The Organ Music of Richard Purvis, Vol. 2
    H. T. FitzSimons [Fred Bock], 2004
        Romanza (for Roland Diggle)
        Wedding March (To Gifford Coombs) [*sic*; Combs] [previously unpublished]
        Communion (for Alexander McCurdy)
        Melody in Mauve (for Bill Thomson)
        An Erin Lilt (for Patricia O'Leary)

Partita on the Easter Chorale "Christ ist Erstanden"[25]
    M. Witmark & Sons, 1952
    (for E. Power Biggs in sincere admiration)
        Prelude
        Canzone
        Capriccio
        Lento
        Toccata

Romanza (1943)
    see *Leeds' Organ Selections by Richard Purvis*, Leeds, 1957

St. Francis Suite: Impressions on the Writings of St. Francis[26]
    J. Fischer & Bro., 1964
        Ascription (for Dr. Philip Steinhaus)
        Hymn to the Moon (for Dr. Searle Wright)
        Earth Carol (for William Duncan)
        Canticle of the Sun (for Dr. Robert Baker)

Seven Chorale Preludes on Tunes Found in American Hymnals[27]
    Carl Fischer, 1949
        Fantasia (Ton-y-botel) (to Ruth Barrett Arno)[28]

Pastorale (Forest Green) (to George Henninger)
Canzona (Liebster Jesu) (to Frederic Freeman)
Grand Choeur (Austria) (to Porter Heaps)
Contemplation (Tallis' Canon) (to Alma Morse)
Poeme Mystique (Manna/Mercy) (to Sally Harris)[29]
Toccata Festiva (In Babilone) (to Clarence Snyder)

Seven Folk Tone Poems for the Organ
  Sacred Songs, 1968
    Of Moor and Fen (for Frank Taylor)
    Brigg Fayre (for Tom Hazleton)
    Of Sea and Skye (for Lyn Larsen)
    A Highland Ayre (for Keith Chapman)
    Of Banks and Braes (for John Seng)
    A Sussex Lament (for Roy Darley)
    From the Hebrides (for Jerry Borrevik)

A Solemn Music
  H. W. Gray, 1971
  "Commissioned by David McK. Williams on the occasion of the International Congress of Organists, 1957, London, England"
  "In Memoriam, The Right Rev. Karl Morgan Block, late Bishop of the Diocese of California"

Suite for a Musical Clock, For the Organ, by George Friedrich Handel[30]
  Flammer, 1952
  Edited by Richard Purvis
  I. Prelude; II. Air; III. A Voluntary on a Flight of Angels; IV. Sonata (for Bells); V. Menuet; VI. Gigue

Sylvan Idylle, A (for Gaylord Carter)
  Gentry, 1973[31] (originally published as "Idyl," Ditson, 1943)
  With registrations for Concert Organ, Theatre Organ, and Hammond Organ

Three Carol Preludes
> Gentry, 1985
>> Contemplation (Picardy) (for Ted Alan Worth)
>> Poème Mystique (It Came Upon a Midnight Clear)
>> (for Charles van Bronkhorst)[32]
>> Caravan of the Three Kings (We Three Kings) (for Terry Charles)

Three Christmas Preludes (reissue of *Three Carol Preludes,* Gentry, 1985)
> Fred Bock, 2006
>> Contemplation: Let All Mortal Flesh Keep Silence
>> Poème Mystique: It Came Upon the Midnight Clear
>> Caravan of the Three Kings: We Three Kings

Three Fanciful Concepts
> Flammer, 1967
>> Fête joyeuse (for Rodney Hansen)
>> A Lamentation of Jeremiah (for Dr. Fred Tulan)
>>> First Performance Salisbury Cathedral, July 31, 1965
>> Rondo (For Pedals alone) (Homage à Moscheles) (Respectfully inscribed to Signor Antonio Ruffatti, Fratelli Ruffatti, Fabrica Organi, Padova)[33]

Three Pieces for Organ[34]
> J. Fischer, 1954
>> Prayer for Peace (for William Teague)
>> Elegy (In memoriam Richard Ross, head of Organ Department Peabody Conservatory 1941–1954)
>> Capriccio (On the Notes of the Cuckoo) (for Thomas Warren)

A Trio of Contrasts[35]
> Flammer, 1965
>> Pax vobiscum (for Jeanette Bartlett-Devine)[36]
>> Eklog (for Marlan Allen)
>> Fanfare (for Lewis Bruun)

Two Liturgical Dances (in *Mixture IV*, compositions by Elmore, Purvis, Wyton, Young)
Flammer, 1970
  Sarabande for a Day of Solemnity (for George Wright)
  Passepied for a Joyous Festival (for George Wright)

Published Works for Organ with Other Instruments

Larghetto Cantabile, for classical guitar and organ
  Apogee Press, 1971; World Library, sole distributor
  Arranged by Purvis from Petit Concert Champêtre (1972)

Lyra Davidica, for brass, tympani and organ
  Leeds, 1943

Petit Concert Champêtre (Hommage à Boccherini), organ and harp, or organ and harpsichord or piano
  Apogee Press, 1972; World Library, sole distributor
  (for Linda Hargis and Dale Wood)
    Allegretto rustico
    Larghetto cantabile
    Allegro giocoso

Suite for Piano and Organ: From the Sierra
  Gentry Publications, Theodore Presser, 1970
  Reprinted in 1977, Gentry; front cover gives title as "Sierra Suite," but contents the same
    I. Bell Prelude (Mountain Majesty) (for Hal Schutz)
    II. Pastorale d'Été (Laughing Waters) (for Kay Chenoweth)
    III. Capriccio Espagnole (Echoes from an Abandoned Hacienda) (for Bud Iverson)
    IV. Harmonies du Soir (The Forest at Eventide) (for Art Chenoweth)
    V. Scherzo (Burlesca) (Of Wind and Rain) (for Dewey Cagle)

The Published Organ Works of Richard Purvis
Alphabetical List of Individual Works and Movements

Title	Dedicatee	Publisher or Collection
Adoration (Adoro devote)	John W. Shields	Four Prayers in Tone, Witmark, 1951
Air for Flute Stops (Arne)		Five Baroquisms, Gentry, 1972
All Glory, Laud and Honor	The Very Reverend C. Julian Bartlett	Introduction and accompaniment to SATB hymn Leeds, 1963
Andante Sostenuto (Bach)		Five Baroquisms, Gentry, 1972
Andante Cantabile	Douglas Metzler	From Pièce Symphonique, unpublished; this movement arranged for solo organ and published by Apogee Press, 1971
Aria (Handel)		Five Classical Airs, Sacred Songs, 1966
Arioso (Bach)		Five Classical Airs, Sacred Songs, 1966
Ascription	Philip Steinhaus	St. Francis Suite, Fischer, 1964
Autumn Soliloquy	Larry Vannucci	Gentle Moods, Gentry, 1971
Brigg Fayre	Tom Hazleton	Seven Folk Tone Poems, Sacred Songs, 1968
Canticle of the Sun	Robert Baker	St. Francis Suite, Fischer, 1964
Cantilena	Harrold Hawley	Four Dubious Conceits, Flammer, 1952
Canzona (Liebster Jesu)	Frederic Freeman	Seven Chorale Preludes, Fischer, 1949
Canzone	E. Power Biggs	Partita on "Christ ist Erstanden," Witmark, 1952
Capriccio	E. Power Biggs	Partita on "Christ ist Erstanden," Witmark, 1952
Capriccio (On the Notes of the Cuckoo)	Thomas Warren	Three Pieces for Organ, Fischer, 1954
Caprice (Greene)		Five Classical Airs, Vol. 3, Word, 1972
Caravan of the Three Kings (We Three Kings)	Terry Charles	Three Carol Preludes, Gentry, 1985; Three Christmas Preludes, Fred Bock, 2006
Carillon (Puer Nobis Nascitur)	Joseph Whiteford	An American Organ Mass, Flammer, 1953
Carol Rhapsody	Floyd Wright	Leeds, 1941 (single); Leeds' Organ Selections by Richard Purvis, Leeds, 1957; Eleven Pieces for the Church Organist, MCA, 1957; The Organ Music of Richard Purvis, Vol. 1, FitzSimons, 2004
Chartres	Marshall Bidwell	Sprague-Coleman, 1946 (single); Four Carol Preludes, Leeds; Leeds' Organ Selections by Richard Purvis, Leeds, 1957; Eleven Pieces for the Church Organist, MCA, 1957

Title	Dedicatee	Publisher or Collection
Communion	Alexander McCurdy	Sprague-Coleman, 1941 (single); Five Pieces on Gregorian Themes, Leeds; Leeds' Organ Selections by Richard Purvis, Leeds, 1957; Eleven Pieces for the Church Organist, MCA, 1957
Communion (Gevaert)	Joseph Whiteford	An American Organ Mass, Flammer, 1953
Contemplation (Picardy)	Ted Alan Worth	Three Carol Preludes, Gentry, 1985; Three Christmas Preludes, Fred Bock, 2006
Contemplation (Tallis' Canon)	Alma Morse	Seven Chorale Preludes, Fischer, 1949
Cortège	Alma de Bretteville Spreckels	Organ Music from Grace Cathedral, Sacred Music Press, 1969; Sacred Organ Folio, No. 1, Lorenz, 1970; Organ Music for Lent and Easter, Sacred Music Press, 1971
Dialogue Monastique	Earl Ness and William Whitehead	Apogee Press, 1972
Dies Irae	Virgil Fox	Sprague-Coleman, 1942 (single); Five Pieces on Gregorian Themes, Leeds; Leeds' Organ Selections by Richard Purvis, Leeds, 1957; Eleven Pieces for the Church Organist, MCA, 1957
Divinum Mysterium	Richard Keys Biggs	Leeds, 1942 (single); Five Pieces on Gregorian Themes, Leeds; Leeds' Organ Selections by Richard Purvis, Leeds, 1957; Eleven Pieces for the Church Organist, MCA, 1957
Earth Carol	William Duncan	St. Francis Suite, Fischer, 1964
Eklog	Marlan Allen	A Trio of Contrasts, Flammer, 1965
Elegy	Richard Ross	Three Pieces for Organ, Fischer, 1954
Elevation (Vom Himmel hoch)	Joseph Whiteford	An American Organ Mass, Flammer, 1953
Erin Lilt, An	Patricia O'Leary	Gentle Moods, Gentry, 1971; The Organ Music of Richard Purvis, Vol. 2, FitzSimons, 2004
Fanfare	Lewis Bruun	A Trio of Contrasts, Flammer, 1965
Fantasia (Ton-y-botel)	Ruth Barrett Arno	Seven Chorale Preludes, Fischer, 1949
Fête joyeuse	Rodney Hansen	Three Fanciful Concepts, Flammer, 1967
From the Hebrides	Jerry Borrevik	Seven Folk Tone Poems, Sacred Songs, 1968
Grand Choeur (Austria)	Porter Heaps	Seven Chorale Preludes, Fischer, 1949

Title	Dedicatee	Publisher or Collection

Greensleeves	Claribel G. Thompson	Leeds, 1944 (single);
		Four Carol Preludes, Leeds;
		Leeds' Organ Selections by Richard Purvis,
		  Leeds, 1957;
		Eleven Pieces for the Church Organist, MCA,
		  1957;
		Oxford Book of Christmas Organ Music, Oxford,
		  1995;
		The Organ Music of Richard Purvis, Vol. 1,
		  FitzSimons, 2004

Gwalshmai [sic; Gwalchmai]	C. Harold Einecke	Leeds, 1948 (single);
		Four Carol Preludes, Leeds;
		Leeds' Organ Selections by Richard Purvis,
		  Leeds, 1957;
		Eleven Pieces for the Church Organist, MCA,
		  1957;
		The Organ Music of Richard Purvis, Vol. 1,
		  FitzSimons, 2004

Highland Ayre, A	Keith Chapman	Seven Folk Tone Poems, Sacred Songs, 1968
Hymn to the Moon	Searle Wright	St. Francis Suite, Fischer, 1964
Idyl	Gaylord Carter	Oliver Ditson, 1943; republished as "A Sylvan Idylle," Gentry, 1973
Interlude (Corner)	Joseph Whiteford	An American Organ Mass, Flammer, 1953
Introit (Christe Redemptor Omnium)	Joseph Whiteford	An American Organ Mass, Flammer, 1953
Introspection		In Quiet Reflections, Sacred Music Press, 1994
Joyous Procession, A	Darwin Wolford	In "In Retrospect," Artists' Performance Collection, Sonos, 1984

Kyrie Eleison	Charles M. Courboin	Sprague-Coleman, 1943 (single);
		Five Pieces on Gregorian Themes, Leeds;
		Leeds' Organ Selections by Richard Purvis,
		  Leeds, 1957;
		Eleven Pieces for the Church Organist, MCA,
		  1957

Lamentation of Jeremiah, A	Fred Tulan	Three Fanciful Concepts, Flammer, 1967
Larghetto (Handel)		Five Classical Airs, Vol. 2, Sacred Songs, 1967
Largo (Vivaldi)		Five Classical Airs, Vol. 3, Word, 1972
Lento	E. Power Biggs	Partita on "Christ ist Erstanden," Witmark, 1952
Les Fifres (d'Andrieu)		Five Baroquisms, Gentry, 1972
Les Petites Cloches	Sister M. Carola	Four Dubious Conceits, Flammer, 1952
Lilliburlero	Donna Parker	Gentle Moods, Gentry, 1971; The Organ Music of Richard Purvis, Vol. 1, FitzSimons, 2004
Lyra Davidica	David Forbes	Leeds, 1963

Title	Dedicatee	Publisher or Collection
Marche Grotesque	Carl Mueller	Four Dubious Conceits, Flammer, 1952
Meditation on "Rockingham"		In "Impressions," Organ Service Music, Vol. 1, Fred Bock, 1985
Melody in Mauve	Bill Thomson	Gentle Moods, Gentry, 1971; The Organ Music of Richard Purvis, Vol. 2, FitzSimons, 2004
Musette en Rondeau (Rameau)		Five Baroquisms, Gentry, 1972
Nocturne (Night in Monterey)	Janie Craig	Four Dubious Conceits, Flammer, 1952
Noel (Balbastre)		Five Classical Airs, Vol. 3, Word, 1972
Novelette [I]	Reginald Greenbrook	Organ Music from Grace Cathedral, Sacred Music Press, 1969; The Sacred Organ Journal, Vol. 42, No. 5, Lorenz, 2008
Novelette II	Reginald Greenbrook	Organ Music from Grace Cathedral, Sacred Music Press, 1969
Novelette III	Reginald Greenbrook	Organ Music from Grace Cathedral, Sacred Music Press, 1969; The Sacred Organ Journal, Vol. 39, No. 6, Lorenz, 2005
O Sacred Head, Now Wounded		The Organ Music of Richard Purvis, Vol. 1, FitzSimons, 2004
Of Banks and Braes	John Seng	Seven Folk Tone Poems, Sacred Songs, 1968
Of Moor and Fen	Frank Taylor	Seven Folk Tone Poems, Sacred Songs, 1968
Of Sea and Skye	Lyn Larsen	Seven Folk Tone Poems, Sacred Songs, 1968
Offertory (Resonet in Laudibus)	Joseph Whiteford	An American Organ Mass, Flammer, 1953
Partita on the Easter Chorale "Christ ist Erstanden"	E. Power Biggs	Witmark, 1952
Passapied for a Joyous Festival	George Wright	Mixture IV, Flammer, 1970
Pastorale (Forest Green)	George Henninger	Seven Chorale Preludes, Fischer, 1949
Pax Vobiscum	Jeanette Bartlett-Devine	A Trio of Contrasts, Flammer, 1965
Plaintive Blue	Helen Dell	Gentle Moods, Gentry, 1971
Poème Mystique (It Came Upon a Midnight Clear)	Charles van Bronkhorst	Three Carol Preludes, Gentry, 1985; Three Christmas Preludes, Fred Bock, 2006
Poeme Mystique (Manna/ Mercy)	Sally Harris	Seven Chorale Preludes, Fischer, 1949
Prayer for Guidance, A (Jesus Savior, Pilot Me)		Five Folk Hymn Orisons, Sacred Songs, 1966
Prayer for Peace	William Teague	Three Pieces for Organ, Fischer, 1954
Prayer of Aspiration, A (Beulah Land)		Five Folk Hymn Orisons, Sacred Songs, 1966

Title	Dedicatee	Publisher or Collection
Prayer of Confidence, A (Dwelling in Beulah Land)		Five Folk Hymn Orisons, Sacred Songs, 1966
Prayer of Consecration, A (Have Thine Own Way, Lord)		Five Folk Hymn Orisons, Sacred Songs, 1966
Prayer of Patriotism, A (America, the Beautiful)		Five Folk Hymn Orisons, Sacred Songs, 1966
Prelude	E. Power Biggs	Partita on "Christ ist Erstanden," Witmark, 1952
Prélude Solennel (Veni Emmanuel)	Joseph Whiteford	An American Organ Mass, Flammer, 1953
Psalm XVIII (Marcello)		Five Classical Airs, Vol. 2, Sacred Songs, 1967
Psalm XIX (Marcello)		Five Classical Airs, Sacred Songs, 1966
Repentance (La Trobe)	John W. Shields	Four Prayers in Tone, Witmark, 1951
Retrospection, A	Richard Thomasson	Organ Music from Grace Cathedral, Sacred Music Press, 1969; American Organ Music, Vol. 2, Sacred Music Press, 1975
Rigaudon (Campra)		Five Classical Airs, Sacred Songs, 1966
Rimembranza	Joyce Jones	In "In Retrospect," Artists' Performance Collection, Sonos, 1984
Romanza	Roland Diggle	Sprague-Coleman, 1943 (single); Leeds' Organ Selections by Richard Purvis, Leeds, 1957; Eleven Pieces for the Church Organist, MCA, 1957; The Organ Music of Richard Purvis, Vol. 2, FitzSimons, 2004
Rondo (for pedals alone)	Antonio Ruffatti	Three Fanciful Concepts, Flammer, 1967
Roundelay	Dan Semer	In "In Retrospect," Artists' Performance Collection, Sonos, 1984
Sarabande for a Day of Solemnity	George Wright	Mixture IV, Flammer, 1970
Siciliano (Bach)		Five Baroquisms, Gentry, 1972
Sicilienne (van den Gheyn)		Five Classical Airs, Vol. 3, Word, 1972
Sketch in D Flat (Schumann)		Five Classical Airs, Vol. 2, Sacred Songs, 1967
Solemn Music, A	Karl Morgan Block	H. W. Gray, 1971
Spiritual	Claude Murphee [actually Murphree]	Leeds, 1947 (single); Four Carol Preludes; Leeds' Organ Selections by Richard Purvis, Leeds, 1957; Eleven Pieces for the Church Organist, MCA, 1957
Suite for a Musical Clock (Handel)		Flammer, 1952
Supplication (Eisleben)	John W. Shields	Four Prayers in Tone, Witmark, 1951

Title	Dedicatee	Publisher or Collection
Sussex Lament, A	Roy Darley	Seven Folk Tone Poems, Sacred Songs, 1968
Sylvan Idylle, A	Gaylord Carter	Gentry, 1973 (Originally "Idyl," Ditson, 1943)
Thanksgiving	John W. Shields	Four Prayers in Tone, Witmark, 1951
Toccata	E. Power Biggs	Partita on "Christ ist Erstanden," Witmark, 1952
Toccata Festiva (In Babilone)	Clarence Snyder	Seven Chorale Preludes, Fischer, 1949
Toccata Marina	George Thalben-Ball	Organ Music from Grace Cathedral, Sacred Music Press, 1969; Toccatas! Toccatas! Seven Brilliant Pieces for Organ, Lorenz, 1977
Trumpet Tune (Purcell)		Five Classical Airs, Sacred Songs, 1966
Trumpet Voluntary (Purcell)		Five Classical Airs, Sacred Songs, Vol. 2, 1967
Trumpet Voluntary (Stanley)		Five Classical Airs, Vol. 3, Word, 1972
Undulato	Bill Thomson	Organ Music from Grace Cathedral, Sacred Music Press, 1969; The Sacred Organ Folio, No. 1, Lorenz, 1970
Vexilla Regis	Palmer Christian	Leeds, 1943 (single); Five Pieces on Gregorian Themes; Leeds' Organ Selections by Richard Purvis, Leeds, 1957; Eleven Pieces for the Church Organist, MCA, 1957
Wedding March	Gifford Coombs [*sic;* Combs]	The Organ Music of Richard Purvis, Vol. 2, FitzSimons, 2004

Works for Organ and Other Instruments

Larghetto Cantabile (for classical guitar and organ)		Apogee Press, 1971 (arranged from Petit Concert Champêtre)
Lyra Davidica (for brass, tympani, and organ)	David Forbes	Leeds, 1943
Petit Concert Champêtre (for organ and harp, or organ and harpsichord or piano)	Linda Hargis and Dale Wood	Apogee Press, 1972
Suite for Piano and Organ: From the Sierra		Gentry, 1970; Gentry, 1977

Unpublished Manuscripts for Solo Organ and Multiple Organs

The Four Elements (Earth, Air, Water, Fire), 1980
> Commissioned by Kenneth Starr
> Premiered at Washington National Cathedral, May 24, 1981; Kenneth Starr, organist

Heraldings
    MS [no date]

Kalevala Mists (Kalevalan Usva), based on a [Finnish] Runo melody, 1984
    For David Laukkanen

La Danza: Suite for Two Organs [no date]
    I. Bourrée
    II. Mazurka
    III. Serenata
    IV. Gondolieria
    V. El Ranchero: Early Spanish Californian Dance
    VI. Tarantella

Melita Suite, 1978
    "Respectfully dedicated to the Faculty and Student Body of the U.S.
    Naval Academy, Annapolis, Md."
    Premiered by James Dale, September 22, 1978, Naval Academy Chapel
    "Commissioned for this concert in memory of Mrs. Polly Slayton, and
    dedicated to the Midshipmen and Faculty of the Naval Academy"
    I. Introduction and Theme
    II. Maestoso Bravura
    III. Scherzetto
    IV. Cantabile
    V. Finale

Symphonic Suite for Three Organs, 1991[37]
    For Tom Hazleton, Donna Parker and Jonas Nordwall
    1. Fêtes Joyeux
    2. Rushing Rivulet
    3. Cancion Catalan
    4. Tarantella-Valsante

Unpublished Manuscripts for Organ with Other Instruments

Deliusness [no date]

    Hommage à Frederic Delius

    Fantasy for Organ and Harpsichord

        1. Prologue

        2. Primavera

        3. L'Hiver

        4. Epilogue

Deux Esquisses (Clair de lune, Jeu d'eaux) for harp and organ, 1991

    Commissioned by Kenneth Starr

    Premiered at Methuen Memorial Music Hall, Methuen, MA, September 25, 1991; Kenneth Starr, organist, Susan Robinson, harpist

Feu d'Artifice, in memory of Virgil Fox, 1990[38]

    For organ, 3 trumpets, 2 trombones, and timpani

    Commissioned by Kenneth Starr

    Premiered at Old South Church, Boston MA, October 21, 1990; Kenneth Starr, organist (program for the 10th anniversary of Virgil Fox's death)

Pièce Symphonique [no date]

    Organ, strings, harp, and timpani

    Premiered at Grace Cathedral on April 25, 1969; Richard Purvis, organist; The Oakland Symphony, Gerhard Samuel, conductor

        Grave e molto maestoso

        Allegro con brio

        Andante cantabile [in E][39]

        Allegretto scherzando

Soliloquy, 1991

    Commissioned by Lamont Crape

    "Dedicated to Dr. La Monte [*sic,* actually Lamont] Crape in friendship and admiration"[40]

Wedding Processional
    For Gifford Coombs [*sic;* Combs]
    MS [no date]
    Organ, 2 trumpets, 2 trombones

Other Unpublished Arrangements

Adagio for Organ and Strings, Albinoni-Purvis
Aria con Variazione, Handel-Purvis
Fanfare, Lemmens-Purvis[41]
A Solemn Melody, Walford Davies-Purvis
The Summer Knows

Fragment

Organ solo on "Slane" [no date]

Other manuscripts may exist in the Archive of Recorded Sound at Stanford University.

Notes

1. *New York Times,* November 4, 1995. He also named his son Leeds. See www.nmpa.org/aboutnmpa/levy.asp.

2. *The Billboard,* June 22, 1946, 20.

3. *New York Times,* November 4, 1995.

4. *Overtones,* Vol. X, No. 2, April 1940, 62.

5. More likely in 1941. Biographical Data, 3.

6. *The Diapason,* December 1, 1941, 1.

7. *The Diapason,* August 1, 1942, 5.

8. **Foreword:** Throughout America worshipping throngs annually pay homage to the Infant King in many types of Christmas Eve devotions. These devotions are called by numerous names, such as "The First Mass of Christmas," "Choral Eucharist in Celebration of the Holy Nativity," "Christmas Communion Service" or simply "The Lord's Supper," and the Liturgy and Ritual vary greatly. But without measurable variance is the adoration brought by faithful worshippers to the altar of cathedral or chapel; and in the hearts of men, there is kindled a new hope for the coming of His Kingdom and "peace on earth to men of good will."

    As a humble, albeit sincere tribute to the undying faith in a better world that lives in men's souls, and to the spirit of Christian brotherhood that makes America great, this American Organ Mass was written.

The work may be used "in toto" or "in part" in conjunction with any Christ-mastide Service. Several numbers lend themselves readily to recital purposes, and a most unique use was suggested to the composer by the Rt. Rev. Karl Morgan Block, Bishop of the Diocese of California. Since the tunes used as canti fermi are readily available, the Bishop suggests that each section of the Mass be preceded by a choral rendition of the Hymn or Carol on which it is based. This results in an interesting program of "Carols and Carol Preludes."

In order that the canti fermi [*sic*] be readily found, a cross-index derived from a variety of Hymnals widely used in America lists the various tunes. It is hoped the inter denominational nature of this index will suggest the democratic and unbi-ased spirit which prompted the writing of this composition.

> Richard Purvis
> Feast of Saint James, 1952
> Grace Cathedral
> San Francisco

9. Recorded in 1965. *Two-Organ Recital,* Rs-1003, Rittenhouse Book Distributors, Philadelphia).

10. **Foreword:** These little "encores" were conceived originally as improvisations while I was on a trans-continental tour, and were later written down from tape recordings and altered to their present versions.

They are called "dubious" because it is doubtful if they are organ music in its tru-est sense, and "conceits" because they are whimsical imaginings of their composer.

It is hoped that they will find a place in the organist's repertoire where organ music of a not-too-serious nature is needed. Perhaps it is well that the "King of Instruments" can bring forth a chuckle as well as a mood of exaltation.

> Richard Purvis

11. In a memo dated September 7, 1951, Purvis wrote to June Townsend: "On the enclosed MSS. will you please make one copy each of 'Marche Grotesque' and 'Les Petites Cloches.' I would like to have these just as soon as possible as Virgil Fox wants to use them on his tour starting in October." Cited in Townsend, 31.

12. Richard and John vacationed often in the Monterey area. Donna Parker, e-mail, September 27, 2010.

13. Donna Parker said that Purvis considered *Four Prayers in Tone* his favorite work. Donna Parker, e-mail, September 27, 2010.

Foreword: These Chorale-Fantasies (if such they may be called) were written at the request of many of my colleagues from churches of varying denominations who desired Service Preludes of greater length than the preludial selections found in the composer's "Seven Chorale Preludes on Tunes Found in American Hym-nals." Because the *canti fermi* used herein are less popular than those used in the aforementioned collection, they preceded each Fantasy.

> Richard Purvis
> Organist and Master of the Choristers
> Grace Cathedral, San Francisco
> The Feast of Saint Luke, 1950

14. Originally titled "A Cheerful Earfull—Five Vignettes for Residence Organs." Musical Notes, *The Organ Music of Richard Purvis*, Vol. 1 (FitzSimons, 2004), 5

15. Also in *Leeds' Organ Selections by Richard Purvis*, 1957; in *Eleven Pieces for the Church Organist*, MCA, 1957; and in *The Oxford Book of Christmas Organ Music*, Oxford University Press, 1995.

"The famous setting of *Greensleeves* was actually composed during WWII as Richard sat under fire in a foxhole." Musical Notes, *The Organ Music of Richard Purvis*, Vol. 1, H. T. FitzSimons, 2004. See more details in Chapter 3, "War Years."

16. According to June Townsend, "Idyl" was also published in *The Etude* magazine. Townsend, 28. Issue unknown.

17. On March 27, 1987, over lunch in San Francisco, Purvis told me that he had written "Carol Rhapsody" for a faculty Christmas party at The Curtis Institute, where he was a student 1936–1940. He said he wrote it "in the style of a Radio City organist."

The following suggests a different provenance for this piece: "Tom Hazleton's memories of Richard's comments about many pieces in these collections provide insight into their creation. *Carol Rhapsody* was written for Floyd Wright in the 1940s. He asked Richard to compose a medley of Christmas carols that he could play for his program on radio station KPO. Richard often played this piece on his own theatre organ program, performed under the nom-de-plume, Don Irvin [*sic*; actually Don Irving]. 'Don's' program was played on Oakland's Chapel of the Chimes Mortuary Wurlitzer (with English Post Horn). It was often included at Richard's legendary Advent Concerts at Grace Cathedral." Musical Notes, *The Organ Music of Richard Purvis*, Vol. 1, H. T. FitzSimons, 2004, 5.

18. Also in *The Sacred Organ Folio*, No. 1, Lorenz, March 1970, 13; and in *Organ Music for Lent and Easter*, Sacred Music Press, 1971, 7. Notation on manuscript copy reads: "First performance at the funeral of Alma de Briqueville Spreckles [*sic*] at the California Palace of the Legion of Honor, Lincoln Park, San Francisco, August 12, 1968." Grace Cathedral archives.

19. Also in *The Sacred Organ Journal*, Vol. 42, No. 5, May/June 2008, Lorenz.

20. Also in *The Sacred Organ Journal*, Vol. 39, No. 6, July/August 2005, Lorenz.

21. Also in *The Sacred Organ Folio*, No. 1, Lorenz, May 1970, 46.

22. Also in *Toccatas! Toccatas! Seven Brilliant Pieces for Organ*, compiled by David H. Hegarty, Lorenz, 1977.

23. Also in *American Organ Music*, Vol. 2, p. 18, Sacred Music Press, 1975.

24. "*The Organ Music of Richard Purvis*, Vols. 1 & 2, and *Three Christmas Preludes* are published by Fred Bock using the FitzSimons banner. Fred was really into the process of publishing as much Purvis as he could obtain permission to do when he passed away. His son Steve and the main editor Allen Petker picked up the pieces and the first two books were released in 2004 during the LA AGO convention and the Christmas book a while later." Jonas Nordwall, e-mail, 2009.

25. **Foreword:** This PARTITA was written at the suggestion of E. Power Biggs that I "compose something" for the "classical" organ. This venture into the realm of neo-classicism is a sincere attempt to create a contemporary American Work which will characterize the brilliant and colorful idiom of the classical organ. Though the

registration suggested is for an instrument of this type, the work will lend itself to performance on any organ worthy of the name. Registration for less severe designs is indicated by italics, in parentheses.

The magnificent hymn, "Christ ist Erstanden", which serves as a *cantus firmus*, is fast being admitted to many American hymnals; arranged as an anthem or Easter carol, it is finding a place in the repertoire of many choirs.

The various movements of the PARTITA picture the mood suggested by the various verses of the hymn.

> Richard Purvis
> Feast of All Saints, 1951
> Grace Cathedral
> San Francisco

"At the suggestion of E. Power Biggs, Purvis composed the Partita on "Christ ist Erstanden" which was first played by Mr. Biggs in the Germanic Museum, Harvard University, Boston, over a national radio hook-up (CBS). Due to audience response, Mr. Biggs repeated the work twice during the same year." Biographical Data, 6.

26. According to the Biographical Data, in 1956 Purvis composed and first performed at Grace Cathedral "The Song of St. Francis," an extended organ work. In 1963 "The Song of St. Francis" was rewritten and renamed "St. Francis Suite," and accepted for publication by J. Fischer. Biographical Data, 7.

Preface: The following pages embody a sincere effort to portray through tone a few of the verses found in the magnificent *Hymn of Saint Francis*. The text which suggested the various movements follows:

I. ASCRIPTION: O most high, almighty, good Lord God, to Thee belong praise, glory, honour and all blessing.

II. HYMN TO THE MOON: Praised be our Lord for our sister the moon ... which he has set clear and lovely in the heavens.

III. EARTH CAROL: Praised by our God for mother the Earth, the which doth sustain and keep us, and bringeth forth divers fruits and flowers of many colours, and green grass.

IV. CANTICLE OF THE SUN: Praised be my Lord God with all his creatures, and especially for our brother the sun, who brings us the day and who brings us the light; fair is he and shines with great splendour: O Lord, he signifies to us, Thee!

The composer is well aware that the inspired words of Saint Francis might suggest to some a more archaic idiom, but the timelessness of this great paean lends itself to any vernacular. Perhaps, too, it is fitting that a native of the City of Saint Francis should attempt to capture the mood o these verses in some degree.

He also wishes to express to Elizabeth Goudge his gratitude for inspiration gleaned form her compelling and poetic book, *Saint Francis of Assisi*.

> Richard Purvis
> Feast of Saint Francis
> Grace Cathedral
> San Francisco

27. **Foreword:** The following pieces were written for organist who have felt the composer's "Five Pieces on Gregorian Themes" too austere for non-liturgical services. The principle on which these preludes were composed is one suggested by Wallace Arthur Sabin of San Francisco. Mr. Sabin opined that music for American church services should be of a devotional nature, with a freshness and spontaneity of conception unhampered by limitations induced through a strict adherence to an orthodox ecclesiastical style, but without any suggestion of triteness or mere sentimentality descending to the level of the mundane or secular. The following pieces are a sincere attempt to realize this ideal.

  Richard Purvis, England—1944

  Notes for Hammond Organists: In playing these pieces on the Hammond organ disregard registration and manual indications for pipe organ. The pre-performance set-up appears in the upper right hand corner of the first page of each selection, and the registration changes are given at the proper places.

  The composer has made no attempt to duplicate organ timbre in electronic registration, but has conscientiously sought the most colorful and effective Hammond "stops" for each prelude, treating the instrument as individual on its own merits.

  The pre-sets indicated are those for the standard Hammond consoles—A, B, C, D, and E. Organists playing the model G console (designed for the armed forces) will have to make the usual modifications.

28. In verbal program notes to a 60th anniversary recital of the Kimball organ at the First Church of Christ, Scientist, San Francisco, on May 5, 1985, Purvis said that he had mailed the corrected proofs of *Seven Chorale Preludes* to Ruth Barrett Arno while he was engaged in the Battle of the Bulge. The packet never arrived, but Ruth Barrett Arno was later helpful in the publication process of the collection. Recital recording courtesy Douglas Metzler.

29. Purvis published another piece entitled "Poème Mystique" (an arrangement of "It Came Upon the Midnight Clear") in his 1985 collection *Three Carol Preludes*.

30. **Preface:** Sometime early in the reign of George I of England, Charles Clay built a most ingenious mechanical clock which contained bells and a miniature pipe organ. It is evident that this machine created quite a sensation in London and no less a person than Handel wrote and arranged at least one and probably two sets of tunes for it. ... From these two sets, Mr. Purvis has arranged a most charming "Suite."

  —John W. Shields May 1, 1952

31. The cover states "Arr. by Richard Purvis," although it is an original composition, not an arrangement.

32. Purvis composed another piece entitled "Poeme Mystique" (an arrangement of the hymn tune *Manna/Mercy*) in his 1949 collection *Seven Chorale Preludes on Tunes Found in American Hymnals*.

33. On June 27, 1966, Purvis wrote the following letter:

My Dear Signor Ruffatti:

  I am sending you a copy of the "Rondo for Pedals" which I have composed for Mr. Worth to play at the Dedicatory Recital of your new instrument in Saint Mary's

Church, Wayne. As you can see, I have taken the liberty of inscribing the work to you and I sincerely hope you will be gracious enough to accept the dedication.

I have long felt the organ repertoire needed a virtuoso work in the manner of Moscheles, Tausig and Hummel. The present "Rondo" is an attempt (on my part) to eradicate that lack. I am greatly looking forward to playing the Wayne [PA.] organ on November 16 and I want you to know some very good reports have filtered West regarding the organ you placed in Atlanta for the A.G.O. Convention. Congratulations!!

With every good wish for your continued success, I am

Sincerely yours,

Richard I. Purvis

34. **Foreword:** This "mixture of three" presents music which may be registered effectively on two-manual organs of moderate means. Numbers one and three have proven to contain that indefinable quality known as "audience appeal" when used in recitals throughout the United States. The significance of the "Elegy" needs to no comment. Richard Ross [head of organ department, Peabody Conservatory, 1941–1954] was one of America's finest organists—at no time did he ever forsake his ideals for showmanship, popular appeal or passing trends. His death is a great loss to the American organ world. R.I.P.

Richard Purvis

Feast of Saint Matthias, 1954

Grace Cathedral, San Francisco

35. **Foreword:** These three contrasts were originally written as wedding music for young couples who wanted music that was unhackneyed at their nuptials; the first two are preludial music and the last, a recessional. In their present form they make an interesting "Suite" for recitals, being highly colorful and widely diversified. The composer has so used them with signal success on numerous occasions and hopes organists will enjoy playing them as much as he did writing them!

Richard Purvis

Grace Cathedral

San Francisco

Ascensiontide 1964

36. Written in 1963 for the wedding of Dean Bartlett's daughter. Biographical Data, 7.

37. This suite, evoking scenes of San Francisco, including Chinatown and a Spanish mission, was the catalyst that started the musical group Trio Con Brio, composed of Donna Parker, Jonas Nordwall, and Tom Hazleton. They included it on their 1992 CD, *Not Just Another Organ Recording,* Triple Play Recordings.

Regarding the Suite, Purvis wrote the following undated letter to Tom Hazleton: Hi, Tom!

I'm taking your suggestion in composing a work for 3 organs. The problem is to write it (and registrate it) so that it sounds like three entities and not one massive glob of sound. I hope it turns out to be something you, Donna and Jonas enjoy playing! Do you think you could prevail upon Rodgers to commission the work?

It would do a lot to give my morale and prestige a boost right now. (They both could use a lift.) . . .

> All the best, Dick

Wednesday, Nov. 6, 1991

> Hi, Tom!

Here is my messy manuscript—many hours of thinking and scribbling. . . . The greatest problem was to preserve 3 entities, so that it did not fall into Reger's trap of becoming a huge glob of sound. . . .

> Dick

Both letters courtesy Donna Parker.

38. A Concerto for Organ, Brass, and Timpani in memory of Virgil Fox was also commissioned by Kenneth Starr. "Feu d'Artifice" was to become the third and final movement of this concerto. Purvis was working on the first two movements at the time of his death, but no sketches or drafts survived; hence this concerto remains unfinished. Kenneth Starr, e-mail, April 8, 2011.

39. This movement was also arranged for organ solo in the key of F and published in 1971 by Apogee Press.

40. In a letter to Lamont Crape, dated Thanksgiving 1991, Purvis writes:

Here's your piece [Soliloquy]! I hope you enjoy playing it with as much pleasure as I had writing it. This one did not come easily at first, but once the conception solidified, it progressed with greater ease. I've tried to use the organ's colors to the greatest advantage, but don't hesitate to change any registration you deem fit.

As usual I have to apologize for my terrible manuscript. I hope with the aid of a magnifying glass and two pairs of glasses you may be able to decipher my hieroglyphics. I have not employed many expression marks and no phrasing, leaving this up to your own good taste.

41. Written for Tom Hazleton; performed by Purvis and Tom Hazleton on the main church and Chapel organs at Grace Cathedral. Donna Parker, e-mail, April 26, 2011.

chapter 8

Dedicatees of
Purvis's Organ Works

With only a few exceptions (such as the *Five Folk Hymn Orisons* and his arrangements of classical pieces in *Baroquisms* and *Five Classical Airs*), almost every organ piece published by Purvis was dedicated to a friend or colleague. These include teachers, students, fellow organists (both classical and theatre), clergy, organ builders, and others.

Allen, Marlan Eklog	Student, Organist, St. John's Presbyterian, Berkeley[1]
Arno, Ruth Barrett Fantasia (Ton-y-Botel)	Organist, The Mother Church, Boston, 1932–1961
Baker, Robert Canticle of the Sun	Director, Union Theological Seminary, New York; Founder, Yale Institute of Sacred Music
Bartlett, the Very Reverend C. Julian All Glory, Laud, and Honor	Dean of Grace Cathedral, San Francisco
Bartlett-Devine, Jeanette Pax vobiscum	Daughter of Dean Julian Bartlett
Bidwell, Marshall Chartres	Organist, Coe College; Cedar Rapids, Iowa, and Carnegie Institute of Music, Pittsburgh
Biggs, E. Power Partita on the Easter Chorale "Christ ist Erstanden"	Concert organist
Biggs, Richard Keys Divinum Mysterium	Organist, Blessed Sacrament Church, Hollywood, California
Block, The Right Rev. Karl Morgan A Solemn Music (in memoriam)	Bishop of the Diocese of California
Borrevik, Jerry From the Hebrides	Unknown

Bruun, Lewis Fanfare (from Trio of Contrasts)	Student, organist in Maryland
Cagle, Dewey Scherzo (Burlesca)	Theatre organ enthusiast
Carola, Sister M. Les Petites Cloches	Unknown
Carter, Gaylord Idyl A Sylvan Idylle	Theatre and radio organist
Chapman, Keith A Highland Ayre	Student; Wanamaker organist; organist, First Methodist Church, Wayne, Pennsylvania
Charles, Terry Caravan of the Three Kings	Organist, Kirk of Dunedin, Florida; Allen dealer
Chenoweth, Art Harmonies du Soir	Rodgers Store Manager, San Francisco
Chenoweth, Kay Pastorale d'Été	Rodgers Store Manager, San Francisco
Christian, Palmer Vexilla Regis	Organist, Hyde Park Presbyterian Church, Chicago; Professor, University of Michigan
Coombs, Gifford [*sic;* Combs] Wedding March (Recessional)	Chorister at Grace Cathedral
Craig, Janie Nocturne (Night in Monterey)	Organist, Ft. Worth, Texas; student
Courboin, Charles M. Kyrie Eleison	Organist, St. Patrick's Cathedral, New York City
Dale, James Melita Suite	Organist, US Naval Academy, Annapolis, Maryland
Darley, Roy A Sussex Lament	Organist, The Mormon Tabernacle, Salt Lake City
Dell, Helen Plaintive Blue	Theatre and radio organist, Los Angeles; organist for Los Angeles Dodgers
Diggle, Roland Romanza	Organist, St. John's Episcopal Church, Los Angeles
Duncan, William	Assistant to Richard Purvis, Grace Cathedral
Einecke, Harold Gwalshmai [*sic;* Gwalchmai]	Organist, St. John's Episcopal Cathedral, Spokane
Forbes, the Reverend Canon David Lyra Davidica	Headmaster, Grace Cathedral School for Boys
Fox, Virgil Dies Irae	Concert organist

Freeman, Frederic Canzona (Liebster Jesu)	Organist, First Unitarian Church, Oakland; Dean, Northern California Chapter AGO (in 1951)
Greenbrook, Reginald Three Novelettes	Organist in San Jose and San Francisco[2]
Hansen, Rodney[3] Fete joyeuse	Student; organist in Baltimore and Connecticut
Harris, Sally Poeme Mystique (Manna)	Unknown
Hawley, Harold [*sic,* actually Harrold] Cantilena: Green Boughs	Organist, Chapel of the Chimes, Oakland, California
Hazleton, Tom Brigg Fayre	Theatre and church organist; student
Heaps, Porter Grand Choeur (Austria)	Concert organist for Hammond Organ Company
Henninger, George Pastorale (Forest Green)	Theatre and radio organist for ABC, New York City
Iverson, Bud Capriccio Espagnole	Organist, Walnut Creek, California; Conn Dealer
Jones, Joyce Rimembranza	Concert organist; professor, Baylor University
Larsen, Lyn Of Sea and Skye	Theatre organist
McCurdy, Alexander Communion	Purvis's professor at Curtis Institute of Music
Metzler, Douglas (Cortright) Andante Cantabile (from Pièce Symphonique)	Student, chorister, assistant
Morse, Alma Contemplation (Tallis' Canon)	Unknown
Murphree, Claude[4] Spiritual	Organist, University of Florida 1925–1958
Mueller, Carl Marche Grotesque	Composer and organist, Montclair, New Jersey
Ness, Earl Dialogue Monastique	Organist, First Baptist, Philadelphia; Professor, Temple University, Philadelphia
O'Leary, Patricia An Erin Lilt	Unknown
Parker, Donna Lilliburlero	Student, theatre organist

Ross, Richard Elegy	Head of organ department, Peabody Conservatory; Organist, Brown Memorial Presbyterian, Baltimore
Ruffatti, Antonio Rondo (for pedals alone)	Owner, Fratelli Ruffatti, Padova, Italy; built console for Grace Cathedral in 1968
Schutz, Hal Bell Prelude	Baldwin dealer in Northern California
Semer, Dan Roundelay	Student in Los Angeles
Seng, John Of Banks and Braes	Theatre and radio organist for NBC, Chicago
Shields, John W. Four Prayers in Tone	Purvis's partner; choir member and teacher at Grace Cathedral
Snyder, Clarence Toccata Festiva (In Babilone)	Curtis classmate; organist, Longwood Gardens 1956–1978
Spreckels, Alma de Bretteville Cortège	Palace of the Legion of Honor benefactress
Steinhaus, Philip Ascription	Organist, St. John's, Lafayette Square, Washington, D.C.; Peabody Conservatory; Church of the Advent, Boston
Taylor, Frank Of Moor and Fen	Organist, Scottish Rite Temple, Oakland, California
Teague, William Prayer for Peace	Organist, St. Mark's Episcopal, Shreveport, Louisana
Thalben-Ball, George Toccata Marina	Organist, Temple Church, London
Thomasson, Richard A Retrospection	Organist, Belmont Methodist, Nashville, Tennessee
Thomson, Bill Melody in Mauve Undulato	Organist and studio musician in Los Angeles
Thomson, Claribel (Gegenheimer) Greensleeves	Curtis classmate; organist, First Presbyterian, Ardmore, Pennsylvania
Tulan, Fred A Lamentation of Jeremiah	Organist in Stockton, California
Van Bronkhorst, Charles Poeme Mystique (It Came Upon the Midnight Clear)	Organist, Bidwell Memorial Presbyterian, Chico, California
Vannucci, Larry Autumn Soliloquy	Theatre and jazz organist, San Francisco

Warren, Thomas
  Capriccio (On the Notes of the
  Cuckoo)
	Chorister at Grace Cathedral; former owner of Balceta
	  home, San Francisco

Whiteford, Joseph An American Organ Mass	Executive of the Aeolian-Skinner Organ Co.
Whitehead, William Dialogue Monastique	Organist, Fifth Avenue Presbyterian, New York City

Williams, David McK.
  A Solemn Music (commissioned by
  Williams)
	Organist, St. Bartholomew's, New York City

Wolford, Darwin A Joyous Procession	Professor, Ricks College, Rexburg, Idaho
Worth, Ted Alan Contemplation (Picardy)	Student, concert organist, Rodgers dealer
Wright, Floyd Carol Rhapsody	Theatre and radio organist for CBS, San Francisco

Wright, George
  Sarabande for a Day of Solemnity
  Passapied for a Joyous Festival
	Theatre, radio, and television organist, San Francisco,
	  New York, and Hollywood

Wright, Searle
  Hymn to the Moon
	Organist, St. Paul's Chapel, Columbia University, New
	  York City

Dedications to Richard Purvis

Among Purvis's papers was an original manuscript of Flor Peeters' "Lied to the Ocean," Op. 66, no. 1, inscribed as follows:

"To my dear friend Richard Purvis, organiste [*sic*] at Grace Cathedral, San Francisco"

"Lied to the Ocean," published in 1950 by C. F. Peters (6002b), is dedicated to Purvis.

Fred Bock dedicated two of his compositions to Purvis: "Postlude on Old Hundredth," in *Organist Sounds for Worship,* Sacred Music Press, 1971; and "Fantasia on 'On Christmas Night,'" in *The Organ Music of Fred Bock,* Vol. 1, Fred Bock Music Co., 1997.

Also in Purvis's library was a copy of Aaron Copland's Symphony for Organ and Orchestra, autographed by the composer in February 1963 (although not specifically to Purvis).

Notes

1. Stephen Loher, e-mail, June 3, 2009.

2. See obituary, *The American Organist,* August 1994, 37.

3. According to Stephen Loher, Hansen was one of Purvis's favorite students. Stephen Loher, e-mail, June 3, 2009.

4. Misspelled in score as "Murphee."

CHAPTER 9

CHORAL AND
OTHER VOCAL WORKS

This compilation of titles of works for choir or solo voice by Purvis is based on available scores as well as on references to scores. Some details are missing, and some may be inaccurate. However, the list provides insight into the nature and scope of Purvis's works for the voice. Additions and corrections are welcomed by the author.

Given Purvis's large output of choral works, as well as his arrangements of hymns by other composers, it is surprising that Purvis never composed a hymn. The 1940 Episcopal hymnal was in use during his tenure at Grace Cathedral. Neither the hymn nor service music volumes of *The Hymnal 1982* that replaced it contains anything by Purvis.

Many copies of the sheet music and manuscripts of the choral works are now in the Archive of Recorded Sound at Stanford University.

Choral

Advent Carol (Conditor Alme Siderum)
    Flammer, 1970
    Latin 9th century—based on Sarum plainsong
    Adapted from a translation by John Mason Neale
    unison choir (optional descant) with organ and optional instruments
    For James Weeks and the Choirs of First Congregational Church, Long Beach, California

All Glory, Laud and Honor (Processional)
    Leeds Music Corp., 1963
    Organ solo with SATB or unison chorus; also available for organ, brass
    choir, tympani and chorus (unison or SATB)
    For the Very Reverend C. Julian Bartlett, Dean of Grace Cathedral

Alleluias I, II, and III
    Unpublished MS
    SATB, organ, with chancel and gallery brass (3 trumpets)

The Ballad of Judas Iscariot
    Elkan-Vogel, 1940
    SATB
    Poem by Robert Buchanan

Benedictus es Domine
    H. W. Gray, 1949
    SATB/TTBB; for mixed voices in the key of E flat
    To Joseph Ragan and the choir of All Saints' Church, Atlanta, GA

A Carol for the Unity of All Mankind
    1971 (?)
    choral with organ, unison or two part

A Canticle of Light
    Flammer, 1967
    SATB
    Short anthem or introit; SATB, accompanied; based on vs. 105, 106, 109
    of Psalm 119
    For Conrad Eden and the Choir of Durham Cathedral, England

Canticle of Trust
    1979 (?)
    SATB and organ, handbells optional

Carol of the Bamboo Flute
   J. Fischer & Bro., 1965
   Christmas carol for unison voices with descant and organ, accompaniment for piano, celesta or harp
   For Dr. William Jones and the Choir of Redlands University

Carol of the Little King
   H. W. Gray (?)

A Cheer for the New Age
   Gentry Publications, 1971
   Unison or two part, accompanied
   For Dr. Sue Sikking in admiration and appreciation

Christians Awake!
   Sacred Songs, Waco, Texas, 1968
   Unison and two-part
   For Anna Harland and the Choirs of Portalhurst Presbyterian Church, San Francisco, California

A Cradle Carol
   J. Fischer & Bro., 1965
   Unison, two-part or mixed choir with organ, piano, harp or celesta optional
   Melody based on W. J. Kirkpatrick's "Away in a Manger"
   For Dale Wood and the Choir of Eden Lutheran Church

David and Goliath
   MS, notated "Tioga Pass, July 11, 1971"

De Profundis (Out of the Depths)
   Leeds Music Corp., 1964 (in Four Anthems)
   Psalm 130; for chorus of mixed voices SATB with organ and optional trumpet solo accompaniment
   For Jack Schneider and the Choir of Calvary Presbyterian Church, Riverside, California

A Festival Anglican Eucharist
   Cited in Townsend thesis, p. 24; could be the same as "Mass of the Holy
   Nativity"
   For four-part male choir (TTBB), congregation and organ

Festival Mass to Promote Ecumenicism
   McLaughlin & Reilly, 1967
   "Official text of the National Conference of Bishops"
   For four-part male choir, congregation and organ

Five Carols for the Church Year (An Advent Carol, A Manger Carol,
   A Passiontide Carol, An Easter Alleluia, A Carol for the Unity of All
   Mankind)
   Flammer, 1971 (?)
   unison with descant

Five Joyous Canticles (A Canticle of Joy, A Canticle for God's Kingdom
   on Earth, A Canticle of Praise, A Resurrection Canticle, A Canticle of
   Brotherhood)
   Word Music Co., 1971 (?)
   Unison with descant

Four Anthems (A Psalm of Ascents, Judica Me Deus, De Proundis [with a
   Hebrew shofar call], Unto Us A Child is Born)
   Leeds, 1964
   SATB

The Four Seasons Suite
   Includes: Autumn, "Thanksgiving"; Christmas, "A Little Carol"
   MS, 1977
   SATB
   For the Men and Boys Choir of the Chapel of the Four Seasons, Santa
   Cruz, California

A Graduation Song
   MS
   For Grace Cathedral School?

A Hymn of Faith for these Days "Trust in the Lord"
   MS
   Unison Choir and Organ
   For Rev Frederick Lattimore, Mr. Derrison Symonds and the Choir of
   St James Episcopal Church, Oakland, California

Iam Hiems Transiit (see Winter Passes Over)

A Joyous Christmas Roundelay
   1986

A Joyous Psalm of Praise
   1970 (?)
   SATB

Jubilate Deo
   Sprague-Coleman 1943, MCA Music, 1943; Leeds, 1943
   "Unison", "In the manner of a stately procession"
   For the Choir of the Episcopal Academy

Judica Me Deus (in Four Anthems)
   Leeds Music Corp., 1964
   Based on Psalm 43
   For choirs of mixed voices SATB with organ and trumpet solo
   accompaniment
   For Jack Ossewaarde and the Choir of Saint Bartholomew, New York
   City

Laudate Dominum
   Sacred Songs, 1966
   SATB (complete score and brass parts available from publisher)

Written for the Festival Evensong and Blessing of the Organ of the new
Ruffatti organ at Saint Mary's, Wayne, Pennsylvania, November 29, 1966

A Lenten Carol
Flammer, 1969
Two part (or unison) voices, unaccompanied; based on an English folk
song
For Richard Thomasson and the Choir of Belmont Methodist Church,
Nashville, Tennessee

A Little Carol
1982 (?)
SATB

Lonesome Valley
Summy-Birchard Co., 1963
For unison and descant; secular; for mixed voices; white spiritual, freely
arranged by Richard Purvis

Long, Long Ago
MS
choral, strings, harp, organ, celesta

The Lovelorn Sailor
MS, 1970 (?)
For unison voices or choir and guitar or piano

Lyra Davidica (Processional)
Leeds Music Corp., 1963
For organ, brass, and tympani

Magnificat
G. Schirmer, 1941
SATB

Mass in Honor of Saint Francis[1]
  McLaughlin & Reilly, 1967

Mass of Saint Nicholas[2]
  Coleman-Ross, 1947 (composed around 1940)
  SATB

Mass of the Holy Nativity[3]
  Flammer, 1951
  Festival Anglican Communion Service
  For male voices
  "Devotedly inscribed to the Rt. Rev. Karl Morgan Block, Bishop of the
  Diocese of California"

The Mass of the Holy Resurrection[4]
  Flammer, 1962
  For four-part mixed chorus (SATB) and organ; three trumpets, two
  trombones and tympani optional
  Dedicated to the Rt. Rev. James Albert Pike, Bishop of California

Missa Festiva[5]
  McLaughlin and Reilly, 1967
  For two male choirs TTBB, with organ, brass, and timpani

On the Street Car
  Galaxy, 1943[6]
  SSA
  To the Wednesday Morning Chorale of Oakland, CA; words by Merrill
  Moore[7]
  Text by American poet Craine[8]

Our Brother is Born
  J. Fischer & Bro., 1954
  Carol for male voices
  Text by Eleanor Farjeon (from Oxford Book of Carols)
  Inscribed to the Loring Club of San Francisco

Paean of Praise
  J. Fischer & Bro., 1967
  "Text from the Scriptures"
  Arranged for mixed voices with baritone solo
  Written for the 300th anniversary of Old First Church, Newark, New
  Jersey

A Passiontide Carol
  1971 (?)
  Choral with organ, unison or two-part with descant

A Psalm of Ascents (in Four Anthems)
  Leeds Music Corp, 1964
  Psalm 121
  For chorus of mixed voices SATB with organ and trumpet (optional)
  accompaniment
  In memoriam Mary Duncan Bayer

A Psalm of Hope for These Times (Our Days)[9]
  MS
  For Unison Choir and Organ
  For Rev. Earnest Wilson and the Choir of Unity Temple, Kansas City,
  MO

Prophecy
  Flammer, 1940, 1954
  A cappella SATB
  Poem by Harriet Knight Salvage
  For Richard Helms and the Choir of the Second Presbyterian Church,
  Kansas City, Missouri

Purvis a la Jazz Hot
  1965

"Purvis a la Jazz Hot" appears in the printed program of the Duke Ellington "Sacred Concert" at Grace Cathedral, September 16, 1965. The program states that it was orchestrated by Louie Bellson and Duke Ellington. However, there are no known copies of the score, if such a work exists. There are various commercially released recordings of the concert, but none include this piece. On one recording Duke Ellington is heard to say, "Thank you. And now we will have the privilege of providing a certain amount of ornamentation for Richard Purvis and the Grace Cathedral Choir." What follows is an slow instrumental piece of a few minutes in length. No choir can be heard.

David Worth writes, "I still think the 'Purvis a la Jazz Hot' was the Ellington accompaniment to Purvis' 'Lonesome Valley' (a clever conflation of that tune with 'Deep River' and a descant all going together so neatly). I was singing in the choir at that Grace Cathedral concert and well-remember the 'stumble' getting it started, with Ellington coming over to Richard, saying a quiet word to him, and then the band re-started the single bar intro (the Saturday Review article on that concert mentions that moment)."[10]

Mark Harvey, a jazz trumpeter who has worked on a number of projects involving Duke Ellington's music, responds:

> My speculation is that [1] the intro is for the Purvis piece but that [2] the composition played is, first, a piano, impressionistic sort of piece, followed by, definitely, "In the Beginning God", a premiere at this concert, which does feature choir and soloist. I cannot believe Ellington would have introduced his own new composition as a mere "decoration." So, either the intro happened, and they deleted the Purvis piece, or something else was going on, which I have no clue about.
>
> Hopefully some other source will turn up an actual concert recording of the Purvis piece, which both David Worth and I agree was most likely that "Lonesome Valley" arrangement done up for jazz orchestra. But until we have some recorded, or other, evidence...[11]

The Road's End
  Elkan-Vogel, 1943[12]
  SSA

Scottish Carol[13]
  Birchard, 1940[14]
  Text by Charlotte Lockwood Garden

A Soldier's Prayer[15]
  Galaxy Music Corp., 1943, and J. Fischer & Bro., 1970
  Medium voice; for unison or two equal voices
  Poem by Joyce Kilmer
  Tempo marking reads: "In slow march time, with weary ponderousness"

A Song
  Coleman-Ross, 1943
  SSA
  Text by Christina Rossetti

A Song for Commencement
  Flammer, 1970
  Text by Charles Wesley; based on an English folk song
  Two-part or unison voices, unaccompanied

The Song of Simeon (Nunc Dimittis)
  J. Fischer and Bro., 1965
  SATB + instrumental parts

Te Deum
  MS (?)

Three Timely Anthems (A Psalm of Hope for These Times, A Hymn of
  Faith for These Days, A Carol for Our Times)
  Music Corp. of America
  Unison with descant

Three Psalms (may be A Psalm of Ascents, Judica Me Deus, De Profundis)
  Leeds Music Corp., 1963 (?)
  SATB

Unto Us a Child is Born [in Four Anthems]
  Leeds Music Corp., 1964; MCA
  for choirs of mixed voices SATB with organ and trumpet solo (optional)
  For William Barnard and the Choir of Christ Church Cathedral, Houston, Texas

Welcome Happy Morning
  Art Masters Studios, 1968
  Unison voices with organ
  From a poem by Fortunatus (530-609 AD), translation by John Ellerton, 1868

What Strangers are These? (Noel Ecossais) "Old Scottish Carol"
  Summy-Birchard Co., SATB 1946; two-part treble voices, 1954

Winter Passes Over (Iam Hiems Transiit)
  Text from *Brother Petroc's Return* by Sister Mary Catherine, 1937
  Leeds Music Corp., 1940
  SATB/SSA)
  To the Choral Art Society of Philadelphia

Published Orchestration for Organ, Brass, and Tympani

Lyra Davidica (Processional)
  Leeds Music Corp., 1963
  For organ, brass, and tympani; not a choral accompaniment

Published and Unpublished Orchestrations of Choral Works Used in Christmas Vesper and Easter Concerts

Most of these manuscripts and parts are now in the Archive of Recorded Sound at Stanford University.

Alleluia! Christus Surrexit, Campbell. 5-part brass, tympani, organ

Ave Maria, Bach-Gounod. 8-part strings, piano, harp, bells, organ

A Cradle Carol (Away in a Manger), Fischer 1965. 5-part strings, harp, celesta, organ

A Carol for Our Times (Purvis). Organ and harp (or piano?)

Carol of the Drum, Katherine K. Davis. 8-part strings, celesta, harp, drums, choir, organ

Christians, Awake! 5-part strings, harp celesta, organ

Christmas Day, Holst. 7-part strings, harp, drums, choir, organ

Dirge for Two Veterans, Holst. 5-part brass, snare and bass drums

An Easter Laud, Pizarro. 5-part brass, tympani, choir, organ

Festival Procession, R. Strauss. Organ, trumpets, trombones, tuba, tympani

Greater Love Hath No Man, Ireland. 5-part brass, tympani, choir, organ

Hosanna to the Son of David, Hannahs. 5-part brass, tympani, choir, organ

I Was Glad, Parry. Organ and brass

Long, Long Ago (Christ Came to Bethlehem). 5-part strings, harp, celesta, organ

Manger Carol (Gevaert), Sowerby. 5-part strings, organ, harp, celesta.

Many Years Ago, Evelyn Sharp. 5-part strings, celesta, harp choir, organ

Masters in This Hall, Candlyn. 5-part strings, harp, chimes, choir, organ

Myn Lyking, Terry. 5-part strings, celesta, harp, organ, choir

O How Amiable, Vaughan Williams, 5-part brass and tympani.

Old Hundredth Psalm Tune, Vaughan Williams. 5-part brass, tympani, choir, organ

On This Day, Stewart. 5-part strings, organ

Processional, Shaw. 5-part brass, tympani, choir, organ

The Promise Which Was Made, Bairstow. 5-part brass, tympani

A Scotch Lullaby, Garden. HW Gray, 1946. 5-part strings, organ, harp, celesta.

Sing Gloria, Katherine K. Davis. 5-part strings, celesta, harp choir

Sing We Merrily Unto God Our Strength, Sidney Campbell, Novello, 1962. Brass

Sleeps Judea Fair, Mackinnon. 5-part strings, organ, harp, celesta

Torches, Joubert. Organ, strings, harp, chimes

Tyrley-Tyrlow, Warlock. 5-part strings, celesta, harp, organ drums, choir
What Strangers are These? Purvis. Strings

Vocal Solos

Discovery
   Elkan-Vogel, 1945
   Words by Anne Campbell

Dream-Vision[16]
   Oliver Ditson (Theodore Presser), 1943
   Solo, high voice
   Poem by Clair Upschur[17]

A Gypsy Jingle (?)
   1947 (?)

John Anderson, My Jo
   Sprague-Coleman-Ross, 1946[18]
   Low voice, and piano
   Lor Katherine Merle

A Soldier's Prayer
   1943
   "In slow march time with weary ponderousness"
   Poem by Joyce Kilmer

Notes

1. "Bishop Hugh Donohoe commissioned Purvis to write a Unison Mass for the new Roman Catholic Liturgy. It was to be performed first at the R.C. Cathedral in Stockton." Townsend thesis, 41.

2. "Richard Purvis (graduating in Organ) has composed works for organ and church chorus: *Communion, Suite on Gregorian Themes*, three Christmas Carols, *Mass of St Nicholas*, and a *Magnificat*." *Overtones*, Vol. X, No. 2, April 1940, 62.

3. Performed at midnight services at Grace Cathedral, 1947 . Townsend thesis, 28.

4. Foreword to this Mass can be read in Townsend thesis, 37.

5. Commissioned in 1965 for the 175th anniversary of St. Mary's Seminary, Baltimore, Maryland. Townsend thesis, 40.

6. Composed 1941. Corbett, 24.

7. Townsend thesis, 28.

8. Corbett, 28.

9. In possession of Douglas Metzler.

10. David Worth, e-mail, May 19, 2011.

11. Mark Harvey, e-mail, June 1, 2011. See www.jazz.com/encyclopedia/harvey-mark.

12. Composed 1942? Corbett, 24.

13. The same as "What Strangers Are These?" Donna Parker, e-mail, April 20, 2011.

14. Townsend thesis, 28.

15. Of this song, June Townsend wrote, citing a letter from Purvis dated October 9, 1942:

Purvis sent it to me [for copying] with: "Here's the best song I ever wrote. Going to pull some strings to see if John Charles Thomas will sing it...

Can you make two copies very pronto? ... Don't hurry—just rush.

Will appreciate your helping out a "poor Sodjer".

In Townsend thesis, 28.

16. "A youthful song, written for George Lapham." Townsend, 27.

17. Corbett, 25.

18. Townsend says 1940. Townsend, 28.

chapter 10

compositions for other instruments

Piano

A Waltz Fragment
    Theodore Presser, 1944

Four Encore Solos for Piano
    Elkan-Vogel, 1941–42 (?)
        Barcarolle
        Scintillation
        Solitude (A Study in Monotony)
        Monterey

Harp or Piano

Noel Pastorale (on Silent Night)
    MS [no date]

Published Orchestration for Organ, Brass, and Tympani

Lyra Davidica (Processional)
    Leeds Music Corp., 1963
        For organ, brass, and tympani (not a choral accompaniment)

Other Orchestrations

See orchestrations of Christmas and Easter choral works in Chapter 9.

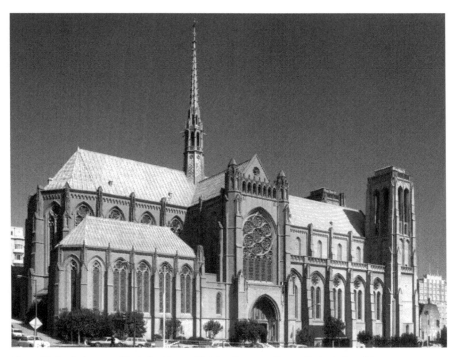

Grace Cathedral, 1970s. Photo by George Knight. Courtesy Grace Cathedral archives.

chapter 11

purvis as recitalist,
1946–1994

Richard Purvis played the most colorful, alive, and interesting recital in the Saint Louis Meeting. He's a master of suspense, contrast and intensity control, with a real sense of heartwarming beauty in his approach.

—The American Organist—New York

Throughout the recital there was not a perfunctory measure. A well planned build-up in the Reubke Fugue resulted in a thrilling climax, which earned a spontaneous ovation from the audience.

—The Diapason Magazine—Chicago

Purvis was active as a performer during his early years as a student at Curtis, and when circumstances permitted, while serving in the army. Virtually from the moment he was discharged and had recovered, he was in demand as a recitalist both locally and nationally.

Performance Style

June Townsend wrote:

> Thus we see that Purvis' recital programs cover the range of organ literature from Bach, through the English School, with an interest in the French composers, Franck and Peeters (French at heart), Dupré (with whom he had his picture taken in his youth),[1] Widor, Louis Vierne, and the modern blind composer Jean Langlais, who played at Grace Cathedral on an American tour. Karg-Elert, an impressionistic German, is also a favorite.

Purvis reflects this Neo-Romantic style in his own compositions which he includes in his concerts to the delight of his audiences.[2]

Purvis consistently programmed the music of Franck. Donna Parker claimed that Purvis had inherited from Tournemire a knowledge of Franck's performance style, recalling the following comment by Purvis: "There's the way the music appears on paper, and there's the way they played it. I got it from Tournemire, I got it from the horse's mouth."[3]

Promotional Literature

Townsend continued, "Under the concert management of Eric Parsons, The Chatham [Hotel, adjacent to Curtis], Philadelphia, the following brochure was issued when he was in the East. Since coming West, and with his many duties, he handles his own concert work." She cited the following brochure:

Richard Purvis,
Concert Organist, Dynamic American Virtuoso

Sample Program

Fantasy in F minor	Mozart
Prelude and Fugue in G Major	Bach
Pastorale	Cesar Franck
Intermezzo (Symphony VI)	Charles-Marie Widor
The Soul of the Lake	Sigfrid Karg-Elert
Canon in B minor	Robert Schumann
Finale (Symphony I)	Louis Vierne
Improvisations on Given Themes	

Richard Purvis is widely known as a front-rank recitalist. His playing is distinguished by a brilliant technic and magnificent interpretation which has won for him the highest praise from press and public.

A major attraction of each recital is an impromptu improvisation on themes given by members of the audience. Mr. Purvis has been acclaimed the foremost American born exponent of extemporisation of his generation. An additional feature is the careful planning of each program to suit the locale in which it is played. This permits a more intimate recital in smaller auditoriums and programs of greater magnitude in larger edifices. Hence, every program is created in such a manner as to insure the greatest possible popular appeal.

Press Comments

"Emotional warmth, complete technical and interpretive mastery and a flair for arousing and sustaining the interest of his listeners characterized his playing … One of the leaders in that small group of highly gifted and alert young American organists who are achieving popular recognition for the organ as a concert instrument." *Diapason* (Chicago)

Publicity photo used to promote Purvis's concerts in the late 1940s and early 1950s.

"Admirable skill and musical perception." *Philadelphia Evening Ledger*

"Foremost figure in the organ concert field today." *Lynchburg* (VA) *Advance*

"Justly entitled to the excellent reputation which had preceded him." *Orlando* (Fla.) *Journal*

"Thrilled a large number of music-lovers." *Pottsville* (Pa.) *Journal*

"Superb artistry and interpretative ability have received enviable comment from press and public alike." *Musical Advance* (New York)[4]

A similar promotional brochure, undated, includes the following information:

RICHARD IRVEN PURVIS
Concert Organist
DYNAMIC AMERICAN VIRTUOSO

What the Press Says …

Richard Irven Purvis returned to San Francisco last night after several years' military service and a long stretch as organist of Philadelphia churches, and gave one of the most brilliant organ recitals this city has ever had the privilege of hearing. And it is worth pointing out, at a time when the organ recital is supposed to be in decline, that Calvary Presbyterian Church held an extremely large audience for this occasion. Unlike some of his colleagues, Purvis did not choose to stress any one phase of the literature, but touched on many phases, from Bach to Frederick [*sic*] Freeman of San Francisco, with works of the French school and the inevitable Karg-Elert. All this Purvis set forth with absolutely flawless manual and pedal technique, with subtle and highly effective registration, and with the utmost in intelligent musicianship. But what one particularly took away was a sense of youthful vitality, of resilience and enthusiasm and delight in playing the organ and playing it well, such as one takes away all too seldom from such events. *Alfred Frankenstein — San Francisco Chronicle*[5]

A capacity audience filled a large church auditorium and showed its delight with enthusiastic applause, demanding several encores at the close of the program. Besides an astonishing technical facility, Mr. Purvis' playing has the elan and drive which characterize the performance of other top-ranking organists, as well as solid musicianship and sensitive feeling. Another quality, however, which is perhaps more important in public performance than any of these, is the ability to make his playing interesting. Throughout the recital there was not a perfunctory measure. A well planned build-up in the Reubke Fugue resulted in a thrilling climax, which earned a spontaneous ovation from the audience. *The Diapason Magazine—Chicago*

Richard Purvis played the most colorful, alive, and interesting recital in the Saint Louis Meeting. He's a master of suspense, contrast and intensity control, with a real sense of heartwarming beauty in his approach. *The American Organist — New York*[6]

The brochure also includes the legendary line regarding his "obituary": "Purvis was captured in Wiltz, Luxemburg in December, 1944, and was a prisoner of war until liberated near Munich in May, 1945. As a consequence of his being listed as 'missing in action' his obituary was erroneously printed by a leading music publication."

Purvis and Organ Registrations

Jonas Nordwall wrote:

> As a student he was allowed by Wallace Sabin to observe Karg-Elert practice at the San Francisco auditorium. Sabin insisted that Dick bring his copies of Karg-Elert's music and carefully note all of the registrations that Karg-Elert used on the Austin. In the "Mirrored Moon," Karg-Elert made about 10 registration changes on one page alone not marked in the score. Additionally, Karg-Elert's daughter assisted him at the console as a registrant. Dick notated all of Karg-Elert's changes on his music, as he did on the Franck scores, which makes them very valuable as a key resource to how things were really played versus their publication.[7]

Purvis marked most of his performance scores with detailed registrations, phrasings, and articulations, often using a variety of colored pencils and ink. He also developed his own system of color-coded registration sheets for pieces he played frequently. These pages, which he kept in a small three-ring binder, show precisely the registrations he used on the organ at Grace Cathedral and on several other organs as well.

The Editions Purvis Used

Purvis owned and performed from a variety of editions. He apparently did not favor any particular edition, even for Bach or Franck, whose music he played frequently. Throughout his career he used Novello editions of Bach that he may have acquired in England during his Curtis years, but he also owned editions published by Peters and Schirmer. His copy of the Riemenschneider edition of Bach's *Orgelbüchlein* was particularly well-used. Although he owned many original French editions, for the music of Franck he appears primarily to have used the Schirmer edition. (Purvis's library of performance scores is now housed in the Archive of Recorded Sound at Stanford University.)

Purvis on the Performance of His Own Music

Donald Corbett wrote about a typical Purvis dialogue with his audience: "Often he would play compositions of his own which had been requested

Purvis - Carol Rhapsody

*Ped. Lieb. 16'
Sw. Fl. Cel. Super OR (V.C. 8')
   Sw/Ped   Ch/Gt
Gt Blank
Ch. Harp (Super.) Sub

* Gen Ⓘ Ped Lieb 16'
Sw Fl Cel Super. Sub. Unison
   Sw/Ped.   Main Trem
Gt. Fl. 8
Ch Krummhorn 8'

Gen Ⓘⓘ
   Ped Violone 16' Fl. 16'
   Sw. Geigen, V.C. 8, Fl. 4'
   Sw/Ped Ch/Gt Chiff On

Gt. Blank
Ch. Fls. 8' + 2'
Gen Ⓘⓘⓘ
   Ped. Full minus Bombarde Sw. Full + Super
   Ch/Ped 8+4   Sw/Gt 8+4   Sw/Ch 8'
Gt Full
Ch Princ 4', Fls 4'+2', Trumpet

* See Alternates

Registrations for "Carol Rhapsody" on the organ at Grace Cathedral. Courtesy Donna Parker.

Purvis - Fantasia (Ton-y-Botel)

Start Ped. Princs. 16' 8' 4'
           Viol. 16', Fls 8' + 4'
     Sw. (4)
Sw./Pd.   Ch./Ped. 8'+4'   Sw./Gt.
     Gt. Princs., Fls. 8', 4', 2' (4)
     Ch. Blank

Gen (I) Ped. (3)
     Sw. 3
   sw/Gt
     Gt. (2) + Fl. 8'
     Ch. (5)

Gen (II) Ped (3) + Foy. 16'
     Sw. (3) + Fl. 2' Reeds. 8' + 4'
     Sw/Ped.   sw./Gt. 8'+4'
     Gt Princs., Fls 8' 4' 2'
     Ch. Princs. 8', 4', - Fls. 8', 4', 2 2/3
       Rd 8' Sub

Gen (III) Ped. Violone 32' + 16'
      Princ., Lieb., 16' Fl 8'
   Sw. (5) minus 16'
     sw/Gt. 8'+4'
   Gt. (4) + Mix
   Ch. Same as Gen (II)

Registrations for "Fantasia (Ton-y-Botel)" on the organ at Grace Cathedral. Courtesy Donna Parker.

by colleagues in the audience. His keen sense of humor would then evince itself. Purvis would state this program would raise two questions. First, he would say, "How will I interpret my own composition? Will it be a radical departure from your interpretations? Secondly, how much real sensitivity and skill will I be able to bring to my performance, assuming that I can even play?"[8]

Douglas Metzler also recalls Purvis making the following observation:

> There's nothing worse than a composer who plays his own music. There are three reasons why I do it:
>   1. Because of a request to play it
>   2. To see if it sounds like what you're used to hearing
>   3. To see if I can still play it[9]

The "Three-Note Encore"

Often at the end of his recitals, Purvis would ask for three random notes from the audience; he would then proceed to improvise an encore on these notes. A recorded example of this is the encore to his recital on May 5, 1985, at First Church of Christ, Scientist, in San Francisco. Although his improvisation on this occasion was in the form of a romantic ballad, Douglas Metzler said that Purvis would sometimes improvise a more involved piece.[10]

Recollections of Purvis as Performer

When asked if Purvis improvised, Stephen Loher wrote: "He did improvise, in the "mid-century" style. His improvisations sounded like his compositions. I think his sense of composing was similar to his sense of organs—he seemed to try to find something good. His repertoire was broad in range, styles, and periods. He never played from memory in public."[11] Loher recalls Purvis playing Flor Peeters' "Lied to the Ocean," which Loher considered "the epitome of Richard's playing."[12]

June Townsend reminisced: "Someone invited Richard to give an organ recital at Pacific Union College, my alma mater. He said he got lost in the middle of Bach's Toccata & Fugue in D minor and for awhile it was Dick Purvis instead of Bach."[13]

Purvis's Managers

Purvis used the services of two managers during his career. The first, Eric Parsons, of Philadelphia, is alluded to only in the above-quoted promotional brochure, probably from the late 1930s. There are no other details regarding this manager.[14]

Purvis's second and more important manager was Richard Torrence, who had lived in San Francisco from 1959 to 1962, before returning to New York to manage the concerts of Virgil Fox. For 8–10 months in the mid-1970s, he managed Richard's concert arrangements as well. In a telephone conversation Torrence told me that Purvis appeared shy when it came to asking for or getting a good fee. On one occasion Torrence had booked a concert and master class for Purvis in Wilmington, Delaware; the fee was $1,200. Torrence's assistant Dorothy Lake had gone to the concert to help. When the sponsor handed Purvis his fee payment, Purvis objected (perhaps ironically): "Give it to her [Dorothy]. You've paid too much already."[15]

Donna Parker also recalls hearing Purvis say, "I don't need that much money," after his manager had already negotiated a higher fee for a performance.[16]

Recitals through the Years

Purvis maintained an active performance schedule throughout his career. Surprisingly, however, it appears that he kept no log of his recitals; no collection of past recital programs (in a 1935 letter to The Curtis Institute at the time of his application he wrote, "I do not make it a habit of keeping programs…"); and no scrapbook of clippings or reviews.

The recitals and reviews listed in this chapter were collected from various sources: the majority were located in the archives at Grace Cathedral; a few were found in Purvis's papers; the remainder either came from other private collections or were mentioned by other sources. In some cases recitals were cited in correspondence or other writings. This listing is admittedly incomplete; additions to the list are welcomed by the author. Nevertheless, it gives a good idea of Purvis's concert repertoire and performance venues.

As in the case of most performing artists, Purvis had a core repertoire, but it evolved slowly through the years, with new pieces added occasionally and other pieces retired. Unfortunately, space limitations prohibit inclusion of many of the highly imaginative program notes that he wrote for concerts he played.

1946

In the fall of 1946, Purvis played at First Presbyterian Church for a regional convention of the AGO in Houston, Texas.[17]

1947

March 2, 1947, Grace Cathedral, Post-Evensong Recital[18]

Bach	Toccata and Fugue in D minor
Scheidt	When on the Cross our Savior Hung
Bach	Christ Lay in the Bonds of Death
Karg-Elert	Prepare Thyself, O My Soul
Purcell	Trumpet Tune
Haydn	The Musical Clock
Widor	Adagio, from Symphony VI
Maleingreau	The Tumult in the Praetorium (Passion Symphony)
Purvis	Communion; Toccata on the Kyrie

March 21, 1947, Central Methodist Church, Stockton, California

Dedicatory Recital, Elsie D. Wallace Memorial Organ

Purcell	Trumpet Tune
Handel	Concerto V
Bach	Fugue in G minor
Haydn	Suite for a Mechanical Clock
Reubke	Sonata on the Ninety-fourth Psalm
Karg-Elert	Invocation
Maleingreau	The Tumult in the Praetorium
Parker	Allegretto
Purvis	Romanza
Vierne	Finale, from Symphony I

April 6, 1947, Easter Sunday, Grace Cathedral

Farnam	Toccata on "O Filii"
Handel	Concerto V

Bach	Fugue in G minor
Vaughan Williams	Rhosymedre
Franck	Pièce Héroique
Schumann	Sketch in D-flat
Bonnet	Angelus du Soir
Vierne	Symphony I (Allegro vivace, Andante, Final)

May 4, 1947, Grace Cathedral

Vivaldi	Allegro, from Concerto in A minor
Bach	Three Chorale Preludes
Bach	Passacaglia and Fugue
Franck	Pastorale
Vierne	Scherzo, from Symphony II
Bairstow	Evensong
Purvis	Divinum Mysterium

June 1, 1947, Grace Cathedral

Bach	Toccata and Fugue in D minor
Daquin	Noel in D
Franck	Prélude, Fugue, and Variation
Vaughan Williams	Rhosymedre
Vierne	Intermezzo, from Symphony III
Bonnet	Angelus du Soir
Widor	Toccata, from Symphony V

July 13, 1947, Grace Cathedral

Bach	Three Liturgical Pieces
Purcell	Trumpet Voluntary
Peeters	Suite Modale (Adagio, Scherzo)
Karg-Elert	The Legend of the Mountain
Alexander Russell	Song of the Basket Weaver
Dallier	Electa ut Sol

The following recital on September 14, 1947, was mentioned in *The Cathedral Chimes*[19]:

"As announced in the Grace Cathedral newsletter, MR. PURVIS' ORGAN RECITAL promises to be another outstanding musical treat. A glance at the program on Page Four will make one feel he should not miss it. We are happy to announce that the recital is to be broadcast."

Bach	Prelude and Triple Fugue
Franck	Cantabile
Widor	Symphony VI (Allegro, Adagio, Intermezzo)
Philip James	Méditation à Sainte Clothilde
Vierne	Carillon de Westminster

October 12, 1947, Grace Cathedral

Purcell	Trumpet voluntary
Byrd	Pavane
Daquin	Rondeau le Coucou
Franck	Prelude, Fugue, and Variation
Peeters	Suite Modale
Dupré	Berceuse (In dulci jubilo)
Boellmann	Marche-Final (Deuxième Suite)

November 9, 1947, Grace Cathedral

Franck	Chorale in E major
Bach	Sonata in E-flat, Passacaglia and Fugue
Bonnet	Angelus du Soir
Haydn	Suite for a Musical Clock

The Biographical Data states: "In the fall of 1947 he toured extensively throughout the Pacific Northwest as a recitalist for the Moller Organ Company, playing in many towns where recitals had never been given."[20]

1948

The following notice was published January 5, 1948, in the *Philadelphia Bulletin*:

Music in Review

"The "Mass of St. Nicholas" by the American composer, Richard Purvis, was sung excellently by the Oratorio Choir last night under Walter Baker's leadership at the First Baptist Church, 17th and Sansom Sts...."

January 11, 1948, Grace Cathedral

Bach	In Dulci Jubilo (two settings)
Jean Huré	Communion sur un Noel
Franck	Chorale in A minor
Handel	Concerto V
Karg-Elert	Two Cathedral Windows (Adeste Fideles, Ave Maria)
Vierne	Scherzetto, Carillon

February 8, 1948, Grace Cathedral

Bach	Fantasia and Fugue in G minor
Peeters	Aria
Franck	Pièce Héroique
Handel	Concerto I
Purvis	Greensleeves, Chartres, Spiritual, Gwalshmai [sic; Gwalchmai]

April 11, 1948, Grace Cathedral

Vivaldi	Allegro, from Concerto in A minor
Scheidt	When on the Cross our Savior Hung
Bach	Christ Lay in the Bonds of Death
Brahms	O Sacred Head, Now Wounded
Purcell	Trumpet Tune
Bruce Simonds	Iam Sol Recedit Igneus
Vierne	Symphony One (Allegro Vivace, Andante, Final)

May 9, 1948, Grace Cathedral

Mendelssohn	Sonata VI
Schumann	Canon in B minor, Fugue on BACH, Sketch in D-flat
Brahms	Three Chorale Preludes
Liszt	Introduction and Fugue (Ad nos, ad salutarem undam)

June 13, 1948, Grace Cathedral

Vivaldi	Allegro, from Concerto in A minor
Franck	Pastorale
Widor	Intermezzo, from Symphony VI

Reubke	Sonata on The Ninety-fourth Psalm
Haydn	Suite for a Musical Clock
Nevin	Dirge "In Memoriam"
Purvis	Toccata Festiva "In Babilone"

Purvis performed at the 1948 National Convention of the American Guild of Organists held in St. Louis, Missouri. His recital on July 7, 1948, was given at our Lady of Sorrows Church, St. Louis. Following is his program, with samples of his program notes:

Vivaldi-Bach: Allegro from Concerto in A minor

Franck: Pastorale
("This delightful country scene from the pen of the Belgian Mystique has all the idyllic color of a Corot paysage. In the middle section, The Midsummer Night revels of a fairy band are suggested, after which the peaceful calm of the original theme returns. The tinkle of sheep bells can be heard just before the conclusion.")

Widor: Intermezzo from the Sixth Symphony
("From the great Sixth Symphony of a superlative French master comes this scintillating scherzo.")

Reubke: Sonata (complete)

Procter: Elegy ("This impressive dirge constitutes the slow movement of a meritorious organ sonata by a contemporary English organist.")

Purvis: In Babilone ("A toccata which is the final number of 'Seven Preludes on Tunes Found in American Hymnals' to be released by Carl Fischer")[21]

The Biographical Data states: "Due to the impact of this [St. Louis] recital, he was engaged for a comprehensive tour of North America in the spring of 1949."[22]

September 12, 1948, Grace Cathedral

Bach	Toccata and Fugue in D minor
Bach	Three Schübler Chorale Preludes
Franck	Chorale in E major
Handel	Allegro, from Concerto IV
Peeters	Lied to the Ocean[23]

Whitlock	Scherzo
Freeman	The Wistful Shepherd
Dallier	Toccata "Electa ut Sol"

"Masterpieces of Organ Literature"

Early in his tenure at Grace Cathedral, Purvis instituted a monthly "Masterpieces of Organ Literature" concert series.

October 10, 1948, Grace Cathedral, "Masterpieces of Organ Literature"

Buxtehude	Prelude and Fugue in F major
Bach	Three Liturgical Pieces
Roger-Ducasse	Pastorale*
Dupré	Scherzando
Whitlock	Fidelis
Franck	Final in B flat

October 15, 1948, Grace Cathedral

Portola Festival Musical Service, with the San Francisco Oratorio Society
   In addition to accompanying the choral works, Purvis played Bach's Toccata and Fugue in D minor.

November 4, 1948, Grace Cathedral, "Masterpieces of Organ Literature"

Dunstable	The Agincourt Hymn
Walond	Introduction and Toccata
Brahms	Three Chorale Preludes
Dupré	Prelude and Fugue in G minor

---

* In Purvis's collection of scores was a well-used copy of the "Pastorale" by Jean Roger-Ducasse, published in 1909. The score shows detailed red and blue pencil markings in Purvis's handwriting, with registrations for a four-manual organ, probably that of Grace Cathedral. It also shows, on the final page of the score, Purvis's notation "Cancel Choir (Knee)," suggesting that he used his knee to press a choir piston at that point in the piece. This 1948 recital is the only known instance of his performing the work. Score courtesy Leslie Wolf Robb.

   Also in Purvis's files was a heavily marked copy of Thalben-Ball's "Variations on a Theme by Paganini for Pedals." Although this piece does not appear on any known recital programs, he may well have programmed it.

Vierne   Symphony I (Allegro vivace, Andante, Final)

December 12, 1948, Grace Cathedral, "Masterpieces of Organ Literature"

Bach   Prelude and Fugue in G major
D'aquin   Noel in D
Bach   Two settings of In dulci jubilo
Egerton   Prelude-Improvisation "Veni Emmanuel"
Milford   Pastorale
Karg-Elert   Saluto Angelico
Purvis   A Carol Rhapsody

The archives also show that Ludwig Altman, the organist of Temple Emanu-El, accompanied at various concerts at Grace Cathedral in 1948.

1949

January 9, 1949, Grace Cathedral, "Masterpieces of Organ Literature"

Purcell   Trumpet Tune
Bach   Three Chorale Preludes
Bach   Toccata and Fugue in D minor
Franck   Pastorale
Handel   Allegro Concerto IV
Karg-Elert   The Legend of the Mountain
Vierne   Scherzo, from Symphony II
Purvis   Communion; Toccata Festiva "In Babilone"

February 13, 1949, Grace Cathedral, "Masterpieces of Organ Literature"

Dupré   Cortege et Litanie
Bach   Three Chorale Preludes
Bach   Fugue in G minor ("The Lesser")
Brahms   Lo How a Rose
Schumann   Sketch in D-flat
Franck   Pièce Héroique
Purvis   Greensleeves, Chartres, Spiritual, Gwalshmai [sic;
Gwalchmai]

March 13, 1949, Grace Cathedral, "Masterpieces of Organ Literature"

Franck	Chorale in A minor
Marcello	Psalm Nineteen
Vivaldi	Largo
Dandrieu	Les Fifres
Bach	Passacaglia and Fugue
Freeman	Elegiac Romance
Vierne	Intermezzo, from Symphony 3
Reubke	The Ninety-fourth Psalm

March 25, 1949, Central Methodist Church, Stockton, California

With the Grace Cathedral Choristers, Purvis presented a concert entitled "The Church Year in Music." The program consisted of 14 choral anthems, including Purvis's "Magnificat." As part of the program Purvis performed three organ solos: Bach, Toccata and Fugue in D minor; Karg-Elert, O God, Thou Eternal God; and his own Toccata Festiva.[24]

April 10, 1949, Grace Cathedral, "Masterpieces of Organ Literature"

Purvis	Vexilla Regis
Scheidt, Bach, Brahms	Three Passiontide Chorales
Bach	Fantasia and Fugue in G minor
Vaughan Williams	Rhosymedre
Vierne	Scherzetto
Franck	Prelude, Fugue, and Variation
Maleingreau	The Tumult in the Praetorium, from Passion Symphony

May 8, 1949, Grace Cathedral, "Masterpieces of Organ Literature"

Vivaldi	Allegro, from Concerto in A minor
Franck	Pastorale
Widor	Intermezzo, from Symphony VI
Reubke	The Ninety-fourth Psalm
Purvis	Divinum Mysterium, Contemplation "Tallis Canon," Toccata Festiva "In Babilone"

According to the Biographical Data, in May 1949 Purvis gave a recital and taught master classes for the Regional Convention of the AGO in Houston, Texas.[25]

June 12, 1949, Grace Cathedral, "Masterpieces of Organ Literature"

Dupré	Cortege et Litanie
Bach	Three Chorale Preludes
Bach	Passacaglia and Fugue in C minor
Haydn	Suite for a Musical Clock
Philip James	Meditation à Sainte Clothilde
Vierne	Scherzetto
Purvis	Communion on a Gregorian Theme
Mulet	Toccata

October 9, 1949, Grace Cathedral, "Masterpieces of Organ Literature"

Purcell	Trumpet Voluntary
Byrd	Pavane
Daquin	Rondeau "Le Coucou"
St.-Saëns	Prelude and Fugue in B major
Peeters	Song to the Ocean (Lied des Meers)
Bossi	Scherzo Burlesca
Hillemacher	Pastorale
Purvis	Fantasy Ton-y-Botel, Pastorale on Forest Green
Dallier	Toccata Electa ut Sol

November 13, 1949, Grace Cathedral, Bach-Franck Cycle I

Bach	Allegro, from Concerto in A minor
	Four Liturgical Pieces
	Prelude and Triple fugue
Franck	Chorale in E major
	Grande Piece Symphonique
	Final in B-flat

December 11, 1949, Grace Cathedral, "Masterpieces of Organ Literature"

Bach	In dulci jubilo, three settings
D'Aquin	Noel in D

Huré	Communion sur un Noel
Bonnet	Variations on the Magnificat
Handel	Allegro from Concerto VI
Langlais	La Nativité
Milford	Pastorale
Karg-Elert	Ave Maria
Purvis	Divinum Mysterium

1950

January 8, 1950, Grace Cathedral, "All Request Program"

Bach, Toccata and Fugue in D minor, three chorale preludes, Fugue in G minor; works of Handel, Schumann, Brahms; and Purvis, Four Carol Preludes

February 12, 1950, Grace Cathedral, Bach-Franck Cycle

March 12, 1950, Grace Cathedral

Works of Mendelssohn, Maleingreau, Scheidt, Bach, Brahms, Widor, Karg-Elert, Bach

April 9, 1950, Easter, Grace Cathedral

Works of Bach, Dandrieu, Vivaldi, Marcello, Dupré, Benoit, Vierne

May 4, 1950, Grace Cathedral, Bach-Franck Cycle

June 11, 1950, Grace Cathedral, "Contemporary Organ Music"

Works of Dupré, Fickenscher (Lament), Peeters (Suite Modale), Frederic Freeman, Purvis (Supplication, Toccata Festiva)

September 10, 1950, Grace Cathedral, Bach-Franck Cycle

October 8, 1950, Grace Cathedral

Works of Handel, Brahms, Schumann, Purvis (Three Prayers in Tone)

November 12, 1950, Grace Cathedral, "Masterpieces of Organ Literature"

Works of Dunstable, Schlick, Cabezon, Palestrina, Byrd, Sweelinck, Scheidt, Kerll, Frescobaldi, Buxtehude

December 10, 1950, Grace Cathedral

Works of Bach, Handel, Daquin Langlais, Karg-Elert, Dupré, Purvis

1951

January 14, 1951, Grace Cathedral

Works of Handel, Franck, Bach, Purvis (Three Prayers in Tone)

February 14, 1951, First Methodist Church, Shreveport, Louisiana[26]

Presented by the North Louisiana Chapter of the AGO

Handel	Concerto I (Larghetto, Allegro, Adagio, Andante con Variazione)
Franck	Pastorale
Bach	Prelude and Fugue in G major
Purvis	Three Prayers in Tone (Repentance, Thanksgiving, Supplication)
Purvis	Toccata in Babilone

Improvisation on Given Themes

February 25, 1951, First Baptist Church, Philadelphia, Pennsylania

The following review appeared on February 26, 1961, in the *Philadelphia Bulletin*:

> Richard Purvis, American organist and composer, gave his first local recital in several years at the First Baptist Church, 17th and Sansom Sts., last night. In a sense the occasion was a "homecoming" for him, since he was formerly associated with the musical life of Philadelphia, first as a student at the Curtis Institute and later as organist in various mid-city churches. He now holds a post at Grace Episcopal Cathedral in San Francisco.
>
> Mr. Purvis placed Handel's First Concerto at the top of his program and set it forth skillfully enough as to technique. The interpretation, however, was disappointing to one listener, mainly on points of registration,

overemphasis of some tonal contrasts, and various details of the stylistic approach to the score.

As the second number, Franck's "Pastorale," went much better as to the qualities of musical delineation and the tasteful colorations realized. Next came Johann Sebastian Bach's great Prelude and Fugue in G major, the statement of the Fugue being especially excellent for the contrapuntal clarity and balance of the several voices, the stability of pace, and the telling buildup of climaxes.

The latter part of the roster embraced some of Mr. Purvis' own pieces, in the performance of which the organist seemed on his finest levels. Brilliance marked a vigorous "Toccata in Babilone" and there were numerous things to gain the attention and liking in "Three Prayers in Tone"—"Repentance," "Thanksgiving," and "Supplication." The recitalist also demonstrated notable capacity as an improviser, exploiting effectively themes submitted by two Philadelphia musicians, Constant Vauclain and Robert Elmore.

In addition to the organ numbers, the recital presented Roy Wilde, baritone, vocally admirable in Bacharach's setting of the Eighth Psalm. Charles Alan Romero served as organ accompanist.

—W. E. S.

March 14, 1951, The Mormon Tabernacle, Salt Lake City, Utah

In March 1951, Purvis visited Salt Lake City, where he was undoubtedly eager to try out the organ installed in 1948 at the Mormon Tabernacle, one of G. Donald Harrison's masterpieces.[27] Not only did Purvis give a recital on that occasion, but he also came away with ideas that would result in several changes to the Alexander Memorial Organ at Grace Cathedral.

On March 11, 1951, the *Salt Lake Tribune* reported:

Organist Slates Utah Concert

Richard Purvis, organist of Grace cathedral, San Francisco, is being presented in an organ concert by the Utah chapter American Guild of Organists in the Salt Lake Tabernacle on Wednesday, at 8:30 p.m. The concert is free to the public, and all lovers of fine music are cordially invited to attend.

Since his debut in San Francisco's Exposition auditorium at the age of 13, Mr. Purvis has been ranked as an organist of most unusual ability by critics and public alike.

After several years of intensive study with Wallace Sabin in San Francisco, Purvis was awarded the much coveted Cyrus H. K. Curtis memorial

scholarship of the Curtis Institute of Music. He was also granted a fellowship for European study by the same school. While in England he appeared
in concert at the school of English church music, the British Broadcasting
Co. and historic York Minster.

Upon his return to this country he appeared as organist with the Philadelphia Orchestra, the National Broadcasting Co. and the Curtis Symphony
Orchestra. He began a military career in March, 1942, when he enlisted in
the army. He was appointed bandmaster of the 28th division and was sent
to the European theater of war. He was captured in Wiltz, Luxembourg, in
December, 1944, and was a prisoner of war until liberated near Munich in May,
1945. As a consequence of his being listed as "missing in action" his obituary
was erroneously printed by a leading music publication. Following his return
to civilian life, he was appointed organist and master of choristers of Grace
Cathedral, San Francisco.

A feature of every Purvis concert is an impromptu extemporization of
themes submitted by the audience. He is considered the foremost improvi-
sator of his generation in America.[28]

On the same day, the *Deseret News* printed an identical article, with the
following additions:

Noted Coast Organist Dates Concert in S.L.

... He is one of the few individuals given an opportunity to read his own
"obituary." ...

In addition to playing the organ, he also is a composer, and has written
several selections.... He also designs every program for the specific organ
on which he is to play.[29]

On March 15, 1951, the following review appeared in the *Deseret News*:

Acclaim Accorded Organist
by CONRAD B. HARRISON

An electrifying young San Francisco organist by the name of Richard
Purvis carved an impressive niche into local concert records Wednesday
night at the Tabernacle.

There have been few organists, if any, among those sponsored by the
Utah Chapter, American Guild of Organists, to match Mr. Purvis in
dynamic production. He won unqualified acclaim from his audience of
organ students and devotees.

CHOICE EXCELLENT

The San Franciscan's choice of program was in excellent taste and closely allied with his aggressive style at the keyboard. He projected his enthusiasm into the Handel Concerto No. 1, bringing spontaneity and spirit to the refreshing work. His technique from the beginning was clean and accurate.

Tonal brilliance of the woodwinds in the big Aeolian-Skinner organ was a feature of the Cesar Franck "Pastorale," while the full power of the instrument was applied to an uplifting and glorious performance of the joyous Prelude and Fugue in G Major by Johann Sebastian Bach. Counterpoint was clearly defined by the organ and the tonal mass was sensational in its brilliance.

NUANCES EFFECTIVE

The same coloring that marked the first half of his program came out in the second half performances of the organist's own works. Nuances were particularly effective in the "Three Prayers in Tone" described as "Repentance, Thanksgiving and Supplication." Full, broad and dynamic was his "Toccata in Babilone," reflecting power and driving spirit of the organist-composer.

Equally brilliant were his improvisations on given themes at the close of the program.[30]

April 8, 1951, Grace Cathedral

Mendelssohn, Sonata III; Schumann, Brahms; Liszt, Ad Nos

May 13, 1951, Grace Cathedral, Bach-Franck Cycle

June 10, 1951, Grace Cathedral, "Masterpieces of Organ Literature"[31]

"Contemporary American Composers"
Robert Russell Bennett Sonata in G

Camil van Hulse	Meditation (Symphonia Mystica)
Leo Sowerby	Fantasy for Flute Stops
Philip James	Meditation à Sainte Clothilde
Seth Bingham	Roulade
August Meckelberghe	De Profundis Clamavi
Frederic Freeman	Three Pieces (Elegiac Romance, Puppets, The Wistful Shepherd
Reginald Greenbrook	Fanfare

September 9, 1951, Grace Cathedral

Works of Bach: Fantasie and Fugue in G minor, Duetto, Passacaglia, O Mensch bewein, Trio in C minor, Toccata in F

October 14, 1951, Grace Cathedral, "English Composers"

Works of Purcell, Tallis, Gibbons, Byrd, Handel, Goodhart, Wolstenholme, Whitlock, Vaughan Williams, Martin Shaw

November 11, 1951, Grace Cathedral, "Medieval and Baroque Composers"

Works of Perontius, Dunstable, Schlick, Cabezon, Sweelinck, Frescobaldi, Scheidt, Kerll, Pachelbel, Buxtehude

December 9, 1951, Grace Cathedral, "French Composers"

Works of Dupré, Couperin, Daquin, Bonnet, Jean Huré, Dallier, Guilmant, Vierne

1952

The *Philadelphia Bulletin* reported on January 5, 1952, that "The Mass of the Holy Nativity, composed by Richard Purvis, a former Philadelphia organist, will be sung for the first time in this city at St. Mark's Episcopal Church, 1625 Locust, tomorrow morning at 11." It is not known if Purvis was present.

January 13, 1952, Grace Cathedral, "American Composers"

Works of Purvis, Healey Willan, Frances McCollin, Bruce Simonds, Horatio Parker, Frederic Freeman, Robert Russell Bennett

February 10, 1952, Grace Cathedral, "Original Compositions"

Works of Purvis: Partita on "Christ ist Erstanden," American Organ Mass, Les Petites Cloches, Three Prayers in Tone, Marche Grotesque, Communion

March 9, 1952, Grace Cathedral

Works of Bach, Bonnet, Karg-Elert, Purvis, Boellmann (Suite Gothique)

April 13, 1952, Grace Cathedral

Works of Marcello, Bach, Mozart, Franck, Benoit, Purvis (Partita on "Christ ist Erstanden")

May 11, 1952, Grace Cathedral

Works of Reger, Handel, Brahms, Bach, Schroeder, Pepping, Reubke

June 8, 1952, Grace Cathedral, "Request Program"

Bach	Fantasie and Fugue in G minor
Kauffmann	Harmonische Seelenlust
Franck	Prelude, Fugue, and Variation
Rinck	Rondo
Vaughan Williams	Rhosymedre
Liszt	Ad nos

The Biographical Data states:

> After the Cathedral organ was completed in 1952, Purvis set himself the task of producing a new program which he entitled "Worship Through Music." At the National Convention of the AGO in San Francisco in 1952, his Grace Cathedral Choristers and members of the San Francisco Orchestra performed this program, which embodied a historical survey of sacred music from Gregorian chant to contemporary compositions. An honored guest, Sir William McKie, organist and Master of the Choristers at Westminster Abbey, was in the audience. He declared this program "the most comprehensive survey of an art ever produced in one hour and fifteen minutes."[32]

June 30, 1952, Grace Cathedral, San Francisco National AGO Convention

"Worship Through Music"

Purvis conducted a plainsong hymn and various choral works by early composers (Cavazzoni, Redford, Corelli, Schütz, Byrd), followed by his Partita on "Christ ist Erstanden."[33]

September 28, 1952, Grace Cathedral, "Music of the Baroque Era"

Works of Bach, Kauffmann, Handel, Byrd, Martini, Buxtehude

October 12, 1952, Grace Cathedral

Works of Dupré, St.-Saëns, Widor, Gigout, Dallier, Guilmant, Vierne

November 9, 1952, Bach-Franck Cycle

Bach   Movements from Clavierübung
          Prelude & Fugue in E-flat major
Franck   Chorale in E major, Piece Héroique

December 14, 1952, Grace Cathedral

Works of Redford, Sicher, Schlick, Bach, Balbastre, Daquin, Jean Huré, Kauffmann, Purvis

1953

The Biographical Data states, "During 1953 Purvis embarked on a transcontinental recital tour of the United States, playing in New York City, Boston, Philadelphia, Baltimore, Detroit, and St. Louis."[34] No details regarding these recitals are available.

January 11, 1953, Grace Cathedral

Works of Walond, Redford, Tallis, Gibbons, Byrd, Handel, Bridge, Whitlock, Martin Shaw

January 26, 1953, Grace Cathedral, "The Evolution of the Chorale Prelude"

February 8, 1953, Grace Cathedral, Bach-Franck Cycle

Bach   Prelude and Fugue in B minor, Trio in C minor, Pastoral Suite,
          Passacaglia and Fugue
Franck   Prelude, Fugue and Variation; Chorale in A minor

March 8, 1953, Grace Cathedral

Works of Bach, Beethoven, Brahms, Boyce, Fickenscher, Frederic Freeman

April 12, 1953, Grace Cathedral, "Original Compositions"

Works of Purvis: Partita on "Christ ist Erstanden," Anno belli III Prayer for Peace/Dirge, Capriccio on the Notes of the Cuckoo, Song of Saint Francis

May 10, 1953, Grace Cathedral, Bach-Franck Cycle

Bach	Concerto in C major, four liturgical pieces, Prelude and Fugue in G major
Franck	Chorale in B minor, Final in B-flat

May 25, 1953, Grace Cathedral, "Ecclesiastical Chamber Music"

Works of Walond, Van den Gheyn, Bach, Handel, Isaak, Dufay, Martini, Kerckhoven, Loeillet

September 28, 1953, Grace Cathedral, "Forerunners of Bach"

Works of Dunstable, Schlick, Redford, Gabrieli, Byrd, Frescobaldi, Sweelinck, Kerll, Kuhnau, Buxtehude

October 11, 1953, Grace Cathedral, Bach-Franck Cycle

Bach	Prelude and Fugue in E-flat, four chorale preludes, Toccata and Fugue in D minor
Franck	Pastorale, Chorale in B minor

November 8, 1953, Grace Cathedral, "Spanish and Italian Masters"

Works of Vivaldi, Cabezon, Frescobaldi, Banchieri, Cabanilles, Martini, Casanovas, Valdés, Bossi

November 29, 1953, Grace Cathedral, "Masterpieces of Organ Literature"

Works of Bach: Three Schübler Chorales, Prelude and Fugue in B minor, Trio Sonata ("Allegro moderato, Adagio alla Siciliano and Allegro"), "O Mensch bewein," Prelude and Fugue in G major

December 13, 1953, Grace Cathedral, "Masterpieces of Organ Literature"

Works of Bach, Balbastre, Kauffmann, Daquin, Hillemacher, Mozart, Donald Morrison, Purvis (An American Organ Mass)

December 20, 1953, Grace Cathedral, Carol Vespers

Works of Bach, Purvis, Shaw

1954

In about 1954 Purvis played the dedicatory recital on the new Casavant organ at All Saints' Episcopal Church in Beverly Hills, California.[35]

Clarence Snyder, a Curtis classmate of Purvis, wrote, "Richard played at my church in Montclair, NJ, the First Congregational, circa 1954. Here he improvised pieces later published, including The Little Bells."[36]

January 10, 1954, Grace Cathedral, "Flemish and English Masters"

Works of Boyce, Tallis, Stanley, van den Gheyn, Sweelinck, Handel, Jongen, Whitlock

February 14, 1954, Grace Cathedral, Bach-Franck Cycle

Bach   Fantasia and Fugue in G minor, Duetto, Passacaglia
Franck   Chorale in E, Pièce Héroique

February 22, 1954, Grace Cathedral, "Bach's Contemporaries"

Works of Vivaldi, Homilius, Loeillet, Telemann, Handel, Czernohorsky, Walter, Lübeck

March 14, 1954, Grace Cathedral, "Bohemian and French Composers"

Works of Czernohorsky, Seeger, Brixi, Messiaen (The Ascension), Dandrieu, Couperin, Daquin, Vierne

April 11, 1954, Grace Cathedral, "Passiontide Music"

Works of Bach, Purvis, Frances McCollin, Krebs, Maleingreau, Reger, Reubke

April 17, 1954, Grace Cathedral, Eve of Easter carillon concert

May 9, 1954, Grace Cathedral, "American Composers"

Works of Purvis, van Hulse, Arthur Howes, Everett Titcomb, Frederic Freeman

May 24, 1954, Grace Cathedral, "The Sons of Bach"

Works of Wilhelm Friedemann, Karl Philipp Emanuel, Johann Ludwig Krebs, Homilius, Doles ("became Kantor of St. Thomas after Bach")

September 14, 1954, St. Paul's Episcopal Church, Salinas, California

One of three inaugural recitals on the church's new Aeolian-Skinner organ. The others were performed by Virgil Fox and Alexander Schreiner.[37]

September 20, 1954, Grace Cathedral, "Music of the Baroque Era"

Works of Stanley, Byrd, Arne, Martini, Vivaldi, Frescobaldi, Cabezon, Casanovas

October 10, 1954, Grace Cathedral, "Masterpieces of Organ Literature"

Works of Fickenshur, Freeman, Purvis

October 18, 1954, Grace Cathedral, "German Composers"

Works of Isaak, Sicher, Schlick, Handel, Krebs, Kauffmann, Teleman, Homilius, Lübeck

November 14, 1954, Grace Cathedral, Bach-Franck Cycle

Bach	Prelude and Fugue in B minor, Duetto from Clavierübung, O Mensch bewein, Toccata in F
Franck	Chorale in E major, Cantabile, Final in B-flat

November 22, 1954, Grace Cathedral, "Masterpieces of Organ Literature"

Music of Perontius, Dufay, le Beque, Couperin, Daquin, van den Gheyn, Loeillet, van den Kerckhoven

December 12, 1954, Grace Cathedral

Works of Bach, Davies, Gigout, Purvis (Adoration, An American Organ Mass, Chartres, Les Petites Cloches, Greensleeves, Carillon)

1955

January 9, 1955, Grace Cathedral, "Masterpieces of Organ Literature"

Mendelssohn, Sonata VI; Schubert, Fugue in E minor; Brahms chorale preludes; Schumann, three pieces; Liszt, Ad nos

February 13, 1955, Grace Cathedral, Bach-Franck Cycle

Bach   Excerpts from Clavierübung
Franck   Prelude, Fugue, and Variation; Chorale in A minor

March 13, 1955, Grace Cathedral

Works of Brahms, Mendelssohn, Schumann, Reubke

Saturday April 9, 1955, Grace Cathedral, Eve of Easter

Carillon Concert

April 10, 1955, Grace Cathedral, Bach-Franck Cycle

Bach   Allegro from Concerto in A minor, Pastorale Suite, Passacaglia
Franck   Pastorale, Pièce Héroique

May 8, 1955, Grace Cathedral, "Contemporary Composers"

Works of Dupré, Schroeder, Pepping, Peeters, Langlais, Donald Morrison

September 26, 1955, Grace Cathedral, "Evolution of the Chorale Prelude"

Works of Dunstable, Redford, Sicher, Schlick, Cabezon, Kuhnau, Bach, Kauffman, Homilius, Doles, Brahms, McCollin, Schroeder, Pepping

October 9, 1955, Grace Cathedral, Bach-Franck Cycle

Bach   Prelude and Fugue in B minor, three chorale preludes, Passaca-
               glia and Fugue
Franck   Chorale in E major, Cantabile, Pièce Héroique

October 18, 1955, St. Paul's Episcopal Church, Salinas, California[38]

November 13, 1955, Grace Cathedral, "From English Quires and Chancels"

Works of Whitlock, Stanley, Tallis, Arne, Walond, Byrd, Purcell, Vaughan Williams, Davies, Martin Shaw

November 28, 1955, Grace Cathedral, "The Bach Family"

Works of J. S. Bach, Johann Bernhard Bach, Karl Philipp Emanuel Bach, Wilhelm Friedemann Bach

December 11, 1955, Grace Cathedral, "In Memoriam Wallace Arthur Sabin (1869–1937)"

Bach	Before Thy Throne, O God, I Stand
Davies	A Solemn Melody
Gigout	Grand Choeur Dialogué
Jean Huré	Communion sur un Noel
Bach	Three settings of In dulci jubilo
Balbastre	Noel Varié
Langlais	La Nativité
Daquin	Noel in D
Purvis	Greensleeves, Christmas Cradle Song, Forest Green, Divinum Mysterium

1956

In 1956, Purvis composed and first performed in Grace Cathedral his extended organ work, "The Song of St. Francis," later rewritten, renamed, and published as the "St. Francis Suite."[39]

February 12, 1956, Grace Cathedral, Bach-Franck Cycle

Bach	Prelude and Triple Fugue, O Man Thy Grievous Sin Bewail, Duetto II from Clavierübung
Franck	Chorale in B minor, Final in B-flat

March 11, 1956, Grace Cathedral, "From French and Belgian Organ Lofts"

Dupré	Cortège et Litanie
Franck	Prelude, Fugue, and Variation
Maleingreau	The Tumult in the Praetorium
Peeters	Aria
Vierne	Divertissement, Scherzetto

| Peeters | Song to the Ocean |
| Gigout | Grand Choeur Dialogué |

April 8, 1956, Grace Cathedral, "Masterpieces of Organ Literature"

Dupré	Vepres du Commun
Camil van Hulse	Meditation
Peeters	Suite Modale
Freeman	Three pieces
Purvis	Partita on "Christ ist Erstanden"

May 13, 1956, Grace Cathedral, Bach-Franck Cycle III

| Bach | Prelude and Fugue in G major, Sonata in E-flat, Toccata in F |
| Franck | Pastorale, Chorale in A minor |

1957

January 28, 1957, Grace Cathedral

Bach	Credo
Corelli	Sonata da Chiesa
Krebs, Pachelbel, Bach	Preludes
Loeillet	Trio Sonata
Martini	Aria con Variazzione
Telemann	Trio Sonata

February 10, 1957, Grace Cathedral

Buxtehude	Prelude and Fugue in F major
Brahms	Three chorale preludes
Haydn	Suite for a Musical Clock
Mendelssohn	Sonata III
Schumann	Three pieces
Reger	Introduction and Passacaglia

February 25, 1957, Grace Cathedral

Works of Bach, Handel, Kauffmann, van den Gheyn, Loeillet, Krebs, Telemann

March 10, 1957, Grace Cathedral

Dupré	Vepres du Commun
Reger	Benedictus
Vierne	Intermezzo and Adagio from Symphony III
Bach	Prelude and Triple Fugue
Brahms	O Traurigkeit
Dallier	Toccata Electa ut Sol

April 14, 1957, Grace Cathedral, "Masterpieces of Organ Literature"[40]

Dupré	Cortège et Litanie
Bach	O Man Thy Grievous Sin Bewail
Bach	Passacaglia and Fugue
Peeters	Aria
Maleingreau	The Tumult in the Praetorium
Elmore	Pavanne
Reubke	The 94th Psalm

1958

March 9, 1958, Grace Cathedral

Works of Campra, Daquin, Rameau, Dandrieu, Bach, Maurice Greene, Marcello, Jongen (Prière), Vierne, Vaughan Williams, Gigout

April 12, 1958, Grace Cathedral

Corelli	Sonata da Chiesa
Bach	Four chorale preludes from the *Orgelbüchlein*
Handel	Trio Sonata
Walcha	Three chorale preludes
Mozart	Three Organ Sonatas

October 12, 1958, Grace Cathedral

Stanley	Voluntary in A minor
Homilius	Chorale Prelude
Handel	Concerto I

Peeters	Song to the Ocean
Carvalho	Sonata for Flute Stops
Lidon	Sonata for Trumpet
Purvis	Repentance, Capriccio on the Notes of the Cuckoo, Toccata on the Kyrie

1959

February 8, 1959, Grace Cathedral, Bach-Franck Cycle

| Bach | Concerto in C major, O Mensch bewein, Prelude and Fugue in G major |
| Franck | Chorale in B minor, Cantabile, Pièce Héroïque |

March 8, 1959, Grace Cathedral

Brahms	Three Chorale Preludes
Dupré	Cortège et Litanie
Scheidt, Homilius, Bach	Three Passiontide Chorale preludes
Maleingreau	The Tumult in the Praetorium
Peeters	Aria
Reubke	The 94th Psalm

May 10, 1959, Grace Cathedral, "Music by Richard Purvis"

Purvis	Partita on "Christ ist Erstanden"
	Introit and Elevation from "An American Organ Mass"
	March Grotesque
	Three Prayers in Tone
	Les Petites Cloches[41]
	Spiritual
	The Song of Saint Francis

September 6, 1959, Grace Cathedral, "Let There Be Light"

The first major public showing in America of "Son et Lumière," the revolutionary new concept of dramatic presentation that originated in France in 1952.

Music of Richard Purvis

October 11, 1959, Grace Cathedral

Martin Shaw	Processional
Frank Bridge	Adagio
Purcell	Voluntary in C major
Tallis	Funeral Dirge
Arne	Air for Flute Stops
Stanley	Adagio and Fugue
Harold Darke	A Fantasy
Maurice Green	Voluntary in C minor
Walford Davies	A Solemn Melody
Whitlock	Fanfare

1961

January 30, 1961, Grace Cathedral

Concert Honoring the 111th Convention of the Episcopal Diocese of California
Richard Purvis and William Duncan, Organists[42]
Works of Handel, Arne, Homilius, Dandrieu, Mozart (Church Sonata), Marcello, Poulenc (Concerto)

February 12, 1961, Grace Cathedral

Works of Stanley, Harold Darke, Maurice Greene, Bach, Franck, Vierne

March 12, 1961, Grace Cathedral

Works of Stanley, Bach, Handel, Flor Peeters, Bossi, Langlais, Purvis

During the months of April, May, and June 1961, Fernando Germani performed the complete organ works of Bach in 14 recitals.

November 12, 1961, Grace Cathedral

Works of Peeters, Schroeder, Bach, Karg-Elert, Vierne, Franck, Bridge, Purvis

June 29, 1961, Grace Cathedral[43]

American Guild of Organists Far Western Regional Convention

Langlais	Suite Médiévale
Maurice Green	Voluntary
Thomas Arne	Air for Flute Stops
Claude Dandrieu	Les Fifres
Peeters	Song of the Ocean
Dupré	Scherzando
Darke	A Fantasy
Purvis	Fanfare

In the early fall of 1961, Purvis performed in Houston, Texas, on the new Moller organ at St. Luke's Methodist Church and conducted a diocesan choral festival at Christ Church Cathedral (Episcopal). He played at St. Luke's on Friday night, conducted an all-day rehearsal on Saturday, and directed the choral festival on Sunday.[44] According to the Biographical Data, it was at this festival that his "Mass of the Resurrection" received its first performance outside San Francisco.[45]

December 28, 1961, Cathedral of Mary Our Queen, Baltimore, Maryland[46]

AGO Winter Conclave

Langlais	Suite Médiévale
Arne	Air for Flute Stops
Greene	Voluntary for Double Organ
Stanley	Trumpet Voluntary
Bach	Passacaglia and Fugue in C minor
Franck	Pastorale
Dupré	Scherzando
Karg-Elert	The Soul of the Lake, Rigaudon
Purvis	Earth Carol, Fanfare

1962

January 29, 1962, Grace Cathedral, "Music for Organ, Brass, and Tympani"

Works of Marcello, Bach, Martin Shaw, Flor Peeters, Lully, Campra, Sowerby, Purvis

February 11, 1962, Grace Cathedral

Richard Purvis and William Duncan, Organists

Marcello	Two Psalm Paraphrases (XIX, XX)
Bach	Prelude & Fugue in G major
Handel	Organ and Oboe Concerto III (Steve Cohen, oboe)
Schumann	Two Sketches (Maestoso in F minor, Scherzando in D-flat major)
Lully	Grand Choeur (2 organs)
Sowerby	Ballade for Organ and English Horn (Steve Cohen, English horn)
Freeman	Pastorale
Campra	Rigaudon (two organs)

March 11, 1962, Grace Cathedral

Works of Bach, Scheidt, Kuhnau, Krebs, Widor, Franck, Handel, Reubke

April 8, 1962, Grace Cathedral

Reger	Benedictus, Introduction and Passacaglia in D minor
Bach	Three Chorale Preludes
Franck	Chorale in A minor
Philip James	Meditation à Sainte Clotilde
Purvis	Spiritual, Toccata on the Kyrie

May 13, 1962, Grace Cathedral

Works of Bach, Walton, Vaughan Williams, Shaw, Davies, Purvis

October 14, 1962, Grace Cathedral, "Music for Two Organs"

William Duncan at the Crocker Memorial Organ (in the Chapel of Grace)
Richard Purvis at the Alexander Memorial Organ

Stanley	Voluntary for a Double Organ
Kauffman	Three Chorale Preludes
	O God, Look Down in Mercy
	Praise God, the Source of Blessing
	How Brightly Shines the Morning Star
Handel	Concerto V
Satie	Messe des Pauvres
Purvis	Dialogue Monastique
Gigout	Grand Choeur Dialogué

October 30, 1962, Grace Cathedral, "Music for Organ and Instruments"

Works of Handel, Loeillet, Mozart

November 11, 1962, Grace Cathedral, "English and American Composers"

Works of Tallis, Whitlock, Bridge, Milford, Walton, Cyril Scott, Darke, Searle Wright, Purvis

1963

In her book *The History of the Organ in the United States,* Orpha Ochse wrote about a recital Purvis played in 1963 on a historical organ in Paso Robles, California:

> Californians continued to send to the East for some of their organs. Typical is the story of the organ William Stevens built in 1863 for Trinity Episcopal Church, San Jose. This two-manual, twenty-four stop organ was transported by boat to the Isthmus of Panama, taken by cart across the isthmus, again loaded on a boat for San Francisco, and finally taken by wagon to the church. The organ cost about $1,200 and the freight added $800. The old organ was given to the St. James' Episcopal Church, Paso Robles, in 1924, where its centennial was observed in 1963 by a recital played by Richard Purvis.[47]

January 13, 1963, Grace Cathedral, "German and Spanish Composers"

Works of Cabezon, Pachelbel, Bach, Carvalho, Pepping, Torres, Casanovas

February 10, 1963, Grace Cathedral, "Flemish and Italian Composers"

Works of Franck, Frescobaldi, Scarlatti, Martini, van den Gheyn, Peeters

March 10, 1963, Grace Cathedral, "French and Scandinavian Composers"

Works of Buxtehude, Vierne, St.-Saëns, Dupré, Widor, Gabriel Dupont, Boellmann

March 24, 1963, Grace Cathedral

With members of the San Francisco Symphony, Purvis accompanied the University of California Chorus in what was billed as the San Francisco premiere performance of Monteverdi's "Vespers," under the direction of Denis Stevens.

The Biographical Data states:

> The summer of 1963 provided a welcome change to Richard. He vacationed for two months in England and visited many of the places which he had frequented as a young student. However, his need for relaxation gave way to his love of music. He could not refrain from examining extensively most of the English Cathedral choir schools; he spent the greatest part of his vacation in observation and study.[48]

October 1, 1963, Grace Cathedral, "Music for Violin and Organ"
Violinist Eugene Stoia
Works of Handel, Bach, Walcha

October 13, 1963, Grace Cathedral, "From English Chancels and Choirs"
Works of Stanley, Arne, Greene, Tallis, Handel, Bridge, Cyril Scott, Darke, Shaw

November 10, 1963, Grace Cathedral, Bach-Franck Cycle

Bach   Agnus Dei, Trio in C minor, Passacaglia
Franck   Pastorale, Chorale in B minor, Final in B-flat

1964

On April 26, 1964, Purvis directed at Grace Cathedral the second Northern California performance of his "Ballad of Judas Iscariot." Tom Rhoads, organist; David Worth, carillonneur; Harrold Hawley, celesta

June 21, 1964, St. Mark's Church, Philadelphia, Pennsylvania

Pre-convention "Festival Choral Evensong" at the AGO National Convention in Philadelphia, Pennsylvania[49]

The *Philadelphia Bulletin* reported on June 20, 1964:

Organists To Meet Here Next Week

Upwards of 1,500 members and associates of the American Guild of Organists will hold a biennial convention here next week, with the 62-year-old Philadelphia chapter as host....

Purvis to Conduct

Richard Purvis, noted organist-composer of Grace Episcopal Cathedral, San Francisco, will conduct a massed choir and orchestra in some of his own works at a 5 P.M. Evensong tomorrow at St. Mark's Church, 4442 Frankford Avenue. Purvis was graduated from Curtis Institute in 1940 and played in several center city churches.[50]

In *Virgil Fox (The Dish)*, Ted Alan Worth gives an effusive report of this Festival Choral Evensong which he coordinated in honor of Purvis, complete with "a choir of thirty, plus brass and tympani drawn from the Philadelphia Orchestra."[51] Purvis conducted and Ted was the organist. Purvis composed a new Nunc Dimittis for the occasion and dedicated it to the Choir of St. Mark's Church. The concert included Purvis's "Lyra Davidica," "Prophecy," "Magnificat," "A Psalm of Ascents," "Unto Us a Child is Born," "The Mass of the Holy Resurrection," and "Lonesome Valley." Also on the program was music by Duruflé, Widor, Bairstow, Wesley, and Vierne.[52]

The Biographical Data states: "During this same year he was chosen as one of the organists to represent the United States in a series of organ recitals honoring the 1964 New York World's Fair. While in New York he played on the outstanding organs of that city."[53]

One of these organs was at The Riverside Church in New York, where he played on July 14, 1964. Fred Swann recalls:

> I remember it well! He arrived at the church 30 minutes after the program was to begin. I played a piece and kept the audience entertained—hoping he would show up.
>
> He played (once he finally arrived at the church!):
>
> Franck Chorale in A minor, Prelude, Fugue and Variation, Final in B-flat
>
> Bach Two chorale preludes: Out of the Depths, Thou Prince of Peace
>
> Purvis Fanfare, Supplication, Saint Francis Suite[54]

Upon returning to San Francisco, Purvis organized the first men and boys' choir festival held under the auspices of the Episcopal Diocese of California.[55]

1965

January 15, 1965, San Mateo Performing Arts Center, San Mateo, California

With the Peninsula Symphony, Aaron Sten, conductor
Handel Concerto No. 5 in F major and Poulenc Organ Concerto

January 16, 1965, Flint Center, DeAnza College, Cupertino, California

Repeat of the January 15, 1965, concert.[56]

March 14, 1965, Grace Cathedral, "The Church Year in Music"

Grace Cathedral Choristers; David Worth, organ; Douglas DeForeest, celesta

Advent	Charles Wood, Expectans Expectavi
Christmas	Bach, O Little One; Kirkpatrick-Purvis, Cradle Carol
Epiphany	Bach, How Brightly Shines the Morning Star
Lent	Byrd, Ave Verum
Passiontide	Purvis, Lonesome Valley; Martini, In Monte Olivetti

Easter	Candlyn, Christ ist Erstanden
Ascension	Handel, Lift Up Your Heads
Whitsuntide	Titcomb, I Will Not Leave You Comfortless

1966

In May 1966, Purvis performed as the lead artist in a series of dedicatory recitals on the new Moller organ at Eden Lutheran Church in Riverside, California.[57] Dale Wood was the organist at this church from 1959 to 1968.

November 15, 1966, Trinity Lutheran Church, Hagerstown, Maryland

Cumberland Valley Chapter AGO

Bach	Prelude, Clavierübung
Handel	Larghetto Grazioso
Stanley	Trumpet Voluntary
Arne	Air for Flute Stops
Greene	Voluntary
Brahms	O Sacred Head; Ye Saints Forever Blessed
Schumann	Sketch in D Flat
Franck	Chorale in A minor
Purvis	A Lamentation of Jeremiah, Fete Joyeuse, Of Moor and Fen, Capriccio on the Notes of the Cuckoo, Fanfare[58]

1967

April 23, 1967, Christ Church, Winnetka, Illinois

Purvis conducted a Festival of Purvis Music with soloists, choir, organ, brass, percussion, harp, and flute.[59]

Celebrating Purvis's 20 years of service at Grace Cathedral, the Grace Cathedral Choir Guild sponsored a concert and tea on Mother's Day, May 14, 1967. The program featured the West Coast premieres of "Paean of Praise" and "Laudate Dominum," composed and directed by Purvis. Assisting were David Worth at the organ, Stephen Loher on the celesta, and a brass and percussion group from Pacific Union College.[60]

November 15, 1967, Longwood Gardens, Kennett Square, Pennsylvania

Longwood Gardens released the following publicity on November 3, 1967:

RICHARD PURVIS IN ORGAN CONCERT
AT LONGWOOD GARDENS

Richard Purvis, Organist and Master of Choristers at Grace Cathedral, San Francisco, will be guest organist at Longwood Gardens on Wednesday, November 15. His program will include works by Bach, Brahms, Reubke, Franck, Schumann, and his own composition, "Partita on 'Christ ist Erstanden.'"

Purvis is one of America's truly great organists and is regarded as a composer and conductor of the highest caliber. He has appeared in concert with the Philadelphia, Houston and Oakland Symphonies and has performed Festivals of his own music in Chicago, Philadelphia, Houston and San Francisco. Among his most recent works is a Festival Mass commissioned for the 175th anniversary of Saint Mary's Seminary in Baltimore, and "Paean of Praise" for the 300th anniversary of Old First Church, Newark, New Jersey.

Purvis arranges every program for the organ on which he is performing so that both the instrument and the music performed will be heard to the greatest advantage. He has been called "a sound musician who is truly interested in the 'Art of Sound.'"

The conservatories will be open at 7:30 p.m. and will remain open for an hour after the conclusion of the concert. There is no admission fee. Parking will be in the conservatory parking area.

December 17, 1967, Grace Cathedral, Carol Vespers

Works of Shaw, Holst, Vaughan Williams, Purvis

1968

January 21, 1968, Civic Auditorium, San Francisco

Marcello	Psalm XVIII, Psalm XIX
Handel	Larghetto Espressivo
Bach	Credo

Franck   Cantabile, Pièce Héroique
Purvis   Earth Carol, Thanksgiving

March 1968, First Methodist Church, Huntington Park, California

Dedicatory recital on the church's renovated Skinner organ.[61]

April 21, 1968, Grace Cathedral, Dedication of the Ruffatti Console

In place of the sermon at the 11 a.m. service, Purvis performed the following inaugural program on the new Ruffatti console:

Bach   Toccata & Fugue in D Minor
Whitlock   Fidelis
Wolstenholme   Allegretto[62]
Davies   A Solemn Melody
Purvis   Toccata Festiva

April 26, 1968, Grace Cathedral[63]

For the inaugural concert on the new Ruffatti console, Purvis performed
with members of the Oakland Symphony under the direction of Gerhard
Samuel.

Bach   Prelude in E-flat major
Handel   Concerto in B-flat major
Franck   Chorale in A minor
Mozart   Sonata in C major
Purvis   A Lamentation of Jeremiah, Toccata Festiva, Of Moor
                 and Fen
Poulenc   Concerto in G minor

May 5, 1968, Grace Cathedral, "From Plainsong to Folksong"

The Grace Cathedral Choristers
Including Plainsong, Byrd, and a "Canticle in the manner of a folksong"
(Jubilate Deo)

October 23, 1968, Church of St. John the Divine, Houston, Texas[64]

October 31, 1968, Trinity Church, New York City[65]

Works of Purvis

During December 1968 or January 1969, the Australian Broadcasting System in Melbourne produced a special television program based on Grace Cathedral's "Carol Vespers." Purvis probably performed for this event.[66]

1969

February 9, 1969, Grace Cathedral

Works of Marcello, Handel, Bach, Dupré, Karg-Elert, Schumann, Purvis
   This concert also may have featured the world premiere of "Five Pieces on Famous Bell Themes" (including the Grace Cathedral Chime composed by Purvis in 1956).[67]

March 9, 1969, Grace Cathedral

Reger	Introduction and Passacaglia
Martini	Aria con Variazzione
Franck	Chorale in E major
Karg-Elert	The Soul of the Lake
Widor	Scherzo, from Symphony VI
Purvis	Communion, A Highland Ayre, Toccata Festiva

April 25, 1969, Grace Cathedral

Premiere of Purvis's "Pièce Symphonique" for organ, harp, strings, and tympani. With members of the Oakland Symphony under the direction of Gerhard Samuel.[68]

Corelli	Concerto Grosso in F major
Handel	Concerto No. 1 in G major
Hindemith	Five Pieces for Orchestra
Debussy	Danse Sacrée et Profane (harp)
Barber	Adagio for Strings
Purvis	Pièce Symphonique

October 13, 1969, Grace Cathedral

Works of Dupré, Widor, Boellmann, Vierne, Franck, Purvis

November 9, 1969, Grace Cathedral, with pianist C. W. Iverson[69]

Works of Bach, Franck, and Purvis, including the San Francisco premiere of "Suite for Piano and Organ: From the Sierra"

November 10, 1969, Grace Cathedral

Works of Bach, Pachelbel, Handel, Peeters, Dandrieu, Franck, Purvis

December 21, 1969, Grace Cathedral, Carol Vespers

With Chico State College Choir

The following three "Recent Press Reviews" were cited in "The Published Music of Richard Purvis":

"Richard Purvis, brilliant American organist, provided Galveston with an evening of superlative music Monday night at St. Mary's Cathedral. His inspired playing exhibited a clarity and range of color seldom heard in organ recitals here, and envoked [sic] unsuspected resources from the Cathedral organ." (E. Stavenhagen, *Galveston News*)

"One of the most interesting and impressive organ concerts of the season. ... The audience was rewarded by a stunning exhibition of musicianship and dazzling technique." (William J. March, *Fort Worth Star Telegram*)

"As a virtuoso, Mr. Purvis is in the very select aristocracy of the organ in this age." (Hubert Roussel, *The Houston Post*)[70]

1970

April 1970, Westminster Presbyterian Church, Wilmington, Delaware

On April 20, 1970, the *Evening Journal,* Wilmington, Delaware, included this notice: "Since 1947 [Purvis] has been organist and master of choristers at San Francisco's historic Grace Cathedral, which has become a Western mecca for fine Anglican ecclesiastical music."[71]

Franck	Piece Heroique
Dupre	Cortège et Litanie
Peeters	Aria
Boellmann	Ronde française
Bach	Fantasia & Fuga
Purvis	A Prayer for Peace, Partita on "Christ ist Erstanden"

The following review by David B. Kozinski appeared:

Purvis Brilliant in Organ Recital Here

Richard Purvis, organist, who enhanced the musical season with his own music, Bach's, and four composers' from the French school, has become an American version of the successful composer-organist from the same French school of organists.

A near capacity audience at Westminster Presbyterian Church last night enjoyed minor works by Franck, Dupre, Peeters, and Boellmann. In the same order, "Piece Heroique" was notable for Purvis' clear, immediate registrations, "Cortege" with its punctuating chimes and "Litanie" by Dupré with its seven-note recurring theme contrasted sharply with the simple, quiet "Aria" by Peeters.

Boellmann's light-textured, 6-8 meter "Ronde Francaise" set off the "piece de resistance," Bach's magnificent "Fantasia and Fugue in G Minor" that concluded the opening half.

The florid, dramatically powered "Fantasia" with its magnetic portion of never-ending descending pedal notes against rising manual lines that spells the listener with its illusion of exhilarating expansion suddenly gives way to the ingeniously conceived architecture of the fugue.

Purvis encored in Bach's aristocratic, long-lined "Arioso," stating that this composer was not only a great contrapuntalist, but also a good tunesmith.

After a short intermission came Purvis' compositions. "A Prayer for Peace," a quietly dissonant expression, contrasted with the Partita "Christ ist Erstanden" in five short movements.

The composer-organist, in his Longwood recital in November 1967 also programmed the same work. At that time we were impressed with his fruitful eclecticism, craftsmanship and identification with the audience.

We can repeat these impressions today. The partita is a cyclical work in that each movement's inspiration comes from the ancient hymn tune. The composer skillfully uses such contrapuntal devices as canon, passacaglia, and ostinato. The partita is a listenable work as a whole.

Purvis, who has published many practical musical works that thousands of church musicians depend on, is organist and master of choristers at San Francisco's historic Grace Cathedral, noted for its Anglican ecclesiastical music.

Church music is in good hands if Purvis' influence prevails. His sensitivity to church-oriented ears is needed today when so much "trial-by-error" giddiness envelops changes in musical values in the church...."[72]

1971

December 19, 1971, First Congregational Church, Los Angeles, California

Purvis performed on the church's Third Annual Recital series. Other organists on the series were Flor Peeters, Maurice Duruflé, Wilma Jensen, E. Power Biggs, Robert Anderson, Pierre Cochereau, and Lloyd Holzgraf. No program is available.[73]

1972

April 30, 1972, The Church of the Brethren, Bakersfield, California
Rodgers organ

Purcell	Trumpet Tune
Handel	Aria con Variazzione
Balbastre	Noel Varié
Bach	Symphonia "I Stand on the Threshold of Immortality"
Boellmann	Ronde Française
Elmore	Pavane
Bach	Toccata and Fugue
Purvis	Fanfare, A Highland Air, Capriccio on the Notes of the Cuckoo, Pastorale (Greensleeves), Les Petites Cloches, Nocturne, Toccata "In Babilone"

1973

March 25, 1973, Sacred Heart Chapel, Loyola University, Los Angeles, California

Franck	Piece Heroique
Dupre	Cortège et Litanie
Handel	Aria con Variazzione
Bach	Andante Sostenuto, Fantasia e Fuga
Karg-Elert	Harmonies du Soir
Vierne	Deux Morceaux (Divertissement, Scherzetto)
Purvis	Of Moor and Fen, Greensleeves, Toccata Festiva

April 1, 1973, First Baptist Church of Castro Valley, California

Dedication Recital, Reuter organ

Works of Marcello, Bach, Purcell, Arne, Balbastre, Handel, Mendelssohn, Schumann, Bonnet

December 16, 1973, First Congregational Church, Los Angeles

Bach	Overture (from the Clavierübung)
Handel	Aria con Variazzione
Franck	Pastorale, Final
Widor	Intermezzo
Reger	Weihnachten
Dupré	Cortège et Litanie
Huré	Communion sur un Noël
Vierne	Deux Morceaux
Purvis	Adoration, Noël Varié, Greensleeves, Toccata Festiva

The following review by Richard Slater appeared in the *Los Angeles Times:*

Purvis Plays Organ at First Congregational

Every series has its lighter side—its "Pops Concert." For the 5th Annual Organ Series at First Congregational Church the moment came Sunday afternoon with Richard Purvis presiding over the 214-rank Schlicker-Skinner organ from the front chancel console.

The veteran recitalist, recently retired after 25 years as organist at San Francisco's Grace Cathedral, programmed a pastiche of morceaux and movements from larger works, topped off by a generous portion of the recitalist's own compositions.

All of the right names were on the program: Bach, Handel, Franck, Widor, Reger, Dupre, Hure, Vierne. But, except for the opening Prelude in E Flat (not "Overture" as listed in the program) by Bach, all were represented by lightweight, insignificant efforts that left the listener longing for something to sink his musical teeth into.

Purvis is a player in the grand Romantic tradition. Taken on his own terms he can have much to say. He is well versed in handling large sounds in large rooms. And, above all, he is an astute colorist who seldom repeats the same musical idea with the same registration.

Most of his message was lost Sunday, however, because of flabby rhythms (the Bach); blurry, inconsistent articulation (Widor's Intermezzo from Symphony No. 6 and Vierne's Divertissement); and long boring waits before every piece that added up to an excessively long program (2 hours and 20 minutes).[74]

1974

A series of three services honoring Richard Purvis was presented in New England:

May 4, 1974, All Saints Church, Worcester, Massachusetts, Works of Purvis

The service included Purvis's "Canticle of Light," "Song of Simeon, "Song of Mary," and "Ballad of Judas Iscariot." David Worth was the organist.[75]

May 5, 1974, Trinity Church, Boston, Massachusetts

Repeat of the May 4 program.

May 6, 1974, 8 p.m. Trinity Church on-the-Green, New Haven, Connecticut

Purvis provided a "Prelude Recital," performing his own works at the organ, followed by a repeat of the May 4 program at which Stephen Loher was the organist.[76]

A review of the program in the New Haven *Telegram* was written by Raymond Morin:

An audience of about 350 heard a program of early works by Richard Purvis, conducted by the composer. ... The program consisted of three canticles— "Magnificat," "Song of Simeon," "A Canticle of Light" — and "The Ballad of Judas Iscariot." ... Purvis is a conservative composer by contemporary standards. Melodies of the "Ballad" follow elemental courses. Harmonic backgrounds support rather than conflict. Some are derivatively reminiscent. Rhythms are straightforward and depart from the norm only to increase momentum.... Purvis conducted with obviously knowledgeable purpose, good appraisal of resources and instructive clarity."[77]

May 10, 1974, Trinity Church on-the-Green, New Haven, Connecticut

Purvis performed for the New Haven Chapter of the AGO

Bach	Overture (Clavierübung)
Franck	Cantabile, Pastorale, Chorale III
Purvis	Supplication; Partita on "Christ ist Erstanden"

May 26, 1974, All Saints' Episcopal Church, Long Beach, California

Dedication recital of the Abbott and Sieker organ

Bach	Overture (Clavierübung)
Handel	Concerto I (Adagio, Aria con Variazione)
Stanley	Trumpet Voluntary
Arne	Air for Flute Stops
Greene	Capriccio
Mendelssohn	Andante
Schumann	Two Sketches (Maestoso, Scherzando)
Vierne	Deux Morceaux (Divertissement, Scherzetto)
Bonnet	Angelus du Soir
Purvis	Partita on "Christ ist Erstanden"

Martin Clark wrote the following review of a recital at First United Methodist Church in Portland, Oregon, around 1974:

Small wonder the works of Richard Purvis are in such demand. According to a news release, "Organ and choral compositions by Richard Purvis are heard more frequently than those of any other American composer."

I can understand why, after hearing his recital Sunday night at First United Methodist Church, along with an audience of three or four hundred (quite an audience for organ recitals and choir concerts).

His works (at least the ones I heard in the first half) are not atonal, row, serial, 12-tone or any other system outside the framework of music language. He does not belong to that cop-out school of composers I have often described as "It-may-not-be-difficult-but-you-can-rest-assured-it's-plenty-difficult."

Mr. Purvis is not afraid to compete. Members of the above non-talent school of composition would probably call him "commercial." I hope so. Coming from them, it would mean that people who love music want to hear his music.

This is not to say that the Purvis compositions I heard Sunday night are hackneyed and merely imitative. Quite the contrary. "Of Moor and Fen," "Passepied for a Church Festival," and "Fanfare" bear the unmistakable stamp of Purvis—but in the recognizable language of music. Unlike the counterfeit would-be composers mentioned previously, Purvis does not evade competition by creating a gibberish of his own.

And the man is an impressive organist. This he demonstrated, in addition to his own works, with Franck Chorale in A Minor, Bach's "Fantasia e Fuga" and, among others, the utterly delightful "Noel Varié" by the 18th century composer, Claude Balbastre.

I missed his choral compositions as performed by the Chancel Choir in order to hear the quaint instruments of the Whirling Dervishes of Turkey.

No disrespect intended, but I should have stuck with the Methodists.[78]

1975

Longwood Gardens released the following publicity on March 21, 1975:

RICHARD PURVIS IN RECITAL
AT LONGWOOD GARDENS ON APRIL 2

Richard Purvis, one of the most eminent organists before the public today, will play at Longwood Gardens on April 2. His program will include *Prelude and Fugue in B minor* by Bach, *Priere du Christ* from *L'Ascension* by Messiaen, *Aria con Variazzione* by Handel, *Choral II* by Franck, and selections by Karg-Elert and Schumann, ending with several of his own compositions.

Concert artist, composer and conductor, Purvis has distinguished himself in all three facets of his career. A graduate of the Curtis Institute of Music, he is the only organist to win the C.H.K. Curtis Memorial Scholarship awarded for study in Europe. From 1947 until his recent retirement, he was Organist and Master of Choristers at San Francisco's historic Grace Cathedral. He has recently been commission by the "American Choir" of London to write an extended work for choir, organ, brass and tympany in honor of the Bicentennial.

April 2, 1975, Longwood Gardens, Kennett Square, Pennsylvania

J. S. Bach	Prelude and Fugue in B minor
Messiaen	Prière du Christ, from l'Ascension
Handel	Aria con Variazzione
Franck	Chorale II
Karg-Elert	Saluto Angelico
Schumann	Sketch in D flat
Purvis	Supplication, Toccata on the "Kyrie"

The following review of the recital appeared in the *Evening Journal*, Wilmington, Delaware:

With French Pastry
Organist Is Too Accessible

by David B. Kozinski

Longwood Gardens' guest organist last night was Richard Purvis. You might call him the people's organist, so accessible does he make his program and he packed them in. The excess audience had to be accommodated in the azalea room that adjoins the ballroom where the organ is located.

The most satisfying work was an air and variations by Handel. The organist played with a direct, unfussy registrated manner, true to baroque style.

The opening Bach Prelude and Fugue in b was another story. Accommodating tempos and reduction to two voices in the fugue simply gets too accessible. Please, Mr. Purvis.

Messiaen's Priere du Christ from L'Ascension had creamy caramel-flavored tone clusters better suited to a French pastry shop than to the grand Longwood organ.

Frank's Chorale II needed more thrust over-all, even though the second section came on dramatically enough. Here again, the registrations had an accessible homogenous quality de trop.

Karg-Elert's Saluto Angelico had excessive, saccharine impressionistic touches, even including vibraphone that were all too much.

Schumann's Sketch in D-Flat sounded like Radio City Music Hall, and Purvis' own Supplication and Toccata on the Kyrie were harmless rhetoric and fluff.

Purvis said that it was conceited of a composer to play his own music. He played it because, as he said, some people want to see if the composer plays it as it is written, others, to see if he plays it like they play it, and still others, to see if he (the performer) can play it at all. Who cares? He said the same thing a few years ago at Longwood.

Those who publish and perform (and buy it) obviously do care. The final recital of the 1974–75 organ series will be on April 16 with Clarence Snyder at the console.[79]

May 4, 1975, Chapel of the Four Seasons, Santa Cruz, California

Works of Lemmens, Karg-Elert, Vierne, Martini, Bach, Franck, Boellmann, Davies, Purvis

1976

From September 10 to 26, 1976, Ted Alan Worth promoted a concert series entitled "A Festival of Organ Virtuosos & Illuminations" at St. Mary's Cathedral in San Francisco.

September 10 and 19: Virgil Fox

September 12: Joyce Jones with Dance Spectrum

September 17: Anthony Newman

September 18: Richard Purvis

September 21: Diane Bish with Dance Spectrum and Synthesizer

September 24: Ted Alan Worth

September 26: A Tribute to Richard Purvis: Festival Choir, Brass, Tympani, Harp, and Organ, conducted by Richard Purvis.[80]

1977

April 22, 1977, Woolsey Hall, Yale University, New Haven, Connecticut

Works of Franck[81]

Tom Whittemore, who assisted Purvis at this recital, recalls: "I turned pages for the recital at Woolsey Hall for Purvis. It was all Franck. At one point, he was playing a soft section on the manuals. The pedal was loaded and his foot slipped off the swell shoes and landed on full pedal. He said, 'Bats! Bats!' That is all I remember, except that it was a beautifully orchestrated performance."[82]

November 5, 1977, Immanuel Lutheran Church, San Jose, California[83]

With the San Jose Camerata. Purvis also conducted an organ clinic.

1978

April 23, 1978, The United States Naval Training Center, North Chapel, San Diego, California

Rodgers Series 250 Pipe Organ
Works of Bach, Handel, Brahms, Schumann, Franck, Vierne, Francis Jackson, Karg-Elert, Boellmann, Purvis

June 18, 1978, Trinity Church on-the-Green, New Haven, Connecticut

1979

January 28, 1979, Church of St. Paul in the Desert (Episcopal), Palm Springs, California

Dedication of Rodgers organ

Marcello	Two Psalm Paraphrases
Bach	Symphonia
Handel	Andante con Variazione
Franck	Cantabile
Vierne	Deux Morceaux (Scherzetto, Carillon)

Sabin	Bourree
Fletcher	Fountain Reverie
Boellmann	Ronde française
Purvis	A Highland Ayre, Capriccio on the Notes of the Cuckoo, Romanza, Toccata Festiva

Late 1970s, Holy Spirit Parish, Berkeley, California

Dedication concert of Rodgers Cambridge 850 organ

Bach	Prelude (Clavierübung)
	Andante Sostenuto ("freely transcribed by Richard Purvis")
Handel	Andante con Variazione
Franck	Cantabile
Vierne	Scherzetto, Carillon
Purvis	Thanksgiving
Bonnet	Angelus du soir, Romance sans paroles
Purvis	A Scottish Carol, Divinum Mysterium, Pastorale-Greensleeves, A Carol Rhapsody

1980

Beginning in the early 1950s and continuing through at least 1985, Purvis performed annually at the Lakeside Temple of Practical Christianity in Oakland, California. Purvis's mother was a friend of the founding minister of the Lakeside Temple.[84]

At one of his last recitals there, possibly in 1980, Purvis performed his "Melita Suite" (Partita on the Navy Hymn).

Vierne	Allegro, from Symphony 2
Reger	Benedictus
Bach	Fantasia e Fuga in G minor
Karg-Elert	Claire de lune
Franck	Final in B-flat
Purvis	Partita on the Navy Hymn (1978)[85]

March 9, 1980, University Presbyterian Church, Fresno, California

Dedication of the three-manual, 55-rank Aeolian-Skinner organ, Op. 1294 (built originally in 1954 for Trinity Episcopal Church in Princeton, New Jersey) Works of Handel, Bach, Boellmann, Franck, Vierne, Davies, Purvis

1984

May 20, 1984, Louise M. Davies Symphony Hall, San Francisco

To celebrate the five-manual, 147-rank Ruffatti organ installed that year at Davies Symphony Hall, 14 local organists joined forces for a concert. Performers included Eileen Coggin, Fred Tulan, David Babbitt, Edwin Flath, Herbert Nanney, Richard Bradshaw, Robert Walker, Richard Webb, Ralph Hooper, Pamela Decker, Robert Newton, Susan Summerfield, Eric Stevens, and Richard Purvis. Purvis played the "grand finale" of the program.

Heuwell Tircuit, in a review in the *San Francisco Chronicle*, wrote:

> There were a number of other classic pieces of 'the organ's greatest hits' variety. Particularly outstanding among these were Edwin Flath's sensationally serious performance of Bach's A minor Prelude and Fugue, Richard Webb's virtuoso bash in the fugue of Julius Reubke's Wagnerian Sonata … , and Richard Purvis' masterly strength when closing the program with Franck's Chorale No. 3.[86]

In a copy of the program, David Worth's mother made the following handwritten notation next to Purvis's entry: "Wonderful—He received a tumultuous welcome. He bowed & smiled nice. Over & over finally threw up his hands as if he didn't know how to stop all the noise & at the conclusion loud Bravos. The place was filled. We were right behind the organ, Row D. He & Shields acted real pleased to greet me afterwards."[87]

June 10, 1984, Grace Cathedral

Purvis performed a joint recital with John Fenstermaker to mark the 50th anniversary of the Grace Cathedral organ.

John Fenstermaker:

Bach	Fantasia and Fugue in G minor
Peeters	Hymn to the Ocean
Karg-Elert	Saluto Angelico
Franck	Chorale No. 3

Richard Purvis:

Arthur Goodhart	Darwall
Wallace Arthur Sabin	Bourree
Percy Whitlock	Fidelis
Purvis	Partita on "Christ ist Erstanden"

Heuwell Tircuit of the *San Francisco Chronicle* wrote the following review:

"50 Years for Cathedral Organ"

The organ boom bellowed on Sunday, with yet another occasion for organ festivities here. June 10 marked the 50th anniversary of the first recital given on the grand organ of Grace Cathedral, which still ranks as one of the magnificent monsters on the American scene.

The cathedral is presenting a series of five Sunday programs of organ and choral music honoring the anniversary, running through July 4. To open the series, Sunday's program highlighted music historically associated with Grace Cathedral, played by John Fenstermaker and Richard Purvis.

Fenstermaker, who has been cathedral organist since 1971, opened the afternoon proceedings with Bach's Fantasia and Fugue in G minor, Flor Peeters' "Hymn to the Ocean," Karg-Elert's "Saluto Angelico" and Franck's Chorale No. 3. (The Peeters piece was written for this particular instrument, and is dedicated to Purvis.)

Purvis, who was cathedral organist from 1947 to 1971, played even more obscure music for the second half.

He began with Arthur Goodhart's "Darwall," a piece given its first American performance in the Chapel of Grace in 1931, four years before its composer's death. Then came Wallace Arthur Sabin's "Bourree" (a piece on the 1934 dedication concert), Percy Whitlock's "Fidelis" (also from the first concert) and Purvis' own Partita on "Christ is Erstanden" in five movements.

The large audience seemed enthusiastic for everything, a situation no doubt engendered by the excellent performances as well as a sense of occasion.

Both organists know the instrument intimately, where its greatest strengths lie—namely, variety of color and the big orchestral-organ sound. But more than that, each clearly has a keen appreciation of the instrument in relation to the room's enormous and lengthy echo effect.

I have not often heard a concert in Grace where the proportions were delivered with such finesse. Much of the music was clearly selected to maximize the sound, but there was more to it than that.

The Bach, while hardly getting a true Baroque sound, was especially impressive. Fenstermaker made no effort to hurry through bravura effects.

And while emphasizing the depth of dignity in the music—its strong point—he managed to get the complicated contrapuntal writing to sound out in high clarity.

The unusual pieces, all on the ultra-conservative side, were either outright English (Whitlock was organist in Bournemouth), or quasi-English. Even Peeters and Karg-Elert sounded distinctly Vaughan Williams-ish.

Of these, Purvis' Partita was easily the best of the lot, showing a sense of backbone. The others were mostly fodder for showing off the instrument: neatly made, reasonable to a flaw, and apparently scared of their own shadow.

It left one wondering. Has the cathedral made no more substantive contribution to liturgical music in 50 years? The organ is there and admirable, and the performances were excellent, but too much of the program amounted to little more than musical pandering.[88]

June 24, 1984, Grace Cathedral, National Convention of the AGO, San Francisco

Pre-convention recital

Works of Franck: Choral in E major, Cantabile, Choral in A minor, Pièce Héroique, Pastorale, Final in B-flat major[89]

October 28, 1984, Overbrook Presbyterian Church of Philadelphia, Pennsylvania

Celebration of the 95th Anniversary of the church. Included a performance of Purvis's "Paean of Praise"

November 4, 1984, Bidwell Presbyterian Church, Chico, California

November 25, 1984, Seventh Day Adventist Church, Sonora, California

December 9, 1984, Lakeside Temple of Practical Christianity, Oakland, California[90]

Annual Christmas Organ Recital

1985

January 25, 1985, Church of the Immaculate Heart of Mary, Denver, Colorado
Dedicatory Concert

January 26, 1985, Wells Music Co., Lakewood, Colorado
Master Class

April 21, 1985, First United Methodist Church, Portland, Oregon
Festival of Purvis Music

April 22, 1985, Rodgers Organ Co., Portland, Oregon
Master Class

May 5, 1985, First Church of Christ, Scientist, San Francisco, California
"Tribute to Wallace Sabin," celebrating the 60th Anniversary of the four-manual Kimball organ designed by Sabin (a "Twenties Program"). Works of Bach, Handel, Hollins, Rheinberger, Lemare, Sabin, Karg-Elert, Batiste, Purvis, and Purvis's "Three-Note Encore"[91]

October 13, 1985, Walnut Creek Presbyterian Church, Walnut Creek, California
Concert for the church's "Christian Performing Arts Series"

December 8, 1985, Lakeside Temple of Practical Christianity, Oakland, California[92]
Annual Christmas Organ Recital

1986

February 2, 1986, Trinity Episcopal Church, San Francisco
Tom Hazleton joined Purvis in a benefit concert for the restoration of the E. M. Skinner organ.

Purvis at the Ruffatti console, Grace Cathedral, about 1986. Photo by Ed Mullins. Courtesy Martin Lilley.

February 23, 1986, Grace Cathedral

Organ Recital by Richard Purvis, Organist Emeritus, Grace Cathedral

Bach	Chorale Prelude (Lord Jesus, We Await Thy Presence)
Bach:	Overture (Clavierübung)
Dupré	Cortège et Litanie
Vierne	Scherzetto
Jongen	Prière
Franck	Chorale III

Music of Richard Purvis (b. 1915 [*sic*])

Two Prayers in Tone (Thanksgiving, Supplication)
Roundelay
Of Moor and Fen
Toccata Festiva

April 1, 1986, San Francisco Civic Auditorium

The San Francisco Chapter of the AGO presented A Celebration of the Panama-Pacific
Exposition Austin Organ. After opening
remarks by Jack Bethards and Charles Swisher,
Purvis performed a recital of works "by organists who have played this instrument since its
installation in the Civic Auditorium."

Purvis at the Austin organ, San Francisco Civic Auditorium, April 1, 1986. Courtesy Paul Motter.

Wallace Sabin	Bourrée
Joseph Bonnet	Deux Morceaux, Angelus du Soir, Romance sans Paroles
Edwin H. Lemare	Sundown, Toccata in D minor
Marcel Dupré	Cortège et Litanie
Alfred Hollins	Spring Song
Sigfrid Karg-Elert	Aus tiefer Not; O Gott, du frommer Gott
Louis Vierne	Sortie (Messe Basse)[93]
Encore: Bach	Arioso

April 12, 1986, Grace Lutheran Church, Butler, Pennsylvania

May 4, 1986, Grace Lutheran Church, Escondido, California

July 29, 1986, San Anselmo Organ Festival, San Anselmo, California[94]

Lecture and Demonstration on Purvis compositions

1987

September 13, 1987, Grace Cathedral

Benefit recital for Senior Resources, Inc., an outreach program

Bach	Lord Jesus, We Await Thy Presence, BWV 730
	Prelude and Fugue in B minor, BWV 544
Peeters	Song of the Ocean ("Written for the Grace Cathedral Organ and dedicated to Richard Purvis")

Vierne	Divertissement, Legende, Scherzetto
Karg-Elert	Saluto Angelico
Franck	Chorale in A minor
Wallace Sabin	Bourrée[95]
Walford Davies	A Solemn Melody
Purvis	Roundelay, Supplication, Toccata Festiva[96]

1989

February 19, 1989, St. Pius Church, Redwood City, California

Works of Bach, Marcello, Dupré, Boellmann, Davies, Franck[97]

Purvis at the Fisk tracker organ, Pony Tracks Ranch, Portola Valley, California, late 1980s or early 1990s. Courtesy Paul Motter.

Notes

1. This picture has not survived.
2. Townsend thesis, 15.
3. Donna Parker, e-mail, September 27, 2010.
4. Undated brochure; probably from the late 1930s; cited in Townsend thesis, 12–13; original unavailable.
5. Excerpted from Alfred Frankenstein, "Purvis Gives A Brilliant Organ Recital." *San Francisco Chronicle*, March 20, 1946.
6. Undated promotional brochure.
7. Jonas Nordwall, e-mail, 2009.
8. Corbett, 13.
9. Douglas Metzler, interview, June 24, 2010.
10. Recital recording, courtesy Douglas Metzler.
11. Stephen Loher, e-mail, May 30, 2009.
12. Stephen Loher, e-mail, September 27, 2010.
13. Townsend "Memories," 1995.
14. Townsend thesis, 12–13; original unavailable.
15. Richard Torrence, telephone conversation, November 23, 2010.
16. Donna Parker, interview, September 27, 2010.
17. Robert Bennett, telephone conversation, November 29, 2010.
18. This was probably his first recital following his appointment at Grace on February 1, 1947.

19. *The Cathedral Chimes,* September 14, 1947.

20. Biographical Data, 5.

21. AGO Convention Booklet, 1948.

22. Biographical Data, 5.

23. Dedicated to Purvis and published in 1950.

24. Concert program.

25. Biographical Data, 5; could not be verified.

26. Recital program courtesy William Teague (who was dean of the chapter in 1951).

27. See more details on this visit and his encounter with Tabernacle organists Alexander Schreiner and Frank Asper in Chapter 4, "Grace Cathedral."

28 *Salt Lake Tribune,* Sunday, March 11, 1951, page 6-M. Courtesy Harry Cross.

29 *Deseret News,* Sunday, March 11, 1951, page F-2. Courtesy Harry Cross.

30. *Deseret News,* Thursday, March 15, 1951, page B-8. Courtesy Harry Cross.

31. *The Cathedral Chimes,* June 10, 1951.

32. Biographical Data, 6.

33. Convention booklet, 11.

34. Biographical Data, 6.

35. Biographical Data, 6.

36. Clarence Snyder, letter to James Welch, November 1, 2010.

37. *The Apostle,* newsletter of St. Paul's Episcopal Church, September 5, 1954.

In a memo from the St. Paul's parish files, dated July 15, 1952, Purvis offered to G. Donald Harrison the following nine suggestions regarding the specification of this organ. Most were followed:

1. Swell stops should run to 73 pipes.

2. The 4' Flute Harmonique on the Swell should be a Koppelflote.

3. The 2' Octavin on the Swell should be a Blockflote.

4. A 16' Hautbois of 97 pipes should be added to the Swell. This would mean that the alternative presented in the Swell between a Rohr Schalmei or Hautbois would end up as a 4' Hautbois of 73 notes.

5. The Plein Jeu should be on the Swell instead of the Great to obtain a true English Swell of Reed Chorus plus Mixture.

6. In place of Sesquialtera could there be an independent Nazard 2-2/3 (flute) and a Tierce 1-3/5 (flute)?

7. If possible, the Swell Reeds of 16' and 4' should be separate ranks.

8. There should be at least one and if possible two more combination pistons on the swell.

9. There should be a "swell unison off" and a "great unison off" among the couplers.

In 1973, the centennial of St. Paul's, historian Robert Johnston wrote, "With the installation of the new organ in the summer of 1954, Mr. Coombs [rector] made plans for its use to bring 'the finest organ music' to Salinas. St. Paul's learned that Richard Purvis, Organist of Grace Cathedral, considered the new organ as 'unquestionably the finest of its size in the United States.' St. Teresa's Chapter of the Women's Auxiliary agreed to sponsor a series of recitals of organists of national and international renown. A series of performances was scheduled for 1955, including Virgil Fox of the Riverside Church in New York, and Alexander Schreiner of the Tabernacle, Salt Lake City." Robert B. Johnston, *St. Paul's Episcopal Church, 1873–1973: A Centennial History* (Watsonville, California: Pajaro Press, 1973), 86.

38. *The Apostle,* newsletter of St. Paul's Episcopal Church, October 16, 1955.

39. Corbett, 15.

40. This is the last recital to be designated officially as part of the "Masterpieces of Organ Literature" series.

41. Program note for this piece states that it "has a distinctly Dutch atmosphere."

42. The program does not specify the pieces Duncan played.

43. San Francisco AGO Convention booklet, 1961.

44. Robert Bennett, telephone conversation, November 29, 2010.

45. Biographical Data, 7.

46. Recital program courtesy of Charles Corson.

47. Orpha Ochse, *The History of the Organ in the United States* (Indiana University Press, 1975), 314.

48. Biographical Data, 7.

49. AGO Convention booklet.

50. *Philadelphia Bulletin,* June 20, 1964.

51. Richard Torrence and Marshall Yaeger, *Virgil Fox (The Dish),* 186–187.

52. Recital program courtesy Richard Elliott.

53. Biographical Data, 8.

54. Fred Swann, e-mail, August 30, 2010.

55. Corbett, 16.

56. http://www.peninsulasymphony.org/history.html?season=1965

57. Corbett, 17.

58. *The Diapason,* January 1967; cited in Townsend thesis, 15; original unavailable.

59. Townsend thesis, 11.

60. Concert program.

61. Corbett, 18.

62. The program states, "These two miniatures were played at the original Inaugural Recital of the Alexander Memorial Organ by J. Sidney Lewis on Sunday, June 3, 1934. They are significant witness to change in musical taste. The Whitlock was unpopular with the audience and was called 'strange', 'bizarre' and 'dissonant'. In contrast, the Wolstenholme was the best received number on the program." Concert program.

63. A letter dated May 6, 1968, from Frank Roseberry (who managed various events in the diocese) to David Worth mentions this performance: "I am so sorry you and Donna did not make it to Richard's concert on the 26th. It was glorious and I believe you would have enjoyed it immensely. We had 25 pieces from the Oakland Symphony for the orchestra, Gerhard Samuel conducting." Letter from Frank Roseberry to David Worth, May 6, 1968.

64. Extra Curricular Program of Richard Purvis, 1968–1969.

65. Extra Curricular Program of Richard Purvis, 1968–1969.

66. Extra Curricular Program of Richard Purvis, 1968–1969.

67. Extra Curricular Program of Richard Purvis, 1968–1969.

68. The Extra Curricular Program of Richard Purvis 1968–1969 lists the date of this concert incorrectly as April 24, 1969. It also states that the program included the American premiere of Czech composer Jan Hanus's 1954 "Symphonie Concertante," but that work was not performed. This program may also have been repeated the same week at St. Mary's Roman Catholic Cathedral in Stockton, California, but there is no confirmation of such a concert.

69. "Bud" Iverson, to whom Purvis dedicated the movement "Capriccio Espagnole" from the Suite.

70. "The Published Music of Richard Purvis," typescript, September 1, 1969; originals unavailable.

71. *Evening Journal*, Wilmington, Delaware, April 20, 1970.

72. *Evening Journal*, Wilmington, Delaware, April 23, 1970.

73. Season flyer, First Congregational Church, Los Angeles.

74. *Los Angeles Times*, December 19, 1973.

75. "All Saints Choristers Plan Fund-Raising Concert," Worcester *Sunday Telegram*, April 21, 1974, 32A.

76. Service and recital programs.

77. New Haven *Telegram*, n.d.

78. *The Oregonian*, Portland, Oregon, about 1974.

79. *Evening Journal*, Wilmington, Delaware, April 3, 1975.

Colvin Randall, organist at Longwood Gardens, remarked on Kozinski's review: "David Kozinski could be annoying sometimes … and I think this is an example! But at least he came to our recitals and wrote about them. It would have been unusual to have the overflow crowd that he describes, so maybe he was just jealous. His son was (is) an organist/composer, so he had a particular interest in organ music. I don't recall many negative reviews over the decades, however, although he seems not to like the registrations at this concert. Nothing wrong with creamy caramel tone clusters for Messiaen! But note he says that the public obviously did like Purvis. Let's just assume David was having an off night." Colvin Randall, e-mail, November 1, 2010.

80. Series poster.

81. Vincent Oneppo, e-mail, November 22, 2010.

82. Tom Whittemore, e-mail, November 22, 2010.

83. Concert flyer.

84. Donald Sears, telephone conversation, June 22, 2011.

85. Recital program, no date.

86. Hewell Tircuit, "14 Organists at Davies," *San Francisco Chronicle*, May 22, 1984.

87. Recital program, courtesy David Worth.

88. Heuwell Tircuit, *San Francisco Chronicle*, June 12, 1984, 46.

89. *The American Organist*, April 1984, 27.

90. Concert Schedule for Richard I. Purvis, Season 1984–1985.

91. Recording courtesy Douglas Metzler.

92. Concert Schedule for Richard I. Purvis, Season 1984–1985.

93. Concert program. When Purvis played here in 1986, the Austin organ Opus 500, built for the Panama-Pacific International Exposition of 1915, had been almost completely restored under the leadership of Charles Swisher of The Citizens' Committee to Preserve the San Francisco Municipal Pipe Organ. As a result of the Loma Prieta earthquake on October 17, 1989, the damaged instrument was dismantled and sent back to Hartford, Connecticut, for repairs. Since 1994 the fully restored instrument has remained in storage in Brooks Hall beneath San Francisco's Civic Center. A detailed history of the San Francisco Exposition Organ, with references to related articles and an accompanying documentary film, can be found at http://www.ExpositionOrgan.org. Vic Ferrer, e-mail, October 25, 2012.

94. Concert Schedule for Richard I. Purvis, Season 1986.

95. The program stated: "1987 marks the 50th Anniversary of the death of Wallace Sabin. He was the founder of the San Francisco chapter of the American Guild of Organists and a designer of the Grace Cathedral Organ. He played the Bourrée at the Dedication Service of this organ in 1934."

96. Recital program.

97. Recital program.

chapter 12

purvis and
the theatre organ

Although Purvis made his mark mainly in the world of church music, his heart was equally in the world of the theatre organ. As detailed in Chapter 1, "Early Years," he heard at a young age the great theatre and symphonic organists of the day, absorbing their styles of playing. The harmonies, techniques, and drama of the theatre organ would emerge in nearly all of his organ compositions, whether for church, recital, or home use. The following statements about Purvis's connection to the theatre organ world come from several people who knew him well in that setting.

Ed Stout

Ed Stout was keenly aware of Purvis's interest and abilities in theatre playing. In Ed's words,

> He straddled the fence and worked both sides, but professionally he didn't work both sides, other than when he was young and played at KRE. Not very many musicians were comfortable playing both classical and theatre, because their teachers would tell them, "Well, you don't want to stoop to the theatre organ." In my opinion, most of the teachers who had disdain for the theatre organ didn't have enough rhythm to play it and didn't understand it. They couldn't take it on its own terms because they tried to compare it to the church organ. The only similarity is that they both have keyboards and pipes that are excited by wind pressure. He had a deep passion and understanding of it and knew all the techniques of theatre playing. If that field had continued, he might have gone with it.

After his retirement, he attended most of the theatre organ conventions and was often at the Castro [Theatre in San Francisco] for silent films and concerts.[1]

Stout continued: "He and George Wright were very close friends. It was not uncommon for a buzz to be going around the Cathedral, 'George Wright's in the audience!' George Wright sold so many records in the 50's, 60's, and 70's that his was a household name. He'd come up to hear Dick play and then Purvis went to everything George played at the Fox and the Paramount."[2]

Stout acknowledged that Purvis never played public theatre organ concerts or accompanied silent films. However, he recalls Purvis getting on the bench at San Francisco's Paramount Theatre for midnight parties during organ conventions, along with "a lot of the top players. I can remember 'Diane,' and 'Tea for Two.' He was playing multiple tunes at the same time, the primary tune and on second touch playing the second tune."[3]

In his column "Professional Perspectives" in the May 2008 issue of *Theatre Organ*, Ed Stout wrote the following expressive account of Purvis's relationship with the theatre organ:

Reflections About Richard Purvis,
The Renowned Organist, Composer and Teacher

Richard Purvis' life and career deeply touched and affected the lives of both church and theatre musicians. Having been professionally and socially associated with Dick for some thirty-five years, there is an opportunity in Professional Perspectives to share some insights about the magnificent organist who managed to compose and perform touching and descriptive "photoplay" music for the weekly drama unfolding for the Sunday matinee in "Saint Richard's" Cathedral, less popularly known as Grace Cathedral. The honorary holy order was awarded Purvis by some of his students and long-time friends. The fact is, Richard Purvis understood his job, and his music was the magic carpet upon which the service rode. Sonic enchantment was created while the devoted found their way to the communion rail, in the form of mini-symphonettes. Hauntingly beautiful melodies were exchanged from one solo voice to another, with seamless control of the expression shutters. You hardly noticed the high heels clomping across the polished marble.

The association of Purvis' compositions to that of photoplay scoring is not in any way disrespectful, nor does it devalue his music. While listening to a Purvis composition you are treated to vivid images created by his highly developed harmony, fump-fump-fump-fump Pedal rhythms and orchestral registrations. Just listen to his Easter "Partita on Christ Ist Erstanden" and you know you are hearing the ultimate score for the not so silent version of Ben Hur. "March Grotesque" could be depicting the cathedral's gargoyles frolicking at a rooftop ball. The brilliant Tom Hazleton freely used Purvis' music for his film scoring at the Avenue, Castro and Stanford Theatres.

Richard Purvis fell in love with the sound of a great theatre organ at the age of ten while attending San Francisco's Granada Theatre with his grandmother. He sat in the very front row in order to study how the legendary Iris Vining commanded the massive six-chambered style 285 Wurlitzer. From that day on, the Granada's organ was his favorite unit orchestra. One year later he began his organ studies with Wallace Sabin on the newly installed W. W. Kimball orchestral organ in the First Church of Christ, Scientist. That wonderful four-manual, twenty-seven rank organ boasted nine sixteen-foot stops in the Pedal. Sabin agreed to instruct the eager lad if he promised to continue his piano studies. He also was in contact with other prominent San Francisco organists like Ben Moore and Uda Waldrup. These gentlemen provided Richard with the opportunity to play the finest instruments in Northern California, including the four-manual Skinner organs in Trinity Church, Temple Emanuel, and the orchestral giant in the California Palace of the Legion of Honor. That (impressively) scaled symphonic Skinner included a large percussion and trap assembly. Civic organist Uda Waldrup played the Legion organ and a weekly "theatre organ" program over the radio.

Upon completing his primary education in the Bay Area, Richard Purvis attended and graduated from the esteemed Curtis Institute in Philadelphia. Curtis offered him a rare scholarship to further his classical organ studies in Europe. Prior to the United States' involvement in World War II, Purvis returned to the Bay Area for a short time and during that era he was able to further investigate his longtime love for the theatre organ. He played a weekly theatre organ program from Oakland's Chapel of the Chimes, which had an expanded style EX Wurlitzer. As a matter of fact, the relay that controlled that organ was manufactured in February of 1939. Dick played the weekly program under the name of Don Irving and his peppy opening tune was "I'll Take An Option On You."

Upon his return from the war, Richard Purvis was invited to be the Organist and Master of Choristers at San Francisco's Grace Cathedral. That began his long love affair with the great Alexander Memorial Aeolian-Skinner, installed in 1934. The four-manual, ninety-three rank masterpiece became identified with Dick's masterful playing, and his emotion-stirring music was written for an "American Classic" styled organ.

Purvis knew the important role tremulants played in bringing romantic music to life and he insisted on having all of the tremulants set in what we called "the natural state," which of course meant in harmony with theatre organ settings, which remind the listeners of other musical instruments or in some cases, the uttering from a great singer. Ninety percent of classical organ tremulant settings are morbid. How can something have excursion after rigor mortis has set in?

Much has been written about Richard Purvis' insight and ability to evoke the soul out of every whistle, but his very special contribution was in playing music from the French Romantic period. Many devoted music fans traveled from all parts of Northern California to attend his legendary Franck to Bach recitals in Grace, the instant Cathedral, "just add water, mix and pour." Now and then the Nave was abuzz with the realization that George Wright was present. George and Richard held each other in the highest professional regard and they were longtime friends.

What was Richard Purvis' greatest contribution to the vibrant world of the theatre organ? It was in the role of a great teacher. Every Friday and Saturday Richard taught gifted students from morning until 5:00 PM. We all have been the beneficiaries of his intuitive weekly sessions. Young Tom Hazleton began his studies with Richard at the age of twelve and he continued with the banter into his mid-twenties. Tom was always the last student and the week's review was seldom about the notes, but was about subtle phrasing and issues over registration. Having sat through several of the lessons out in the house, it was clear Hazleton had well-developed tonal concepts. It was marvelous to hear two magnificent musicians tossing about ideas. Beginning students were always cycled through the Chapel of Grace's two-manual, eighteen-rank organ before being allowed to touch the Cathedral organ. Also grazing within the Purvis corral were many gifted organists, including Keith Chapman, Jonas Nordwall, Lyn Larsen,

Bill Thompson, Donna Parker, Larry Vannucci and Chris Elliott. The wonderful musicians noted above are not in any specific order relating to their musical ability, height, or how much they drink. They just rolled out on the bar in that order, but all Purvis students had one very important attribute and that is, they were all taught how to listen. Purvis was often heard, in his Stentorphone-like voice, "listen with your ears and not your eyes."

Another ATOS highlight was the Regional Convention in 1965, where the guests were allowed to attend his Grace Cathedral recital and they were allowed to sit in the Choir near the console. Until that event, guests were never allowed to sit within that special area where the organ is most clear.

On the personal side, Richard Purvis was somewhat shy and he compensated by playing the "Wizard of Oz," pontificating from behind the green curtain. When strangers or clergy approached him, they received an unexpected Diaphonic blast in the form of remarks such as, "Well, there is nothing I can do about that" or "your mother dresses you funny and your ears are too big." In truth, he was a gentle, generous and loving friend who loved to party and dine with close friends. He also enjoyed burning a few ice-cubes while listening to Larry Vannucci play the blues on the charming style 216 Wurlitzer installed in the Lost Weekend Cocktail Lounge, which was located not far from Dick's San Francisco home.

We will never see another Richard Purvis, George Wright or Tom Hazleton, because the civilization that allowed them to gain the experience required for their blossoming is no longer a part of the American culture. On the positive side, we are fortunate to have several magnificent theatre organists sharing their considerable talents. The theatre organ seems to have not lost its Pied Piper quality of attracting a few gifted youngsters who are so drawn to the sound, you could not keep them away.

Thank you, Richard Purvis, for your contribution in opening so many doors for the young organists in your charge.[4]

Stephen Loher

Stephen Loher recalls, "[Purvis] loved real theater playing and spoke from time to time of the artistry of Jesse Crawford. He and George Wright were great friends. One time during my assistantship George was visiting. We not only got George to play both organs (Cathedral and Chapel) in theater style, but we got him up to the bells where he played 'Winchester Cathedral.'"[5]

Lyn Larsen

In an interview in December 2010, Lyn Larsen, a student of Purvis's and a successful theatre organist, offered his insights into Purvis's life with the theatre organ.

Larsen, a Southern California native, decided early in life that he wanted to be an organist. He performed jazz and popular music on Hammond organs at restaurants, played for churches, and worked for an Allen organ dealership. His first recital for an ATOS convention was given in 1968 at the Wiltern Theatre in Los Angeles.

In 1962 or 1963, Larsen traveled to San Francisco to hear George Wright perform at the closing organ concerts at the Fox Theatre. While in San Francisco, he went to Grace Cathedral to attend a service. He didn't meet Purvis, but he was impressed: "He had even more talent than I thought got utilized there. He had the same talent as Max Steiner and Eric Korngold. He handled a church service not like a church service. If there was a lull, nine times out of ten Richard would improvise soft accompaniment. He played a church service like a film score, very brilliant."

Around 1963 or 1964, a friend told Larsen about Purvis's Carol Vespers, an unusual concert with organ, choir, and orchestral musicians that was well worth hearing. For the second time, Larsen made the long drive from Southern California. Fortunately, he was warned to bring a snack, attend the 11 a.m. church service in the seat he wanted, and wait until the concert at 4 p.m. This time he met Purvis, told Purvis how much he enjoyed the experience, and returned for the Vespers in 1965 and 1966.

Larsen said about Purvis: "At Grace Cathedral he was very no-nonsense. He could even be cross at the keyboard when he was working. It was a defense to weed out visitors, organ nuts, interested choral people, tire kickers, and you learned to leave him alone. When you visited Richard away from Grace, over dinner, he was 100% the reverse, warm affable, a really great guy."

Like Los Angeles, San Francisco had a vibrant theatre organ scene. In 1967 Larsen was asked to play the 13-rank Wurlitzer organ at the Avenue Theatre in San Francisco, where he performed for much of that year.

While Larsen was on staff at the Avenue Theatre accompanying silent films, Purvis often came to hear him perform:

Purvis told me what he liked about the playing—and what he didn't—in a nice way. He said, "You were floundering there. Listen to a section from Holst's 'The Planets' or Vaughan Williams to get a sound or shape." After a couple of films, I told Richard I couldn't get a handle on it. He said, "How about if I come out on Tuesday or Wednesday, get some dinner, let me see the film," and he had really good suggestions. He mentioned something out of "The Planets," not something famous, but a small passage with celesta, sustained notes, etc.—absolutely a great idea for what that spot was. Every now and then during the week, he'd come over, give some suggestions, not organ lessons, but sharing music ideas. He was a huge help.

What was interesting to me was that Richard was far more involved with *music* first, and secondarily he ended up using the organ as a vehicle that he played and composed for. Richard loved to go to the St. Francis Hotel on Union Square to hear a fantastically talented pianist named Frank Denke. He was the head piano instructor at a small college in San Francisco or maybe across the Bay. He taught classical piano, and played classical piano in the lounge. Instead of playing "Misty" and show tunes, he'd play fantastic, elegant, complicated, stride-based piano. He played it immaculately, variations on "Tea for Two" to make your jaw drop. People with developed musical tastes came in. He'd play Gershwin preludes, then "Body and Soul," and someone would ask for the Rachmaninoff G minor prelude, everything from memory. Purvis loved to go there, staying for two or three hours. They were good friends. We'd do dinner and go back to his place, and I'd learn something. It was the first time I'd heard the Vaughan Williams Sea Symphony. It was always some new revelation. In that respect he was like George Wright, who was far more rounded and versatile than the rest of the theatre organ crowd. They both knew there was a lot more to the organ than just manuals and pedals.

When asked if Purvis played theatre organ, Larsen responded:

Yes, he knew all the basics of registrations, how to get all the sounds. After he retired, he'd do a program for one of the ATOS chapters. He wouldn't do a whole program of pop, but he'd play more transcriptions. He always included "I'll Take an Option on You," and always finished with a section of four or five of his own pieces.

He improvised well in a service as well as in theatre in a pop song. He didn't use it like 50s–60's jazz style, start out with the chord basis, go off on wild tangents—plenty of frosting, but where's the cake? He enjoyed playing theatre, Wurlitzers, Kimballs.

In 1968 Purvis published his collection "Seven Folk Tone Poems for the Organ," dedicating each piece to an organist friend, including Larsen, to whom Purvis inscribed "Of Sea and Skye." Larsen noted that Purvis surprised everyone with these dedications: "This was his little way of doing something to express friendship."

In 1973 Larsen moved to Phoenix, Arizona, where he played at Organ Stop Pizza for five years. Although he was also busy touring, he encountered Purvis fairly frequently at conventions of the American Theatre Organ Society, particularly when Purvis performed:

> By then the ATOS realized that their members liked hearing romantic classical music, the kind of stuff Richard or Virgil would do, so sometimes for variety they would have someone like Richard. If the city had a really nice old E. M. Skinner or a nice romantic symphonic type organ, they'd have him present a light program, a nice contrast to the theatre. This gave us a chance to spend some time together. He was getting up in years, so I'd rent a car and I'd be wheels and a right arm for him. I'd take him to the practices, and that's when he'd ask, "Will you turn pages?" I realized how little he ever looked at it, but mentally he wanted it sitting there.[6]

Jonas Nordwall

Jonas Nordwall, another close organist friend of Purvis's, offered the following reflections:

> There are several non-classical organ elements that influenced Richard Purvis's musical tastes. He began as a well-schooled pianist who understood the stylistic differences between classical and popular music. He also liked all forms of instrumental and choral ensembles plus classical and popular organ music.
>
> When looking at the repertoire in his listening library, there are recordings from early Gregorian chant through '50s and '60s popular recordings by Percy Faith and the 101 Strings. He had a fondness for English and Gaelic orchestral and choral works plus Spanish and Russian instrumental compositions. He had many different recordings of the same work by

various artists which I'm sure he used as references for his interpretations. His recording library included the major organ and choral works of J. S. Bach.

As a child Dick frequently went to San Francisco's Granada Theatre (later called the Paramount). The organist who intrigued him the most was Iris Vining. He would reference her very often when talking about great musician-organists. Iris Vining was a consummately trained organist who performed many orchestral transcriptions as well as the tunes of the day and was very skilled at improvising music for silent films.

It is important to understand the influence that the Granada organ had in developing Dick's concepts of organ tone. This organ was ensemble oriented, rather than a few solo voices speaking simultaneously, which was the norm for small theatre organs. It spoke very clearly and cleanly into a 2000+ seat auditorium.

A very important part of the Purvis sound was tremulant settings. Listening to the recordings of Grace Cathedral during Dick's tenure, you notice the tremulants were set faster and slightly deeper than most classical organs. They were somewhat akin to the tremulant settings of the 1920's Wurlitzers, which were far more conservative than the tremulant settings of most present day theatre organs.

Dick desired a more orchestral quality than classical organ quality for tremulants. In his opinion, the settings for Swell Oboes and Solo Flutes were to approximate the sound of the real instrument's tremolo. This was also a most important element of organ sound for Virgil Fox. Virgil would have organ technicians change the tremulant settings prior to a recital if they did not meet his expectations.

Purvis also influenced many of his contemporary colleagues. When Ted Alan Worth was studying with Virgil, Fox would frequently ask Ted how Purvis registered a particular piece, as Virgil did admire Purvis' playing. While both men were of the same generation, and their performance styles were similar in choices of color and use of swell pedals, Dick was the more scholarly performer.[7]

The Jesse Crawford Theatre Organ Society

Richard Purvis was a charter member of the Jesse Crawford Theatre Organ Society, founded as a chapter of the American Theatre Organ Society in

1987. Purvis joined on June 18, 1987, and remained a member until his death seven years later.

The president of the Society, Steve Plaggemeyer, wrote: "Our organization is based in Billings, Montana, so Richard never performed for us here, nor was he ever an officer. He was a friend of our founder, the late Dr. Edward J. Mullins."[8]

Performances by Purvis at Theatre Organ Conventions

On August 8, 1965, as part of the San Francisco convention of the American Theatre Organ Enthusiasts (in 1970 renamed the American Theatre Organ Society), Purvis performed at Grace Cathedral for the convention's "Hi-Jinks." The convention booklet reads:

> Mr. Purvis is one of the country's leading classical organists, and possesses a feeling for melody that is sure to surprise and please ATOE'ers. Mr. Purvis arranged this concert expressly for the theatrically-oriented ear. The organ is one of the best ever produced by Aeolian-Skinner ... due to a number of factors: the design and finishing was done by one of the greatest men ever involved in organ affairs, the late G. Donald Harrison; the placement of the voices in the building is extremely advantageous; the maintenance is carried out under the personal supervision of Edward M. Stout. His acute musical sensitivity and mechanical ability combine to keep these 100-odd ranks and the 4-manual console producing the kind of music for which they were intended. We thank Mr. Stout for his special attention to the organ for this concert.[9]

In the May/June 1984 issue of *Theatre Organ*, Purvis's upcoming concert in Indianapolis, Indiana, was announced: "1984 ATOS Convention attendees will tour the Scottish Rite Cathedral and assemble in the Auditorium for one of the Convention highlights, a concert by renowned composer, teacher and performer, Richard Purvis. This will be Mr. Purvis' first ATOS convention appearance and promises to match an outstanding talent with a unique and historic instrument, the 1929 5/88 E. M. Skinner pipe organ."[10]

Of this recital, given on July 9, 1984, convention reviewer Grant Whitcomb wrote:

Having been introduced to his attentive audience, Richard Purvis immediately endeared himself to all by announcing that San Franciscans were not acclimatized to mid-western summer temperatures, and removed his jacket. The program commenced with a request—Bach's *Toccata and Fugue in D Minor*. As the stately descending octaves spoke forth from the beautiful E. M. Skinner pipes, there seemed to be something lacking, and it was reverberation. Because of carpeting throughout the auditorium, plus numerous drapes and a large curtain across the stage, much of the glorious sound was being depleted before it had the chance to bounce off the woodwork. Nevertheless, it was a magnificent sound and a stunning performance of this familiar work.

The program continued with a lighter Bach Symphonette, a Minuet by Handel, and a Chorale by Cesar Franck, the latter being well-suited to this romantically voiced instrument. Following a brief intermission, Richard Purvis returned to play many of his own compositions. Exhibiting some dry wit, he noted that it may be the height of conceit to perform your own works, but your students insist because they want to find out if: 1) You play it as it was written; 2) You play it like *they* play it; and 3) You can play it at all! Highlighting this portion, we heard "Thanksgiving," "Scottish Aire," and the more familiar "Fanfare" which provided the opportunity to use the Stentorphone, Tuba Mirabilis and the 32' Bombarde, displaying the ultimate power and volume which this organ is capable of producing.

In evaluating such a concert what can one say other than that Richard Purvis' performance was awesome, the musical fare well selected and the organ impressive—with or without adequate reverberation. So the majority of the audience departed knowing that they had heard the biggest played by the best in the most palatial environment—a fitting conclusion to the third day of Convention.[11]

Notes

1. Ed Stout, e-mail, May 29, 2009.
2. Stout interview.
3. Stout interview.
4. Ed Stout, "Reflections About Richard Purvis, The Renowned Organist, Composer and Teacher," in "Professional Perspectives," *Theatre Organ*, May 1, 2008, 46–47. Reprinted by permission.

5. Stephen Loher, e-mail, June 6, 2009.

6. Lyn Larsen, telephone interview, December 1, 2010.

7. Jonas Nordwall, "Additional Notes about Dick Purvis," e-mail, January 25, 2011.

8. Steve Plaggemeyer, e-mail, August 5, 2011.

9. ATOE convention booklet, August 1965, 8-9; courtesy Tom DeLay.

10. Mary Drake, "Indianapolis' Scottish Rite Cathedral and its 5/88 E. M. Skinner," *Theatre Organ*, May/June 1984, 12.

11. Grant Whitcomb, *Theatre Organ*, September/October 1984, 35–36.

chapter 13

PURVIS AS RECORDING ARTIST

In light of Purvis's huge output of organ and choral compositions, the six long-playing records of his music produced during his lifetime seem small in number. Nonetheless, the recordings sold well and were cherished widely. Some have now been re-released on CD.

This chapter includes playlists and liner notes from the recordings, as well as selected press reviews.

Published Recordings

1. Aeolian-Skinner Presents The King of Instruments [1953]

Volume V—The Music of Richard Purvis
Played on the Organ of Grace Cathedral, San Francisco, California
Played by the Staff Organist[1]
Made by the Aeolian-Skinner Organ Company, Inc., Boston 25, Mass.

There are no identifying numbers on the record jacket. On the disc itself, the following numbers are shown: Side 1: F80P6967; Side 2: F80P6968

Side One

I: Partita on Christ ist Erstanden
  Prelude, Kanzone, Capriccio, Lento, Toccata
II: Pastorale (Forest Green)

Side Two

I: Adoration
II: Divinum Mysterium
III: Capriccio on the Notes of the Cuckoo
IV: Introit
V: Elevation

The Organ

Built by the Aeolian-Skinner Organ Company in 1934, and modified in 1952, the Grace Cathedral organ was planned with the prime purpose of accompanying the Cathedral Service. Typical of the American Classic organ, however, it is equally well suited to the diverse requirements of the Classic, Romantic and Modern periods of organ literature, and is afforded excellent musical possibilities by the superb acoustical atmosphere of Grace Cathedral.

The Composer

Beginning his musical career at the age of 13 with an appearance in San Francisco's Exposition Auditorium, Richard Purvis early in life earned for himself a high reputation for virtuosity at the keyboard. Purvis studied with Dr. Alexander McCurdy at the Curtis Institute of Music in Philadelphia, and was the only organist ever to receive the much coveted Cyrus H. K. Curtis Memorial Scholarship. Upon completion of his studies there, he was granted by the Institute a scholarship for further studies abroad.

Following his return to civilian life at the end of World War II, he was appointed Organist and Master of the Choristers of Grace Cathedral, San Francisco, California.

A distinguished composer, he has written such noteworthy music as "The Ballad of Judas Iscariot," "The Mass of St. Nicholas," "A Festival Anglican Eucharist," "Five Pieces on Gregorian Themes," "Seven Preludes on American Hymns," in addition to numerous anthems, piano solos and songs.

The Music

Music is usually written because there is an irresistible creative urge to express on the part of the composer or because there seems to be a need for certain types of composition which the composer feels he can fulfill with some degree of success. The latter type bears the somewhat mundane "canard" of "utilitarian" and it is in this category that Richard Purvis classifies himself. Every composition heard on this record was written, either because someone requested he write a specific type of piece, or because he himself needed a definite type of composition for a particular occasion.

With the exception of the Pastorale on "Forest Green", every work heard on this recording was composed with the Alexander Memorial Organ of Grace Cathedral in mind and the registration heard is of the composer's own choosing. This gives the music an air of authenticity not often encountered in performance.

Partita on "Christ Ist Erstanden"

Prelude - Kanzone - Capriccio - Lento - Toccata

Perhaps reviving an old art form is similar to "pouring new wine in old skins" but when one considers that the freedom of style encountered here is in no way restrained by the medium of expression, the idea proves a happy one. The words of the hymn were written by Michael Weisse (1840–1534) and the tune (which appears as No. 134 in the English Hymnal) is a twelfth century German Melody. The English translation of the poetry is by Catherine Winkworth (1827–1878). (The entire hymn appears as No. 129 in the English Hymnal.) Following are the words which suggested the mood of the various movements.

Prelude	Verse 1	Christ the Lord is risen again.
		Christ has broken every chain.
Kanzone	Verse 5	Now He bids us tell abroad
		How the Lost may be restored.
Capriccio	Verse 2	We too sing for joy and shout,
		Alleluya.
Lento	Verse 3	He who bore all pain and loss
		Comfortless upon the Cross.
Toccata	Verse 2	He who gave for us His Life,
		Who for us endured the strife
		Is our Paschal Lamb today.

Pastorale on "Forest Green"

Phillips Brook's [sic] charming American "O Little Town of Bethlehem" is often sung to the English Folktune, "Forest Green." The resulting happy wedding of "Words and Music" was the inspiration of the charming pastorale. The disarming simplicity and harmonic color of this miniature finds an immediate response in the average listener. This is the second of "7 Chorale Preludes on Tunes Found in American Hymnals."

Adoration

This is one of "Four Prayers in Tone" and employs the thirteenth century plainsong "Adoro Devote" as its principal motiv. Of great intensity and ardour, this music finds its natural medium in comprehensive instruments of modern design. (The plainsong may be found at number 204 in the Episcopal Hymnal.)

Divinum Mysterium

The cantus of this work (one of Five Pieces on Gregorian Themes) is among the loveliest of plainsong melodies. In fact, its charming warmth has made it the gateway through which many laymen have entered the realm of Liturgical Chant. The mood here is bucolic and the crashing chords of the finale suggest the joyous clanging of church bells. The careful listener will hear in addition to the plainsong cantus (No. 20 in the Episcopal Hymnal) an allusion to Adeste Fidelis [sic].

Capriccio on the Notes of the Cuckoo

"Cuckoo pieces" have been written by organists since the dawn of free organ composition. Perhaps the reason for this is that stopped flute pipes give a most reasonable facsimile of the silly, repetitious call of our "little feathered comedian."

From "An American Organ Mass"

Introit - Elevation

The Organ Mass uses as its canti-firmi, Liturgical Melodies associated with Christmastide. Its music is devotional and permeated with an aura of childlike simplicity. The Introit is based on the Sarum Plainsong on "Christe Redemptor", and the Elevation employs the Chorale "Von [*sic*] Himmel Hoch." (These may be found in the 1940 edition of the Episcopal Hymnal as numbers 485 and 22.)

The Registration

Partita

Prelude

Section A:	Solo	Reeds 8' and 4'	
	Great	Diapason 8', 4', 2⅔', 2', Fourniture, Cymbal	
	Pedal	Diapason 16', 8', 4'	
		Violone 16', 8'	
		Posaune 16'	
Section B:	Great	(R.H.) Flutes 8', 4', 1⅗'	
	Swell	(L.H.) Flutes 4', 4', 2', 1'	
	Pedal	Violone 16', 8'	
		Flutes 16', 8', 4'	

Kanzone

Choir	(R.H.) Clarinet 8', Trompette 8'
Swell	(L.H.) Gamba 8', Harmonic Flute 4', Spitz Flute 4'
Pedal	Diapason 16', 8'
	Violone 16', 8'
	Flutes 16', 8', 4'

Capriccio

Reeds and Mixtures on all manuals and pedals (R.H. on Great, L.H. on Choir)

Lento

Section A:	Solo	French Horn 8'
	Swell	Flute Celeste 8'
	Great	Swell and Choir to Great 8'
	Choir	Kleine Erzahler 8'
	Pedal	Gemshorn 16'
		Lieblich Gedackt 16', 8'

Section B: Solo   English Horn
            Swell   Flute Celeste 8' and
                     Stopped Diapason 8' (L.H.)
            Choir   Flute 8', 4', 2⅔'
                     Solo to Choir 16'
            Pedal   As in Section A + Bourdon 16,
                     + Swell to Pedal

Toccata

            Reeds and Mixtures on all manuals and pedals
                     (Flutes added last page)

Forest Green

Choir   Soft Foundations then Flutes 8', 4', 2⅔' (R.H.)
Swell   Soft celestes (L.H.)

The Choir Melodia 8' and the Solo English Horn are used in a Kaleido-scopic manner.

Adoration

The Solo Gamba Celestes—Swell Oboe and Choir Foundation Stops and the Pedal 32' Diapason are heard in the opening section. In the development, the full organ is reached at the climatic [*sic*] point.

Divinum Mysterium

The first part uses the softer registers such as the Solo Flauto Mirabilis 8', Choir Trompette 8', Great Flûte Harmonique 8' and soft celestes. In the second section the long pedal point utilizes the Diapason 32' and the pedal reeds are heard to an advantage at the finale.

Cuckoo

Section A: Swell Spitzfloete 4' (Played octave lower)
            Great Flute 4'
            Choir Clarinet 8'
            Pedal Open Bass 16'
                     Bourdon 16', Flute 8'

Section B: Great Flute 4'
             Choir Flutes 8', 4', 1'
             Pedal Flute 8' (alone)

Organ Mass

   Introit

             Solo   French Horn
             Swell Foundation 8', 4'
             Great Light Foundations 8', 4' (Swell to Great)
             Choir Kleine Erzahler 8', Flute 4'
             Pedal Solo to Pedal only (Later Foundation 16', 8')
   Elevation

   Uses only the softest registers on the organ. The Pedal solo is the Swell 8' Oboe coupled. The "quasi French Horn Chords" are played on the Great Flûte Harmonique.[2]

———

This recording was reissued on CD around 2001 by JAV Records as *King of Instruments*, Vol. 1, CD-JAV 121. It is no longer available.[3]

Lorenz Maycher of the Vermont Organ Academy reports that the entire unedited tape of this recording session has surfaced and will be re-released at a future time.[4]

In 1967, 14 years after its release, G. C. Ramsey wrote the following review of this recording:

> Really of more interest than the music itself on this recording is the fact that all of the pieces (with the exception of the Forest Green Pastorale) were composed with this organ in mind, and thus represent an American series of compositions inspired by the instruments of an American organ builder.... The instrument, this reviewer thinks, is one of the best played in the series. It is a pre-war one, but now has two Great mixtures, undoubtedly more choir mixture work than it did in 1934, and so forth. It does not sound like a French, English, German Romantic, or German Baroque organ. It sounds like an American organ designed with all periods in mind, yet with a unity of its own, and an ensemble sound. The only additions that

this reviewer would like to see (and hear) are more Baroque reeds. In addition, of course, to the reeds already there.[5]

2. A Richard Purvis Organ Recital in Grace Cathedral, Vol. I [1956]

HIFIRECORD
High Fidelity Recordings, Inc.,
7803 Sunset Blvd., Hollywood 28, Calif.
Album No. R-703

Trumpet Tune (Purcell)
Arioso (J. S. Bach)
Greensleeves (Purvis)
Processional (Shaw)
Supplication (Purvis)
Pavanne [sic] (Elmore)
Cappricio [sic] on the Notes of the Cuckoo (Purvis)
Toccata (5th Symphony, Widor)

San Francisco boasts Grace (Episcopal) Cathedral, visited by thousands of tourists each year. High atop a hill on the west side of the city, this imposing edifice, a monument to the Christian faith, seems to possess the Old World charm of antiquity. Its towered, Gothic mass of concrete and gray-stone appears at once friendly and austere, cavernous yet inviting. Inside, the vaulted severity is warmed with many-colored daylight through intricately fashioned art-glass windows. By night, great myriad-lighted chandeliers suspended by dozens of feet of chain cast a candle-like glow upon seemingly endless arches, pillars and girders.

The Cathedral seats thousands, has nothing to deaden its live, natural sound and is therefore an ideal housing for a great Pipe Organ. Reverberation time is nearly five seconds. The Aeolian-Skinner Pipe Organ (judged one of the manufacturer's finest installations) consists of 5,794 pipes and a four manual conventional draw knob type console. The largest pipes are 32' long and may be seen in the adjoining photographs of the casework in the center turrets. These pipes are 32' open diapasons, playable from the pedal board. Lowest "C" speaks 16 cycles per second. Tiny pipes [of] 1' pitch, no larger than a pencil, located in back of the casework, extend to 16,000 cycles per second. Another 32' stop, the 32' Bombarde pedal reed, is housed behind the casework. Pulsations of the reeds in these lower pipes seem so slow as to almost permit counting. Low "C" of the 32' pedal Bombarde also speaks at a frequency of 16 cycles per second. Extreme clarity of sound is made possible by the ideal surroundings, so much so that you will hear piston combination changes, certain mechanical sounds from the organ chamber mechanisms and slight wind sounds which are part of the "attack" in pipe organs.

Richard Purvis, organist and master of the Choristers at Grace Cathedral, is a serious, dedicated young musician who has already created an enviable reputation for playing the organ classics with feeling and dexterity. His outstanding musical talent extends to composition as well as interpretation. You will note many of the numbers included are Richard Purvis' own. Mr. Purvis achieves brilliance without overemphasis of "highs" (a common abuse among those who play in the so-called "baroque" style), and thunderous might that thrills. Yet, in the quieter numbers programmed, his subtlety, unusual tone colors, and expression of feeling are equally inspiring.

Remarkable realism and fidelity was achieved in the master recording by use of two Telefunken type C-12 condenser microphones and one AKG acoustically variable condenser microphone in connection with an Ampex three track Model 350 magnetic tape recorder recording on Scotch Type 111A magnetic recording tape. Tape to disc transfer employed an automatically variable pitch Scully lathe with Westrex feedback heated stylus cutting head. Pressings are Custom pure Vinyl.

USE STANDARD RIAA TREBLE ROLL-OFF & BASS BOOST[6]

———

A digital copy of this recording is offered (as of September 2012) by Essential Media Group on Amazon.com as a "manufacture on demand" product. According to a review posted on the site, it is a digital copy of an LP.

3. A Richard Purvis Organ Recital in Grace Cathedral, Vol. II [1956]

HIFIRECORD
High Fidelity Recordings, Inc.,
6087 Sunset Blvd., Hollywood 28, Calif.
Album No. R-704

Marche Grotesque (Purvis)
Sheep May Safely Graze (J. S. Bach)
Pièce Héroïque (Franck)
Cortège et Litanie (Dupré)
Nocturne (Purvis)
Les Petites Cloches (Purvis)
Adagissimo (Dupré)
Toccata Festiva (Purvis)

Liner notes identical to those of Vol. 1, above.

A digital copy of this recording is offered (as of September 2012) by Essential Media Group on Amazon.com as a "manufacture on demand" product. According to a review posted on the site, it is a digital copy of an LP.

4. Music For Christmas: Richard Purvis at the Organ in Grace Cathedral [1959]

HIFIRECORD
High Fidelity Recordings, Inc.,
6087 Sunset Blvd., Hollywood 28, Calif.
High Fidelity Records R-705

Adeste Fidelis [sic] (Traditional)
Lo, How a Rose (Praetorious [sic]-Brahms)
It Came Upon a Midnight Clear (Willis)
In Dulci Jubila [sic] (Dupré)
Joy to the World (Traditional)

O Little Town of Bethlehem (Purvis arr.)
O Little Town of Bethlehem (Redner orig.)
Cortège et Litanie (Dupré)
Christmas Cradle Song (Purvis)
The First Noel (Traditional)
Carol Rhapsody (Purvis)

Liner notes identical to those of Vol. 1, above, with the addition of the following:

"The Carillon heard consists of real cast bells hung high in the great towers of Grace Cathedral. They may be heard for miles when played."

This recording was reissued in 1997 on CD by Tradition, TCD 1057, under the title *Music for Christmas: Richard Purvis*.
1. Joy to the World
2. It Came Upon a Midnite [*sic*] Clear
3. The First Noel
4. Lo, How a Rose
5. Adeste Fidelis [*sic*]
6. O Little Town (Purvis)
7. Cortege Et Litanie
8. Christmas Cradle Song,
9. O Little Town (Redner)
10. In Dulci Jubila [*sic*]
11. Carol Rhapsody

Liner notes to the CD:

Master organist Richard Purvis performed this selection of festive Christmas songs on the mammoth organ in San Francisco's Grace Cathedral. The organ boasts 5,794 pipes ranging in size from 32 feet tall to the size of a pencil. This is a surprisingly dynamic, historic recording which will treat your subwoofer to a full workout. Recorded in 1959.

The Tradition reissue of this album includes the original liner notes. The master tapes were digitally restored and remastered for this release.

5. Richard Purvis at the Grace Cathedral Organ [1969]

Word Records, Waco, Texas

WST-9033-LP [Purvis's only stereo recording]

SIDE I

1. Fanfare - 3:40
2. Brigg Fayre - 3:42
3. Les Petite [*sic*] Cloches - 2:10
4. Greensleeves - 4:00
5. Thanksgiving - 4:55

SIDE II

1. Nocturne - 4:46
2. Supplication - 8:23
3. Of Moor and Fen - 5:39
4. The Cuckoo [*sic*] - 2:08

Fred Bock wrote the following liner notes for this recording:

I first met Richard Purvis on a Tuesday morning in 1965, in the coffee shop of the Fairmont Hotel in San Francisco. I was on a sales trip for the music publishing division of Word, Inc. Over a glass of fresh-squeezed orange juice (I said fresh-*squeezed*, not fresh-frozen!), toast and coffee, we discussed the kind of writing he could do for us. Since that first meeting we have shared many new and exciting ideas about possible musical endeavors. This record is one of them.

To record in Grace Cathedral is not as easy as it might appear. First, we had to clear the time with the main office. Grace Cathedral is not your run-of-the-mill church. This place is bustling all the time, almost 24 hours a day! The dates were set: October 24, 25, and 26th, if we needed it. The time: 11 P.M. to 4 A.M. Why so late? Well, for one thing, those fabled cabled cars make so much noise as they run along California Street that they would be clearly evident on the tape. Cable car service stops at 11 P.M. Very nearby is the local fire station. Since it is not possible to pre-schedule fires, we had to work around that one. You wouldn't believe all the fires in San Francisco!

We did the recording on a three-track Ampex. Microphones were placed close to the shutters on either side of the chancel area, and one was put farther away for "air" sounds, reverberation (all 8 seconds of it absolutely natural) and leakage from the other two mikes. No apologies for noises peculiar to organ music: air sounds, swell shades opening and closing, piston changes, and the like. These make our record more authentic.

The organ at Grace is a rare beauty. Originally built in 1934 by Aeolian Skinner, it was rebuilt in 1951 by G. Donald Harrison of the same firm. In 1967 a new five manual console was added making it totally new or remodeled in every respect. Before we started recording, while the tuners were still putting on finishing touches, I had opportunity to try the organ out for myself. It was like too much of a good meal. A myriad of stops are available on every manual at any pitch level (the organ is 100 ranks). The reeds are snarly, flutes soft or metallic with little, a lot, or no chiff; and then, there are the strings! Strings are my favorite, and the organ at Grace has string sounds, beautiful and bountiful. Just listen and you'll see what I mean. Now the music. At times Purvis is a scholar, at other times an artist, and at other times, a romanticist. It is amazing to me how all of these traits fit so well into one gentle man. Purvis' activity centers around the organ in the Church. His music on Sunday morning, as well as his writing reflect practical usefulness in aiding worship; sometimes scholarly, sometimes artistically, and sometimes romantically. He communicates through them all. All of the selections we've recorded are published and available, and can sound equally as effective on a small electronic organ as they do on the organ at Grace. However, it's rather nice to hear music played by the composer on the instrument for which he wrote it.

The excitement of working on this project will be long remembered. I remember the kindnesses of Charles Agneau, the verger; Douglas Cortright [Metzler] who assisted by turning pages, and keeping us well supplied with coffee, cakes, and Cokes; and Magnificat, the Church Mouser who hungrily, though silently, stalks about keeping *that* department in good order. Just writing these liner notes has made me feel the excitement that comes when you're making a record, and it has me thinking about album #2. If you're reading this, Dick, what do you think? We could meet in the coffee shop at the Fairmont and talk over a glass of fresh-squeezed (I said fresh-*squeezed*, not fresh-frozen) orange juice.

6. *The Organ Plays Golden Favorites*

© 1972 The Readers Digest Association, Inc.
Produced for Readers Digest by RCA.

This was a 5-LP (10-side) set; Purvis's music is on Record No. 4.
Numbering on the record jacket: 17 RM 14864, RDA 054-D4
The actual disc No. 4 is numbered RD4-054-4/ WIRS-9730 on side 1 and
RD4-054-4/ WIRS-9729 on side 2.
A cassette tape version of this recording, RD6A-123-1, was also produced.

Richard Purvis. Some years ago, in Berkeley, California, theater-organ buffs discovered a wonderfully talented high school boy named Don Irving, who played fabulously for a while and then disappeared. Actually he didn't disappear at all. His name was really Richard Purvis, and he is still very much of the organ world—currently in San Francisco where he holds the post of organist at Grace Cathedral, and has for many years. It was in San Francisco that he made his concert debut when he was only thirteen. Later he won a scholarship to the Curtis Institute of Music in Philadelphia, beginning there a course of organ playing and composition that took him to a succession of the finest teachers in the world, among them Alexander McCurdy (at Curtis) and Charles Courboin (organist of Saint Patrick's Cathedral in New York City). Besides his success as a recitalist, Purvis is particularly famous for his own compositions, at least two of which, "Communion" and his setting of "Greensleeves," are already American classics. Purvis shares with American humorist Mark Twain the dubious distinction of being once pronounced dead. While he was serving in Germany in the Second World War, misinformation about an untimely end was accepted as truth by one of our major musical journals, and Purvis's obituary was published. Fortunately, however, he still composes, plays and conducts in exuberantly good health.[7]

Record 4

Side One

Aeolian-Skinner Organ, Symphony Hall, Boston[8]

Serenade from "The Student Prince" (Romberg)
March of the Toys (Herbert)
Love Sends a Little Gift of Roses (Openshaw-Cooke)
Musetta's Waltz, from "La Bohème" (Puccini)
My Heart at Thy Sweet Voice, from "Samson and Delilah" (Saint-Saëns)
Grand March, from "Aïda" (Verdi)

Side Two

Alexander Memorial Organ, Grace Cathedral, San Francisco

Overture to Act III, from "Lohengrin" (Wagner)
Clair de lune (Debussy)
In a Monastery Garden (Ketèlbey)
Bridal Chorus, from "Lohengrin" (Wagner)
Prize Song, from "Die Meistersinger" (Wagner)
Goin' Home (Dvorak-Fisher)

Side One

Aeolian-Skinner Organ, Symphony Hall, Boston

This organ, designed by G. Donald Harrison, is a wonder among so-called classic American instruments … which means that it is perfectly put together, perfectly proportioned in look and sound, designed tonally to produce either a rich texture of combined sounds ("texture" is a favorite word among organ devotees) or a brilliant range of individual solo voices. There are four manuals and a pedalboard playable from a large oak-trimmed mahogany console which is movable and will even disappear if necessary. Most of the pipes are spotted metal (a combination of lead and tin), an enthusiasm of Harrison's; the wooden ones are California pine. There are 4802 speaking pipes, in six divisions (Great, Swell, Choir, Positiv, Bombarde, Pedal).

Serenade from "The Student Prince" (Romberg)

Sigmund Romberg (1887–1951), Hungarian master of the Viennese operetta, scored his greatest and most lasting triumph in 1924 when he produced *The Student Prince*, and of that lovely score the brightest ornament is the "Serenade."

March of the Toys (Herbert)

Though he was doing very nicely as a cellist in the Metropolitan Opera orchestra, Victor Herbert (1859–1924) wanted to compose more than he wanted to play. Many of his works were very serious and classically meaningful, but that irrepressible sense of popular melody overcame him and he flowed into the warmer world of the operetta. From one of these light entertainments, *Babes in Toyland*, comes the whimsically stiff-legged and strutting "March of the Toys."

Love Sends a Little Gift of Roses (Openshaw-Cooke)

Ever since roses were red and violets blue, flowers have been helping romance along, and in 1919 two songwriters added one more charmingly sentimental tribute with their "Love Sends a Little Gift of Roses." John Openshaw contributed the music, Leslie Cooke the words, and in its quietly ballad way the song has been consistently popular ever since.

Musetta's Waltz, from "La Bohème" (Puccini)

Giacomo Puccini's (1858–1924) opera *La Bohème* is notable not only for its unforgettable music but because it presents two heroines rather than the usual one. Caught up in the spell of the plot, we are just as concerned about the frivolous Musetta, who falls in love with poet Marcello, as we are about the seamstress Mimi and her artist lover Rodolfo. Musetta's gay waltz song proclaims her a "new" woman, interested in money and fun. When Musetta is feeling marvelous, the whole world, thanks to Puccini, knows it!

My Heart at Thy Sweet Voice, from "Samson and Delilah" (Saint-Saëns)

Seldom has such a beautiful melody accomlished such a sinister purpose as does "My Heart at Thy Sweet Voice." In Camille Saint-Saëns' (1835–1921) opera *Samson and Delilah*, Delilah's beautiful aria is a song of allurement without love, of promises fated to be unfulfilled … and yet, how entrancing!

Grand March, from "Aïda" (Verdi)

Solemn, majestic, the "Grand March" in Giuseppe Verdi's (1813–1901) opera *Aïda* accompanies the parade of a conquering Egyptian army. One of the mightiest monuments to the genius of Verdi, the "Grand March" has become a classic in its own right, used whenever stately ritual and dignity reign.

Side Two

Alexander Memorial Organ, Grace Cathedral, San Francisco

One of the glories of the pipe organ in Grace Cathedral, San Francisco, is its Italian console, made especially for the instrument by the Ruffatti Organ Company of Padua. Like many theater organs (but not many church organs) it is in what organists call a horseshoe shape; that is, as the player faces the keyboards, the ivory tablets which bring on or take off various voices of the organ spread from the left to the right in a semicircle which also rises in the center and descends on either side. Each individual voice of the organ is a stop; each stop has a tablet, and there are other tablets as well which control other devices. Much of the coloristic effectiveness of the organ depends on specially selected sounds which are the combinations of multiple stops sounding together; little buttons called pistons magically assemble these combinations when pressed—this organ contains fifty-six. Directly in front of the player lie the keyboards, four of them, arranged in a tier. The lowest, that is, closest to the performer, is the Choir, so-called because its stops are fairly gentle and hence useful for accompanying. Next is the Great, with the sturdiest and most majestic-sounding stops. Next is the Swell, which gets its name from being enclosed in a large box with one side made of louvers which can open and close, making the sound louder or softer gradually. Finally, topmost, is the Solo, made up chiefly of melodic voices used alone, or solo. The Grace Cathedral organ was first built in 1934, designed by G. Donald Harrison of the Aeolian-Skinner Organ Company and rebuilt by him in 1952, somewhat enlarging its resources to 101 stops, with well over 7000 pipes.

Overture to Act III, from "Lohengrin" (Wagner)

A flurry of trumpets, a crescendo of strings, and the Overture to Act III of *Lohengrin* explodes into one of the most exciting of Richard Wagner (1813–1883) excerpts, preluding all the action of the final scenes. At the premier of the opera in 1850 the Overture to Act III was singled out for special praise.

Clair de lune (Debussy)

The famous composer of pictures in music, Claude Debussy (1862–1918), loved the moon as do all Frenchmen and other lovers. Early in his career he wrote a suite of piano pieces called *Suite bergamasque*, the most famous portion (and indeed perhaps his most famous single piece) being "Clair de lune" ("Moonlight"). So perfectly did he catch the romantic hush of the silvery night that his original piano version has been transcribed for nearly every instrument. It is especially effective on a fine organ.

In a Monastery Garden (Ketèlbey)

Albert Ketèlbey (1875–1959) was a master of the exotic, but he did not discover this for some years. After a childhood full of musical promise, he graduated to conducting in theaters for musical shows, meanwhile earnestly composing serious works for posterity. It was not until he began to write in a lighter vein that such beautiful pieces as "In a Monastery Garden" began to flow from his pen.

Bridal Chorus, from "Lohengrin" (Wagner)

The "Bridal Chorus" is certainly the best-known excerpt from Richard Wagner's (1813–1883) *Lohengrin*, that mysterious opera story of a knight who arrives from nowhere, borne on a swan-drawn barge, to champion a damsel in distress whom he does not know but has only heard of. The damsel, Elsa, and he fall in love, of course (this is opera), and after their marriage ceremony are escorted by a chorus of peasants singing the simple, sedate "Bridal Chorus."

Prize Song, from "Die Meistersinger" (Wagner)

Music was a noble profession back in the sixteenth century, and song contests could bring fame, riches, and even a bride, as in Wagner's opera

Die Meistersinger. Young Walther is determined to be a musician and to marry Eva, but he must first win a competition with an original song which he will himself sing and play. And win he does with this broadly flowing "Prize Song."

Goin' Home (Dvorak-Fisher)

Antonín Dvořák (1841–1904), the great Czech nationalist composer, came to America to write his finest symphony—in Iowa, where he had discovered a community of other Czechs singing, dancing, cooking and enjoying an Old World heritage in a New World prosperity. The Symphony No. 5, which he called *From the New World*, includes the beautiful slow movement known everywhere today by the title "Goin' Home."

Unpublished Recordings

There are numerous unpublished recordings of concerts and services played by Purvis. Many are in the possession of Ed Stout, Douglas Metzler, Donna Parker, and Jonas Nordwall; most are on open reel tapes or cassettes. A partial listing of the known unpublished recordings is provided to give readers a sense of the treasures of "the Purvis sound" that survive:

Organ and Orchestra Concert, San Mateo Performing Arts Center, January 15, 1965. Poulenc: Organ Concerto for Organ, Strings, and Timpani. Richard Purvis, organist; Peninsula Symphony. Aaron Sten, conductor

Grace Cathedral Choir Concert, 1966. Purvis: Song of Simeon, Ballad of Judas Iscariot.

Easter Service, Grace Cathedral, April 14, 1968. Purvis conducting and playing the Rodgers electronic organ. Purvis: Alleluia; Christ our Passover; Lyra Davidica.

Choir Room Rehearsal (partial) at Grace Cathedral, November 7, 1968.

Easter Service, Grace Cathedral, April 6, 1969, Skinner organ. Includes Dirksen's "Christ is Risen from the Dead."

First recording of Richard Purvis's "Petit Concert Champetre" for Organ and Piano, recorded in the summer 1969 at the home of Bud Iverson.

Festival Choral Evensong at Grace Cathedral, 1969.

World premiere of "Pièce Symphonique for Orchestra and Organ," Grace Cathedral, April 25, 1969. Oakland Symphony, Gerhard Samuel, conductor; Richard Purvis, organist.

Trial tape for "Supplication" by Purvis. Played at Grace Cathedral, 1969.

Christmas Carol Concert, Grace Cathedral, 1970. Richard Purvis, conductor; Steven Loher, organist.

Tribute to Richard Purvis. St. Mary's Catholic Cathedral, San Francisco. September 26, 1976. Tom Hazleton, Diane Bish, Ted Alan Worth, organists; Richard Purvis, conductor; San Francisco Civic Chorale, and members of the San Francisco Symphony.

Organ Recital at Rodgers store, San Francisco, February 18, 1980. Selections by Bach, Handel, etc., and Purvis's "Melita" Suite.

Richard Purvis, organ recital, Grace Cathedral, October 3, 1982.

Organ Recital at Grace Cathedral, June 10, 1984. Richard Purvis and John Fenstermaker, marking the 50th anniversary of the Alexander Memorial Organ.

AGO Convention, June 24, 1984. Richard Purvis at Grace Cathedral. Franck: Chorale in E major, Cantabile, Chorale in A minor, Pièce Héroique, Pastorale, Final in B-flat; Bach, Arioso.

May 5, 1985, First Church of Christ, Scientist, San Francisco, California "Tribute to Wallace Sabin," celebrating the 60th Anniversary of the four-manual Kimball organ designed by Sabin. Includes the "Three-Note Encore."

Organ Recital at Grace Cathedral, August 13, 1987, Richard Purvis. Bach, "Lord Jesus, We Await Thy Presence," BWV 730; Prelude and Fugue in B minor, BWV 544; Peeters, Song of the Ocean; Vierne, three pieces; Karg-Elert, Saluto Angelico; Franck, Chorale in A minor; Sabin, Bourrée; Davies, A Solemn Melody; Purvis, Roundelay, Supplication, Toccata Festiva.

Evensong at Grace Cathedral to honor Richard Purvis on his 80th birthday, August 15, 1993.

Memorial Service for Richard Purvis Memorial at Grace Cathedral, January 25, 1995.

Richard Purvis plays his "Don Irving" theme on a Rodgers Organ. (Purvis composed and played this theme during his KRE radio years 1925–1930.)

Recordings of Music by Purvis

There are undoubtedly hundreds of recordings by various artists that include compositions by Purvis, but the following hold particular interest:

"Not Just Another Organ Recording"
Trio con Brio (Jonas Nordwall, Donna Parker, Tom Hazleton)
Triple Play Recordings, 333-01CD, 1992
Includes Purvis's "Symphonic Suite," "Dialogue Monastique," and "Thanksgiving"

"Still Having Fun After All These Years"
Trio con Brio (Jonas Nordwall, Donna Parker, Tom Hazleton)
Triple Play Recordings, 333-02-CD, 1995
Includes Lemmens-Purvis "Fanfare in D"

"A Tribute to Richard Purvis"
Thomas Hazleton, Organist
The Organ at Saints Peter & Paul Church, Naperville, Illinois
Allen Organ

Arkay Records, AR6172R, 2004
Includes Fantasia on Ton-y-Botel, Supplication, Thanksgiving, Of Moor and Fen, St. Francis Suite, Dies Irae, Fanfare, Night in Monterey, March Grotesque, Partita on *Christ ist Erstanden*

Notes

1. "Charles Shipley [Verger at Grace Cathedral] tells me that Purvis was listed on The King of Instruments set as the 'staff organist' due to contractual obligations to another recording company at the time." Michael Lampen, e-mail, April 20, 2011.

2. Record jacket; author unknown; possibly Purvis himself.

3. Joe Vitacco, e-mail, April 30, 2011.

4. Lorenz Maycher, e-mail, September 11, 2012.

5. G. C. Ramsey, "The Aeolian-Skinner Record Series," *The American Organist,* March 1967, Vol. 50, No. 3, 21–23.

6. Record jacket; author unknown; possibly Purvis himself.

7. Author unknown.

8. Having never come across any other reference to Purvis's recording at Symphony Hall in Boston, I asked Ed Stout what he knew about it. He replied: "As to your question about the recording on the Boston Symphony Hall organ, I believe I recall his making mention of having to go back there for some recording session, but he had little to say about that to me. You also mentioned the numbers [on this recording] were not what you might expect from Purvis, but he had a remarkable memory for all kinds of music. I remember one night we were having drinks in his place and he asked me if I knew the score to the motion picture 'Wuthering Heights.' I said, 'No, I do not recall the score.' He went to this Steinway B and sat down and re-created the entire score of the film. You could just hear the orchestra sawing away as he played. It was pure magic." Ed Stout, e-mail, April 23, 2011.

chapter 14

purvis as teacher

A person could get more valuable, solid musical information from Dick over cocktails and one dinner than many teachers could provide in a year.

—*Jonas Nordwall*

Purvis was revered by the many organists who studied with him. While at Grace Cathedral, he taught on the Alexander Memorial Organ or in the Chapel of Grace. After leaving the Cathedral, he taught at his home studio on Balceta Avenue, and for a number of years he traveled to Rodgers studios in Los Angeles, San Diego, Fresno, and other California locations to give private lessons.

In 1981 Nelson Barden interviewed Purvis about his experiences with Edwin H. Lemare, who, like Purvis, was a legendary performer and teacher. In the course of the interview, Purvis spoke about his own style of teaching, comparing it with some of Lemare's techniques:

RIP: I heard him [Lemare] at the Civic Auditorium … The registration was beautiful. The build-up in "Sundown" I still remember. Building it up and letting the thing down—it was so meticulously smooth. You didn't hear a stop come on or go off, but it happened.... He was a great colorist, as I remember him. It was flexible playing with a delight in color. Not color for color's sake, but color used as a vehicle through which you express the music. You have to listen to what you're doing, and he certainly listened. I make it a point to have my students listen to what they're doing—they don't want to listen!

NB: What did Wallace [Sabin] do with you to get you over that place of not being able to hear?

Purvis at the Rodgers 925 organ in his home studio, 1988. From a Rodgers Organ Company promotional brochure, 1991. Courtesy Ken Brown.

RIP: I have a theory about that. Most organists don't like music. They like the organ....

NB: How did Wallace teach?

RIP: Architecture in music. Before you played a note, where is the high point? Where do you think the lesser high points are? It we start on the Swell strings and you see a fortissimo, would you go to full organ, or a loud orchestral sound? Everything had to be reasoned out before you played anything. He wouldn't take anyone without a piano background. Once he wrote some fingering in for me, just once. He said, "This is not permanent. I'm helping you, but what I write won't fit your hands." ... You had to have a thorough background in scales and arpeggios, you had to have some harmonic knowledge. He took a few old ladies because they had jobs and couldn't do any better, but if you really went to study with him you approached it this way. He said a thousand times, "The music is only the blueprint. You have to make the building."

NB: Do you teach the same way he did?

RIP: Not quite; I'm not as choosy over my students. I have a feeling that if people need help, I'm going to help them. With some of my students I feel it's more music therapy than anything else. They get a lot from it; they're older people, you see. Now he would never have done that. His idea in taking a pupil was to make a disciple, and he did make disciples of all of us....

NB: How does your teaching vary from what he taught you?

RIP: It doesn't vary terribly much except I think I am a little more interested in the individual's conception of the thing than he was. In other words, I don't expect any two of my students to play alike, and I certainly don't want them to play like me.[1]

The interview continued:

NB: How do you get an organ student over the hump into the music, to be a musician?

RIP: I go back to what I said before: in the first place they don't like music. I'm sure you've read that comment of E. M. Skinner's, someone was doing the slow movement from the [Widor] Gothique, and there was a beautiful contrast between flutes and strings. Skinner went up and said, "That was just beautiful, that's inspiring." And the organist replied, "Yes, but is it SERIOUS enough?" I don't think you can GET those people over it.

NB: There is a place where you have to stop talking words about music, and what comes after is "soul."

RIP: You amuse me talking about "soul." That would just kill organists! I know just what you mean, but you don't hear that very much anymore. Don't you think it's partly our civilization? Everything is white and black.... Myra Hess played a recital here once, and afterwards at Margaret Tilley's house ... she said one thing I never forgot: "Mr. Purvis, I hear so much brilliant piano playing, but almost no beautiful tone." That's what we're talking about, aren't we?

NB: Can you spot it in a student?

RIP: ... There are those that have it.... There's a kid that came to me, I won't tell you where he graduated, studied with a very fine teacher, he played flawlessly, note-wise, a performance of the Fantasie and Fugue in G minor and asked what I thought. I wasn't going to say, because I knew who his teacher was, so I said, "Well, what do you think?" He said, "Well, that's what I've been taught, but there's GOT to be more to it than that." I said, "God bless you, let's go to work."

Some of them are aware, but—I hate to say this—you can only teach so far. It's like you don't really teach anybody anything. What you really do is open doors, and people walk through them or they don't. There are certain people who are not going to play much differently. It's like Lhevinne used to say, "A man's music is the sum total of what he is." If you're dull, you're going to play dully, and that's all there is to it. If you have no imagination there will be no imagination, no matter what you do. It has to come out from inside. "Educare" means to lead forth, and that's true. You can't pour it into them. You can give certain guidelines, you can help them, but if they have something you can set up comparisons. "Do you think this? How do you feel about this?" But a person who just plays the notes—how can you talk to them that way? You are speaking Sanskrit as far as they're concerned."[2]

Purvis was proud of his McCurdy connection and was quick to spot it in others. In 1978, for example, the choir of Virginia Heights Baptist Church in Roanoke, Virginia, performed Purvis's "The Ballad of Judas Iscariot." After listening to a copy of the recording, Purvis wrote to Richard Cummins, organist and director for the performance:

I was particularly interested in your playing of Judas. As I, you have McCurdy (and thru him Courboin and Farnam) written all over you. (Thank God!)

I've had it with the "cultist organist" who plays from the "knuckles down" and has the imagination of a cremated horse! Music, after all, is an expressive art and language no matter what instrument is the medium![3]

A number of Purvis's students have shared their reminiscences of lessons with their teacher. Their statements describe his approach to teaching and the literature they studied with him. But they also testify to Purvis's unique style, personality, and signature statements, particularly those that he was wont to make during lessons.

Walter Bahn

"While I was music director at St. Mary's Cathedral in San Francisco in the early 1960's, I studied with Purvis for several years. Some people thought he wasn't friendly, but he really had a great sense of humor."[4]

Robert Bennett

"I studied with Purvis in the summer of 1962. I worked on Purvis's '7 Pieces,' and also Liszt's Ad Nos and the Reubke. The way he used the organ was not theatrical but was amazingly beautiful. He didn't play by recipe, but it was always colorful and beautiful, and he used the organ to its best advantage."[5]

Michael T. Carney

I started playing the organ as a junior in high school, around 1985. My dad was an organ enthusiast, and he took me to Capn's Galley [in Redwood City] to hear the organ. The theatre organist there [Tom Hazleton] gave me Purvis's phone number. I had about year's worth of lessons at his home on Balceta. He had me work out of Everett Jay Hilty's *Principles of Organ Playing* [1971].

Purvis told me that he had studied with Dupré for a period, and he mentioned something about pedal technique. Purvis said, 'When I was studying with Marcel Dupré, he used to have students put a belt around their knees to keep them together. That was Dupré's preferred style.' But he didn't support that technique, thought it too heavy-handed. I probably had asked if I should keep my knees together. But the upshot was that whatever is comfortable or works well, that's what you should do.

He told me that when he played his degree recital at Curtis, he started out with one of the trio sonatas and said that was a mistake, because all the voices are exposed, a risky proposition.

Purvis was a kindly man. As a teacher, he was efficient, stuck to the schedule, and didn't watch the clock. He always had a few interesting stories, but didn't go off track.

When I started college at Gonzaga in Spokane, I wasn't sure my organ technique was up to getting into that program. Purvis wrote me a nice letter of encouragement. I ended up getting a bachelor's degree in music at SMU, where I studied with Bob Anderson.[6]

Steve Cohen

In addition to being a chorister, Steve Cohen studied the organ with Purvis. At one of his lessons, Steve hadn't adequately prepared. As he started to play a piece for Purvis on the organ in the chancel, Purvis began to walk toward the nave to listen from farther away. Suddenly, he turned on his heel and headed back to the console, where he turned off the organ and declared that the lesson was over. Steve reported that this was the last time he ever showed up unprepared for a lesson. Later, in 1954 or 1955, Cohen prepared to play his first service in the Chapel of Grace. He had practiced diligently and set pistons for the service. But when he hit a piston he'd set for a soft, subtle sound, he was shocked by the full-organ combination it activated. After the service, Purvis asked him how it had gone. When he admitted that one of the combinations was far from what he thought he had set, marring the service and embarrassing him, Purvis responded, "So what have you learned from this? You must always check your pistons before you play!" Obviously, Purvis had sabotaged Cohen's settings to teach him a lesson that he didn't anticipate. Steve says he has never again failed to check his piston settings before he played publicly for anything.[7]

Don Corbett

I was a piano major at the Royal Conservatory in Toronto. One of my theory teachers there was also an organist and encouraged me to go to an organ concert. After that I couldn't wait to start studying the organ. My last organ teacher in Canada suggested that I look up Purvis when I went to the Bay Area. I did, and when Purvis asked if I had a master's or doctorate, I said no. He then said, "You do have a bachelor's, don't you?" I said, "Yes, a degree from the conservatory." He then said, "Good, then we'll get on together." He didn't like people with all sorts of academic ideas.

Although I was working for an airline and didn't have much time, I studied with Purvis from 1966 to 1969. I had my lessons on the Skinner organ at the cathedral. I worked on standard literature with him, Bach, but no Franck. I also studied his Easter partita with him. With Purvis you could do your own interpretation of the music, not be told it had to be a certain way.

When I hit a wrong note, and he'd poke me in the back and say, "Quit composing, Don." Another line of his: "Don't just play notes, play from the heart."

For a while I tried lessons with Ludwig Altman. He was strictly a Bach interpreter, and it had to be his way or no way. I only lasted four months with him.

I later moved to Southern California, where I received a Master's Degree in 1969 from Long Beach State.[8]

Christian Elliott

I learned as much about *music* from Richard Purvis as I learned about the *organ*. The music was most important, not the organ. Richard was first and foremost a superb musician. In his teaching, it was clear that he was interested in beautiful music: careful phrasing, thoughtful expression, colorful yet tasteful registrations.[9]

I studied the Bach D Major Prelude and Fugue, several Schumann works, and a lot of Purvis's own compositions with him. One of the recitals I did at Menlo Presbyterian was an all Purvis one, and Dick very kindly gave me a copy of his Partita on Christ is Risen, which I learned and studied with him, as well as other pieces of his. Lessons were at his home in San Francisco.[10]

Jim Hansen

In 1961 we stopped in San Francisco for a couple of days. I had to see Grace Cathedral, so I went in and looked at the Aeolian-Skinner, looked in the chapel, walked around, and saw the artifacts. The sexton was there, and he noticed I was interested in the organ. He asked if I'd like to meet Mr. Purvis. He said, "Go upstairs, he's in his office, go and meet him." I was about 15–16. Purvis asked, "Would you like to play the chapel organ?" and he gave me a note of permission written on Union Pacific Railroad stationery ...

I got to know him later when we had the music store [Rodgers dealership, Southland Music Center] in Lemon Grove. Purvis was teaching up in San Francisco, and then Phil Wickstrom, the L.A. dealer, asked if he could come down and teach in L.A., and we asked him to teach in San Diego. He taught 10 hours a day in San Diego! Between 1973–79 or '80, he would come down Thursday and Friday. He would stay at my home, in the Kensington area of San Diego. He liked to go to the Starlight Room at El Cortez Hotel in San Diego; his favorite thing was half a charcoal-grilled chicken.

I studied with him 6–7 years myself. I studied Anglican music, a Chadwick piece (variations). It was classical only: Franck, Bach, Purvis's own music, Vierne, Mendelssohn, Reubke, Liszt Ad Nos.

When we went out to dinner we had fun. In a lesson he wasn't stern but was all business. If he knew something about the composer or had a story to tell, he would impart that to you, but lessons were an hour long and we got a lot accomplished. He knew what he was doing.[11]

Tom Hazleton

Jackson Borges, who studied with Tom Hazleton, remembers hearing Tom say that Purvis, in a moment of exasperation during a lesson, asked Tom, "Who ever taught you how to play the organ?" Tom replied, "You did!"[12]

Vaughn Jones

His knowledge of music of all types was so impressively enormous. He once compared a section of some organ piece I was learning to a similar section in one of the Hindemith string quartets. "You do know the Hindemith string quartets, don't you?" Well of course I didn't but I bought a recording of them that week and listened to it before my next lesson. I have never known anyone else in my life who was as knowledgeable as he was about so many different aspects of music. He could also expertly discuss and critique the scores of *South Pacific* or other Broadway shows of the 1920s through the 1950s.[13]

Lyn Larsen

While Lyn Larsen was not strictly speaking a student of Purvis's, he credits Purvis with numerous important influences on his playing.[14]

When Larsen was on staff at the Avenue Theatre, accompanying silent films, Purvis came to hear him often.

He told me what he liked about the playing (and what he didn't, in a nice way). He said, "You were floundering there. Listen to a section from Holst's Planets or Vaughan Williams to get a sound or shape." After a couple of films, I told Richard I couldn't get a handle on it. He said, "How about if I come out on Tuesday or Wednesday, get some dinner, let me see the film," and he had really good suggestions. He mentioned something out of *The Planets*, not something famous, but a small passage with celesta, sustained notes, etc.—absolutely a great idea for what that spot was. Every now and then during the week, he'd come over, give some suggestions, not organ lessons, but sharing music ideas. He was a huge help."[15]

Stephen Loher

He was a superb teacher—I never left a lesson in five years when I was not on cloud nine. I don't know if you could say he had a "style" of teaching. He could articulate the magic of phrasing: i.e., in a dominant-tonic progression he would say that the tonic should be softer because the listener is expecting that resolution so we should not hit them over the head with it. He would make inspired comments about this or that which would seem to open doors to new vistas—or he would tell a story about a former performance or an experience he had or someone else had that just set the tone of what we were working on.

He usually taught more advanced students but he certainly loved the challenge of taking a beginner and molding him into something.

He used no method books! He did not require memorization because he never played from memory himself.

Articulation was important but never in a formula—it would depend on the piece, the architecture of the piece, the rhythm, tempo, etc. He was big on bringing out a counter-melody, or highlighting a theme in an inversion, etc.

Registration demonstrated his mastery of orchestration—enough said!

He was both friendly and a taskmaster! You would not dare go into a lesson unprepared, but the session was always uplifting. He never browbeat but encouraged. It was always an hour of inspiration.[16]

Douglas Metzler

He hit me over the head with a hymnal during lessons. As a teacher, he would often get on the bench and demonstrate.

He said, "Don't play from the knuckles down" (use your heart). "Think about it. It's in there. God gave it to you, use it!"[17]

Jonas Nordwall

I first knew him in the early 70's but never formally studied with him until a few years before his death. A person could get more valuable, solid musical information from Dick over cocktails and one dinner than many teachers could provide in a year. My interests were his concepts about performing Franck that he learned with Tournemire. Dick's words were: "Here's what is written, but this is how they played." There were more registration changes than published as each performance was always a new experience and a work in progress.

A famous phrase of his was, "Have you ever thought about this?" He could win you over to his way with this.[18]

Richard would sometimes say, "I was there when this happened." An example of this: Wallace Sabin had arranged for four or five of his students, including Purvis, to watch Karg-Elert practice at the Civic Auditorium in San Francisco during his 1929 U.S. tour. When I looked at the markings on Richard's original copy of Karg-Elert's "The Mirrored Moon," there were 10 to 12 additional registration changes written on the score, nothing to do with the printed suggestions. I asked, "What's that?" Richard said, "I wrote those down because I was there when Karg-Elert was practicing and that's what he did." Karg-Elert was using all of the vast tonal resources of the Austin to achieve his desires. There was one combination action system and Karg-Elert's daughter was her father's console assistant, making the additional changes when all of the pistons had been used.

During the early 1990's, Donna Parker and I had business trips for Rodgers Instruments which took us to San Francisco about once a month. Ted Worth had told us to get as much information from Richard as possible that reflected the playing styles of the earlier American 20th century. We knew Richard's health was not what it once was and took every opportunity to gather information. Donna and I would meet Richard and John for lunch at one of their favorite restaurants, Original Joe's in Westlake, followed by sessions in his home studio. One time we were curious about his deft skills with hand registrations which he had developed during the earlier years at Grace and on other instruments. Richard played two pages of the Franck Chorale No. 3 with multiple hand changes and the crescendo pedal. It was absolutely seamless, masterful. We asked, "Could you do that again?" Purvis laughed and did the whole thing again. As Ted had said, "You get him to show you how he did this. They don't play that way anymore. Where would you go to learn that?"[19]

Donna Parker

Donna Parker studied with Purvis longer than any other of his students. She was particularly close to him, and when he died she rescued many of his papers and books moments before they were discarded.

JW: When did you begin studying with Purvis?

DP: In 1968, I was 12 almost 13. He came down once a month to the Rodgers studio in Burbank. My teacher Bob St. John and a good friend of Dick's said, "You need to have a good classical background." Richard was teaching at Bill Thomson's home in Woodland Hills. I went in and played the Bach Prelude in F Major. I'm sure it was hideous, and all he said, "Well, we have some work to do." The guys would have "gotten it," but I was the baby and I was the girl, and he was kinder to me, didn't hit me over the head with books. I was the baby, and the girl, so he was taking care of me. I didn't want him to take care of me like that, but he did.

JW: What about your college studies?

DP: I was studying at Cal Poly Pomona, and I was granted the right to study with Dick off campus. I did all my work with him. They didn't have an organ program, so it was arranged that Dick could grade me.

In 1975 I moved to Arizona to go to ASU. There's a letter he wrote [see below], in which he warned that the university setting is not aimed at the individual, it's on a pretty broad scale, and he talked about mediocrity. I named certain universities and he shook his head and said, "That's not for you. I know who you are, and that's not the path I would suggest."

Robert Clark was teaching there at ASU. I realized it wasn't what I wanted to do, and I went into theatre playing. He was always disappointed, and said, "You would have made a fabulous classical organist. Why don't you want to be a classical organist?" I said, "Because you just read what's there on the page." But he said, "No, there's more to it than that…" He wished I'd gone on in the classical field.

JW: Did you continue to study with Purvis? Did you study classical or theatre music?

DP: While I was at Rodgers in Oregon, between 1990 and 1993 I went to Bay Area once a month to study, to go over concert pieces. I did mostly classical. He didn't want to do big long works. We did a lot of Orgelbüchlein, and he loved Flor Peeters. He and Peeters were good friends. You knew it was a personal thing when he was teaching Flor Peeters. As a kid I wanted to play the flashy stuff, but he was good about teaching hymn playing and the chorale-based works. I wasn't doing church work, but when I went back in, it all kicked in. As I looked back, it was the things he taught me as a kid. It's back in there somewhere. He covered how to play for church, not just being a concert organist, and play the "party pieces." It's really come in handy when I've done church work.

JW: Where did you have your lessons? What were the lessons like?

DP: At the Cathedral when I was up in San Francisco, but often on electronic organs at the Rodgers studios. At lessons, you had to be prepared. I heard him absolutely yell at other students before me who weren't prepared. If you asked him to register the organ for you, he would say, "Teacher, teacher, teacher, someday the teacher will not be there." You had to learn to be independent. But he did love to set up the organ the way he wanted it, and then you would play it that way.

JW: What other pieces did you study?

DP: Once I prepared the Fanfare from A Trio of Contrasts. I did it exactly like he'd recorded it, and he said, "You played it much too fast." I answered, "But I played it the way you recorded it." He stood there and said, "We're not going to play it that fast." We backed up and went from there. The same with Widor Toccata: He said, "Your left hand isn't strong enough." I worked on it, came back, and he was favorably impressed.

The thing I loved was that Dick never ever treated you as if you were an underling to him. You were a musician on the same path, the same journey. He may be ten miles down the road from you, but he was glad to share what he knew. As a student he would allow me to talk. We talked about things, I argued and we'd discuss, and we'd correct it. He didn't say, "Shut up, we're going to do it this way and that's that." His other students said the same thing about him.

Ted [Alan Worth] told a story about that the first time he went to Grace with his grandmother to try out for lessons. After Ted played the music he had prepared, Dick said, "What do you want to do?" Ted answered, "I want to play the pipes." To which Dick answered, "Let's see if we can get him a career as a plumber!" Ted explained that "I was so full of myself, and that's probably why he said what he did." But then Dick said, "Let's get busy." In lessons he'd smack Ted over the head with a hardcover book and say, "We're not going to do it that way!" You can't use the "book method" today. Maybe part of it was from being in the military—a different era.

But he always wrote notes to his students. He was always kind. He might come across with a gruff exterior, but he had a heart as big as all outdoors.[20]

Purvis wrote the following letter to Parker, who was studying in Arizona at the time.

May Fifth 1975

My dear Donna,

Thank you for your letter. I was pleased to hear of your decision and certainly wish all success for you in your new locale.

Don't expect <u>too</u> much from Arizona State—it has a good department, but like <u>All</u> schools there are limitations as to what can be done for an individual. Remember the curriculum of most schools is <u>NOT</u> designed for the person of talent, individuality and imagination! This is the downfall of our current education—a cheap glorification of mediocrity. Bear in mind, the so-called "norm" is always mundane and banal—and that is what educators exploit presently.

Enclosed are a couple of recital programs. The Longwood recital is (without doubt) the best concert I've ever played. I got a standing ovation at the end of the César Franck B minor Chorale!

I'll save an hour for you in September. I'm in Burbank Sun, Mon, Tue....

My best to your Dad and Mother and the very best of everything to you. Sincerely,

Richard Purvis[21]

Tom Rhoads

When I studied with Richard, from about 1956 to 1960, I worked on standard repertoire: Franck Chorales, Bach preludes and fugues, chorale preludes, some Hindemith, Karg-Elert, and Purvis's music. I was quite excited about Purvis's music at the time, and every time something new came out, I'd study it with him. I remember doing the "Four Prayers in Tone" and the "7 Chorales."

He was such a fine teacher, although sometimes he wouldn't let students learn by doing—he wanted to dictate it all. He paid a lot of attention to detail in phrasing and articulation.

He was brusque, but very kindly and helpful. I could call him anytime and get information.

My lessons with him were on Saturdays, every week or two. I was living in Palo Alto at the time and drove up to San Francisco in my '31 Model A, a gutsy little car. I think he charged $35 for a lesson, a lot of money then. I generally got scheduled last on lesson days, and we always ate out after the lesson—Mayes Oyster House, at Fisherman's Wharf, and other places.

I did several duo recitals with him, at Grace Cathedral and also at St. Mark's in Palo Alto. I recall doing the "Dialogue Monastique" with him at St. Mark's.

We always came an hour before our lessons to listen to what was going on. One day I was sitting out [in the nave] with Doris Shively. Purvis was busy dictating phrasing and stop changes. This one day he had a little nun from Dominican Convent in San Rafael. She was playing along quite nicely, and he became more and more intense: "Now put that on, now Solo to Pedal 4', and this and that one," and the next thing I heard was, "My God, Mr. Purvis, I only have two hands!"[22]

Donald Sears

Some of his leading students were Rodney Hansen, Lewis Bruun, Keith Chapman, Lyn Larsen, Ted Alan Worth, Tom Hazleton and others I never met, such as David Worth. I was in a different category from these famous organists but I did work with Richard from 1966 to 1994.

I began study with Purvis in April 1966 and took my lessons in the cathedral until 1971 when he opened his study downstairs in his home. He was very difficult and occasionally very rude to me during lessons. This was shared by all or almost all of his students. He was an excellent teacher if you could take the abuse he dished out. In my own case I heard such one-liners as "Sloppy Joe playing," "That's your excuse, now do you want to hear mine?", "That had about as much sparkle as a cremated horse," "You can't count to three!", and on and on. However, when the happy moment came when he was truly satisfied with my playing, he never failed to tell me.

He insisted that all Bach ornamentation be very controlled, every trill had to be counted, some getting seven, some eight, some twelve and some sixteen. He didn't allow just a rapid trill, ever. Also he was very conscious of the linear movement of the music, the forward thrust of Bach's counterpoint, for example. He was just as demanding about the organ music of Franck, as he had studied Franck with Charles Courboin in New York who had in his turn studied with a pupil of Franck. He always said you had to know the sounds of the organ at St. Clotilde in Paris to registrate Franck's music.[23]

Ed Stout

In his more gifted students he instilled the following: "Listen with your ears, not your eyes. The name on the drawknob doesn't mean anything! Listen with your ears."

Here's a funny story about Tom Hazleton, who started lessons with Purvis when he was 12 years old. Tom came up from Pacific Grove on Saturdays for lessons and somehow Dick said something that Tom took great offense to. Tom had a lot of tenacity—he was a gutsy fellow—and Tom quit! He told him to go to hell. As a teenager, yes. He was 14, I think. So he went over and studied with Harold Mueller at Trinity, a sweet man and a fine musician. That probably was a good thing—it would give him a slightly different perspective and take on things. Then Purvis asked Tom to please come back, and he did.[24]

Barbara Tonsberg

I met him around 1956–57; I was living in Angwin at the time. I would go to his recitals at Grace. In the summer of 1957 I went to San Francisco State to take classes and study with him for a summer. It was fun, and no pressure on him. He could teach when he wanted any day. He was very relaxed, but very thorough. He was always right on top of things. He could be funny, but not always. If I did something stupid, he'd make a joke about it. I'm short, so the Cathedral organ was a problem. He'd tease me about it. "You have to climb to the top!" He'd let me stay and practice on the organ as long as I wanted. I had another summer with him, and then I would go down every other week for a couple of years. I quit for a while, but later took lessons at his home. My last lesson with him was in winter 1993 or so.

I studied the Bach-Vivaldi A minor, Vierne, French things. He had his own way of registrations, short cuts for getting around difficult spots. He said, "I have my own way of doing things," and he wrote in notes here and there.

Richard came to PUC [Pacific Union College] as a visitor, but didn't play any recitals on the Rieger.[25]

June Townsend

The following is excerpted from June Townsend's 1967 thesis:

> Since this writer has studied with Mr. Purvis, both at the beginning and
> the height of his career, the following insights have been gained.
>
> To the outsider, his personality seems a little on the Beethovenesque
> side. He has no patience with laziness and incompetence, and demands
> the same perfection from his students that he does from himself. He wants
> them to be able to "THINK!" He holds his Boy Choir until he can hear a
> pin drop.
>
> On the other hand, to his pupils he is the soul of kindness. His philosophy
> seems to be that exemplified in the *Magnificent Obsession* of Lloyd Douglas—
> of unselfish giving with no thought of return. He has loaned out his music to
> his students and given free lessons to those he felt were deserving.
>
> He inspires his pupils (not without a little awe), and his own effortless
> playing sets a beautiful example of what he wants done. He wants the music
> to "say something" to the hearts of the listeners. His playing is registrated
> beautifully and he thinks of tone color orchestrally.
>
> His students go forth to make names for themselves, in the church
> and concert world, some of them being: Ted Alan Worth, Tom Hazleton,
> Lewis Bruun, Garnell Copland, Robert M. Quade, Walter Bahn, and David
> Worth.[26]

In her "Memories of Richard Irven Purvis," written in 1995, Townsend's
memories were still bright:

> He [Harry Ingling] was only around 19 or 20 but Harry and I wanted to
> study with him. At my first lesson at his home in San Leandro (Oakland) I
> played Mendelssohn's "Consolation." He informed me that when a phrase
> repeats, "Don't say the same thing the same way twice." Later he said that I
> sounded like a little mouse crawling over the keys. I had learned to play on
> a little Melodeon organ at home and preferred the organ touch. He wanted
> to know how I acted when I got mad and I said I went into a gloomy silence.
> He would have wanted me to show more passion in my playing, but his
> personality was intimidating and demanding and since Harry and I were
> both nervous, he said "Next Lamb to the Slaughter," which wasn't very
> encouraging. One time I came early for a lesson and he was upstairs getting
> dressed. I started practicing and when he came down he said, "Why don't

you play like you did while I was putting on socks and tying a shoe?" He didn't miss a beat. His later students can probably agree.

He introduced me to BACH with the Two-Part Invention in F which does decidedly different things in each hand. I said this is like trying to pat your head and rub your stomach at the same time. He said, Yes but patting your head and rubbing your stomach is very simple compared to BA-CHH (German accent). He also gave me some simple Chopin studies. One was marked "Sotto Voce." In explaining "Sotto," he said it was like "Saute." My mother couldn't understand what slow cooking had to do with music. When I called him on it he thought it had to do with cutting up into little pieces—hence "small or low tone." Maybe his mother was cooking chopped up onions. So much for Julia Child....

He inspired in his pupils a sort of unasked-for Hero Worship.[27]

Jean White

I studied with Richard on and off at his home in later years. I started at the Cathedral when they were putting in the Ruffatti, so lessons were in the Grace Chapel at first, and later on the Ruffatti.

I studied Franck and Purvis's music. He didn't teach me much about registration because I played a very small organ that was not a pipe organ. We had a model 5 Baldwin organ, and Richard simply set the stops for me, so I didn't learn a lot that way from him, except from listening. Of course listening was the thrill because he was so musical.

I've heard other organists who played technically better than he did in his later years, but his musicianship was so wonderful. That was what I was thrilled with. People would say to me, "How could you study with him, he was such a mean man, he lit into you." But with me he was as sweet as could be and we got along famously, partly because I was a musician. Some of his students were players, but I was a musician, so we got along very well and I just adored the man and I still miss him.

He was so kind to me and appreciated the fact that I continued to study even with all the things that were happening with my family. I had four children to raise, my husband had died, I had cancer and we went through some difficult years, and he appreciated that.

In later years I'd say, "How are you?" and he'd say, "Better you shouldn't ask!"[28]

Ted Alan Worth

One of Purvis's more flamboyant students was Ted Alan Worth, who had moved to the San Francisco area from Chicago when he was 14. Ted would have had many stories to tell about Purvis today, but he died in 1998. Fortunately, some of his reminiscences of Purvis can be found in *Virgil Fox (The Dish)*, by Richard Torrence and Marshall Yaeger. Though the following account is mostly about Ted, it paints a colorful picture of Purvis as well.

I first fell in love with the organ when I was 14. I had moved to San Francisco from Chicago to live for a year with my maternal grandmother—whom I adored, while my parents wound up affairs in the Midwest before moving themselves. I later joined my parents, sister, and brother to live in Menlo Park, which is in the San Francisco Peninsula, just south of the city.

One muggy Sunday afternoon in San Francisco I was particularly bored, and "Nana" suggested I take the California Street cable car up to the great stone Episcopal cathedral (then only half completed) that dominated the top of Nob Hill.

The minute I stepped through the side entrance doors to take in the size and height of the building—with but a moment to gaze at the monumental "conic" [*sic*, actually Conique] blue stained glass windows at the crossing— a great cascade of sound stopped me cold.

There was an organ recital in progress!

I was amazed! After the initial shock, I walked over to one of the great cathedral pillars to catch my breath and generally take it all in.

I had always loved classical music, and had sometimes dreamed of a career as a concert pianist. I was fortunate to have studied with a couple of fine church organists in Chicago who taught piano to some of the interested choirboys. I didn't like the drudgery of practice, however, and didn't progress rapidly because of it. The experience in Grace Cathedral that Sunday afternoon changed everything.

How auspicious that an impressionable youth should have been in that glorious place at just that moment!

The concert was a recital of the music of Brahms, Schumann, Mendelssohn and Liszt.... This concert was a revelation that would have lasting effects on my entire life.

That afternoon's performer was the Resident Organist and Master of Choristers, Richard Purvis. He was internationally known, and he was playing one of the most extraordinary and famous Aeolian-Skinner pipe

organs in America. He was also performing some of the greatest masterpieces of Romantic organ literature; but I didn't understand, yet, what he
was doing. I was simply entranced.

The concert ended with the great "Fantasia and Fugue on 'Ad nos, ad
salutarem undam,'" by Franz Liszt.

After the final chorale played on the full organ concluded, and the final
chord reverberated down the nave of the cathedral, a new convert had been
made for the organ. I knew that if this experience was as life transforming
as it felt, this determined boy had set out to become an organist!

I can't remember whether it was after that first concert or the following Sunday after the services that I introduced myself to Richard Purvis
and explained my determination to be an organist. Mr. Purvis was almost
abrupt with me, saying that I would have to audition for him first on the
piano before we even discussed moving on to the organ.

Following my audition, Mr. Purvis told me that I would have to study
the piano (especially technique), the Bach "Inventions," and so forth with
him for several months. Only then could I proceed to study the organ.

Mr. Purvis was right, of course; for an organ student has to prepare
properly on one keyboard before progressing to multiple keyboards—to
say nothing of adding both feet! Mr. Purvis also suggested that I join the
Grace Cathedral choir.

I jumped at the chance.

In the wondrous months that followed, a new world opened to me. I
lived for every rehearsal and service, especially Thursday nights and Sundays when we were in the Great Choir (the area of the church between the
crossing and the altar) and heard the sounds of that wonderful organ in the
hands of Richard Purvis.

Mr. Purvis was a magnetic and powerful person. He ran the choir—
indeed the whole cathedral—in an autocratic, strict fashion. He brooked
interference with no one, and led the choir like an army drill sergeant. You
had to address him as "Sir." He, in turn, referred even to an 8- or 9-year old
probation chorister as "Mr. Kelly," or just "Mister."

He could be harsh, and sometimes cruel ("You are all idiots! Who ever
told you that you could sing?"); but the boys in the choir adored him
because he got the right results; and we were all proud of those results.

His extreme musicality and vitality shone through his sternness, however. When he got the sound effect he wanted, a look of love and approval
would come over his face, completely erasing the terrible scowls and

frequent rages into which he flew when someone sang the wrong note or committed some other grievous sin.

When he began to teach me the organ, although I practiced diligently, I would sometimes make a foolish error at my lesson and he would say, "Mr. Worth, perhaps your mother should let you be a plumber; then you could still play with pipes! You surely can't play the organ!"

They were harsh words, but Mr. Purvis had an uncanny sense of what would make people mad enough to work hard for him and give him what he wanted. He knew the people who needed strong words (which I guess included me), and those who needed gentler prodding. It always worked....

Undaunted by his rejections, I worked ever harder at the organ, devouring every book or periodical I could read on the organ or organists; and anything related to organ or to the great cathedrals, churches, and concert halls that housed those wondrous musical machines. As I recall, I was almost rabidly interested and in love with the organ—and I idolized my teacher.

I was fortunate to be able not just to study with him formally, but to watch Mr. Purvis at choir rehearsals, at cathedral services (where I was sometimes asked to turn pages, which was a signal honor), and generally whenever the organ motor was running.

We students learned much by osmosis—like a sponge—watching a master perform before our eyes: how he made this sound or that; how he achieved astonishing crescendos and de-crescendos; how he made playing a mechanical instrument seem as pliable as conducting a symphony orchestra, to say nothing of familiarizing us with the entire gamut of masterpieces written for the King of Instruments.[29]

Ted Alan Worth came under the spell of Virgil Fox at a recital at Calvary Church in San Francisco, further cementing his resolve to become not just an organist, but a concert organist, and one "who could play the organ like Virgil Fox."

I began to practice much more diligently, and tried to do everything Mr. Purvis instructed me to do at my lessons. He was kind enough to give me free lessons, but he still insisted on sticking to the basics on the piano, and then practicing simply on the organ using chorales, pedal exercises, and simple repertoire. The experience was valuable. Without this background, my dreams would never have been possible.[30]

About a year after I first heard Virgil Fox in that concert at Calvary Church, Mr. Purvis announced that the American Guild of Organists would have its Biennial National Convention in San Francisco that coming June [1952], and the cathedral would be the scene of quite a few activities.

What a thrill it would be for me to see and hear all these famous people. I wondered whether Virgil Fox would play at Grace Cathedral. "Indeed not!" Purvis said. "Virgil will play where he belongs, at the Civic Auditorium!"

I thought that was strange for I wanted to hear the greatest organist on what was for me the greatest organ.[31]

After Worth met Virgil Fox at a recital during the Convention and decided to audition for the virtuoso, he began to work on Dupré's Prelude and Fugue in G minor, but without asking Purvis for permission.

Both Virgil Fox and Richard Purvis always stressed slow practice, with marked fingering and pedaling ...

With diligence and determination, plus hours of rehearsal, I could finally play the Dupré work. I remember that after one lesson that didn't go well, I asked to play the work for Mr. Purvis. I thought I played it well; but he flew into a rage, and asked me who gave permission to learn that piece, and why I had been so foolish as to memorize it *all wrong!*

After that daunting experience, I didn't share any more of my extra-curricular pieces; but I did continue to memorize any pieces that I loved.

I'm sure Mr. Purvis knew what I was up to! He always acknowledged that Virgil Fox was a brilliant technician, but he didn't approve of his showmanship, or the way he "carried on—it is not dignified—and those speeches to the audience—cheap!"

Those elements, however, were the very things that drew me (and thousands of others) to Virgil; and I was not about to be deterred. Nor did I care for criticism of Virgil Fox even if it came from Richard Purvis, to whom I owed so much.[32]

The "Master Teacher" Appointment

According to the Biographical Data, Purvis was selected in 1964 by Claremont College, California, as the institution's "Master Teacher" for an intensive summer organ class and workshop.[33]

Purvis and Lesson Fees

Richard seemed sensitive about overcharging his students and clients, sometimes reducing his rates (to the chagrin of his managers who had already negotiated higher fees for concerts). He was particularly reluctant to raise his lesson fees and went out of his way to justify an increase when it was absolutely necessary. In a 1974 memo to his pupils he wrote the following:

> Dear Student:
>
> For the past six years my lesson fee has been twenty-five dollars. During that period plane fares have risen six times, bus fares five times, and motels have almost doubled their rates, to say nothing of restaurant prices. This you all know too well, but after conferences with both my business consultant and my accountant, I find I must raise my rate. Their advice was a thirty dollar minimum fee per lesson but I honestly feel I can operate on less than that. At least, I want to attempt it, so I am effecting a compromise.
>
> As of September 1, 1974, my fee per lesson will be twenty-eight dollars and I will give this honorarium at least a six months' trial before acquiescing to the stipulations of my accountant and business consultant.
>
> I regret economic pressures necessitate this increase, but I must resort to this measure or cease teaching away from my San Francisco studio.
>
> Richard Purvis[34]

Purvis's Workshop Textbook

In 1973 the Rodgers Organ Company published a booklet for use at the company-sponsored organ workshops that Purvis gave throughout the country. In a draft for the preface to this booklet, Purvis wrote:

> Dear Student,
>
> Welcome! Welcome to an "Adventure in learning"; an opportunity to share our combined knowledge and experience. Each of us brings his own individual viewpoint and background, and together we will explore the highways and (even more important) byways of the organ's literature, technic and ethos.
>
> This will be a happy time for us all, a time of mutual sharing and growth. So welcome and happy Learning!
>
> Here's to Music! (I think it's here to stay.)
>
> Richard Purvis

Following were a series of lessons, each with a detailed outline.

Lesson 1: The Organ (A Historical and Esthetic Approach)

A discussion of the organ through the ages

Lesson 2: Rhythm

Lesson 3: Phrasing and "Touch"

Lesson 4: Registration

Lesson 5: Ornamentation

Lesson 6: Performance Versus Practice

1. Projection of musical ideas

2. Communication with audience

3. Conviction in performance

4. Program building

5. "Ear Fatigue" on the part of the listener

6. Style and period in performance

7. Registration as an asset or deficit in performance

8. Daily piano drill

9. To memorize or not....

10. The value of taping both practice and performance[35]

Notes

1. This advice most likely came from Alexander McCurdy. My organ teacher at Stanford, Herbert Nanney, also studied with McCurdy at Curtis, and he often repeated the same line to us.

2. Nelson Barden interview with Richard Purvis, San Francisco, October 1981.

3. Letter from Richard Purvis to Richard Cummins, October 14, 1978.

4. Telephone conversation with Walter Bahn, Houston, Texas, November 30, 2010.

5. Telephone conversation with Robert Bennett, Houston, Texas, November 29, 2010.

6. Telephone conversation with Michael T. Carney, San Mateo, California, November 5, 2010.

7. Telephone conversation with Steve Cohen, June 7, 2011.

8. Telephone conversation with Donald Corbett, September 2010.

9. Christian Elliott, e-mail, October 24, 2010.

10. Christian Elliott, e-mail, September 29, 2010.

11. Telephone conversation with Jim Hansen, November 3, 2010.

12. Jackson Borges, telephone conversation, November 5, 2012.

13. Vaughn Jones, e-mail, March 23, 2012.

14. See further comments by Lyn Larsen in Chapter 12 and Chapter 16.

15. Telephone conversation with Lyn Larsen, December 1, 2010.

16. Stephen Loher, e-mail, June 6, 2009.

17. Douglas Metzler, interview, Bothell, Washington, June 24, 2010.

18. Jonas Nordwall, e-mail, 2009.

19. Jonas Nordwall, e-mail, September 11, 2012.

20. Donna Parker, interview, Aloha, Oregon, September 27, 2010.

21. Letter courtesy Donna Parker.

22. Telephone conversation with Tom Rhoads, Kailua, Hawaii, September 14, 2010.

23. Donald Sears, e-mail, May 30, 2009.

24. Stout interview.

25. Telephone interview with Barbara Tonsberg, Angwin, California, November 3, 2010.

26. Townsend thesis, 23.

27. Townsend Memories, 1995.

28. Telephone conversation with Jean White, Walnut Creek, California, September 20, 2010.

29. *Virgil Fox (The Dish)*, by Richard Torrence and Marshall Yaeger, and based on a memoir by Ted Alan Worth (New York: Circles International, 2001), 5–8. Reprinted by permission.

30. *Virgil Fox (The Dish)*, 16.

31. *Virgil Fox (The Dish)*, 18.

32. *Virgil Fox (The Dish)*, 27.

33. Biographical Data, 8.

34. Memo courtesy Donna Parker.

35. Typescript, no date.

chapter 15

purvis and religion

Although he served as organist in a number of Protestant denominations during his lifetime, Purvis never definitively identified himself as a member of any of them. Following his studies in England, his church work at St. James's in Philadelphia, and his 25 years at Grace Cathedral, he may have felt most at home with the Anglican tradition of liturgy, music, and ecclesiology. After a lifetime in service of the church, one might expect to find Purvis saying or writing something regarding his personal feelings about religion. With one important exception, quoted later, little has surfaced.

Stephen Loher wrote:

> I don't know what religion he was raised in. I remember him talking about his grandmother who I think dabbled in Christian Science—I say dabbled because from what I used to hear it didn't seem as though she was completely into it. He did cite a healing that she had with her leg. Richard found his way into Unity Church. He read the writings of Ernest Holmes and Edgar Cayce—these were in the New Thought movement which was prominent in the 19th century. Cayce was into reincarnation.
>
> He was also an "Anglican" in culture—I think he loved the Anglican liturgy (more matins/evensong than Eucharist I think) and he greatly admired Bishop Pike as a thinker.
>
> I am not sure how his religious sense impacted his compositions. Being a church musician many were liturgical pieces—but there were several secular works and then there is his passion for the theater organ (Sierra Suite!). He never really spoke of how religion impacted his compositions, or playing, for that matter.[1]

In the course of Nelson Barden's 1981 interview, Purvis made the following comments:

NB: You were born in Oakland?

RIP: No, San Francisco!

NB: A thousand pardons.

RIP: Good heavens, you may GO right now! I'm a third generation San Franciscan and a fourth generation Californian, and an Episcopalian. That lets me be quite a snob![2]

In his application to Curtis, dated November 15, 1935, Purvis listed his religion as "Presbyterian." Though he may have considered himself a Presbyterian at that time, this assertion should probably be taken loosely rather than literally. After all, he had most recently been organist at Calvary Presbyterian in San Francisco, and believing that he should list something on the application, he wrote in what came first to his mind.

Many people caught in monumental conflicts like war, as Purvis was, have mentioned religion as a source of strength. Even though Purvis suffered as a German stalag prisoner during World War II, none of his scant correspondence from the period mentions religion.

June Townsend wrote in her memoirs in 1995: "He loaned me a copy of the book 'The Magnificent Obsession,' which emphasizes doing things quietly for others without thought of reward—Cast your bread on the waters and it comes back Cake! Although he played for other churches, his philosophy was along the lines of Unity and Christian Science. He carried out his Magnificent Obsession by lending me his music."[3]

While Lyn Larsen was director of music at a Religious Science church in Phoenix, Arizona, in the early 1980s, he invited Purvis to play a recital for his congregation. But he admonished Purvis first: "Remember, this is for a Religious Science church, we don't chant, we don't have icons. I know you're not familiar with this, although it's similar to Unity.... Purvis sat there and said, 'Really? Really??' Finally he looked up and said, 'I'm an old Unity boy from way back. For music I like the Anglican, but for philosophy I like the Unity.'" Larsen said, "I'd known him for years, and he'd never told me that."[4]

Notably among Purvis's papers were the following quotations about religion copied out in his own handwriting, probably in his later years. Most of the text appears to come from a book entitled *A Course in Miracles*, published by an organization called the Foundation for Inner Peace. It provides the only indication we have about Purvis's personal thinking on the subject of spirituality.

Because I AM, Son of God, I AM ALL and I have ALL.
I AM Health
I AM Wealth
I AM Prosperity
I AM Inspiration
I AM Love

Only the Love of God will protect me in all circumstances. It will lift me out of every trial, and raise me high above all perceived dangers of this world into a Climate of Perfect Peace and Safety. It will transport me into a state of mind that nothing can threaten, nothing can disturb, and where nothing can intrude upon the Eternal Calm of the Son of God.

I AM sustained by the Love of God.

I do not put my faith in illusions which will fail me. I put all my Faith in the Love of God within me; Eternal, Changeless, and Forever Unfailing. This is the Answer to whatever confronts me now Thru the Love of God within me, I AM resolving all seeming difficulties without effort and in Sure Confidence.

Divine Love, flowing thru me like a Mighty, Rushing, Cleansing, Healing Stream, now washes away every particle of excess weight; regenerates, rejuvenates, and renews every atom of each cell in my body; harmonizes, vitalizes and purifies the action of every organ of my body; nullifies and removes all impurities, toxins, disease and pain; and dissolves anything [and] everything unlike Its Perfect Nature. I AM Love, Life, Beauty, Joy and Eternal Youth. Immortality is My Divine Inheritance.

Spiritual Substance is the Only Reality and It Manifests Abundantly in My Life NOW!

Eternal Life is transforming my body into a Perfect Instrument for the Harmonious Expression of Divine Love, Strength, Beauty, and Wisdom.

Remember not the past nor be anxious for the future. The future is taken care of by your living NOW. Eternity is NOW!

Omnipresence knows nothing of past or future but is Eternally Present; the same yesterday, today, and forever.[5]

Notes

1. Stephen Loher, e-mail, May 30, 2009.
2. Nelson Barden interview with Richard Purvis, San Francisco, October 1981.
3. Townsend Memories, 1995.
4. Lyn Larsen, telephone interview, December 1, 2010.
5. *A Course in Miracles* was first published in 1975 by the Foundation for Inner Peace.

cbapter 16

anecdotes
and reminiscences

"We might have griped about his demanding ways; but we loved him."

—*James W. McLeod*

The following anecdotes and reminiscences were shared by people who knew Purvis well. Several were communicated in writing; others were taken in interviews or gathered from publications. Some of the information below has appeared in previous chapters, but much of it has not.

Frances Beniams

Beniams was Dean of the San Francisco AGO Chapter from 1971 to 1973. The following excerpt comes from a history of the Chapter, written by Beniams and published in the April 1984 issue of *The American Organist*.

> Richard I. Purvis, long-time organist and choirmaster at Grace Cathedral, one of Mr. Sabin's most "fair-haired children," was away at the time of his mentor's death. He had received a scholarship to study at Curtis Institute with Alexander McCurdy. Now Richard would join his own contemporaries here in an attempt to help fill Mr. Sabin's very large footsteps. Under Purvis, a great organ in Grace Cathedral was installed by Aeolian-Skinner, with G. Donald Harrison's illuminating guidance and enthusiastic push to get things done before approaching deadlines.[1] Packed services at cathedral performances, daily teaching in the cathedral school, development of men's and boys' choirs, his own organ recitals here and elsewhere kept him

Richard Purvis, 1990s. Courtesy Donald Braff.

rushed. That helped to keep him too busy to dwell on his wartime experiences as captain of a lost battalion and prisoner of war in Germany. It also kept him from the amount of composition he wanted to do—a role he yearned to fulfill. Today he is teaching—commuting to Southern California to do some of it—doing public performances, enjoying his music studio and home, and composing whenever inspiration strikes him.[2]

Jack Bethards

"Richard was invited to speak at the San Anselmo Organ Festival, and he gave an excellent talk. He said in a humble way: 'I am what might be called a *utility composer*—I try to write music that people can use.'"[3]

Donald Braff

Donald Braff was a close friend of Richard and John's. Richard had played for Braff's wedding in 1964 in the Chapel of Grace. Donald offered the following observations:

John Shields liked Yosemite. He had a VW bus, and they often camped there in the summer in the greater Yosemite area. Richard would join him for some of these campouts. John was a great photographer.

Purvis said that the organ at the Legion of Honor was "a very expensive installation, but it speaks through a blanket." He was careful not to denigrate the organ, but the truth was that it spoke through canvas painted like stone.

Richard cooked; John didn't. Don's wife Marian was a gourmet cook. They ate together regularly at each other's homes.

Don had lunch with Dick and John, often up the coast of Highway 1, sometimes at Olema, every Wednesday like clockwork, after Don retired in 1990.

Richard had lived on the top of Hyde St. for a long time. The apartment had a panoramic view. The apartment was too small for both Richard and John—Richard had a big collection of LPs, a hi-fi system, big speakers, etc.

Richard knew how to drive. He had a driver's license, but when he lived on Hyde Street, there was no parking, and no use for a car, so he gave up his car and license. He was chauffeured by John and others.

Regarding their relationship, they were "very discreet and dignified."[4]

Ken Brown

Approximately a year before Purvis died, Ken Brown conducted the following interview, first published in the Daffer Church Organs Newsletter, *Organist News,* Fall 1995.

O.N. [*Organist News*]: Whose work has influenced you the most?

R.P.: In the world of performers, Lynnwood Farnam, Charles Courboin, Wallace Sabin, Marcel Dupré, and Sir Edward Bairstow. In the realm of composers, César Franck, Ralph Vaughan Williams, Johannes Brahms, Frederick Delius, and Sigfrid Karg-Elert.

O.N.: What have been some of the highlights of your career?

R.P.: Playing my Concerto (for organ and orchestra) at Columbia University under the direction of Searle Wright...[5] the festival of music at the Episcopal Cathedral in Houston ... the festival of my music at Saint Mary's Cathedral, San Francisco ... the Franck recital I performed at Yale University and the recital I played at Grace Cathedral for a National Convention of the American Guild of Organists.

O.N.: What are your favorite compositions by other composers?

R.P.: I have no "favorite" composition—every good composer has something valid to say and it's the performer's duty to convey his ideas to the audience.

O.N.: How would you assess the current shortage of young organists?

R.P.: I think that much of the shortage is due to the restrictive musical approach of most teachers. The organ student is often discouraged from either thinking or using his imagination. Instead, he is bombarded with preconceived ideas as to how a piece should sound—too many "don'ts" and not enough "do's"—this stifles young people.

O.N.: What advice can you give to young organists?

R.P.: 1. LISTEN TO WHAT YOU ARE DOING!
  2. Explore the tonal possibilities of every stop on the organ you are playing.
  3. Always treat every organ and every building as an individual.
  4. Listen to as much chamber and orchestra music as possible.
  5. Play both the piano and the organ with other musicians.

O.N.: Who are today's best organists?

R.P.: I don't like the term "best organists"—but performers I greatly respect and enjoy are Thomas Murray, Michael Murray, Charles Callahan, Simon Preston, and David Higgs.

O.N.: How should one judge the success of an organ installation?

R.P.: There are two criteria: Is it the right organ for the building; and does the specification lend itself to the type of music to be performed, either concert or church use. If it is for church use: Will the organ lead congregational singing; artistically accompany the choir; and convey the ethos of the church's liturgy and be adequate for solo performance.[6]

Steve Cohen

Steve Cohen was a chorister at Grace Cathedral from 1947 to 1957. His colorful "Recollections" of summer camp at The Bishop's Ranch in Healdsburg, California, were written in late 2002 and published in the Winter 2002 issue of the *Russian River Recorder*. They are reprinted here in their entirety.

Recollections of a Choir Boy at El Rancho del Obispo

Having read the article in the Summer 2002 Issue 77 of the *Russian River Recorder*, I thought that you, the reader, might be mildly interested in a personal observation of a Grace Cathedral Choir boy who spent many summers at El Rancho del Obispo in the 40's and '50s.

It all started one 1947 day in San Francisco when I, an independent 7 year old, climbed up Golden Gate Heights in the inner Sunset from Jefferson Elementary School. My parents decided to have a chat with me. They had apparently arranged, without, (*of course*), consulting me, an audition with Richard Purvis, the Organist and Master of Choristers at Grace Cathedral.

In my most whining and controlling manner I informed my parents: "*I do not want to go.... They are all sissies and I do not want to be a sissy choirboy.... etc., etc.*" Thus, I went to the audition and was accepted as a treble in the Grace Cathedral choir in 1947. (So much for whining, temper tantrums and protestations.)

As a former Choirboy Ted Worth stated: "Mr. Purvis was a magnetic and powerful person. He ran the choir—indeed the whole Cathedral—in an autocratic and strict fashion. He brooked interference with no one and led the choir like an army drill sergeant." You had to address him as "Sir." He, in turn, would refer even to the youngest 7–8 year-old as "Mr. Cohen," or just "Mister."

He could be harsh, and sometimes cruel (*"You are all idiots! Who ever told you that you could sing?"*); but the boys in the choir respected him because he obtained incomparable results; and we were all very proud of those results.

We came from all over the city on Monday, Tuesday and Wednesday afternoons for rehearsals and on Thursday evenings for rehearsals with the men. A group of us *"angelic"* choirboys would descend on the Cathedral early on Thursdays and play tag up on the catwalks, (*no safety rails—no OSHA!*); drop objects such a nails and tennis balls to see how high they would bounce. Explore the roofs and the creek that ran under the Cathedral. We were not exactly the most pristine, angelical choirboys as, dear reader, you will see later on. (Including reading comic books, which we snuck into the Cathedral chancel during the services in many devious ways and playing "hangman" during the sermon, always under the stern watchful eyes of Mr. Purvis.)

Mr. Purvis's extreme musicality and vitality shone through his sternness. When he achieved the sound effect that he wanted a look of love and approval would come over his face, completely erasing the terrible scowls and frequent rages into which he flew when someone sang the wrong note or committed some other "grievous sin."

One time I will never forget was when one of our numbers committed some grievous sin during the middle of the Sermon. Mr. Purvis left the organ bench, came across the chancel, and literally escorted S.S. out of the chancel and the service by his ear that was in a very tight grip. (Incidentally S.S. is now a retired University of California professor and lives in Visalia.)

His words were harsh, but he had an uncanny sense of what would make people mad enough to work hard for him and give him what he wanted. He knew the people who needed strong words (which definitely included me), and those who needed gentle prodding. It always worked.

Thus 1947 came to a close.

Sometime in 1948 Mr. Purvis mentioned that the choirboys would go to the Bishop's Ranch for two weeks in August. Apparently this had only been done once before. And it WAS FREE! Those of us who were new to the choir experienced a bit of trepidation of the unknown.

My father was a band teacher in the San Francisco Unified School District and as such had the entire summer devoted to my mother and myself. We explored the Sierra and the desert. Camped on the floor of Yosemite Valley in Camp Seven, right on the Merced River, for almost three months. Try getting a campsite in Yosemite for three days this coming summer!

We left the Sierra early so I could attend Choir Camp. My mother sewed nametags in all my clothing, marked my hats, shoes, etc., etc.. All the things mothers have done for their children for time immemorial before summer camp actually took place.

Came the fateful day, with anticipation and butterflies in my stomach I climbed into the sea foam green 1937 Pontiac and off we went to another adventure.

This was quite a trip as Highway 101 was not a freeway. We crossed THE Bridge. We wound through Sausalito, Mill valley over the hill to Corte Madera, over more hills to San Rafael and after several hours we approached Healdsburg through the apple orchards on a two lane concrete highway. There were several motels between Santa Rosa and Healdsburg that had 10 or 15 small cabins. And LOTS of Gravenstein apples. Every trip we would always buy a bushel to take home. We finally got to Healdsburg and turned on Westside Road. Would we ever get there???? I *HAVE......TO...GO !*

Well, we finally turned on to a little road leading to a dairy. The road consisted of two concrete strips, each about a foot in width. Would we fall off of it and get stuck???? We finally came around a corner and there was the main ranch house. It was beautiful. Ivy covered brick with a portico. A place where we could stop and unload out of the sun, but more importantly, I guess out of the rain, which we obviously in August did not have to worry about.

There were several of my fellow choir members running and shouting on the lawn in front and they showed me the swimming pool and wading pool at the end of the wisteria and grape arbor. All of which still exists, all except the wading pool. (I guess the attorney for the ranch, sometime in the future felt that it was too much a liability. As, I guess, was the diving board that has been long gone.)

I assumed with great anticipation and grandeur that we would be staying in the main ranch house. However I was intercepted about two steps from the car as I was heading for *MY* room in the House.

I was shown over to two long huts complete with concrete floors, with drains, where we would spend our two weeks. There was just barely room enough, height wise, for our U.S. Army surplus double-decker bunks with white with blue stripe mattresses, or, were they blue with white stripes or maybe they were invisible mattresses with blue and white stripes? The pillows matched the mattresses. We were given two sheets, and a pillowcase and of course, an olive-drab blanket which said U.S. ARMY across it. Oh well, so much for MY room in the ranch house.

Our days we filled with many activities that did not give us much time to get into trouble, so the camp director, John Shields, and Mr. Purvis thought........ Little did they know!

Reveille....... Can you believe it!!

All the bunks had to be made to military precision. Then we were off to the main ranch house for Breakfast. Then back to the doghouses, I guess, dear reader, that I forgot to mention that we living in the dog kennels that had been built by the previous owner of the ranch who raised Great Danes. (I don't think we were great... and I don't believe we had any Danes in the choir.) But that IS where our temporary home was.

Back it was to the Ranch House for choir rehearsal. CHOIR REHEARSAL??? WE'RE ON VACATION!! We rehearsed in the main room of the ranch house with Mr. Purvis at the grand piano until lunch. From the living room we could look out over the Russian River valley and wonder why we were rehearsing Magnificats, Nunc Dimitai, Psalms, Descants and Anthems when we could be playing in the pool.

If Mr. Purvis caught us day dreaming, the roof fell down: "*MR. COHEN, WHY did you come to this camp? To DAY Dream? If so you can leave right now for Healdsburg and get on the bus to San Francisco! You WILL NEVER be a chorister, let alone a musician!*"

Mr. Purvis was a taskmaster. But when we gave him the results he wanted he positively beamed and he knew, and we knew, that we had accomplished something on a grand scale. We choirboys would do anything for him.

I came into a little more verbal kidding than most other choirboys, because of my musical training. My father had taught me to play clarinet and then oboe and English horn and piano. Five years later the previous Cathedral organist, Phoebe Cole, had been teaching me organ during my 8th–9th grades. When Mr. Purvis heard of that he made several of his "famous remarks," such as: "*Mr. Cohen, you should ask your father to let you be a plumber; then you could still play with pipes! You surely can't play the organ!*" "*You should go back to playing that 'ill woodwind which no one plays well!' etc., etc.*"

It was an honor to turn pages and assist him at the console, either at the Cathedral or at the Legion of Honor, or even once to ride up with him on the mighty Wurlitzer at the old Fox theatre to play for a Teachers meeting. I thought I was in my form of heaven.

However, in 1954 he offered me a scholarship to learn "*How to really play an organ the way it should be played!*" My first lesson was not on the Chapel of Grace 2 manual, but on *the* 4 manual, 102 stop Æolian Skinner organ in the chancel of the Cathedral.

He was a hard taskmaster. It was devastating when I came unprepared for a lesson. *I only did that once!*

Whoops, dear reader I have digressed........ Back to choir camp at El Rancho del Obispo. Let's see, where did I leave off..... Oh yes, one of the most important parts of the day.

LUNCH! Lunches were like lunches in Boy Scout camps, Girl Scout camps (don't ask how I know that!), Fraternity houses, Sorority houses, the Navy, you get the idea, I'm sure. And yes, we had BUG JUICE! Bug Juice came in many different colors: yellow, red, green, purple and, of course, the ever popular orange.

After we had cleared the tables we rehearsed for another hour and a half. During that time it was getting warm in the living room, the pool looked great down there at the end of the arbor.... "MR. COHEN!" "Yes sir," "I lost my place." "You WHAT?" {~~*Saa - ve Me! I just want out of this hot room and to get in the pool~~*}

Finally it was swimming time. The diving board was completely crowded with a line of choirboys doing cannon balls, regular dives, lots of belly flops, and dunking each other in the pool.

"*OUT OF THE POOL!*" came the dreaded cry.

Away we went to clean up for dinner.

After dinner, and in later years, when the rehearsals were cancelled in the afternoon ... *Finally*, we would try our hand at archery and other activities.

Only one chorister ever had an arrow that went into his chest and luckily it bounced off a rib. (By the way, he is still alive and lives in Fresno.)

Other activities consisted of softball in the corral on the hill that is visible from Westside Road and the ever-present ping-pong games in the courtyard of the ranch house. Capture the Flag, and all the other games and activities that make a summer camp enjoyable.

Then there was the INFAMOUS day. Someone, his name shall never be mentioned, although we all know who it was, he actually lives in Visalia and still has "finger-marks" on his ear..., brought some cherry bombs to camp. Then someone had this wonderful idea: What would happen if you lit a cherry bomb and flushed it down the toilet? (This is somewhat on a par with dropping nails from the cat-walks of the Cathedral to see how high they would bounce.)

The infamous moment came—the cherry bomb was lit. The cb was dropped into the toilet. The toilet was flushed. We all ran out of building. There was a muffled WHOMPFF !! The sound of porcelain breaking.... The toilet lay in about 4–500 pieces all over the floor of the bathroom... *OH-OH*, we had *REALLY* done it!

Then it was DINNER! And, of course, BUG JUICE![7]

After dinner we would usually play a game such as capture the flag where the flags were usually several hundred yards apart. Or the highlight of the camp: the treasure hunt. I'll never forget the clue that stumped all of us: "The flag that never waves." The next clue was, of course...., in the ranch mailbox.

Then came either movies in the living room of the ranch house.... Travel logs, cartoons, or actually movies sponsored by "Chiquita Banana" or campfires in the courtyard of the ranch.

At the campfires we were initiated into the rites of the camp, and in later years we did the initiating of the younger members.

Skits: "The Spit Around the World," "Stand-In" complete with fake movie camera and director. I think you get the idea.

Of course there were the usual (?) campfire songs: "Hole in the Bottom of the Sea," "State Song," "Flashing Like Silver," "The Worms Crawl In, The Worms Crawl Out," and the infamous "Mr., Mr. Johnny Rebeck." Ghost stories, on and on and on to the infamous: "Aztec Initiation Ritual."

In the year 1996, the "Old Choirboys of Grace Cathedral held a reunion. We thought that it would be fun to stay a weekend at the modernized, rebuilt, Bishop's Ranch. The author invited the group to his home on Friday for swimming and a BBQ. We then proceeded to the Ranch late that evening and spent the weekend at "El Rancho del Obispo" with our significant others.

We had a campfire, toured the wineries, sang in the living room of the Ranch house and generally had a great time. In fact, we have this reunion every other year. The last reunion was held this year in June. Sadly we have lost two of our members during this period of renewing our friendships.

Two years ago we "Old Grace Cathedral Choir Boys" wanted to contribute something for the ranch that would add to ambiance of the ranch and would be a remembrance of all our good and bad times at the ranch. We decided to build a campfire circle. It took us almost a year to jackhammer out of the side of a hill an area for the campfire. We dedicated it to our camp director, John Shields, who ran all the camp activities when we attend camp in the 40's and 50's.

I have taken many close friends up to the Ranch over the years and shown them what I have talked about for so long. They always come away in awe that such a place does exist.

All of us will carry these fond remembrances of those wonderful, and not so wonderful childhood times and friendships that have held true through these years, while participating in "Choir Camp" at El Rancho del Obispo.[8]

See additional comments by Steve Cohen under "The Old Boys," below.

Tom DeLay

There is a story attributed to Purvis was about some AGO snoot-in-the-air who could not wait to get up to the console after the postlude and introduce herself.

Lady: "Oh, Mr. Purvis, it is such a pleasure to meet you. I'm Lilian Cipher from the East Arkansas Chapter of the AGO."

Purvis: "Well, I certainly can't help that."

Knowing the Purvis disdain for self-appointed prima donnas, I can believe it. Tom Hazleton told me the story one time of where he tried some prima donna nonsense and Purvis reamed him but good. First and last time.

Purvis had a unique way of trying to "disarm" people on a first meeting. So it was with Ed Stout. Purvis started with all sorts of diatribe about "…you organ tuners are all alike.… blah, blah, blah," and then proceeded with some of the most verbose nonsense you could imagine. Ed handled it in his own inimitable way which can only be described by Ed.

Once Purvis was in Fresno for a lesson with his many students down there. I was servicing an instrument on which Purvis was to give a lesson. He started in with the same verbose nonsense directed at me that he had used on Ed Stout 20-ish years earlier! I turned it around and dished it right back to Purvis. He looked at me and sternly admonished, "OK, who got to you?" He knew. We had a good laugh.

Another time, I was flying back from a convention in Portland. A fellow organist and I started chatting about historic old pipe organs, particularly

Murray M. Harris instruments. From the seat directly behind us came a semi-gruff, "Well, it is about time someone recognized how wonderful Murray Harris instruments are!" Of course it was Purvis, and he told of the many Murray Harris instruments he had played in the Bay Area, particularly the four-manual instrument still in First Baptist Church in Oakland.[9]

Christian Elliott

I first met Richard Purvis in 1984 when I played my first solo concert at a national convention of the American Theatre Organ Society. Dick was attending that convention and performing a classical program at the Scottish Rite Cathedral in Indianapolis on a large Skinner organ. I was performing in Fort Wayne on a large Wurlitzer. After attending my performance, Mr. Purvis came up and introduced himself and congratulated me on my performance. He said some very kind remarks about my musicianship and sensitivity. I remember saying "Thank you" and Dick very quickly said: "Don't thank me—Thank GOD!" That was Dick's quick wit coming through, as I would later find out. Later at that convention, Lyn Larsen said I should have responded to Dick with "Well, you're the next closest thing to God!"

Upon graduating from college in 1988 I moved to the Bay Area when I was selected to replace Tom Hazleton as the Menlo Park Presbyterian Church Senior Organist. This opened up the door to study privately with Richard Purvis. I approached Dick about studying, and he was agreeable, with the lessons held at his home where he had a small studio complete with 3 manual Rodgers analog organ.

In the late 1980's, for one of my Lenten recitals I decided to present an all-Purvis program. It was my honor to study all of the pieces personally with Richard. One of the works was his Partita on "Christ ist Erstanden." It was out of print but I was eager to learn it. Dick photocopied the music and sent it to me with a very nice inscription on the cover. I had several lessons with him on that work, and it was a challenging piece. Dick honored me by taking the bus from San Francisco to Menlo Park and personally attended my all-Purvis recital. Needless to say it was an honor having the composer in the audience (and a bit nerve wracking as well!).

Richard was careful in his registration choices, and I remember how he always seemed to prefer an independent pedal as much as possible. He used manual to pedal couplers sparingly. He was very methodical and careful in how he would approach registrations for a work, telling me in advance how he would approach the registrations for a particular piece, and how many combination pistons it would require.

I learned as much about *music* from Richard Purvis as I learned about the *organ*. The music was most important, not the organ. Richard was first and foremost a superb musician. In his teaching, it was clear that he was interested in beautiful music: careful phrasing, thoughtful expression, colorful yet tasteful registrations.

I've heard many stories over the years about Richard's very gruff demeanor in his Grace Cathedral days. People said he'd mellowed significantly after retiring, and I must say that he was always an exceedingly kind, interesting, and warm person to me. It takes a special talent to be a teacher of the organ. Richard was one of the best in my experience, and I shall never forget having had the supreme honor of having studied with him.[10]

Jim Hansen

My dad had a brother in Santa Rosa and in 1961 we were going to visit them, so we stopped in San Francisco for a couple of days. I had to see Grace Cathedral, so I went in and looked at the Aeolian-Skinner, looked in the chapel, walked around, and saw the artifacts. The sexton was there, and he noticed I was interested in the organ. He asked if I'd like to meet Mr. Purvis. He said, "Go upstairs, he's in his office, go and meet him." I was about 15–16. Purvis asked, "Would you like to play the chapel organ?" and he gave me a note of permission written on Union Pacific Railroad stationery ...

Got to know him later when we had the music store [Rodgers dealership, Southland Music Center] in Lemon Grove. Purvis was teaching up in San Francisco, and then Phil Wickstrom, the L.A. dealer, asked if he could come down and teach in L.A., and we asked him to teach in San Diego. He taught 10 hours a day in San Diego! Between 1973–79 or '80, he would come down Thursday and Friday. He would stay at my home, in the Kensington area of San Diego. He liked to go to the Starlight Room at El Cortez Hotel in San Diego; his favorite thing was half a charcoal-grilled chicken.

I studied with him 6–7 years myself. I studied Anglican music, a Chadwick piece (variations). It was classical only: Franck, Bach, Purvis's own music, Vierne, Mendelssohn, Reubke, Liszt Ad Nos.

When we went out to dinner we had fun. In a lesson he wasn't stern but was all business. If he knew something about the composer or had a story to tell, he would impart that to you, but lessons were an hour long and we got a lot accomplished. He knew what he was doing.[11]

Rodgers Jenkins

Purvis was a houseguest at the home of Rodgers Jenkins in Portland, Oregon, when he played recitals in that city. Jenkins, one of the cofounders (with Fred Tinker) of the Rodgers Organ Company, supplied Grace Cathedral with a Rodgers organ in 1968 while the pipe organ at Grace was being rebuilt. Jenkins said that Purvis would retire to Jenkins's home office and compose, without a piano or keyboard.

"He was an interesting fellow, a little slow to get to know him, but once you got past that barrier, he was your buddy. A crusty old guy, but he was nice. He knew a lot of limericks, most of them not publishable."

Jenkins recalled that Purvis played Hammond organs while stationed overseas, and, later, jazz on Hammond organs in the Bay Area.[12]

Joyce Jones

Sometime in the 1970s Colton Piano and Organ, the Rodgers representative in Los Angeles, opened a new showroom. As it happened, the opening was on Super Bowl Sunday that year. People in Los Angeles were crazy with football. It was a big showroom, and there were 2000 people who came to the opening! A bunch of us played—they wanted me to show the organ off, and Richard was also there to play. When he saw that I was going to play his "Les Petites Cloches," he said, "Why are you going to play that trashy thing?" I said, "Well, name me another piece that shows off the harp, the chimes, and flutes, and a few other things, and does it all in three minutes!" He answered, "I'll keep my mouth shut." He then said, "Why don't you play my Partita?" When I told him that it was out of print, he said he'd send me a copy, which he did. It was very thoughtful of him. Those are two of my fond memories of him.[13]

Vaughn Jones

When Ethel Merman was in San Francisco touring with "Gypsy" in the early 1960s, she led a rather notorious life in the late night. There was a pet monkey in the show, and Ethel thought it was amusing to take the monkey with her to every restaurant and nightclub and bar in San Francisco every night. One night Purvis was in a bar called "Gordon's" with Ethel and several other people when the monkey escaped from Ethel's lap, hopped up on the bar, and bit the telephone cord in two. That made Herb Caen's column. Purvis told me that story more than once and thought it was hilarious. Last but not least: Ethel was a devout Episcopalian and frequently attended church at Grace Cathedral when she was in town.

I was practicing the Bach "O Mensch bewein" for Good Friday and I can still hear Purvis telling me, "Vaughn, you would have made a good Chicago gangster. You really machine gun those trills with great energy!"

Once I was practicing a French Baroque fugue (Clerambault? du Mage?) and put a little trill or mordent in the statement somewhere. Halfway through the piece, Purvis said, "You would have made a lousy politician. After the second repetition you completely forget your platform!"

One of the recitals I gave at St. John the Evangelist included the choir doing an anthem or two. Purvis was at the church with me to listen to the balance of the organ and give me advice on the registration, but I had not asked him to help direct the choir. After the choir finished rehearsing one of the anthems, Purvis said loudly from his front row pew, "The altos sound like a flock of seagulls fighting over an orange peel."[14]

Keyes Kelly

Keyes Kelly was a chorister at Grace and keyboard student of Purvis. He joined the choir in 1951 at age 6, the youngest boy Purvis had ever accepted. He also began piano lessons with Purvis when he was about 8, and later studied the organ with him for approximately 10 years. His weekly lessons (which cost $20) were on the Cathedral's Aeolian-Skinner organ: "He was a hard taskmaster, but we became friends as I became older." Kelly's father was the first verger at Grace in the 1930s, and his mother managed the Sunday School at the time Purvis arrived. Kelly recalls that sometime in the late 1940s his mother convinced Purvis to dress up as Santa Claus for the

Sunday School Christmas party. Keyes and his older brother Lloyd were the only pair of brothers ever to receive the Bishop's Cross, a prestigious award given to choirboys based on their musicianship and service of at least five years. Purvis selected the recipients.[15]

Richard Kline

An organ enthusiast in the Washington, D.C., area, Kline sang with McCurdy as a student in Philadelphia.

> I met Purvis several times at Grace where he was kind enough to show me the organ. I was a good friend of Ed Stout's and he demonstrated new things that had been added to the original instrument.
>
> I met him later in Hagerstown, Maryland, where he did a recital. Afterwards I took him to his motel and then continued back across the mountain to Frederick, Maryland, where I live. About a half hour into the trip I realized that he had left his music on the floor of the front seat so I turned back and went to the motel. Purvis had had quite a bit to drink that night and was NOT pleased to be awakened, music or no music. I was amused as there was a similar story about Karg-Elert coming to Washington from NYC years ago to open the new Moller at the GSA building. After a rather extended visit to the club car on the train, he left all his music on board. I feared that Purvis might have had another engagement and would need his scores.[16]

Michael Lampen

Michael Lampen related a story told to him in April 2011 by Verger Charles Shipley about how "Purvis (or was it Bishop James A. Pike?) somehow got locked into the Chapel of Grace. Unable to exit via the vestry he had to climb over the wrought-iron screen at the chapel entrance. The screen's twenty-foot height and spiked top makes this story very improbable."[17]

Lyn Larsen

"Aside from our musical connection and shared interest, we also had a great personal friendship that I enjoyed from about 1966 right up until he passed away."[18]

Larsen said about Purvis, "At Grace Cathedral he was very no-nonsense. He could even be cross at the keyboard when he was working. It was a defense to weed out visitors, organ nuts, interested choral people, tire kickers, and you learned to leave him alone. When you visited Richard away from Grace, over dinner, he was 100% the reverse, warm, affable, a really great guy.

"In 1967 I was 22, Richard was 54. He was an avid walker and hike. He even went to Scotland and hiked around."

Larsen occasionally met Purvis at his home on Balceta for more formal lessons. In the 1980s, Larsen met with Purvis there to work on orchestration. "Richard had very dry sense of humor. He could put you on, then hit you with a zinger."[19]

See additional comments by Lyn Larsen in Chapter 12, "Purvis and the Theatre Organ."

Stephen Loher

An epiphany moment for me (I can still recall it vividly to this day) was my first time walking into St. Gracie's. It was 1952 and I was 11. My parents had decided to bring me to Richard's recital—in this case it was October and hence the Bach-Franck Cycle 1. We parked in the parking lot which in those days was on the liturgical south side of the nave—today we have the new buildings and plaza in that place.

The Church was only half finished—3 of the 6 bays, the crossing, transepts, quire, etc. There was a big iron wall outside the "temporary" end of the nave. The South tower had been built in the 40's, because Dr. Coulsen (I think that is the name) had given a beautiful set of 44 Gillette and Johnson bells and built the tower to house them. There was a garden between the iron wall and the Cathedral House which fronted on Taylor Street. (Two "Cathedral" cats roamed the garden: MagnifiCAT and CATechism).

We arrived at about 4:30 and I couldn't stay in the car. I went right into the Church. Canon Montizambert was preaching and the sight was overwhelming to me. I had never seen such a large space, and the blue of the Connick windows gave a hue to the whole scene. Presently Canon Montizambert concluded the sermon and Richard slid in on the Erzähler celestes, doodled a bit and then went into the offertory anthem: Sheep May Safely Graze. It was a dramatic moment and influenced my own service playing to this day. Eventually, at 14, I began to study with Richard.[20]

Richard was very analytical about other organists, unless they were just fakes. He would point out the good things and the not so good things. He was not a snob. He had a love/hate relationship with Virgil. He loved so much of what Virgil did but was a bit turned off by what he perceived as the commercial aspect.[21]

He was a generalist—was fluent in speaking about many subjects, so I think he must have read constantly.

Did he like food!!! But he was on a kick about "healthy" food, so I think his immense weight was the product of his drinking. He did not smoke, but he drank. He seemed to be able to control his drinking. If something important was coming up, he was able to stop drinking for a few days or even a week. He didn't touch a drop when he came to New Haven to play at Woolsey for the time he was here—about 5 days.

He did not drive. John Shields was the usual chauffeur. He did at one time try to learn to drive a Volkswagen Beetle. I was told of several attempts to negotiate said Beetle on the Jones Street hill. I think they were ultimately unsuccessful.[22]

He liked to eat out and often. One of his favorite places was Al's Papagayo Room at the Fairmont (which closed in the early '60s.) After the Papagayo Room his favorite haunts were on the Wharf—eventually Alioto's (the one not on the water).

I don't recall his taking what we would call a "vacation," but he would go away. I remember playing several Sundays at Grace because he was out of town. He did tour across the Pond at times but that was before my assistantship. During that time I don't recall his taking a "vacation," but he used to love to go over to Sausalito and sit at the waterside.

Some of his favorite phrases, usually delivered during choir rehearsal with the boys (full rehearsals were very formal): "Your wig is on crooked and your mother dresses you funny." "Come to dinner, I will open a can of beans." He did not use "colorful" language—this would have offended his intelligence and his ability to articulate that intelligence.[23]

Richard had a different response to brides on the telephone, depending on whether it was a wedding in Chapel of Grace (in which case he was very gruff, said there would be no rehearsal, got off the phone quickly) or in the main church (in which case he was very polite, "Yes, definitely, I will be at the rehearsal," etc.) [Weddings in the main church paid much better than weddings in the chapel.][24]

Douglas Metzler

In a wide-ranging conversation we had about Purvis, Douglas Metzler offered the following miscellaneous details:

> Purvis and Virgil Fox liked to eat at the Ritz Poodle Dog in San Francisco. His nickname for Virgil was "Virg-hole." He sometimes called Tom Hazleton "Hazle-tone."
>
> He enjoyed swimming (he swam in on the team in high school) and hiking. He suffered from arthritis while still at Grace Cathedral. He invested in Krugerrands. When drinking at restaurants, he would say "Tide's out, captain!" to signal that he wanted another drink.
>
> He didn't get fired at Grace, but he had plenty of conflict with the dean. He finally said he'd had enough and resigned.

Metzler also said that Purvis had told him that he spent the summer of 1952 in England, where he was given the opportunity to attend the coronation of Queen Elizabeth II. However, the only way he could get in was with the choir. He was told not to sing, but just to "stand there and mouth something."[25] (Purvis was probably pulling Metzler's leg, since there is no record that Purvis spent the summer of 1952 in England, let alone attended the coronation.)

See additional comments by Douglas Metzler in Chapter 5, "Later Years."

Jonas Nordwall

I first met Purvis in 1971, when I was playing for Rodgers at the Asilomar organ show. He came up to me, and said "Hi, I'm Dick Purvis; I like the way you play." We started a relationship (I was 23 at the time), and I'd just started at First Methodist in Portland. I never formally studied with him until a few years before his death. A person could get more valuable, solid musical information from Dick over cocktails and one dinner than many teachers could provide in a year. My interests were his concepts about performing Franck that he learned with Tournemire. Dick's words were, "Here's what is written, but this is how they played." There were more registration changes than published, as each performance was always new experience and a work in progress.[26]

A famous phrase of his: "Have you ever thought about this?" He could win you over to his way with this.

When we'd go out to dinner, it was a three-hour event. There was a lot of discussion. We stayed away from politics, but there was a lot of music stuff.

On one occasion Tom Hazleton played Purvis's "Toccata Festiva" really fast, and Richard said, "No, it should be slower." Richard played things much more slowly at Grace Cathedral. He didn't seem to want to understand that on other organs (in recordings, particularly, but also in recitals) tempi would depend on the acoustics of each venue. We had some friendly disagreements with Richard about tempi in his own music.

Once I brought Purvis up to Portland to play a recital. He said he didn't want to do a solo organ recital ("They're a dime a dozen.") He wanted to do some Purvis choral music. He sent up his first program, and said, "I'll be there four days before the concert. When he got there, he asked, "Can I change the program? This is a Purvis organ!" The only two straight things were the Franck A minor and the Bach Fantasie and Fugue in G minor.

You had to watch your tongue. After the concert we went out for drinks. In his mind he was still in Grace Cathedral. He'd played the Fugue so slowly. I said "Why did you play so damn slow?" "You heard every note, didn't cha?"

Purvis was the ultimate organ geek. He had played everything in the Bay area sooner or later.[27]

See additional comments by Jonas Nordwall in Chapter 12, "Purvis and the Theatre Organ."

The Old Boys

On June 7, 2011, at The Bishop's Ranch in Healdsburg, California, I met with "The Old Boys," a group of Grace Cathedral choristers who sang for Richard Purvis for various periods between 1948 and 1960. A couple of them had also attended the Cathedral School, which opened in 1957. Starting in 1948, Purvis took the choristers to The Bishop's Ranch every summer for a two-week choir camp in late August. They bunked in what used to be doghouses—the Ranch had formerly been a Great Dane farm. At this meeting I asked them about their experiences both at the Cathedral and at camp.

Each year since 1994, they have gathered for a reunion at the Ranch. One of the men said, "We're here every year because of the bond we shared with Purvis—we survived him!—but also for the affection we had for him. For sixty years we have known each other."

The Old Boys' Reunion, June 7, 2011, Healdsburg, California. Courtesy Mike Sidwell.
   Back row: Roger Williams, Lloyd Kelly, Steve Cohen, Bob Loshuertos, Alan Chesterman, Greg Klink, Steve Sibbett
   Front row: James Welch, Mike Sidwell, Norm Smith, Tom Chesterman, Jim McLeod, Lester O'Shea

Present at this reunion were Alan Chesterman, Thomas (Tom) Chesterman, Stephen W. (Steve) Cohen, Robert (Bob) Loshuertos, Lloyd Kelly, Gregory Klink, George Mason, James (Jim) McLeod, Lester O'Shea, Steven Sibbett, Michael (Mike) Sidwell, Norman (Norm) Smith, and Roger Williams.

Below are memories shared by The Old Boys.

Tom Chesterman recalled an experience when he was a young priest in 1957 or 1958. "We had the youth vespers at the cathedral in the fall. I was the diocesan youth advisor, and we decided to do the 20th century folk mass (called the 'jazz mass' in those days). We had used it at the Ranch. When I said we wanted to do the Psalm and Lord's Prayer from that as part of the music, Dick said, 'I can't play that on the cathedral organ. If I try, it will sound like a calliope. But I have a friend playing a gig at a nightclub, and I think he can make the cathedral organ sound decent, if you insist on doing this.' And he did. I found this an amazing act of humility, to let someone else come in and play this."

Steve Cohen recalled that Steve Sibbett was causing some kind of disturbance during a service. Purvis left the console, crossed the chancel, grabbed the boy by the ear, and, in view of the congregation, marched him out of the chancel. It didn't stop the boy from returning the next week. Purvis's predecessor, Hugh MacKinnon, could also be stern with the choristers. MacKinnon would later apologize. Not so with Purvis.

(See additional comments by Steve Cohen under his own listing earlier in this chapter.)

Bob Loshuertos remembered that his father came home from a council meeting at St. Mark's Lutheran Church in San Francisco, where his family were members, and said, "We hired an organist, but we won't keep him long, he's too good for here." Still, Purvis organized a children's choir while he was at St. Mark's, and he later played the dedicatory organ recital there.

Loshuertos was for a period a "scribe," responsible for tabulating points for the boys' report cards. He would put music books up on the rack for Purvis, and during the sermon, he'd sit at the console and deduct points from miscreant boys' tallies.

Loshuertos recalled that when his father died during the summer of 1949, Purvis expressed sympathy to his mother, claiming that he too knew the pain of loss because "his fiancée was killed in England during the war." (Steve Cohen added that he also had heard that Purvis was engaged to someone he met in England during the war. There is no documentation to support this.)

Jim McLeod had a vivid recollection of the choir camp in 1948, the year of the 1948 Olympics in London. "It was the first year, and Purvis called it a 'Choir Olympics.' I'll never forget how he arrived at the camp: He came walking down a hill, like he was coming down from Mount Olympus, with sheets wrapped around him like a toga, a laurel wreath on this head, and in his hand a flashlight for a torch. Here he comes down, to start the Choir Olympics, to light the flame. It was lot of fun that year. He was never so loose again after that."

McLeod also recalled that Purvis actively composed while at the Ranch. "He would be up at the Ranch Monday through Friday, and he used to write music—in the Big House. He didn't have a piano or an organ—didn't need it—and he would spend the afternoon up there writing. He might have written some of his organ music there. This would have been 1948, '49, and '50."

McLeod recalled his first rehearsal as a chorister in Feburary 1947. "Jack Chisum and I were late, and he [Purvis] told us so, right away. Mind you, this was my first meeting with this fellow. I said 'OK,' and he said 'OK what?!' He required us to call him Sir. That particular night, he worked us for an hour to say 'Immortal, invisible.' He bashed those tenors. He didn't come in like Mr. Nice Guy."

Several of the Old Boys remember that behind Purvis's back they sometimes called him "RIP [pronounced "rip," not R.I.P.]": "He didn't like it. He didn't know how to deal with it. Or with kids, for that matter. He didn't want anyone to get too close. But for us, calling him 'RIP' was really a sign of affection."

One of the choristers admitted that as a choirboy he sneaked into the pipe chambers of the organ at Grace Cathedral and stole a small flue pipe (which he still has). He added that he thought other pipes may have disappeared in the same way.[28]

Mike Sidwell added this story:

> Normally when the church service got to the point where the sermon was given, Mr. Purvis would shut down the organ, get down from the organ bench, and move down to the stall or bench closest to the chancel facing the choir across the chancel. He would then do some paper work or something like that. After about 20 minutes or so he would gather his papers, move back to the organ bench and get the organ ready to play when the sermon was over. If I remember correctly, when the sermon was over the person giving the sermon would turn towards the altar and say, 'And Now to God the Father, God the Son,' and Mr. Purvis would play a quiet bit of music.
>
> One Sunday Canon Forbes was giving the sermon. Everything was normal except that after about eight minutes he quickly finished the sermon, turned toward the altar and started, "And Now To…" Of course this took Mr. Purvis completely by surprise and he was scrambling to put his papers away, get back to the organ bench, and start playing. I heard later from Canon Forbes that he had been waiting quite a while to do this.

Brad Smith, who was a chorister from 1948 to 1957, has vivid memories of Richard and John both at camp and at the church. He spoke of how important John Shields was as a balance to the sometimes "imperial" Richard Purvis. "Richard was strict and could be denigrating. Maybe he was afraid things would get out of control. John Shields was the guy who did all the nitty-gritty, was always there supporting, taking us out for review sessions, helping us with our parts. Richard didn't teach us how to read music; we had no musical training except memorization. This was actually helpful to me—I can still hear a tune and pick it up very fast, but I can't read music."[29]

Norm Smith recalled that even doing homework was more relaxing and enjoyable than a rehearsal with Purvis. He also recalled that during a conversation between his mother and Purvis, the subject turned to Scotch whiskey. His mother said, "My husband loves Scotch whiskey, you'll have to come over for dinner some night." Purvis accepted the invitation, joining the Smith family every month or two for a few Scotches and dinner.

Roger Williams said that when he was married at Grace Cathedral, Richard played for the service. His fiancée wanted the traditional wedding marches, but Richard was very outspoken in his opposition. "He said that that music was from an opera about an ass." But in the end, the bride got the music she wanted.

One of the men remembered that in 1949 or 1950 Purvis had taken the boys of the choir to do a Christmas program at the California Club, near Grace Cathedral. The businessmen wouldn't stop talking during the music, so Purvis marched the boys off the stage and that was the end of the concert!

One person said that Purvis ran the choir rehearsals himself, directing from the piano. "It was a one-man show."

Two quotable quotes from Purvis, as recalled by the Old Boys:

"He is dead from the neck both ways."

"Were you born in a barn?" (spoken when someone forgot to close the door).

Donna Parker

Regarding her long-time teacher and mentor, Donna Parker said, "Dick had to be guarded. He was gruff. John was the sweetheart. It was a good cop/bad cop relationship.

"He didn't treat his students like underlings. You were a musician on the same path."

Regarding Purvis's authority on the performance of Franck's music, Purvis told Donna, "I got it from Tournemire, I got it from the horse's mouth." She also confirmed that he called the organ at Grace "Gussie."

About the origin of "Night in Monterey," Donna said that Richard and John liked Monterey and the Santa Cruz mountains. They often vacationed in the Monterey area.[30]

James (Bede) Parry

I first met Purvis when I was serving in the Coast Guard and was stationed at Alameda. I began studying with Richard Purvis in May of 1961 when I was discharged from the Coast Guard. I had often stopped by the Cathedral over the years and Charlie Agneau, then Verger of Grace Cathedral, would let me in to play the marvelous Grace Cathedral organ. In 1961, Charlie arranged a meeting with Purvis, and we went over to Purvis' apartment for dinner. Fortunately, Purvis took an immediate liking to me, and, after many Scotches, he told me I had "the right idea" (vis-à-vis Anglican Church music). I was not interested in becoming a concert organist, but I was interested in becoming a good Anglican Church musician. My idols were King's College Cambridge Choir and Grace Cathedral. Ever since I was in grade school, I was drawn to those recordings of Purvis at Grace Cathedral.

My earliest remembrances of Purvis were how he held his mentors in high esteem. This was especially true with Wallace Sabin and Sir Edward Bairstow. Purvis told me he had studied with Bairstow at York Minster (Purvis considered Francis Jackson, Bairstow's successor, his "brother.") Over the years, I have heard many stories about Edward Bairstow, and I am quite sure that Purvis emulated him in more ways than music! The descriptions I have read about Bairstow are mirrors of how Purvis behaved at Grace Cathedral. According to his contemporaries, before the War Purvis was a sweet person. After the War and his studies in England he became very gruff and curt. Some attribute this to his war experience, but I rather believe it was his mentoring with Bairstow that set the tone.

During the time I was at Grace Cathedral, the middle altar had not yet been installed, and, in fact, the Cathedral had only three bays of the nave completed. The acoustics were superb. I don't know if you ever heard Richard improvise at Grace Cathedral, but it was truly heavenly. He played a beautiful service. He did not use free harmonizations on hymns because he felt in the Cathedral they detracted from the singing.

Purvis felt most organists were not musicians. And, of course, with the renaissance of mechanical action organs and E. Power Biggs, all the rage was to play in the "Baroque" style (whatever that meant!). He called these folks "Baroquists." They were not musical, according to Richard. He would often give examples of Léon Goossens, who was a wonderful oboist. Purvis thought that's how the organ should be played.

Which brings to mind another anecdote. In the late 1950s, the First Congregational Church of Long Beach had a large M. P. Moeller installed. One of the pieces Richard had selected was the Concerto in B-flat Major by Handel. He had a habit taking a 16' flute, an 8' flute, and a 2' flute, and playing them an octave higher, giving an 8', 4', and 1' sound. Purvis ran out of notes when he attempted to play an octave higher. It was amusing, but very embarrassing for Richard.

One of the more memorable incidents occurred after I moved to New York. Purvis had come to New York for some special service at St. Paul's Chapel, Columbia University. Searle Wright (another one of Richard's "brothers") was playing a recital. I was sitting with Richard waiting for the program to start, when up walks Virgil Fox. In his usual effusive way, he said, "RICHARD!! What are you doing in New York?!!" To which Purvis answered with a growl, "I'm trying to hear a recital." To which Virgil responded in a stentorian tone, "Richard Purvis, are you always as rude outside of San Francisco as you are in it?!!!" [Compare with Richard Torrence's account, below.]

The last time I saw Purvis was for lunch in 1994. He told me he was not in good health, but he was his usual sharp-witted self. He died on Christmas Day 1994. To this very day, I consider Richard Purvis my mentor and most important musical influence in my life. I love church music. I love choral music. I love playing the organ. And Richard gave me so much in all of these areas. Richard, rest in God's peace![31]

Bill Rhoads

My close connection to Richard went from 1970–1973. After that I would see him for a meal from time to time. I only took a few lessons with him. My main connection was a standing dinner invitation on Wednesday evenings and driving him to places outside of the City—mainly to some friends in Oakland who are now dead. We did take the ferry to Angel Island a few times for a picnic.

We did not talk a great deal about the organ except his conversations that "musical organists" were becoming few and far between. He did mention that a few PhD students approached him about studying and he turned most of them down, saying they were technicians only. On a few Wednesdays, David McK. Williams would join us, and a couple of times Searle Wright was there for dinner. Richard and I would talk a great deal about spirituality, in which he had a passionate interest. He always was pushing me to further studies with the organ.

He was always extremely kind to me and was very much a mentor. At one point, I had just started a new job and after paying the usual fees for a new apartment, I learned of a family emergency in Washington D.C. and needed to fly home immediately but did not have the airline fare. Richard just handed me his credit card and said, "Use this for all your expenses" (you could do this in the early seventies). He had a reputation for gruffness but was one of the kindest individuals I ever met. As time went on, I moved and we did not see as much of each other as we once did, but every few months, Bob Hunt (his former assistant living in Marin) and I would drive to Larkspur, pick Richard up at the ferry terminal, have lunch together, and spend the afternoon walking.

He did have a passion for Gregorian chant which he studied at Quarr Abbey on the Isle of Wight with Father Desroquettes—now long dead. He was so impressed at how the chant was accompanied and how Desroquettes would improvise on the chant tunes. He would always kid me about how my tradition (Roman Catholic) had given so much of its tradition up and would say I needed to help keep it alive. So I am doing just that at St. Stephen's in Sacramento. Unfortunately I did not see much of him in the last few years of his life. The last time I saw him was the celebration of his eightieth birthday at Grace.

The thing Richard did for me was show me how to play a service, and that was my only interest in the organ. And no one played a service like he did with the exception of Cochereau (of course a completely different style), but both outstanding improvisers.[32]

Manuel Rosales

I knew Richard after his retirement from Grace Cathedral and met him during one of his teaching tours of Southern California. He had an entourage of students whom he traveled once a month to teach. Just about that time we had completed the restoration of Los Angeles Art Organ, Opus 46, and the news of that spread to the Bay Area. Purvis was an aficionado of Murray Harris's work and called me to ask if he could see and play the instrument. Our first encounter was accompanied by dinner, and for about a year we met about once a month to chat and dine together. Among his favorite choices for the first course was mock turtle soup.

He was a gentle, gracious and kind person with much to talk about in his career and personal experiences. He was one of kind and of a generation of cultured individuals whose knowledge and taste was not limited to the organ world but could appreciate art, orchestral music, architecture and fine dining![33]

David Rothe

Purvis was certainly a giant among Bay Area organists. I began my organ studies with Val Ritchie and went on to study with Alex Post, Harold Mueller, Richard Purvis and Herb Nanney. I am grateful to have learned valuable things from each one of them. But I would have to say that Richard Purvis was the most memorable teacher and the most colorful performer.

I attended many of his bi-weekly concerts at the Palace of the Legion of Honor and also attended most of his "Bach-Franck" cycle performances at Grace Cathedral. This was when I was in my late teens. He was considered the "top dog" among Bay Area organists, and even though I studied with several others, it was always my ambition to study with him; this eventually happened in 1960 while I was a student at UC Berkeley. I played my senior recital at Grace Cathedral in 1961, and substituted (as Purvis's "Deputy Organist") during the summer of 1962.

Here are a few memories I have of Richard Purvis:

Purvis was a great teacher (especially in the Romantic tradition). Despite his stern demeanor he had the musical development of his students at heart.

Purvis rarely complimented his students on their playing. I remember once when I played a piece for him he surprised me by saying, "Not bad." I said, "Oh, thank you, Mr. Purvis." He replied, "I didn't say it was good!"

Aware that I was studying at UC Berkeley, when he was teaching music of Bach, Purvis would often throw in a few extra tips as to "how the Baroque boys would play it."

I also remember working on a Bach trio sonata with him. During one of our lessons Purvis wandered off (as he often did, to listen from the nave) until I finally bumbled my way to the finish. When he returned to the bench several minutes later he said, "Congratulations, you have just played for the great Virgil Fox!" Apparently Virgil was in town and stopped to pay his respects to Purvis. I was of course mortified at not having played my best for Purvis or, especially, for Virgil. Purvis said, "Don't worry, Virgil knows how difficult it is to master those pieces."

I went to dinner with Purvis once at Caesar's Restaurant in San Francisco, which I believe was his favorite restaurant. Purvis ordered sweetbreads and suggested I do the same; I declined.

In 1964, after I had finished my studies with him, I brought Dirk Flentrop to San Francisco to see Grace Cathedral. (Flentrop had come to Palo Alto to meet the architect for the current All Saints' Church.) Purvis was at the console and cordially welcomed Mr. Flentrop and played the Little G minor Fugue for him (rather more detached than I had ever heard him play before; probably to demonstrate that contrapuntal lines could be heard on the famed Aeolian Skinner, even in Grace Cathedral's acoustics). Flentrop was also polite and cordial but mentioned to me later Grace Cathedral should put one of his (Flentrop's) instruments in the rear gallery if they wanted to hear Bach's music clearly.

I went in a different direction in terms of musical repertoire and interpretation and didn't see Purvis again until the 1990s, when we both attended the OHS convention in San Francisco. We sat together on the bus trip and had a pleasant chat.[34]

Donald Sears

I was a pupil of Richard Purvis from 1966 to 1994. He was a demanding, sometimes unreasonable teacher, but he was also one of the best in the country and always expected as much from himself as he did from his pupils.

When I went to take what was to be my final lesson with him in October 1994, I was making my way down the side of his home to his studio at the back of the house when I heard him improvising on his custom-built Rodgers organ. I was about five minutes early, so I stopped and listened, not revealing my presence. He was playing on the string celestes, and the beauty of hearing him play in solitude almost stopped my heart. There it still was, the gorgeous registration, the divine legato and phrasing, the uncanny ability to embellish a theme with a myriad of colors and variations done so effortlessly I couldn't catch my breath. His death on December 25, 1994, certainly marked the end of an era in the organ life of America.[35]

Clarence Snyder

I was in Dr. Alexander McCurdy's organ class with Richard Purvis, Walter Baker, Claribel Thompson, and Jack Cook from 1935–1936. Richard played on his graduation recital from the Curtis Institute of Music the G Major P&F by Bach, Tu es Petra, among other pieces.

I was his assistant at St. James Church, Philadelphia, PA, for two years.

Richard played at my church in Montclair, NJ, the First Congregational, circa 1954. Here he improvised pieces later published, including The Little Bells [Les Petites Cloches].

I was playing the harp which had been given to me—not seriously. Richard wrote a piece for me for Harp and Soprano. I gave the music to a harpist in Ohio. It was never published.

I visited him in Oakland, CA, when I was in the Navy. He took me to one of his radio programs.

He had perfect pitch, you know, and could play anything he heard. He and I went to see Robin Hood [*The Adventures of Robin Hood,* 1938, score by Korngold]. We came back to St. James and he played most of the score on the organ by ear.

Richard liked to make his anthem accompaniments colorful; he would often have me play on one manual a melody he wanted brought out while he was playing with two hands on another manual.

Richard played organ for the occasional dance held in Casimir Hall at Curtis.

Richard was a fine improviser. He improvised the Xmas Eve service at Dr. McCurdy's church; choral music, harp, strings.[36]

Paul Stephen

Richard Purvis was one of the true "giants" as performer, arranger, composer, teacher, etc., with traditional and theater pipe organs. A "crossover" artist, he also performed popular music under the name of Don Irving because even then, there were those elitists who viewed this genre as "lowbrow."

Richard was very aware of the non-organist audience who loved hearing the organ, especially when playing the things they enjoy. Like many of his contemporaries, he was a great person first, musician second, and organist last, by including the "schmaltz" for those with heavy wallets wishing to donate towards a new organ or enlarging of an existing one.

My last time seeing and hearing Richard was in New Haven CT at Yale's Woolsey Hall. An all-Franck program, partially at the insistence of the university organist in the early-mid 80's; he played very well.[37]

Ed Stout

I interviewed Ed Stout at length at his home in Hayward, California, on August 31, 2010. Ed knew Richard better than almost anyone else and has great stories to tell.

I started working on the organ in 1959 at the cathedral. Purvis started in '48 or '49, so he had been there about 10 years. I started there but he didn't know it because my former boss, William N. Reid, had the contract for the organ in '58–'59, but he didn't like going there. He was in Santa Clara and didn't like going up to the cathedral, so he asked me as a former employee if I'd go up and do these service calls on Saturday nights. I was living in San Francisco at the time. I was introduced to Purvis by Tom Hazleton who took lessons from him on Saturday afternoons. Tom was always the last student and Keith Chapman was usually the next to last.

He insulted me—he loved doing that. We were over at the bishop's door which led out to the parking lot and Tom was going to give him a ride home. He lived in a nice flat on Filbert at the time, not too far from Bay Street. Tom said, "Ed, this is Richard Purvis, and Dick, this is Ed Stout. He's a very fine organ technician." Purvis looked at me and barked, "All organ men are phonies!" I thought, "I'm not going to take this," so I said, "Now I know why the walls in this place are as high as they are, because nothing else could contain your rudeness!" I went out the bishop's door and slammed it, and I remember pushing against the pneumatic closer to make it slam, loud. Well, they didn't come out and it was one of those minutes that went on forever. I thought, "Well, there goes that job, but I'll be damned if I'm going to work for someone like that." Finally they came out, and Purvis was bright red—his ears were red—and I thought, "God, wow." Tom was smirking, and we got into Tom's little Volkswagen. I got in the back seat and Purvis got in the passenger's seat and Tom drove, and Purvis turned around and said, "Your mother dresses you funny." That's all he said. I can remember as clearly as if it were yesterday.

So we went down California Street, out of the lot and up Jones. Tom did a U-turn in front of a place called Marvel Cleaners. Purvis waddled out of the car into the cleaners and came out with a suit on a hanger. He thrust it at me and I said, "Oh, I didn't know you were still wearing short pants." He said, "Your ears are too long." I hung the suit on a hook and we took him home. When we took off after dropping him at his place on Filbert, I said to Tom, "What happened in there?" Tom said that after I said that to him, he went into hysterical laughter and got down on his knees and was slapping his knee, and when he contained himself he said, "Tom, I really like that guy." And that began that long, long, long friendship and working relationship.

When we were up there on the hill, it was all business. It was "Mr. Purvis." It was all business, and he barked at everybody. You know, he was very shy, and the barking and sharp retorts and funny quips that he had, comments about your mother does this and your ears are too long, or whatever—it might be that's the way he survived, because he was quite shy, so he put up this big brick wall. He was like the Wizard of Oz, the little guy behind curtain. He was not little in professionalism and stature and as a human being, but he was shy, and he could hide behind the green curtain with a microphone and bark, and that protected him. But he was through and through a gentleman and one of the sweetest and most generous men I've ever known. I've heard stories about how he helped friends out of difficulties. He was extraordinarily generous as a human being. He just loved music and loved that organ up there. But he was a unique human being.

I worked for him for about four months, and he was sort of sizing me up, I could tell. He would make little remarks and he would say something about how he appreciated that I'd fixed something. It was only about four months and he said, "We really should have dinner." The first time I drove to his place on Filbert, it was on the upper of two flats, and we had a drink at his house. Then we went down the hill to a place called Caesar's. It was a wonderful Italian place on the corner of Filbert and Bay. When we got back and he said, "Oh my God, I've locked my keys in the house. They're on the counter." I said, "Well, what are we going to do?" He said, "You can go over the fence and climb up the outside plumbing and into the bath-room window. The bathroom window's open." And I said, "You want me to climb up to the second floor?" and he said, "You're an organ man, you can do that." So I did. I'd had enough to drink, and I went up the plumbing on the outside of the building and shimmied in head first, down onto the toilet seat, and unlocked his front door. He was simply marvelous. So then we started a ritual of having dinner at least once a month, sometimes more. He would tell me stories about his experiences. He told me about the war situation, and as he became comfortable and learned that he trusted me, if he told me something in confidence, I wouldn't repeat it. It took a while to build up that trust but then it was great.

I was given a sort of official title, and that was a joke, you know. Before I went to Grace Cathedral, you never heard of anybody who takes care of an organ as a "curator." "I'm the curator of a two-rank Wicks!" Now every little piss-pot organ has a "curator." Dean Bartlett liked titles. He was a great dean, and a wonderful gentleman. He always called me "Dr. Stout." When I first started working there, my little tuning bag was a leather bag, and I looked like a little country doctor (or veterinarian might be closer). He said to me one time, "You know, you take care of the chapel organ and you take care of the Alexander organ and now you're starting to take care of the carillon. You're our curator of musical instruments." And so on my early stationery I put "Curator of Musical Instruments" and referred to that title that Dean Bartlett bestowed on me. But it was tongue in cheek. He liked fancy titles, but I didn't take it seriously. It started as a joke at Grace Cathedral in 1960.[38]

Purvis never let anyone sit up in the choir until one event, and it was part of his shyness. He had a modesty guard on top of the big oak console so you couldn't see him at all. It was a piece of oak on three sides which made the top of the console higher. It went away later because one time a dumb clergyman swung around the corner and grabbed it, thinking it was part of console, and it went crashing onto the floor during the service, this big oak thing. Getting back to the modesty screen, out in the church you couldn't see the organist anyway. Maybe he had some music piled up on top of it and didn't want it showing, wanted it tidy, maybe the light, someone in the nave complained about the glare of the light? There could have been any number of reasons.

After the Christmas concert one year, Grace Cathedral's annual gift with the chorus, Purvis threw the party of the year at his Hyde St. flat. It was fabulous. A large crowd, Bishop Pike, Dean Bartlett, George Wright was invited, the place was packed with people he liked, and they all got along. It was his thank you for people who helped, people who copied manuscripts, got the orchestrations ready for the concert every year. Pike would always end up at the right end of the fireplace, telling stories. He was a great story teller, and there was always a group of people around Bishop Pike.

Purvis was very broad musically. I can tell you how broad he was. He loved the organist Larry Vannucci. Larry took lessons with Purvis; he studied classical organ and he never stopped taking classical piano. Vannucci could play the Chopin etudes at the age of 70, and well. But he made his living playing theatre organ, and Dick loved to hear him play at The Lost Weekend, which had a Wurlitzer pipe organ in the bar. It was at 30th and Taraval, and the building is still there. For 15 years it was legendary. Great entertainers would come out to hear him play jazz and the blues on the 10-rank Wurlitzer in the bar. It was like having a music lesson, because he was so musical. When Larry left there, he played at a place called the Harbor Lights in Tiburon on a Hammond. For a while there I had a white hearse I bought from a black funeral parlor in Palo Alto. It was a '49 Buick with a superior body, a great big thing, and the grille looked just like Jane Fonda's mouth, so we called it Miss Fonda. I always knew I could get an 8' pipe crate in the back. It was easy because it had rollers built in. I went downtown and I bought a whole bunch of garlands of plastic flowers, and I would make my friends lie in these flowers all around, and I'd go ripping around town in this thing. Now Purvis just loved this. He would never do that, but we'd ride over and park this damned hearse in front of the bar, and we'd go into the bar and drink and listen to Larry play.

One night Dick and I drove over to Tiburon in my hearse to hear Larry play at the Harbor Lights. It was getting late, maybe 2 o'clock, and we told Larry we were going to head back to the City. Larry begged Dick to stay because "the kids" were coming in soon to have a session. What he meant was the Mexican waiters and kitchen staff came over from Sam's and other restaurants to the Harbor Lights on a regular basis to play some of their "back country folk music" with their guitars and stringed instruments. Larry so was adept, he just "sat in" with them on the Hammond organ. So, Purvis and I stayed, and to be true, the music was very exciting. One kid had a little tap-tap something, castanets, and a pretty girl was singing some of the songs. Dick really was enjoying the music, because I saw his right hand tapping on the bar. Before long, Dick pulled the bar stool next to him and straddled it, and soon he's rapping out rhythm on the bar stool bongos. He was a total musician and every part of his being resonated with music. He had to get into it.[39]

Purvis and Virgil Fox knew each other. I don't think they were close friends, but they knew and respected each other. He didn't talk about Virgil to me very much.

Purvis did dedicate one set of pieces to E. Power Biggs. Dick told me that he thought that Biggs was more musical before he went off the end of the plank on the early stuff. Purvis recognized what Biggs was doing, but he felt his playing was more exciting when he was playing a little more romantically. I think E. Power Biggs made a record at St. George's Church in New York City, some Franck, I think, and I remember Dick commenting that that was darn good playing.

I remember when Bishop Pike ordained the first woman. During her first service at Grace Cathedral she walked out front to read the gospel. I was sitting next to Dick, and she made a Freudian slip: "And here beginning the *sexth* chapter of…" Dick broke out laughing, he grabbed his stomach and chortled. All the rest of the clergy sat there on the other side in stark terror, and here's Purvis bent over in hysterics because of the Freudian slip.[40]

Fred Swann

Richard Purvis was often crusty and impatient with people he felt were invading his space, or ones that interrupted him when he didn't wish to be interrupted.

One example I remember well: At the conclusion of a service in Grace Cathedral many years ago a sweet "little old lady" organist from the Midwest approached the console and gushed, "Oh, Mr. Purvis, I just love your music, and play it in my church whenever I can." He immediately responded, in a *very* gruff voice, "Well, I don't suppose there's anything I can do about that. Good day, Madam." Whereupon he turned and motioned me to follow him as he left, muttering.

Over the years I've played a number of recitals at Grace Cathedral. Once, a few years after his retirement, Dick came to hear me, and at the reception following he was almost gushy in his kind remarks about my playing, handling of the organ "just like I like it," and his demeanor was utterly kind and sincere. I don't know what made me do it, but I got a very severe look on my face, and in my best Purvis imitation growled, "And what would you know about it?!" I continued to glare, and five seconds later we both burst out laughing. He later told several mutual friends about "Swann's comeuppance." He mentioned it to me a number of times in the years before he died, so I knew we were still friends.[41]

Regarding a recital Purvis played at The Riverside Church on July 14, 1964, Swann recalls, "I remember it well! He arrived at the church 30 minutes after the program was to begin. I played a piece and kept the audience entertained, hoping he would show up."[42]

Bob Tall

Alex [Schreiner] and Frank Asper didn't get along too well. Alex was always telling Frank, "I'm a trained organist and I'm the principal organist here." But after radio shows on Tuesday when they'd deliver the mail, 40–50 cards would come to Alex, and there would be a big sackful of mail for Frank. Not great friends.

When Purvis went there to play a recital on the new organ in the 1950's, he was not aware that they didn't like each other. He invited them both to dinner at the Hotel Utah, and they both accepted. When they found he'd invited both of them, neither showed. Purvis waited and waited and that made him angry. The whole experience was a negative one, and he couldn't wait to go back and play his organ.

G. Donald [Harrison] said, "How did you like the [Tabernacle] organ?" Purvis answered, "It's all right, it's the room that makes the sound, but my organ at Grace Cathedral is better." G. Donald was taken aback, since the Tabernacle was his magnum opus.

G. Donald went out to Grace Cathedral and listened to Purvis play for an hour and a half, had dinner with him, and, according to Purvis, G. Donald agreed with Purvis that Grace Cathedral had the better organ.

Once Purvis said to me: "I am the master of intimidation. Your wig's on upside down, your teeth are in backwards."

The last time I saw him was [in 1976] at St. Mary's in San Francisco when Virgil was playing on a big five-manual Rodgers. Purvis also played a recital there. He said to me, "Why didn't you sell me one of these organs?" I was all dressed up for the concert, and when I saw Richard, I said "My eyes are in correct, my wig is not upside down," etc. Richard said, "I'm speechless."[43]

Barbara Tonsberg

See Chapter 14, "Purvis as Teacher."

Richard Torrence

Richard Torrence, who was Purvis's concert manager briefly in the mid-1970s, told of an exchange between Purvis and Virgil Fox that occurred at Columbia University's St. Paul's Chapel. (Compare with James Parry's account, above.)

"When Virgil came over to greet Richard, Richard snapped, "Must you make such a spectacle of yourself?" Virgil answered, "Must you be as rude in New York as you are in California?" Richard said, "You never play any of my pieces." Virgil responded, "That's because they don't develop!"[44]

June Townsend

Of all those who helped chronicle Purvis's life, June Townsend knew Richard longer than anyone else. June was born in 1909 or 1910 (she mentioned in a letter to John Shields in 1995 that she was 85), and she met Richard in 1934. She studied with him, assisted him at recitals, corresponded with him during the war, and helped copy and prepare many of his scores for publication. In 1967, while a student at Pacific Union College in Angwin, California, she wrote her master's thesis on Purvis.[45] That thesis has been a major source of information for this book. In 1995 June suffered a great personal tragedy: for the second time in her life she lost her home to fire. She wrote: "My house burned down and I lost my music in a local forest fire, but since I had loaned some to a friend, I was able to reclaim most of his [Richard's] compositions in my copy books."[46] According to the Seventh-Day Adventist Church in Napa, June died on February 12, 2002.

Although June's thesis is not reprinted here, the following memoir is quoted in its entirety.

"Memories of Richard Irven Purvis"
by June Brown Townsend [1995]

The first time I met Richard Purvis he acknowledged the introduction and promptly turned his back and returned to his friends. He hated to meet admirers.

At the fledgling Seventh-day Adventist Church of Hayward held in the Quaas home I became acquainted with John and Harry [Ingling] who were studying with the same teacher that was tutoring Richard. He had won an award when quite young for his playing and when he did "Humoresque" the teacher asked why he phrased it a certain way—it just came naturally to him. The boy had talent to be cultivated and his parents saw that it was. In his teens he played for an Episcopal Church and a movie theater nearby. Now he was organist at the First Baptist Church in Oakland and studied with Wallace Sabin and accompanied for him as he directed the Chorus of the Tuesday Noon Club and Wednesday Morning Chorale under Wallace Sabin.

He was only around 19 or 20 but Harry and I wanted to study with him. At my first lesson at his home in San Leandro (Oakland) I played Mendelssohn's "Consolation." He informed me that when a phrase repeats "Don't say the same thing the same way twice." Later he said that I sounded like a little mouse crawling over the keys. I had learned to play on a little Melodeon organ at home and preferred the organ touch. He wanted to know how I acted when I got mad and I said I went into a gloomy silence. He would have wanted me to show more passion in my playing, but his personality was intimidating and demanding and since Harry and I were both nervous, he said "Next Lamb to the Slaughter," which wasn't very encouraging. One time I came early for a lesson and he was upstairs getting dressed. I started practicing and when he came down he said, "Why don't you play like you did while I was putting on socks and tying a shoe?" He didn't miss a beat. His later students can probably agree.

He introduced me to BACH with the Two-Part Invention in F which does decidedly different things in each hand. I said this is like trying to pat your head and rub your stomach at the same time. He said, Yes but patting your head and rubbing your stomach is very simple compared to BA-CHH (German accent). He also gave me some simple Chopin studies. One was marked "Sotto Voce." In explaining "Sotto," he said it was like "Saute." My mother couldn't understand what slow cooking had to do with music. When I called him on it he thought it had to do with cutting up into little pieces—hence "small or low tone." Maybe his mother was cooking chopped up onions. So much for Julia Child.

He loaned me a copy of the book "The Magnificent Obsession," which emphasizes doing things quietly for others without thought of reward—Cast your bread on the waters and it comes back Cake! Although he played for other churches, his philosophy was along the lines of Unity and Christian Science. He carried out his Magnificent Obsession by lending me his music. He inspired in his pupils a sort of unasked for Hero Worship. When my father passed away, I sent him word that I'd like him to play for the funeral at the Presidio Chapel, as my Father was a Spanish American War veteran. My girlfriend and I were doing the music when he rushed in out of breath and took over, playing for her to sing "Face to Face" and giving moral support as I watched the mourners pass by. He said, "It's the least I could do." After the service we left him standing on the steps while we went off to the cemetery. My mother apologized to him later that we had left him without transportation.

He liked my music copy work, and showed me one of his first pieces called "Dream Vision"—"I see her face, my lady fair with rose hued hands and silken hair, And through she smiles and beckons to me, I sigh, for 'tis but a Vision I see." He said it was why organists stay awake nights. He said, when half asleep he could hear beautiful music; but if he got up to write it down, it was gone.

After my father died and our house burned down, he said I could do copy work for him to pay for my lessons.

He went back to Chicago for the big exposition, where he saw the new Hammond organ which had just been invented—the beginning of the electric organ age. Our SDA Church in Oakland got the first one, and since they were broadcasting, I got Richard and Harrold Hawley to play for a couple of them. Dick showed me how to set it up and I played for a song service and was told they could hear it clear out on the street. Beware of a heavy foot on the expression pedal!

Someone invited Richard to give an organ recital at Pacific Union College, my Alma Mater. He said he got lost in the middle of Bach's Toccata & Fugue in D minor and for awhile it was Dick Purvis instead of Bach.

I was at his home patching up old music with the radio playing. It was a Woman's Program explaining an apple recipe. "We want rings, not applesauce," I repeated. He countered with "Engagement Rings?" I rejoined with that was "Applesauce" (slang of the day). When she got into more intimate women's concerns, Dick said, "Lady, you're wasting your breath on this audience!" and turned it off.

His grandmother died and I offered my condolences. In typical rebuttal he replied that it was nothing to be sorry about, as it happened to everybody—but of course we miss her.

When he had to drop our lessons because of his studies, I went to the Chapel of the Chimes Crematorium Columbarium in Berkeley and started organ lessons with Harrold Hawley. Richard was also on the staff and played for some evening broadcasts from station KRE. When he played popular music, he went by the name "Don Irving," and sometimes I sat on the organ bench and turned pages for him on a stack of songs of the day, such as "Stars Fell on Alabama" and "Take a Letter, Miss Brown" (my name). Harold introduced me to the pipes in the organ loft and tuning and allowed me practice time, "as it was better for organs to be in use." One Sunday a church service was being broadcast somewhere when it suddenly went off the air. The Radio Man rushed out shouting, "Play Something, Play Something!" I turned to Handel's Largo and started when Harold appeared, climbed over the bench, pushed me aside, and said "You're not being paid for this!" When Dick arrived later, I told him I'd had my Big Moment and he asked, "Who was he?"

Since I lived near Newark (Fremont), I sometimes gave Dick a ride home. We stopped at a White Log Tavern (the McDonald's of the day) and I tried to swallow my peanut butter and jelly sandwich despite my big thrill. Since the Chapel was next to the Cemetery, Dick mentioned climbing over the fence, but thought better of it. There was a big dip in the street I didn't take. He said he used to drive a "Tin Lizzie" named "Elizabeth" and loved to swoop down it with his friends until he forgot one time that his father was on board!

He was Secretary of The American Guild of Organists, SF Chapter, and wanted me to join. He wanted to know if I would stand on my head in the middle of the street if he asked me to. That sounded like Politics and I declined! Later he joined Harrold Hawley in sponsoring me and I was IN regardless! I really appreciated the Guild recitals and the Diapason Magazine which opened up the organist's world to me.

Shortly before he went East, I asked him what he wanted for Xmas. He replied, "A four manual Aeolian-Skinner organ," so I said I'd see what I could do. I went home and carved a tiny organ out of a piece of wood and painted it up. The next time I saw him I said, "Here is the present you ordered." "I ordered?" he replied, and then was overwhelmed when he saw it. He even took it with him.

Soon he was offered a scholarship to the Curtis Institute of Music in Philadelphia. He was worried about finances in order to get there, so I offered him a couple of street-car tokens. He didn't think they would get him very far! He suggested I study with Wallace Sabin, his old mentor. I took lessons at a Berkeley Church and at his home. He informed me that I had a "Beer income and a Champagne appetite," due probably to the rarified atmosphere of music I'd been traveling in.

He informed me, "You'll shed some tears when I'm gone." I told him one time that he wasn't bothered with an Inferiority Complex (like I was). He replied, "Ow! But I'm not easily hurt." I meant it as a compliment. I wrote him at Curtis and said the sky had been crying (rainy season) ever since he left. He sent a card saying "Sledding was great fun."

When he was about to leave I said, "Thanks for making me a great musician." He characteristically replied, "Yes, and you don't know anything, you don't THINK, you never did think.—You'll make a good Church Organist." I wasn't expecting to become another Claire Coci!

My neighbors were going to Philadelphia and Dick was playing for some big event. I sent my regards, and when they saw him he nearly fell off the organ bench. I was equally thrilled when they returned and handed me his autographed bulletin.

I asked him how he could play those big recital pieces by memory, and he said, "My hands just go."

At Curtis he began composing, and sent me his manuscripts to copy for the publishers. He did so well that they gave him a scholarship to study Choirmaster work with the Boy Choirs. On the ship to England, he said there was a costume party, so he borrowed a blanket, painted his face with lipstick, and went as an Indian.

I needed a practice organ, so Harry and I stopped at the home of the pastor of the San Leandro (Oakland) Presbyterian Church. When he saw us he excused himself to change into formal attire and said, "I think I know what you came for." However, Harry and I had no intention of GETTING MARRIED. I only wanted to rent the organ! When I did get married I took George back there and reminded him of it. The organist there passed away and I got the job. Richard's family was rather close as two brothers married two sisters.[47] The other Purvis family attended this church and Beatrice, Dick's beautiful cousin, turned pages for me at an Easter service. I was invited to her wedding.

When Dick came home for a visit after his English experience, I took him over to the church. He said when he was young, they wouldn't let him play it for fear he might "break it," but I think he played one of his first recitals on it. He played his beautiful little arrangement of Bach's "Arioso" which was an improvement, if I can be so bold! I invited him to my home where Mom had "killed the old red rooster" and made chicken & dumplings. I showed him my "Hambone" organ which I had assembled from assorted parts I got from my organ technician. There were little wooden pipes and a blower from the juke box of the day. When he tried it out he decided it was not up to AGO specs. About this time a new lady came to church who could play as well as direct the choir, so I got "dumped." I left a note for Dick, saying I was crying. He replied that "knowledge is power," so I enrolled at San Jose State College and received an A.B. in Art with a minor in music.

World War II was on and Richard enlisted. He went from PFC to Warrant Officer and Chaplain's Assistant. He was in the Honor Guard for the President and the Queen, up close so he could see their faces. He and my brother were sent to Germany. He led his band in procession in the liberation of Paris. I copied his popular "Greensleeves" which he said he "wrote in a foxhole." Unfortunately he received a head wound and was captured by the enemy. There were endless marches and he was helped to survive by a Jewish doctor who hid medication in his shoes. He was Missing in Action and hope for him faded. However, he was liberated and hospitalized. He said the nurse said, Mr. Purvis, "Eat this," and I ate it. When he came home, his mother tried to stuff him, but he was afraid of getting a "spare tire."

By this time I was married and living in San Francisco. I played for our little Seventh-day Adventist Church on Capp St. near 24th and some meetings at the Masonic Hall nearby. Dick said he was born on the "corner of 26th" and his parents went to the Masonic Lodge. He also attended Fremont High School in Oakland where I had graduated. Strange how our paths had crossed. I had tried out for an organ position at St. Mark's Lutheran in SF and mentioned it to Dick. The next thing I knew, he had the job and talked them into bringing the console down from the loft to he main floor. I suggested he should be at Grace Cathedral and he was. Here his Boy Choir experience came into its own as he developed the Choir and Boys' School. His compositions increased as well as organ records.

I moved to Napa to a chicken ranch, but continued doing his copy work and took some lessons at the Cathedral which I paid for with fresh eggs. Since my husband worked in the City while I tried to run the ranch, marital problems developed. Richard encouraged me by writing, "Do something with your music." So I returned to Pacific Union College, not far from Napa, and over several years earned my Masters in Music. I also was given a plaque for forty years of service to the Napa SDA Church.

While playing there, a young boy came up and asked me if he could practice in exchange for playing. David Worth was introduced to Purvis and became his Assistant.

The last time I saw Dick was at his eightieth Birthday concert. We didn't look like we did sixty years ago. I said, "I've got four years up on you," and not to be outdone he answered, "I'll catch up." He didn't.

Rest in peace, Richard Irven Purvis R.I.P.[48]

James Welch

On May 4, 1980, I gave a recital on the Kimball organ at First Presbyterian Church, Oakland, which included Purvis's "Nocturne (Night in Monterey)." I was surprised when Purvis arrived for the recital. This was my first encounter with him. My journal states: "Richard Purvis showed up, which kind of scared me." Newton Pashley, organist of First Presbyterian Church, was also in attendance.

On December 31, 1986, I played Purvis's "Les Petites Cloches" as part of a recital at the Carmel Mission Basilica. In response to a letter and recital program I had sent to Purvis, I received the following letter:

My dear Jim:

Thank you so much for the program from the Carmel Mission and your cheerful breezy note. I'm grateful you played the "Little Bells" and I sincerely hope both you and the audience enjoyed it. You are certainly doing more than your share of keeping the music of Purvis alive, and I'm grateful.

Needless to say, I'm greatly looking forward to your concert here at Sts. Peter & Paul on March 29th. I like very much the work Jack Bethards is doing these days. He certainly has more than redeemed the name of Schoenstein. The old man, Felix, was a master builder from Germany. I remember several of his very fine trackers around the state, and, believe me, they were far better examples of organ building than many of the organs which replaced them.

About the Carol Rhapsody, when you are up here give me a call. We'll have lunch (or something) and I'll tell you the whole story which is much too long to scribble. Since my phone is unlisted I'm enclosing my card. Do call!

May 1987 bring you Health, Happiness, Prosperity and True Progress![49]

Again thank you for your interest and progress. I am truly grateful.

All the best,

Dick Purvis[50]

On March 27, 1987, I had lunch with Purvis in San Francisco. My journal states: "Over to Raffle's at Fox Plaza for lunch with Purvis. He was full of stories about SF, Wallace Sabin, Alfred Hollins, his time in England and studying chant in France, Isle of Wight, his regular disgust for academia, 'BORED' meetings of the AGO, etc. Very modest, didn't want to talk about HIS music—I wanted to, though. The food was awful, but it was fun seeing him and hearing him talk. He's a character, all right. I couldn't tell whether he really likes me, or whether he was just doing this as a favor for my playing his stuff all the time."[51]

In my score of his *Eleven Pieces for the Church Organist,* I recorded what Purvis told me on that occasion about his "Carol Rhapsody": "Written for Curtis Christmas Party to entertain faculty. In style of Radio City organist." When I asked him about his "Greensleeves," he responded, "Oh, yeah, Greenslobs."[52]

April 22, 1987

My dear Jim:

Here are the two works I promised you. Sorry to have been so slow in getting them to you, but things got a bit hectic in the teaching department around Easter. So many students needed extra help.

You truly did a fine job for Jack Bethards [inaugural concert at Sts. Peter & Paul, San Francisco, March 29, 1987]. He was elated and so was I. Thank you for playing my Toccata [Festiva] and thank you doubly for subtracting 5 years from my age! I was born in 1913, not 1918. Somewhere along the line, "3" was taken as "8."

I hope you will enjoy the Four Prayers and the Partita. I'm sorry the copy of the four Prayers is so marked up, but my old battered copy is all I have. In fact, it's been reproduced many times by students and colleagues.

Again thank you for a most enjoyable program—neatly and deftly played.

With every good wish for your continued progress and success, I am
Sincerely yours,
Richard Purvis[53]

In 1988, while University Organist at the University of California, Santa Barbara, I invited Purvis to present a recital there. His response to me:

September first 1988

My dear Jim:

Thank you so much for your letter and your tentative invitation to come to Santa Barbara. I would be most interested in accepting, providing too much is not expected of me. After all, I am no longer 16.

While I don't think I play quite as well technically, people still seem most interested in hearing me play. I just had two great sessions with the grand old Austin at the Bohemian Grove (my old teacher was one of the designers of that unique instrument). And there are scheduled concerts for U.O.P. [University of the Pacific, Stockton, California] and "The Art of the Organ" in Minneapolis.

If we can come up with something that will please and entertain the average audience, I would be most interested—but please no typical A.G.O. "doldrum."

Again, let me tell you how much I enjoyed seeing you at the O.H.S. bash [in San Francisco] and how much I enjoyed your delightful program

September first 1988

My dear Jim:

Thank you so much for your letter and your tentative invitation to come to Santa Barbara. I would be most interested in accepting; providing too much is not expected of me. After all, I am no longer 16.

While I don't think I play quite as well technically - people still seem most interested in hearing me play. I just had two great sessions with the grand old Austin at the Bohemian Grove! (my old teacher was one of the designers of that unique instrument). And there are scheduled concerts for U.O.P. and "The Art of the Organ" in Minneapolis

If we can come up with something that will please and entertain the average audience, I would be most interested — but please no typical A.G.O. "doldrum"

Excerpt of letter to the author, September 1, 1988.

at "Notre Dame de Victoires" [where I performed Purvis's variations on "Chartres," among other works].

> All the best,
> Dick

P.S.: Incidentally I was "rehabilitated" for 2 months at Santa Barbara after my P.O.W. experience in W.W.II. I was billeted at the old "Miramar." Is it still there?[54]

On February 10, 1991, I played the dedication recital on the new Schoenstein Choir Organ at St. Agnes Church, San Francisco. Joining me in a performance of Purvis's "Dialogue Monastique" for two organs was Leonard Fitzpatrick, who played the gallery organ. Purvis attended. I didn't know it at the time, but this was the last time I would see him.

In October 1991, I planned a six-month leave of absence from the University of California, Santa Barbara, for advanced study elsewhere. I thought about studying in Boston, Washington, D.C., or Europe. Having met recently with Purvis, I also considered living in San Francisco and studying with him for a season. I wish now that I had.[55]

On December 15, 1991, in a Christmas concert at St. Agnes, I played Purvis's "Poème Mystique" and "Caravan of the Three Kings," and accompanied the Menlo Park-based Valparaiso Singers in "What Strangers Are These?" Purvis was invited but was unable to attend.

Jean White

See Chapter 14, "Purvis as Teacher."

David Worth

David Worth was Purvis's assistant in the mid-1960s. He recalls the following experiences:

> Princess Margaret and Lord Snowdon, her new husband, came once. They stayed over at The Huntington Hotel, I think, and we had an evening service in her honour. I can see her sitting in the front pew. The cathedral choir sang the Gelineau setting of Psalm 23, to which Richard had written a very simple ostinato/obbligato. I played on the celesta set in front of the choir in the chancel.

Archbishop Michael Ramsey visited the Cathedral [on February 24, 1965]. I remember his very bushy eyebrows! Musically I remember that Richard played the Campra "Rigaudon" for entrance music.

Duke Ellington's first West coast concert tour brought him to Grace Cathedral [on September 16, 1965]. I recall Ellington stretched out on a small couch in the sacristy just before the concert. He seemed very much a quiet, introspective man. I don't recall the cathedral choir rehearsing with Ellington, but I do know that at the concert they sang two choral pieces that Richard had set long before. One was his "Lonesome Valley." There was an awkward moment getting the piece started at the performance; Richard and Ellington were conducting and Richard and the choir didn't seem to know when to start. A CD was recently released of that first concert at Grace, but none of the Purvis things were on it.

The 1960's were times of happenings around Grace. Very much on the cutting edge of social and political issues. I remember Barry Goldwater coming to the 9:00 a.m. service. (I sensed no one at the cathedral wanted him at 11:00. This was at the time of the Republican convention.) I have the 11:00 service leaflet, and Caspar Weinberger was a reader at that service. Richard never spoke about political things to me. I suspect he felt it was beyond our concerns and he was very independent about political stuff. Probably kept those opinions to himself and his few closest friends.

I recall his concept of what worship was all about, though. Early on in my studies we had a very uncharacteristic conversation in which he offered how he saw the intent of his music at the cathedral, suggesting that even little Mrs. McGillicuddy, who was a cook during the week down the street and didn't know a piano from a ballet, would chance in to the cathedral and hear the organ, and be deeply moved by that first encounter to return. It was one of the more spiritual moments of his expressions.

My memory of how he offered me the assistant position was profound. He had been encouraging me to audition at Curtis. I had applied and was awaiting an audition appointment. He had noted on one letter from Curtis what pieces I might start to memorize (and that how sometimes a very introspective piece might be more telling in such an audition, so one of his choices was "O Mensch bewein," something he played uniquely). I got another letter from Curtis saying the appointment was pending my teacher's letter of reference. I took it to him at my next lesson. His response was that we were going to have a brief lesson that day and then go out for a talk. He took me down to Blum's at the Fairmont, ordered a brioche and coffee for both of us, and then told me he felt that I would find a more valuable musical learning experience staying at the cathedral as his assistant! Entirely shocked I was!

Richard was always perfunctory, presumptive and strict. I remember one Sunday morning when the choir came in to rehearse in the chancel before the service that a young chorister was seated alone over on the organ side, clearly in trouble. About ten minutes into the rehearsal that chorister suddenly stood up, took off his glasses, threw them into the middle of the chancel and walked out. Richard seemed entirely unmoved (and John Shields went out to see after the young man). I have no idea what was behind it all.[56]

David Worth recalls that the legendary newspaperman Herb Caen mentioned Purvis in one of his columns in the *San Francisco Chronicle*,[57] but finding such a reference would be a challenge.

Notes

1. The Aeolian-Skinner organ was in fact installed in 1934, more than a decade before Purvis's arrival at Grace Cathedral.

2. Frances Shelby Beniams, "Northern California-San Francisco AGO Chapter History." *The American Organist*, April 1984, Vol. 18, No. 4. 154.

3. Jack Bethards, telephone conversation, November 30, 2010.

4. Interview with Donald Braff, October 5, 2010, Palo Alto, California.

5. This could not be verified.

6. The newsletter stated: "This interview was conducted by ORGANIST NEWS more than a year before his death, but is published for the first time here." "An Interview with the Late Richard Purvis," *Daffer Church Organs Newsletter*, Fall 1995, Vol. 7, No. 3. Daffer Church Organs, Jessup, Maryland.

7. I asked Steve for the recipe for Bug Juice, and he replied:

    Recipe:

        Get in car

        Go up to 280

        Exceed 100 mph for 5 miles

        Go back home

        Scrape bugs off windshield

        Add water and mix

        If it still does not taste as you would wish....

        Add 1 liter of dark rum

    Steve Cohen, e-mail, June 10, 2011.

8. Steve Cohen, "Recollections of a Choir Boy at El Rancho del Obispo. *Russian River Recorder*, Winter 2002. Used by permission. Excerpts were also published in *In Quire, A Newsletter of the Grace Cathedral Choir of Men and Boys*, Volume 1, Issue 10, January 25, 2005, and Volume 1, Issue 11, February 1, 2005.

9 Tom DeLay, e-mail, 2010.

10. Christian Elliott, e-mail, October 24, 2010.

11. Jim Hansen, telephone conversation, November 3, 2010.

12. Rodgers Jenkins, telephone conversation, November 1, 2010.

13. Joyce Jones, telephone conversation, November 22, 2010.

14. Vaughn Jones, e-mail, April 7, 2012.

15. Keyes Kelly, telephone conversation, April 12, 2012.

16. Richard Kline, e-mail, October 30, 2010.

17. Michael Lampen, e-mail, April 28, 2011.

Ed Stout responds to this story: "Richard Purvis could not have climbed over the fence and gate, even with rocket assist! There are many tall tales about the place. I do, however, remember hearing of someone climbing over the chapel gate, but I believe Richard's physical condition would have prevented even considering such a feat. Dick fought a weight problem and he told me directly he was subjected to German experiments while in prison camp and his metabolism was never right after that." Ed Stout, e-mail, April 29, 2011.

18. Lyn Larsen, telephone interview, June 1, 2009.

19. Lyn Larsen, telephone interview, December 1, 2010.

20. Stephen Loher, e-mail, November 8, 2010.

21. Stephen Loher, e-mail, May 30, 2009.

22. Actually Purvis did drive, but he had given up his car when he lived in apartments close to the Cathedral.

23. Stephen Loher, e-mail, June 6, 2009.

24. Stephen Loher, conversation, Salem, Oregon, September 27, 2010.

25. Douglas Metzler interview, June 24, 2010, Bothell, Washington.

26. Jonas Nordwall, e-mail, June 2009.

27. Jonas Nordwall, interview, September 27, 2010, Aloha, Oregon.

28. On June 9, 2011, I received in the mail a small Principal pipe with the following memo: "Here is a memento from the Grace Cathedral organ—collected circa 1950. This, along with several others (maybe 5-6), was removed as a prank by mischievous (aka creative thinking) choristers prior to one of the Thursday night rehearsals (when we normally arrived an hour or so early to play basketball or engage in novel 'activities' as interests dictated at the time—e.g., releasing pigeons in the church that were secured from the spiral stairways leading to the catwalks in the top of the church, or igniting delayed explosion cherry bombs in the church crypt). Of course, the impact of the missing pipes was enjoyed by all of us as a hissing sound in the chancel for some weeks (probably not many) until the pipes were replaced. As I recall, the culprit(s) were never exposed—another 'thorn in the side' of RIP."

29. Brad Smith, telephone conversation, September 27, 2012.

30. Donna Parker, interview, September 27, 2010.

31. James Parry, e-mail, September 14, 2011.

32. Bill Rhoads, e-mail, September 21, 2010.

33. Manuel Rosales, e-mail, November 7, 2011.

34. David Rothe, e-mail, December 21, 2011.

35. Donald Sears, San Francisco Chapter AGO newsletter, July–August 2003; see additional text from this article in Chapter 5, "Later Years," and further comments in Chapter 14, "Purvis as Teacher."

36. Clarence Snyder was organist at Longwood Gardens from 1956 to 1978. Letter from Clarence Snyder to James Welch, November 1, 2010.

37. Paul Stephen, a student of Virgil Fox, is an organ enthusiast in Massachusetts. Paul Stephen, e-mail, October 29, 2010.

38. Ed Stout, interview, August 31, 2010.

39. Ed Stout, e-mail, April 23, 2011.

40. Ed Stout interview, August 31, 2010.

41. Fred Swann, e-mail, September 3, 2010.

42. Fred Swann, e-mail, August 30, 2010.

43. Bob Tall, telephone interview, October 12, 2010.

44. Richard Torrence, telephone conversation, November 23, 2010.

45. Townsend may also have compiled the Biographical Data in preparation for her master's thesis. A number of the dates in the Biographical Data are incorrect.

46. Letter from June Townsend to Donna Parker, October 4, 1995.

47. Richard's uncles or aunts? He had only one sibling, his brother Robert.

48. Townsend Memories, 1995.

49. Compare this line with the passages Purvis copied from *A Course in Miracles,* found at the conclusion of Chapter 15.

50. Letter to the author, January 26, 1987.

51. Personal journal entry of interview with Richard Purvis, March 27, 1987, San Francisco.

52. Interview with Purvis, San Francisco, March 27, 1987.

53. Letter to the author, April 22, 1987.

54. Letter to the author, September 1, 1988.

55. Personal journal entry, October 1991.

56. David Worth, e-mail, September 25, 2010.

57. David Worth, e-mail, April 28, 2011.

CONCLUSION

On September 7, 2003, shortly after what would have been Purvis's 90th birthday, friends gathered once again at Grace Cathedral to hear Tom Hazleton perform an all-Purvis recital—including an encore improvisation on "Somewhere Over the Rainbow." It was the first time Tom had played a recital at Grace Cathedral in nearly three decades, and he too would be gone within three years.

The event was one more manifestation of the lasting impact Purvis had on several generations of American organists, through his compositions, his recordings, his teaching, and his friendship.

Purvis's early life was one of hard work and good luck, studying with fine teachers and landing numerous opportunities to perform both classical and popular music. He soon went from the highs of study at the elite Curtis Institute to the devastating experiences of war, including captivity in a prison camp.

Purvis never married and had no children; references to family were rare. He appears not to have spoken openly about his sexual orientation.

All three areas—war-time experiences, family dynamics, and sexual orientation—may have affected his psyche. His ever-eccentric and sometimes combative personality were well known. But without more first-hand information, the reasons remain conjectural.

A quarter of a century at Grace Cathedral placed Purvis permanently on the musical map of America. From this elegant aerie atop Nob Hill, he performed, taught, and composed. Yet as the international musicologist David Urrows points out, "Purvis' career was on an inevitable collision course with history. He clearly despised vernacular traditions taking over in church music." The consecration of Grace Cathedral in 1964, perhaps the high point in his ecclesiastical career, "occurred at exactly the moment when the very traditions he loved were being suppressed in favor of guitar-wielding clerics with a mission for social (and not principally religious) change.... He was, like so many, born too late in some ways."[1]

Purvis was a loyal San Francisco musician. After studying in the East, he could have remained there and made a name for himself. He later received an offer to take a prominent position in Boston, but turned it down. Clearly, he possessed an independent Western spirit that kept him anchored in California, developing his own unique style and staying true to it throughout his career.

What I can say, and I believe I speak for many others, is that Richard Purvis awakened in me a love for organ music in a way that no one else ever did. Although I never heard him perform in person and never studied with him, he was essential to the inspiration that led me ultimately to pursue a career in organ. For this I thank him.

Note

1. David Urrows, e-mail, October 31, 2011.

ΛPPENÒIX Λ

**"The Secret of Adding Orchestral Color To Hammond Registration"
by Richard Purvis**
The Etude, Volume 63, No. 3 (March 1945), 137.

The article includes a photo of Purvis, in army uniform and at the Hammond organ. (See photo on page 87.) The caption reads: "W/O [Warrant Officer] Richard Purvis, Band Leader, 28th Infantry Division"

In modern orchestration one of the most effective means of adding richness and fullness to a melodic line or an accompaniment is that of doubling. For example, a melody played on the Oboe may be doubled on the English Horn an octave lower; one played on a Trumpet may be doubled by a Trombone, or one played on a Violin may be doubled by a Viola. You will note that the doubling is done by instruments of the same tonal characteristics as the instrument employed in soloing the actual melody. In other words, wood-wind doubles wood-wind; brass doubles brass; and string doubles string. Thanks to the varied possibilities of the Hammond, this same principle may be applied to your own playing in your own home with telling effect.

Let us use "Suggestions for Hammond Registration" (Bulletin No. 2)* as our text book. If you will turn to pages two and three you will find the pitches controlled by the draw bars clearly defined. Those which sound the "key-note" in various octaves are I, III, IV, VI and IX. The interval of the fifth (in various octaves) is sounded by II, V, and VIII. In other words, if I drew I, III, IV, and IX and played C, I should hear C sounding at five different pitches at the same time. However, if I drew II, V, and VIII and played the same C, I would hear G (instead of C) sounding at three pitches. From this experiment we can easily see that I is the double of III, and III is the sub octave (or double) of IV. In similar manner, II is the double of V and V is the double of VIII. This may seem a bit complicated at first, but a few minutes perusal of the chart on page two of our guide and a repetition or two of the afore-mentioned experiment at the console will no doubt clarify matters.

A Practical Application

Now let us proceed to a practical application of doubling (or sub-coupling as it is sometimes called). Turning to pages 8 and 9 of Bulletin No. 2, we find a greatly varied list of Hammond Stops. A simple and colorful example is the Hohl Flute. At 8' pitch (or piano pitch) its designation is 003100000. Now since I is the sub octave of III and III is the sub octave of IV, at 16' pitch (or one octave below piano pitch) the composition of the same stop is 301000000. By the use of a simple bit of addition, we arrive at the conclusion that a Hohl Flute doubled WITH ITSELF would be registered 304100000. The following chart will illustrate this more vividly.

	I	II	III	IV	V	VI	VII	VIII	IX
Hohl Flute 8'	0	0	3	1	0	0	0	0	0
Hohl Flute 16'	+3	0	1	0	0	0	0	0	0
Hohl Flute 16' & 8'	3	0	4	1	0	0	0	0	0

Such a simple problem in addition could be solved by a child and yet this formula—plus a bit of common sense—will greatly enrich your palette of tonal colors.

A problem that is a bit more difficult is forming the true double to the Quintadena. At 8' pitch this delightful stop is formed through setting the draw bars at 003130000; at 16' foot pitch it would appear 331000000; hence at the two pitches its indication would be 334130000.

	I	II	III	IV	V	VI	VI	VIII	IX
Quintadena 8'	0	0	3	1	3	0	0	0	0
Quintadena 16'	+3	3	1	0	0	0	0	0	0
Quintadena 16' & 8'	3	3	4	1	3	0	0	0	0

For our last illustration of doubling at the sub octave, let us consider a type of doubling that calls for a bit of common sense plus mathematics. The composition of a Corno d'Amore is 006751000, hence its sub octave is 657100000. Now if we add these two factors together our result is 6 5 13 8 5 1 0 0 0. "A ha!" you say, "your system isn't fool proof. Since there are only eight dynamic degrees on a draw bar, thirteen is an impossibility." And right you are, but let's try a little experiment. On A set up 006751000 and play middle C and the C one octave lower. Listen to the sound carefully. Now on B set up 658851000 and play middle C only. Is there any perceptible difference in the sound produced by these two means? Under normal circumstances the answer would be negative. From this, we can reasonably conclude that any number greater than 8 may be effectively supplanted by 8.

One word of caution. When using doubles—or sub octaves—avoid the lower range of the manuals. Any pitch lower than a third below middle C is apt to be "muddy" or "growly."

Now let us consider the reverse process—namely, doubling at the super octave. Again let us refer to pages two and three of "Suggestions for Hammond Registration" (Bulletin No. 2). By a bit of perusing we discover that IV is the super octave (pitch sounding one octave higher) of III, VI is the super octave of IV, and IX is the super octave of VI. By the same virtue, V is the super octave of II and VIII is the super octave of V. From this (and the similar paragraph in Part I) one can readily see that whether a draw bar plays the role of a sub or super octave is relative to circumstances.

Let's go back to our old friend the Hohl Flute. At 8' pitch the draw bars are set 003100000. At 4' pitch (one octave higher than piano pitch) we would set our draw bars 000301000. Resorting to simple addition our draw bars would appear 003401000 if we doubled this stop at the super octave.

Another Example

For another example we'll dig up the Quintadena. Its 8' set-up is 003130000, while at 4' pitch its registration is 000301030. Thus, if the super octave is employed with the unison pitch we would set the draw bars at 003431030. Here let me add a word of caution. In most rooms the VIII bar at 3 will be too prominent, so reduce it to 2 or 1. In other words, "voice" the stop to suit the room in which you are playing.

No doubt many of you are wondering if it is not possible to employ the sub octave and the super octave simultaneously. It most certainly is possible and one may obtain a good many Debussy-like effects in this manner. At 8' pitch (piano pitch) an Unda Maris is formed 002100000. Draw the Chorus Control and turn the tremolo on one third of the way. Try a few chords and note the ethereal timbre of this delicate stop. When "spread" the sheer beauty of this stop is greatly enhanced. Let us extend this color over three pitches by use of the sub and super octave.

	I	II	III	IV	V	VI	VII	VIII	IX
Unda Maris 8'	0	0	2	1	0	0	0	0	0
Unda Maris 4'	0	0	0	2	0	1	0	0	0
Unda Maris 16'	2	0	1	0	0	0	0	0	0
Unda Maris 16', 8', & 4'	2	0	3	3	0	1	0	0	0

Set your draw bars at the sum of the three above factors and play a few chords whose lowest note is not far below middle C. It sounds much like the effect derived from muted strings in a very full orchestration, doesn't it?

That you will want to sit at the console and experiment to your heart's content, I know. Try "spreading" your favorite combinations and see if your vocabulary of "effects" is not greatly increased. You will find endless pleasure in the increased color the use of sub and super octaves places at your disposal.

The demand for tonal color is a natural one. The great variety of instruments in the orchestral tonal mass, now heard via the talking machine, the radio, and the cinema, is doubtless responsible for this.

---

* Note: Bulletin No. 2 is given to each Hammond owner at the time of purchase. If you don't possess this helpful pamphlet, it may be obtained by writing to the Hammond Instrument Co., 2915 Northwestern Avenue, Chicago, Illinois.

At the bottom of the page is the phrase "FORWARD MARCH WITH MUSIC"

APPENDIX B

"A History of Grace Cathedral, " 2007
by Michael D. Lampen, Archivist, Grace Cathedral
Used by permission.

Introduction

Grace Cathedral is located on historic Nob Hill in San Francisco, California, adjacent to the California Street cable car line, at 1100 California Street near Taylor Street. It is one of over eighty cathedrals of the Episcopal Church in the United States. The word "cathedral" refers to the bishop's chair, or "cathedra" which makes the church the bishop's official seat. Grace Cathedral is the cathedral church of the Episcopal Diocese of California, originally statewide in area, now comprising most of the San Francisco Bay Area counties. The Cathedral is administered by the dean and chapter, with the support of a board of trustees and the cathedral congregation. Grace Cathedral is San Francisco's largest traditional-style church building and America's third largest Episcopal cathedral. It may be the world's largest all-concrete and steel building in the late Gothic Revival style. A noted tourist attraction, the Cathedral is also a designated city landmark. Grace Cathedral is known for its Ghiberti Doors of Paradise replicas, AIDS Chapel, varied stained glass, renowned pipe organ, carillon and choir, and as the birthplace of the spirituality-based labyrinth revival in the United States.

History

An ancestral parish, Grace Church, was founded on Powell Street in 1849 by the Rev. Dr. John Ver Mehr, during the California Gold Rush. Grace Chapel was replaced by a larger church in 1851. In 1862 an imposing third Grace Church was built, further up the later-named Nob Hill. Bishop William I. Kip, First Bishop of California, served for a short time as rector, and the church was called Grace "Cathedral" during his tenure. This was the second such designation in the Episcopal Church, but being unofficial, it was later dropped. Grace Church was destroyed in the fire that followed the great 1906 San Francisco earthquake. Bishop William F. Nichols, Second Bishop of California, saw in the disaster the opportunity to fulfill his vision of a hilltop cathedral. Railroad baron Charles Crocker and his son, banker/philanthropist William H. Crocker had built adjacent Nob Hill mansions (1876, 1888) on the hill's western crest, and both homes were destroyed in the 1906 fire. Bishop Nichols convinced William H. Crocker and the other heirs of Charles Crocker to donate the property to the diocese as a cathedral site, the cathedral receiving its name and founding congregation from the ruined parish church. A temporary pro-cathedral opened on the site at Easter, 1907.

The first, north-facing, Grace Cathedral design was submitted by English Gothic Revival architect George Frederick Bodley of Bodley and Hare, in 1907, but his subsequent death led to a more imaginative 1909 design by his partner Cecil Hare. The cornerstone for Hare's design was laid in 1910, and the much beloved Dean J. Wilmer Gresham was chosen as the first dean. Plans were changed, and American architect Lewis P. Hobart was appointed cathedral architect. His revised plans placed the cathedral facing west, its façade opening east to the (future) adjacent park and nearby hotels. The crypt portion of Hobart's design was built, and this 'Founders Crypt' served as the cathedral from 1914 to 1930. Design revision continued, resulting in a seismically stronger structure featuring a riveted steel frame, with bare concrete rather than cut stone. Hobart's final design was inspired by the High Gothic cathedrals of Amiens, Beauvais and Paris, but also used Spanish and English Gothic elements. Following a fund-raising campaign, construction began in 1928 and the Chapel of Grace, first completed unit, opened in 1930. A gift of the Crocker family, the chapel stands on the site of their mansion's front steps. Construction continued with the choir, transepts and first half of the nave, but halted as the Depression deepened in 1934. A temporary metal partition closed off the half-finished nave. An adjacent builder's shack, converted into the tiny Wayside Chapel of Saint Francis in 1944, was popular with servicemen and their families. It was moved to a Crocker family ranch in 1973.

English-born San Francisco dentist Nathaniel Coulson donated the Singing (north) Tower and carillon of bells, completed in 1941. The tower stood alone as a 'campanile' until incorporated into the finished cathedral. In 1960 the Golden Anniversary Committee launched the cathedral completion campaign. Weihe, Frick & Kruse, architects, largely followed Hobart's design. Construction resumed in 1961, and included the final half of the nave and the Childrens' (south) Tower. Donors of many denominations, and several faiths, contributed to its completion. The largely completed Grace Cathedral was consecrated November 20, 1964, and the first Holy Eucharist using the new central High Altar was held the following Sunday.

The Cathedral is 329 feet (100 m) long and the façade towers rise 174 feet (53 m) from street level. The central fleche rises 247 feet (75 m) from the adjacent sidewalk. The nave interior is 91 feet (28 m) tall to the vaulting. The elevation of the sanctuary floor is 300 feet (91 m) above sea level. A large portion of the interior vaulting and cast stone walls of Grace Cathedral remain uncompleted. All of the older cathedral lead roofs have been replaced in lead-coated copper, and the building's exterior has been waterproofed.

Organs, Carillon and Choirs

Grace Cathedral is known for its outstanding organs and carillon, as well as its famed choir of men and boys. The cathedral's Aeolian-Skinner organ (1934) is one of the earliest and most acclaimed classic-style American organs, and has been augmented with divisions by Casavant Freres (1974) to 7466 pipes. It is the fourth largest church organ in California. The mobile combination memory console (2000) is by the Schoenstein Company of San Francisco (founded 1877). The smaller Chapel of Grace organ (1929), an Aeolian updated by Aeolian-Skinner, has 1422 pipes. The cathedral's hand-pumped William Davis organ (New York, 1862) is one of the earliest American organs in the west still in use.

The 44-bell carillon, cast by Gillett & Johnston of England (1938) includes the 6-ton bourdon bell, largest in the western United States. Except for the bourdon, the bells are in fixed position (non-traditional carillon) and all are rung by electronic activation of their hammers. They are also played from a keyboard. The carillon hung for a year at the 1939–1940 Golden Gate International Exposition on Treasure Island in San Francisco Bay, while the tower was being completed.

The cathedral men's choir was augmented with boys in 1913, making it the fifth oldest Anglican male choir in the nation, and one of ten still surviving in the Episcopal Church. The choir is known for its mastery of traditional Anglican church music and its high performance standards.

Columbarium

The Chapel of Saint Francis, the cathedral columbarium, occupies two tiers in the gallery level of the Singing Tower. Dedicated in 1986, the columbarium was completed in 1996 (William Turnbull and Associates) and is the first columbarium allowed to be built in San Francisco since 1894. Wall cabinets contain 2992 niches, reserved for individual urns, containing ashes or mementos. Cathedral persons of note inurned in the columbarium are tower/carillon donor Nathaniel Coulson, Bishop Edward L. Parsons, Bishop Henry H. Shires, Dean Stanley F. Rodgers, *and organist-choirmaster Richard Purvis* [emphasis added]. The principal chapel furnishing is the cathedral's former High Altar (in use as such 1907–1964).

Cathedral Close

The Grace Cathedral close, or precinct, occupies a sloping 2.7 acre (1.1 hectare) city block on Nob Hill, part of the historic neighborhood containing the 19th century mansions of San Francisco's "nobs". The Crocker rear carriage gateway and boundary walls (1876) survive along the north and east borders of the close. Diocesan House (Hobart, 1935), the administrative building of the diocese, is at the northeast corner of the close, with the

Cathedral School (Rockrise & Watson, 1966) at the northwest corner, and the Chapter House (cathedral administrative building)(William Turnbull, 1995) between them. The cathedral close was completed in 1993–1995. The project included a front stairway and outdoor labyrinth, central courtyard over an underground garage, a school addition, expanded Diocesan House, and the new Chapter House. The latter building replaced the former Cathedral House, which stood on the site of the cathedral's front steps. Opened in 1912 as the second home of the Church Divinity School of the Pacific (first Episcopal seminary in the west), the Tudor-style building became a postgraduate seminary in 1939, and then the cathedral administrative building, before demolition in 1993. Meeting rooms and a gift shop and café are located in the renovated cathedral crypt, and outdoor landscaping includes a biblical garden.

Cathedral School for Boys

The Cathedral School for Boys (1275 Sacramento Street), established in 1957, is an Episcopal cathedral-affiliated primary school, the first of its kind in the west, and is recognized as one of San Francisco's top grammar schools. The school blends high academic and personal standards with diversity and community values in a spiritual setting. The faculty of 40 teaches 240 students in grades K–8, and the school is open to application for all qualified boys. Several students are on scholarships. Boys with musical ability may audition for the cathedral choir. The school included a rooftop playground and a cathedral crypt gymnasium.

Bishops and Deans

Bishops of the Diocese of California

1. William I. Kip, 1857–1893
2. William F. Nichols, 1893–1924
3. Edward L. Parsons, 1924–1940
4. Karl M. Block, 1940–1958
5. James A. Pike, 1958–1966
6. C. Kilmer Myers, 1967–1979

7. William E. Swing, 1980–2006
8. Marc H. Andrus, 2006–present

Deans of Grace Cathedral

1. J. Wilmer Gresham, 1910–1939
2. Thomas H. Wright, 1941–1943
3. Bernard N. Lovgren, 1946-1951
4. C. Julian Bartlett, 1956–1975
5. Stanley F. Rodgers, 1975–1977
6. David M. Gillespie, 1979–1985
7. Alan W. Jones, 1985–present

(Bishop Block was acting dean in 1943–1946 and in 1951–1956, with Canon Eric Montizambert dean in all but name during the latter period.)

Recordings

The Grace Cathedral Choir has made many CD recordings since their first LP in 1976. Their first DVD, "Sounds of the Season," was issued in 2004. Notable organists who have recorded at Grace Cathedral include cathedral organist-choirmasters Richard Purvis and John Fenstermaker, former organist Susan Matthews, and guest organists Michael Murray and Catharine Crozier. Jazz great Duke Ellington premiered and recorded his "Sacred Concert" at Grace Cathedral in 1965, and Vince Guaraldi recorded his acclaimed jazz mass (the "Grace Cathedral Concert") at the Cathedral the same year. Others who have recorded here include Art Garfunkel, Beaver & Krause, Cal Tjader, Al Stewart, and Bola Sete. Grace Cathedral has hosted famed organists, choirs and musicians from around the world. Numerous concerts, dance and drama performances have also been held at the Cathedral. A complete discography is available in the cathedral web site (under Tales from the Crypt, The Cathedral Sings).

Appendix C

"Winds of God—75 Years of the Great Organ at Grace Cathedral"[1]
by Michael Lampen, Archivist, Grace Cathedral
Used by permission.

To walk into Grace Cathedral with the organ deep into a towering Bach fugue or a mystic Messaien prayer is an awesome, cosmic experience. Even more thrilling is the sudden ending of a great crescendo, when dying reverberations sound through the Cathedral for a full seven seconds. No other musical instrument has the power, the near-orchestral range and the sonic variety of a great organ. Grace Cathedral's 7466-pipe Aeolian-Skinner instrument, the Charles B. Alexander Memorial Organ, is one of the finest American classic style organs, and is among the largest church organs in the west. It is also the largest of Grace Cathedral's three organs, the others being the Chapel of Grace Aeolian-Skinner (1930) and the portable William Davis hand-pumped organ (1862), among California's oldest. May, 2009 marks the 75th birthday of the Charles B. Alexander Organ, Grace Cathedral's "great" organ.

An organ is a dense forest of pipes, part wind instrument and part keyboard instrument, played on one or more 'manuals'. The organ principle can be illustrated by an open-ended whistle. Air is blown into the narrow mouthpiece, past a little side slit that allows a lip or metal tongue to vibrate and give off a note, causing the body of the whistle to vibrate in

sympathy and accentuate the note. The length of an organ pipe, ranging from pencil-sized to 32 feet, controls the pitch. Pencil pipe notes are
near the upper limit of human hearing, while the giant pipes are more felt
than heard. Brass-sounding cylindrical pipes are made of mixtures of zinc,
lead, copper and/or tin, while violin and woodwind tones are produced
by rectangular oak pipes. Pipes of specific tonal qualities have inherited
colorful names such as Echo Gamba and Lieblich Gedeckt. Most pipes
stand in sets on wind chests, and each set is enclosed in a wind chamber,
with moveable shutters to control volume. A large organ has a console
with several manuals to play the several major divisions of pipes, including a keyboard for the feet! An array of white knobs (draw stops) flanks
the manuals. Using a customized computer system, the stops can be set
individually or in groups to mix and match pipe combinations, creating
an almost unlimited palette of sound colors. In addition to the draw stops
there are tilting tablets, pistons, studs and levers. While all pipe organs
were once hand-pumped, electricity has supplied pump power for all but
the smallest organs, for the last century.

Grace Cathedral's great Aeolian-Skinner organ was installed in 1934,
the gift of Harriet Crocker Alexander (1862–1935), sister of William H.
Crocker, principal donor of the cathedral site. The Crockers were a musical family, and stained glass windows in the William Crocker mansion's
music room (that stood on the present organ site before 1906) depicted
composers and instruments. The organ was given in memory of Harriet's
husband, Charles Beatty Alexander (1849–1927), a noted New York attorney, Princeton University figure and Presbyterian elder, and in honor of
their three daughters Harriet Aldrich, Janetta Whitridge and Mary White-
house. In the spring of 1934, workers assembled the organ in the two large
chambers flanking the cathedral choir. The Alexander Memorial Organ
was dedicated on May 20th, 1934 by Bishop Edward L. Parsons. Noted
organ authority Wallace Sabin played Bach's Prelude and Fugue in E flat
major. The inaugural recital on June 3, 1934, by cathedral organist J. Sidney
Lewis, featured works by Bach, Brahms, Rheinberger, Handel, Stanford,
Guilmant, Whitlock and others.

Although listed as Opus 910A of Ernest M. Skinner (1866–1960), America's greatest organ designer of the early 1900s, the Alexander organ was

in fact largely designed by G. Donald Harrison (1889–1956). By the 1930s, Skinner, a genius designer who had never finished high-school, was little more than a figurehead of the Aeolian-Skinner Company, created in 1932 when Skinner bought out Aeolian. The educated English-born Harrison, who had joined the Skinner firm in 1927, soon began to edge out Skinner, as fresh ideas of organ building came to the fore. Harrison's design for the Grace Cathedral organ included contributions by Stanley Williams, War-ren D. Allen, and Wallace Sabin, and consultation with cathedral organist J. Sidney Lewis, and the cathedral trustees of the day. The installation was one Aeolian-Skinner's first major organs in the west, and one of the earliest and finest examples of what Harrison dubbed the "American classic organ". Balancing Baroque and orchestral sounds by using a broad mix of pipes and stops, the classic organ expressed the eclectic repertoire of church music that developed following the more sentimental Victorian era.

An often overlooked aspect of Grace Cathedral's great organ are the two spectacular English oak screens (1935), designed by cathedral architect Lewis Hobart and carved by Romanian-American master carver Samuel Berger. Weighing a total of 14 tons and assembled without metal nails or screws, they rise on either side of the choir, enclosing the two organ cham-bers. Carved detail includes robed figures holding songbirds, angel musi-cians playing instruments, dragons, and a profusion of foliage wreathing the upper portions of the screens. Below, chorister angels with songbooks are joined by blowing figures representing the organ action. On the central bosses, support figures hold shields with the instruments of Christ's Pas-sion. A visitor with binoculars will find even more details. Halfway up the central side mullions are four cheeky monkeys.

When built, the Grace Cathedral organ had five divisions; Choir, Great, Swell, Solo and Pedal, and 6077 pipes. Thanks to the interest and generos-ity of Harrison and his successor Joseph S. Whiteford, additions and minor tonal alterations were made in 1952 and 1956, raising the total to 7286 pipes. Swain & Kates made further alterations ca. 1959. Display pipes in the lower screen openings were removed in 1962. Two new divisions by Casavant Freres of St. Hyacinthe, Quebec, were installed in 1974, one in the distant cathedral gallery and the other (now silent) the bombarde, in the apse. A tuba section was added in 2000 making the current pipe total 7466. The console, too, went through several incarnations. In 1968 the original console was replaced with a solid-state system by Rufatti Fratelli of Padua, Italy. The organ itself was mobilized in 1984, so that it could be rolled down a ramp onto the choir floor and turned to any position for concerts. A thick electrical "umbilical cord" linked it to the 20-horsepower turbine pump in the crypt. In 1998 the venerable firm of Schoenstein and Co., San Francisco organ builders since 1877, created a new mobile digital control console, doing away with the ramp and downsizing the "umbilical cord."

J. Sidney Lewis, fourth cathedral organist (1916–1942), was the first to have the privilege of regularly playing the great organ. Later organist/choirmasters of note were the noted composer Hugh MacKinnon (fifth—1942–1946), and the famed Richard I. Purvis (sixth—1947–1971), who fondly knew the organ as "Gussie." John R. Fenstermaker followed (seventh—1971–2000), and then Christopher Putnam (2000–2001), Jeffrey Smith (2005–2010) and the current Director of Music Benjamin Bachmann. Some of the several assistant organists are of note. Ted Alan Worth (1958, 1967–1969) became a noted concert organist, and Susan Matthews was the cathedral's first woman assistant/acting organist (2001–2005). "The organ is not a machine but an expressive instrument," she noted. "My job is to make it breathe like a real person."

Great premieres have taken place on the Grace Cathedral organ and great organists have played its keys. The complete organ works of Bach, played by Vatican organist Fernando Germani (1960), and Paul Jacobs performance of the complete organ works of Messiaen (2002), have enthralled listeners. Other visiting performers have included Marcel Dupre, Jean Langlais, E. Power Biggs, Karl Richter, Simon Preston, Virgil Fox, Pierre Cochereau, Marie Claire-Alain and many others. The great organ accompanied Duke Ellington in the premier of his Sacred Concert (1965), and Vince Guaraldi's Jazz Mass (1965). As well as serving in thousands of services, hundreds of recitals, and numerous choir and orchestral concerts, drama, dance and new age performances, the organ has featured in such events as The Organ in Sanity and Madness, Totentanz, and The Hunchback of Note Dame and other silent movies. Cathedral organists Fenstermaker and Purvis celebrated the organ's 50th anniversary with a gala 1984 concert featuring works by Bach and Sabin. The great organ is even heard in feature movies such as Hitchcock's *Family Plot* and *Bicentennial Man*, and has had literary cameos in novels such as *Flint* by Charles Norris and Armistead Maupin's *More Tales of the City*.

The first commercial recording of the great organ was in 1953 for an LP set *Aeolian-Skinner presents—The King of Instruments* (v. 5). The unattributed segments were played by Richard Purvis. *A Richard Purvis Organ Recital* (v. 1, 2) were recorded for High Fidelity in 1956, as was his *Music for Christmas* in 1959. A Reader's Digest/RCA set of 1972 also features the organ (LP 14). John Fenstermaker recorded *The Organ at Grace Cathedral* in-house LP in 1979, followed by cassette recordings in 1986 and 1988. The Organ Historical Society's 1988 *Historic Organs of San Francisco* CD set includes the great organ. *A Brass and Organ Christmas* Gothic CD followed in 2000. Susan Matthews recorded *Chosen Tunes*, a Gothic CD, in 2004. Visiting recording organists have included Michael Murray (1973), Catharine Crozier (1990), Cherry Rhodes (1995) and John Weaver (2000).

Like all organs, Grace Cathedral's great organ requires maintenance. Fluctuating temperature and humidity, loosening due to vibration, general wear and tear, occasional earthquakes, all take their toll. Like a living creature, an organ requires constant attention and loving care, including a biweekly tuning of a portion of the many pipes. Edward Millington Stout III, Bay Area organ curator emeritus, now retired, worked with often-limited resources to restore and repair the great organ during his 42-year tenure.

Note

1. http://www.gracecathedral.org/visit/cathedral-history-art/Winds-of-God.php.

selected bibliography

Barden, Nelson. Interview with Richard Purvis, October 1981, San Francisco, California. Transcript.

Baron, Richard, Major Abe Baum, and Richard Goldhurst. *Raid! The Untold Story of Patton's Secret Mission.* New York: Putnam's Sons, 1981.

"Biographical Data." Anonymous typescript, on Grace Cathedral letterhead, covering Purvis's life from about 1925–1964. Possibly written by Purvis himself; may have been compiled by June Townsend.

Corbett, Donald M. "The Life and Works of Richard Purvis." A Thesis Presented to the Department of Music, California State College at Long Beach. In Partial Fulfillment of the Requirements for the Degree Master of Arts. August 1969. 46 pp.

———. The Published Music of Richard Purvis. September 1, 1969. Typescript.

Kershaw, Alex. *The Longest Winter: The Battle of the Bulge and the Epic Story of World War II's Most Decorated Platoon.* Da Capo Press, 2004.

"Lessons with Dr. Courboin: A Conversation with Richard Purvis." *The Erzähler, Journal of the Symphony Organ Society,* January 1995, Vol. 4, No. 3. Interview by Jonathan Ambrosino, 1992. Excerpts of this article also published in "Charles Courboin—A Remembrance." Part 2. Compiled by Ray Biswanger. *The American Organist,* November 1996, Vol. 30, No. 11, 54–56.

Townsend, June Leora Brown. "Memories of Richard Irven Purvis." Typescript, 1995. 3 pp.

———. "Richard I. Purvis: Contemporary American Organist-Composer." A Research Project Presented to the Graduate Division, Pacific Union

College. In Partial Fulfillment of the Requirements for the Degree Master of Arts. August 1967. 67 pp.

Stout, Edward M. Interview by James Welch. August 31, 2010, Hayward, California.

Torrence, Richard, and Marshall Yaeger, *Virgil Fox (The Dish)*, based on a memoir by Ted Alan Worth. New York: Circles International, 2001.

INDEX

Numbers in *italics* reference pictures.

A

Aeolian organs, 19, 42
Aeolian-Skinner organs, 45, 128–130, 358, 368, 381
Alexander Memorial Organ, 120, 122, 124–126, 128–132, 184, 358, 368, 379, 383, 483–487
    50th anniversary program, 343–345
    photographs of, *108, 123, 133, 147, 149*
All Saints Episcopal Church (Worcester), 134, 336
Ambrosino, Jonathan, 63
American Guild of Organists, 18, 62, 74–76, 300, 326
American Theatre Organ Society, 167, 363, 364, 428
Andrews organ, 11–12
Army Music School, 83
army service, 81–105
Asper, Frank, 128–130, 452
assistants, 136–140
Austin organs, 7, 17, *348*

B

Bahn, Walter, 99, 392
Bairstow, Edward, 50, 441
Bakersfield, California, 334
"The Ballad of Judas Iscariot," 45–46, 85, 392
Baltimore, 322
band, infantry, *84, 86, 88,* 89–90, *96, 98*

Barden, Nelson, 7, 17
Bartlett, C. Julian, 150, 172, 177–185
Baum, Abraham, 93
Beniams, Frances, 417
Bennett, Robert, 393
Bernstein, Leonard, 38–39
Bidwell Presbyterian Church, 345
Biggs, E. Power, 451
birth, 1
birthday celebrations, *204, 205, 206,* 216, 469
Bishop's Ranch, 155, 421–427, 436, 438
Block, Karl Morgan, 169–170
Bok, Mary Louise Curtis, 37, 43
Bonelli, Carl, 136
Boys Achievement Club, 7
Braff, Donald, 200, 217, 419
Brown, Ken, 4
Butler, Pennsylvania, 348

C

California Palace of the Legion of Honor.
    See Legion of Honor
California Theatre, 8
Callaway, Paul, 83, 112
Calvary Presbyterian Church, 13, 19–26, *24*
cancer, 205
Capp Street Church, 2
Carney, Michael T., 393
Carruth, William W., 49
Castro Theatre, 356
Castro Valley, California, 335

CHAPTER X

ABOUT THE AUTHOR

James Welch is Organist of Santa Clara University in California. He received the Doctor of Musical Arts degree in organ performance from Stanford University, with further studies in France and Austria. He has concertized internationally, performing recitals in such prestigious venues as Notre Dame Cathedral in Paris, the Leipzig Gewandhaus, National Cathedral in Washington, D.C., and the Mormon Tabernacle in Salt Lake

James Welch and Richard Purvis, San Francisco, February 10, 1991.

City. He has also performed and taught in Beijing, Taipei, Hong Kong, New Zealand, and Jerusalem. A specialist in Latin American organ music, he received a Fulbright award to conduct music research in Brazil; he has also given recitals in Mexico and edited three volumes of organ music by Mexican composers. He has presented lectures and recitals at conventions of the American Guild of Organists and at the International Congress of Organists. Several of his articles about prominent American organists have appeared in *The American Organist* and *The Diapason,* and he has released numerous CDs, recorded on a variety of organs. He lives in Palo Alto, California, with his wife Deanne Everson and their two sons.

In his early teens, James Welch came under the spell of the organ music of Richard Purvis via recordings from Grace Cathedral. Since that time he has performed and recorded many of Purvis's compositions. Although he met Purvis in person only occasionally, those encounters made a lasting impression. He also had the opportunity of playing many recitals over the years on the organ at Grace Cathedral, giving him an opportunity to feel "the Purvis spirit" and experiment with "the Purvis sound." Realizing that there was no biography, Welch undertook the absorbing project of collecting information and interviewing people who knew Purvis well. This book, celebrating the centenary of Purvis's birth, chronicles one of the most colorful and influential organists of his day—or any day.

www.welchorganist.com

—

The Archive of Recorded Sound at Stanford University houses a growing collection of Purvis scores, documents, letters, and recordings. To donate to the collection, please contact the Archive via the following:

soundarchive@stanford.edu

https://lib.stanford.edu/ars

650-723-9312

Made in the USA
Charleston, SC
01 August 2013